The Book Publishing Annual

The Book Publishing Annual

Highlights, Analyses & Trends

1984 Edition

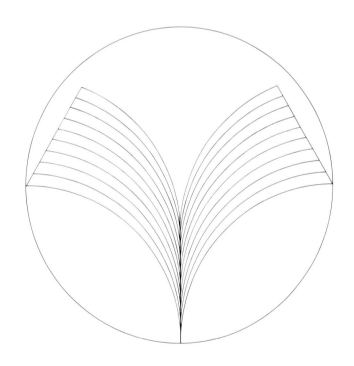

By the Book Division, R. R. Bowker Company,
in collaboration with the staff of *Publishers Weekly*

R. R. Bowker Company
New York and London, 1984

The first volume of this series was published in 1983
under the title *Publishers Weekly Yearbook*.

Published by R. R. Bowker Company
205 East Forty-second Street, New York, NY 10017
Copyright © 1984 by Xerox Corporation
Printed and bound in the United States of America

ISBN 0-8352-1873-2

ISSN: 0000-0787

Contents

Preface

This second volume of R. R. Bowker's annual review of the book publishing industry appears under a new title to reflect a broader scope. *The Book Publishing Annual,* like its predecessor, *Publishers Weekly Yearbook,* consists chiefly of reports by the editors of the book industry journal, *Publishers Weekly.* In order to extend its coverage of the various types of publishing, the current volume has gone outside of the *PW* staff to include reports from the field on scholarly, professional and business, religious, higher education, school, and small press publishing. The new industry overviews, combined with the coverage these publishing areas receive in such chapters as "Book Industry Economics," "Book Design," and "Book Manufacturing," complement the *Annual*'s treatment of trade book publishing and provide a more balanced picture of the book industry.

The intent of *The Book Publishing Annual* is to review in depth and breadth the highlights of the year in book publishing, to analyze and interpret facts and events, to identify trends, to supply new statistical data about the industry, to bring together statistical information that appeared in *Publishers Weekly* during the year, to evaluate the importance of the year's publishing activities and recognize their implications for the future—and in so doing to provide in one concise volume a sharply focused annual profile of the book industry.

The contents of this second volume is similar to that of the first, with the addition of several important new features besides the overviews described above. The critical surveys of the year's books that appeared in the 1983 edition have been replaced this year with two reports on trends, one on hardcover publishing by Joann Davis and one on paperback publishing by Sally A. Lodge. Daisy Maryles and Bette-Lee Fox have compiled for the first time an all-time bestseller list for mass market paperbacks, and have updated the all-time bestseller lists for hardcover and trade paperback books that appeared in last year's volume. To his review and analysis of publishers' operating expenditures in "Book Industry Economics, 1983," John Dessauer has added a survey of 1983 salaries for representative positions in book publishing. In "Book Manufacturing," Jerome Frank has included a section on advances in electronic transmission of manuscripts from author to publisher to typesetter. And in a new chapter, "Software Comes to the Bookstore," Robert Dahlin reports on bookstore experience in selling computer software in 1983.

Several of these new features—the industry overviews, the mass market paperback all-time bestseller list, and the salary survey—were added to broaden the scope of the *Annual.* The review of the year's output of books was changed from a critical study to a survey of trends because the trends approach was seen as more useful in a publication addressed to the business of books. The two reports on the continuing advances of the computer in the book industry have been added as a result of trends monitored throughout the year and judged to have had sufficient impact on the industry to merit attention in a review of the year's activities. It is hoped that the addition of these new features in combination with the *Annual*'s extensive continuing coverage of the book publishing world will provide an even more useful perspective of the book industry.

Preparing *The Book Publishing Annual* is a cooperative endeavor. Thanks are due to the *Publishers Weekly* editors who again took time from their busy schedules to research and write their reports for the *Annual,* to the industry specialists from outside the Bowker Company who cooperated in helping to provide broader coverage for this edition, to Jerome Frank, *PW*'s Book Design & Manufacturing editor, who served as photographer for the *Annual,* and to Paul Doebler, Editor-in-Chief, Professional Books, for providing help and encouragement throughout the planning, compilation, and production of this edition. The editorial production staff of the Bowker Book Division played a key role and their support is very much appreciated: Nancy Leff Bucenec and Iris Topel in seeing the *Annual* through to production, and Corinne Naden in preparing the index.

Jean Peters
Manager, Research and Development
Book Division

LIST OF CONTRIBUTORS

John F. Baker, Editor-in-Chief, *Publishers Weekly.*

Robert Dahlin, contributing editor to *Publishers Weekly.*

Joann Davis, Senior Editor (Trade News), *Publishers Weekly.*

John P. Dessauer, Director, Center for Book Research, University of Scranton, and contributing editor to *Publishers Weekly.*

Robert E. Ewing, Chairman of the Board and Chief Executive Officer, Van Nostrand Reinhold Company, Inc.

Howard Fields, Washington correspondent for *Publishers Weekly.*

Bette-Lee Fox, Audiovisual/Bibliographic Editor, *Library Journal.*

Jerome P. Frank, Editor, Book Design & Manufacturing, *Publishers Weekly.*

Elizabeth A. Geiser, Senior Vice President, Gale Research Company, and Director, University of Denver Publishing Institute.

William Goldstein, Associate Editor (Trade News), *Publishers Weekly.*

Thomas Gornick, Senior Acquisitions Editor for Computer Science, Holt, Rinehart & Winston.

Chandler B. Grannis, contributing editor to *Publishers Weekly.*

William Griffin, Religious Editor, *Publishers Weekly.*

John Huenefeld, President and Senior Publishing Consultant, The Huenefeld Company, Inc.

Sally A. Lodge, Senior Associate Editor (Paperbacks), *Publishers Weekly.*

Herbert R. Lottman, International Correspondent for *Publishers Weekly.*

Daisy Maryles, Senior Staff Editor, *Publishers Weekly.*

John Mutter, Associate Editor (News), *Publishers Weekly.*

Paul S. Nathan, Rights & Permissions columnist, *Publishers Weekly.*

Miriam E. Phelps, Research Librarian, *Publishers Weekly.*

Margaret M. Spier, Developmental Editor, Reference Books, R. R. Bowker Company.

James R. Squire, Senior Vice President Emeritus, Ginn and Company.

Allene Symons, Senior Associate Editor (Bookselling & Merchandising), *Publishers Weekly.*

1983: The Year in Review

1

General Books

JOHN F. BAKER

If 1982 marked the trough of the recession for most American publishers, 1983 was the year when the first tentative signs of recovery began to appear. Beginning sluggishly in the spring, after only a lackluster Christmas, sales began to pick up decisively by early summer, and by fall were running as much as 25 percent ahead of the previous year in some categories. Although there were obviously variations from category to category, the sales improvements ran virtually across all industry lines—with the exception of mail-order sales, which remained depressed throughout the year.

It was also a year in which the number of takeovers and actual disappearances of imprints declined sharply from the previous year. NAL (New American Library) was bought by a group of Wall Street investors for $50 million, and Gulf & Western agreed to purchase Esquire, Inc., but these were the only major changes of ownership in trade publishing. Otherwise most of the takeover activity took place in one direction only—that of publishers gearing up to get into the booming and potentially highly lucrative field of computer-software creation by buying up existing software publishers or, alternatively, by creating their own special divisions to perform the same function.

Investing in Software

In the course of the year, Simon & Schuster, Dutton, Warner, Random House, SFN Companies, Prentice-Hall, and Addison-Wesley were among those making major investments in software, and although there was comparatively little product available in this first year of general gearing up, it seemed clear that 1984 would be an important year for publishers testing the electronic marketplace. In terms of distribution, too, steps were taken to lay the groundwork for a future in which software was made widely available through marketing channels normally reserved for books. Ingram Book Company of Nashville, the wholesalers, began a major software distribution program, and several of the bookstore chains started stocking software merchandise on a limited basis; as they achieved more expertise in the different kind of merchandising required, and became convinced of its viability as a product to sell alongside books (and they had already been scoring a considerable sales success with computer-oriented books in the previous two years), independent booksellers were expected to follow suit in increasing numbers. It remained to be seen whether the enthusiasm—and the considerable sums being spent—for the pursuit of software was justified in the long run.

The increased interest in software was reflected at the American Booksellers Association (ABA) convention in Dallas in early June, where stands promoting software, and seminars explaining its possibilities to booksellers, seemed to be the most prominent features of what was otherwise a rather slow convention in terms of sales and bookseller participation.

Another aspect of the so-called computer revolution was the increasing possibilities publishers saw in being able to relate electronically to an ever-greater degree with both their authors and their printers. Part of the problem hindering further advance of such interfacing, as the computer industry would call it, was their lack of compatibility between various systems, depending at least in part on the availability of a common series of encoding and programming instructions; to this end, the Association of American Publishers launched a major pilot plan to develop a series of such codes to assist in standardizing computer instruction.

The Business Climate

The economic sluggishness of much of 1983, and the year or two that preceded it, did take its toll on the industry. The Brentano's bookstore chain, which had filed for Chapter 11 in 1982, finally went out of business in early 1983. Publishers that took similar refuge from their creditors in the course of the year included A & W Publishers and Hastings House. The Dial Press was folded into Doubleday, and a considerable part of its staff either let go or transferred to its corporate owner. Time-Life Books, which had suffered severely in the Mexican devaluation and with a Japanese enterprise, also let many staffers go and closed a number of offices—though at year's end it was claimed to be in good shape for a return to the black in 1984. Viking Penguin also underwent a minor crisis during the year. President Irving Goodman resigned amid claims that this American branch of a major worldwide, British-based company was suffering from "inadequate profitability," and Penguin chief executive Peter Meyer came in from London to conduct a major restructuring, in place just after the end of the year—but again, with the loss of a number of jobs.

One of the rare attempts to create a coordinated effort to improve book distribution nationwide was also an apparent victim of publishing economics—though perhaps just as much of publisher caution and reluctance to experiment. ZIPSAN, a scheme launched to simplify, as well as cut the costs of, shipping books nationwide was launched in July and dead in less than six months because, said founder DeWitt Baker, it never succeeded in getting enough publishers to try it—though he claimed it succeeded in its promises to cut transportation costs over its chief rivals. Meanwhile, ABA's attempt to streamline and simplify distribution, the Booksellers Ordering Service, moved on toward testing in 1984 with a group of publishers.

Another attempt to fill a long-felt need among New York–based publishers seemed to be making progress during the year. This was a plan spearheaded by Martin Levin, retired president of Times Mirror, to enlist city assistance in preparing a publishing center in which a number of publishers, driven out of prime Manhattan office space by ever-escalating rents, could share resources in a single building or building complex, at advantageous rents. This seemed likely to become a reality by 1985, though the size and final number of occupants remained uncertain. Meanwhile, two more major publishers moved, Abrams from its expensive East 58th Street location to lower Fifth Avenue, and R. R. Bowker from Sixth Avenue to 42nd Street and Third—both in search of lower rents.

Several continuing publishing stories saw new chapters written during 1982. The fate of the American Book Awards, the subject of much speculation in recent years as new formats were tried in turn and dropped in favor of others, became even more embroiled than it had been. At first the awards ceremony was scheduled to coincide with ABA in Dallas; then it was announced that there would be insufficient time for that, so a considerably reduced version was offered at the New York Public Library. Eventually, in face of continuing discussion as to whether the number of categories and entrants was unwieldy, it was agreed that the 1984 version would take place in the late fall, probably with considerably reduced categories.

The suit brought by Harper & Row and the *Reader's Digest* against the *Nation* magazine for alleged misappropriation of part of President Ford's memoirs was an up-and-down affair. The *Nation* lost a court ruling in March but then won an appeal against the judge's decision in November; it now seems that Harper and the *Digest*, who see the case as one of copyright violation while the *Nation* sees it as one of First Amendment rights to publish news, will take it to the Supreme Court.

The publishers' big triumph in their continuing struggle against academic and organizational photocopying without recompense came in 1983 in a court victory against New York University, against which a test case had been brought. In April the university and a closely associated copying shop agreed to abide by guidelines for making use of photocopies. A case brought by paperback publishers against a numbers of dealers in stripped books also survived a court challenge and seemed likely ultimately to be resolved in the publishers' favor.

Authors and the Law

On another front, however, there were new anxieties. California passed a law providing that writers employed on a casual work-for-hire basis were entitled to full benefits, as if they were employees, during the term of their work, and publishers elsewhere in the country were hoping the idea would not spread—or trying to determine whether if they used California-based authors the law applied to them too.

Writers themselves remained strongly committed to setting up a functional national writers union that, they claimed, would be more aggressive in its approach to book and magazine publishers than are existing writers' organizations; but so far, although there have been a number of organizing meetings and the fledgling group makes its voice heard from time to time, it remains far from a force in the industry.

One development of which writers should surely approve—and for which writers' groups have lobbied hard and successfully in a number of other countries, including Australia, the Scandinavian countries, and Great Britain—is the Public Lending Right, by which writers receive a small royalty payment each time one of their books is loaned out by a library. It would obviously be difficult to fund and administer in a country the size of the United States, but a first step toward placing it on the agenda here came in October when aides to Republican Senator

Charles Mathias of Maryland said he would introduce a bill during the next session of Congress to study the possibilities.

One publishing case in which all writers' groups became involved during the year was the case of Dodd, Mead and three of its writers. Recently taken over by Thomas Nelson, a publisher of Bibles and religious books, the house let it be known that it would avoid books containing certain words and expressions the Nelson people found objectionable. The authors of two novels already on the Dodd, Mead list declined to remove offending words from their books and took them elsewhere; but the compiler of an anthology of verse, Richard Coniff, was caught with his book already in print; copies were kept in the warehouse, and at year's end Coniff sued.

Another suit by a writer watched with great attention in the publishing world was that brought by Gerard Colby Zilg against Prentice-Hall. Zilg had written a book critical of the Du Pont family, and alleged in his suit that the publisher, under pressure from the company, had in fact "suppressed" the book by inadequately advertising it and cutting the print order. In 1982 a judge ruled for Zilg, but that ruling was overturned on appeal last September; the appeals court in effect ruled that providing some good-faith effort is made to make the book available, a publisher's judgment as to how extensively to print and promote a book is final.

A somewhat similar case, however, was resolved in favor of the author. Deborah Davis, author of a book on publisher Katharine Graham of the *Washington Post,* had sued her publisher, Harcourt Brace Jovanovich (HBJ) because soon after publication it disavowed the book, ordered copies already printed to be destroyed, and reverted the rights to Davis. She received $100,000 from HBJ in an out-of-court settlement of her suit for $6 million and was also allowed to keep her advance on the book. Legal observers said HBJ's apparent caution probably stemmed from the Zilg ruling.

A more unusual author suit was filed by William Peter Blatty, who claimed that in reporting his book *Legion* on its bestseller lists some time after it had appeared on other lists, the *New York Times* had been guilty of negligence and "trade libel." In its reply the *Times* said that a victory for Blatty would mean the end of its lists. In fact, at the end of the year the *Times* bestseller lists were again in the news, when they were restructured to combine mass market and trade paperbacks in one list, but breaking out how-to, cartoon, and joke books into a group of their own; in hardcover, a similar list of how-to books was added to the existing fiction and "serious" nonfiction lists. This was one of the first moves by Mitchell Levitas, newly appointed editor of the *New York Times Book Review* (previous editor Harvey Shapiro was moved over to the *New York Times Magazine*), who said he was making the change to "reflect an emphasis that has become a larger part of book buying in recent years." Publisher reactions were mixed.

One of the year's odder publishing stories was the recall by Random House of all 58,000 copies it had shipped of *Poor Little Rich Girl,* a biography of Barbara Hutton, after a doctor said to have prescribed drug treatments for Hutton revealed that he had been only 14 years old at the time of the alleged treatments—and threatened to sue unless the book was withdrawn; he also refused to permit correction by insertion of errata slips. The book's author, C. David Heymann, blamed the error on "secondary sources," and at the end of the year was said to be attempting to place the book, purged of error, elsewhere. Random planned to destroy the returned copies.

Personnel Shifts

Some notable shifts of personnel during the year included the resignation of G. Roysce Smith, executive director of ABA, and his replacement by Bernard Rath, who held the same position with the Canadian Booksellers Association; the firing by Hearst of Arbor House president Donald Fine, who set up on his own; the move of Marvin Brown from Atheneum to NAL; of John Macrae III to Holt, Rinehart & Winston; of Joseph Kanon to Dutton; of Erwin Glikes to Macmillan's Free Press; of Seymour Turk from Harry Abrams to Book-of-the-Month Club; and of author Norman Mailer from Little, Brown, his long-time publisher, to Random House, reportedly for a package deal involving $4 million. Former McGraw-Hill president Curtis Benjamin, long an industry guru and commentator, died, and so did Charles Haslam, affectionately known to customers at his famous bookstore in St. Petersburg, Florida, as the Book Man, and much beloved by generations of ABA members.

American publishers have always gone to the Frankfurt Book Fair; 1983 was the year when a large part of the German publishing industry brought its own book fair to New York, to give its U.S. colleagues more of a chance to meet them and to look over their wares than is generally possible at Frankfurt. Most American publishers, with the exception of a handful of largely scientific and technical houses, boycotted the Moscow Book Fair again this year, partly because they felt they would do insufficient business to justify the trip, partly as a protest against Soviet treatment of dissident authors. An argument against this policy, however, was made at a luncheon for two exiled Russians in New York, who declared it was better to lend support to the dissidents by presence in Moscow than simply to stay away.

Amid the recovering hopes of publishers in general, one segment of the industry continued to show remarkable growth and resilience. Smaller presses mushroomed vigorously, adding approximately 200 a month through much of the year (though naturally with some attrition as well). Increasingly they were taking up the slack in serious fiction, poetry, writing by members of minorities, writing of political dissent, and carefully targeted regional nonfiction. It was the obverse of big-dollar publishing, yet, paradoxically, it was succeeding in many ways—building a readership, keeping books in print, making better-looking books—where larger publishers were faltering. By 1983, in fact, small-press publishing had carved out such a distinct niche for itself that R. R. Bowker, the publishers of *Publishers Weekly* (and of this book), launched a new magazine specifically to cater to this universe: *Small Press.*

This was simply one among a number of encouraging developments that enabled the book industry to face 1984 with considerably more equanimity than it had possessed the previous year. True, there were casualties of the long recession, but they were by no means as numerous as many observers had feared or as had been predicted in this space a year ago. Publishers learned that their business was not entirely recession-proof, as has sometimes been rashly boasted; but if they learned anything else during 1983's gradual recovery, it was that books are remarkably resilient—and so are the people who make them.

2

Scholarly Publishing

CHANDLER B. GRANNIS

Scholarly publishing as represented by the nonprofit university presses has, with quiet effort, pulled itself up to perceptibly higher and safer ground than it occupied in the late 1970s. It seemed then that several presses might be swept away and in fact at least two small ones were, while several more had to struggle for survival. Soaring energy costs, falling enrollments, inflation, and declining federal aid to libraries had resulted in crises on many campuses. For the presses all this meant reduced university subsidies for general operations and diminished book purchases by college and university libraries. At the same time, book-production costs and list prices were being forced upward, further affecting both individual and institutional ability to buy.

By the end of 1983 such conditions were still in effect, but the presses had learned how to cope: how to become more self-reliant financially while still demonstrating that some support is in the university's interest; how to market books more widely and effectively; how to begin a sensible transition to microcomputers and word processors; and how, meanwhile, to enliven the title mix without compromising the scholarly mission, the presses' reason for being.

On this final point, presses emphasize that the publication of their very few novels, short story collections, and books of poetry is not undertaken as a way to raise money. Even a showy, apparent success can lose money. Some presses, however, think it is important to encourage creative writing of quality, writing that is not necessarily "commercial." This is all the more true, Leslie E. Phillabaum, director of Louisiana State University Press, suggests, because "the university, partly through its appointments, has become in a sense a patron of writers.

Just as we publish the results of research by the history faculty, we can help the creative writer."

Nevertheless, staff officials of the Association of American University Presses (AAUP), retiring executive director Richard Koffler and assistant director Andrea Teter, pointed out at the end of 1983 that allegations of "a turn to trade books" by university presses are much exaggerated. "Monographs are not an endangered species," they said. As for the 1983–1984 financial situation, they agreed—still using the stark imagery of the era—that "there are no presses on death row."

Facts and Figures

Admittedly, with 1982 university press income roughly estimated at a little over $92 million by the Association of American Publishers, the presses account for slightly over 1 percent of all publishers' receipts in the United States. On the other hand, the AAUP member presses typically turn out 10 to 11 percent of the recorded U.S. title output (including imports).

Moreover, there are more university presses than ever before. AAUP membership by the end of 1983 consisted of 83 members, including 7 international members publishing primarily in non-English languages, plus 7 associate members, presses not yet large enough for full membership. By contrast, at the end of 1980 there were 72 members; affiliate status was not established until 1981. All but a handful of significant U.S. university presses belong to AAUP.

To cite representative figures from recent AAUP statistical reports, total output figures for 67 North

American presses, all books in all editions, were, in 1980, 3,010, and in 1982, 3,268; paperbacks only, 1980, 1,193; and in 1982, 1,364. Overall output for the 67 presses increased about 8 percent over the two years, while paperback output increased over 14 percent.

Professionalism and Other Issues

When asked at the end of 1983 what he considered the most important trend in scholarly publishing since the 1970s, Arthur J. Rosenthal, president of AAUP for 1983–1984 and director of the Harvard University Press, declared instantly: "*Finally*—the presses are being professionally managed."

In the same week, similar views were voiced informally by several university press people at the annual convention of the Modern Language Association, including outgoing AAUP president David H. Gilbert, director of the University of Nebraska Press. Some people from southern presses suggested, also, that with the influx of northern population in recent years, attitudes had become "less parochial." "We're not so exclusively a southern ghetto as we were," said one. The audience for scholarly books in the South has become "more sophisticated," it seemed to Carol Orr, director of the University of Tennessee Press. Academic authors, she added, seem increasingly willing to be published by southern presses, which now enjoy growing prestige.

Bright, competent people have always been attracted to scholarly publishing. In recent years the pool of better-trained applicants has widened and the competition for jobs has therefore become keener. More young aspirants come to the presses with some background in the intensive university institutes in publishing and other special courses in publishing.

AAUP meanwhile has stepped up in recent years its efforts to provide specific training for people already employed at presses by holding program segments or preconvention seminars in, for example, marketing, business management, computer operations, design and technology of book production, editorial operations, and the problems of journal publishing. Workshops dominate AAUP regional meetings.

The professional status of women has been emphasized by the Women in Scholarly Publishing group formed in 1978. The Society for Scholarly Publishing (SSP), a rapidly expanding national organization of individuals (with supportive corporate members), provides intensive forums and workshops on practical problems. SSP involves people working on all kinds of professional publications, both commercial and nonprofit. In addition, many university presses are included in the Professional and Scholarly Publishing Division of the Association of American Publishers (AAP). Some press staff members are able to attend publishing orientation courses and seminars organized in major cities through AAP's education program.

How much all this may have contributed to the presses' ability to surmount the agonizing "crisis of the seventies" would be hard to say. Certainly the squeeze was still on at the beginning of 1984. Two trends were compressing the markets for scholarly books: (1) a continued curtailment of university library book-purchase funds, with announced budgets revised downward, and in one or two rumored instances slashed back by tens or even hundreds of thousands of dollars; (2) the rising value of the dollar relative to foreign currencies, adversely affecting foreign sales of U.S. books, noticeably in Europe, and most severely in Mexico.

Such forces being beyond any publisher's power to control, scholarly presses were working on more manageable areas: (1) control of operating costs; (2) funding for general operations; (3) funding for individual titles and for project development; and (4) improved marketing.

Conventional methods of streamlining personnel, manufacturing, and general costs are of course employed. Pressruns are down. One major press says typical first printings have dropped from 2,500–3,000 to 1,000–1,500. Another says what was formerly a run of 1,500 would now be 1,200 or 1,000. There are additional cost-controlling devices: maintaining rather stringent requirements for authors of highly specialized, short-run academic monographs, and contracting with other presses or agencies for some noneditorial functions. For example, Columbia University Press acts as publishing agent for the New York University Press and as domestic sales representative for the State University of New York Press; warehousing for the Tennessee press is handled by Johns Hopkins; distribution, fulfillment, and warehousing are done for the Missouri and Wesleyan presses by Harper & Row. Many presses have formed cooperative groups for domestic and foreign sales representation. Most presses freely and generously swap information about the availability of outside services in manufacturing, design, fulfillment, computer work, and other services.

The Search for Funding

To make up, in part, for the heavy reduction or complete loss of general operating subsidies, presses look for sources on their own. "Friends" or "Associates" programs are being organized. Massive endowment campaigns, exemplified by a five-year drive under way at the University of Minnesota Press, is another productive device.

Just how to raise funds of this magnitude has become a matter of earnest study. The noble art of cultivating large and, ideally, regular gifts from very wealthy donors—or many generous gifts from the less wealthy—is essential to the support of learned endeavor, and more and more university press executives have been preaching it in the past few years. Efforts are especially directed to potential givers in the city or region of a press and among its alumni and other sympathetic connections. Matt Hodgson, director of the University of North Carolina Press, told colleagues at the AAUP meeting in 1983 that a press has to make contacts with "the rich and powerful establishment" in its state, and then to show that the press is worthy, its need "explicable," and its conduct effective.

Meanwhile, said a Columbia editor, William Germano, university administrations still have to be shown that their presses deserve support as they further the university's aims.

At the national level major grants from the Andrew Mellon Foundation were awarded through the American Council of Learned Societies to 22 presses in the early 1970s and more recently to 11 other presses in a second round. The National Endowment for the Humanities, for FY 1984, increased its scholarly publications funding to $400,000 and offered challenge grants for establishing specific projects. The National Historical Publications and Records Commission (NHPRC) had had its funding withdrawn in 1981, endangering an array of important programs for publishing the documents of the Founding Fathers and other vital source materials in American history. Late in 1983, however, NHPRC was given by Congress a new five-year lease on life, and is awarding grants, according to information reported by John Ryden, Yale University Press director, who heads AAUP's committee on foundations and grants. The funds, he points out, were restored "under massive pressure reflecting the concerns of the scholarly community."

Clearly grants and fund raising retain a vital role. But presses want as many of their books as possible to be self-supporting. "There is an increasing awareness of markets," says Nancy C. Essig, marketing and associate director at the Johns Hopkins University Press. "There is more sophistication, a more businesslike attitude." It probably helps, too, that more staff members come to the presses with some commercial publishing experience or instruction.

Aggressive, resourceful ways of marketing are being applied; AAUP's quarterly *Exchange* is full of short reports in which presses describe local, regional, or disciplinary promotional schemes that work, and tell how they have cultivated relations with stores. Presses systematically look not only for a book's specialized appeal, but also for its retail trade potential and its possibilities for reviews in major media.

Regular advertising in major book media is worthwhile for many presses, and several—Harvard and California especially—have become known for clever, provocative advertising copy. Titling is important, along with an appealing even if inexpensive jacket design. The AAUP-related mailing-list service has been improved and is an important aid to sales. Presses have also stepped up, since the late 1970s, their use of annual newsprint tabloid sale catalogs, which they send to alumni, academic lists, and other buyers. If a press's backlist is large enough and deep enough, it can thereby offer hundreds of titles at reduced prices, adding substantially to income and reducing inventory.

Trend to Paperbacks

The most visible trend in university presses over the past five to ten years has been the proliferation of paperback editions. Scholarly paperbacks have been around since the middle 1950s, when the Indiana University Press, then largely rising on its own bootstraps, put out paperback editions of such politely popular works as the charming Rolfe Humphries translation of Ovid's "The Art of Love"—still a good seller. Other presses came along slowly, but in the very comprehensive *Association of American University Presses Directory, 1982–1983,* the great majority of presses report they issue at least some works simultaneously in hard and paper covers and some in paper only, and many have their own active paperback reprint lines. University press ads in the *Publishers Weekly* spring and fall announcement numbers demonstrate the extent of these editions.

The paperbound editions without question make book purchases possible for students, junior faculty, and general readers who cannot afford hardbound editions. Libraries often turn to university press paperbacks for the same reason, even though the books will have more than light or short-term use. Even some overseas research libraries, which would normally want hardcovers, seem to be ordering paperbounds in order to conserve dollars. This may limit the export trade, but as someone remarked, paperback sales are better than none.

Widening the Title Mix

Debate begins to bubble when presses widen their title mix, cautiously introducing beautiful regional photo collections, guides, and even cookery books along with historical and other regional studies; bringing in titles considered "tradey" because bookstores can sell them; adding art books; venturing into university course books; publishing a lot of poetry and, most recently, here and there, making a bold foray into fiction. University press novels especially have occasioned recent academic head-shaking and journalistic twittering.

Actually, none of these ventures except the novels are new to university presses; some go back 15, 25, or even 65 years. What is new in the 1980s is that the deviations from purest scholarship have become numerous and conspicuous. For example, at Johns Hopkins Nancy Essig says, "Without trying to compete, we look for more opportunities in college-level course books," including a history of Maryland to which seven authorities contributed—a book needed in the schools. "We do more regional trade books, including our big Christmas 1983 book, historical photos of Baltimore." A Vietnam war book, *Without Honor,* by a Baltimore *Sun* writer, was an example of "a trade book that even Walden and Dalton would stock."

Carefully chosen, such trade efforts can bring in some money while serving the press's scholarly aims. Vivid recent examples of this were the new edition of the *Chicago Manual of Style* and the University of California Press's limited and trade editions of the Lewis Carroll classics in lavish formats illustrated by the wood engraver Barry Moser.

Current lists demonstrate that regional studies are a continuing, even a growing feature of a great many presses. They include folklore, arts, biographies, Native

American and other ethnic studies, natural history, migrations, social and economic studies—a vast range. Some need support, some are profitable; all, as a senior editor at Nebraska said, contribute to the study of the nation's development.

Art books are part of and much more than the regional programs. Barbara Braun cites in *PW,* October 21, 1983, the varied programs at Princeton and MIT, some requiring aid from the national endowments and private foundations; Chicago, which has experimented with color reproductions, fiches, slides, and other film materials for professional markets; and California, where James H. Clark, director, formerly of Harper & Row, frankly acknowledged: "In the past five years we have lost the capacity to publish art books on our own"—following completion of the famous work "The Plan of St. Gall," to which much of a major endowment was devoted.

Other notable examples of art publishing are Pacific and Northwest Indian art studies by the University of Washington Press and Asian art published by California, Hawaii, Washington, Stanford, Columbia, and others. Many presses have set up co-publishing programs with museums. Much of this cooperative output is more scholarly than popular or tradey; but co-published catalogs sold in connection with great public exhibitions often span both interests.

Fiction and Poetry

The growth of flexible attitudes toward list building was bound to encourage consideration of fiction. In 1967, the Louisiana State University (LSU) Press decided to commit itself to publishing short story collections, partly because commercial publishers were not doing so and good material was being neglected. The press began to publish also an occasional volume of poetry, and this pattern of short fiction and poetry has been picked up gradually by other presses.

The total number of new novels from university presses remains small, but lightning has struck twice. The first success was in 1980, when LSU issued *A Confederacy of Dunces* by John Kennedy Toole. It had been rejected by New York publishers, in one case after long consideration. The young author later took his own life, but eventually the manuscript came to LSU through the novelist Walker Percy and was enthusiastically accepted. It became a Book-of-the-Month Club (BOMC) choice, the 1980 Pulitzer-prize winner for fiction, and a paperback best seller for Grove Press.

The second bolt of success came as this article was being written. Ohio State University Press had published in 1982 a voluminous novel about small-town Ohio, a work 50 years in the writing, called ". . . *And Ladies of the Club,*" by an 88-year-old author, Helen Hooven Santmyer. The press had published her memoirs earlier. The novel had a very small sale, but it came to the attention of two Hollywood producers, who came to Ohio seeking a deal. Weldon Kefauver, press director at Ohio State, got an agent to represent the press. As a result of five months of intensive negotiations (*PW,* January 27, 1984) the press and the author became equal partners in a majority share of proceeds from the reborn novel, with Putnam as trade publisher (a first printing of at least 50,000 copies scheduled for August), paperback rights set at a $250,000 minimum, and adoption as a BOMC main selection. The two Hollywood producers will use the story as a TV miniseries. Ohio State had published only one other novel, *Solitaire* by Mojmir Drvota (1974), before *Ladies* came along. For the future, Kefauver may publish novels if a very good reason to do so arises, but "will not go out aggressively for them."

LSU expects to continue publishing creative works, about four works of fiction (novels and short stories) a year, along with about six books of poetry. A contemporary play or some translated work may be added from time to time, making 10 or a dozen books out of a total annual list of about 60. Leslie Phillabaum says the reason for such publishing is "because it needs to be done." Trade channels are not readily open to manuscripts that "don't fit into a theme or a genre," but LSU Press has "had no difficulty in publishing quality work" and has had to turn down many offerings. First pressruns of LSU novels may average 2,000 to 2,500 copies all in hardcover and the books are usually short, about 80,000 words. *Confederacy* was LSU's longest novel, 320 pages. Even that one may not have made money. In effect, nearly all university press output of poetry, fiction, and so on is subsidized in that it comes under the press's general support subsidy from the university, except for an occasional grant to aid a specific project.

Arthur Rosenthal, recalling that an attempt at Harvard in 1977 to launch a program in short novels failed in two years to produce enough satisfactory material, is currently considering poetry. He notes that several recent National Book Critics Circle Awards for poetry have gone to university press books. In words similar to Phillabaum's he says, "I think we should do something for the beginning writers in the creative fields as we do for first writers in history or economics."

Other presses suggest further reasons for taking on fiction and poetry: not only because it is new and worthy but because it is old, perhaps forgotten or out of print and still worthy; or because it is a foreign or translated work deserving of literary attention in America.

In this spirit, the University of Illinois Press and the University of Missouri Press have maintained for several years modest programs in short fiction and poetry, typically about four titles annually. The University of Iowa Press is known for its long-accumulating list of titles selected for the Iowa School of Writers Award for Short Fiction. Johns Hopkins began about 1979 to solicit a very few quality manuscripts per year, and now publishes annually two books of poetry and/or short fiction in a total list of 125 titles, more or less. Toronto listed in 1983 a volume of short contemporary fiction and a modern reissued novel. The University of Massachusetts Press continues with its one or two poetry books a year.

Two university presses remain outstanding in their

fostering of poetry. Yale—through its series based on an annual competition, the Yale Series of Younger Poets, begun in 1919—has the longest experience. Wesleyan has carried on its proportionately large poetry program for a quarter-century. In the *Publishers Weekly* spring announcements February 1983, Wesleyan included 7 poetry titles in an advertised list of 19 books.

Princeton University Press, according to its director, Herbert S. Bailey, Jr., may issue as many as half a dozen books of poetry a year, but a work of fiction would be published not as fiction but as a translation, a classic, or a definitive edition. John Ryden at Yale makes the same qualification. Columbia takes a somewhat different view: John Moore, director, sees a function for a university press in publishing top European fiction, in translation, that is ignored by U.S. trade houses. Two books of this sort were published by Columbia in autumn 1983. Moore believes a press will lose no more on these than on translated nonfiction, maybe less, since fiction is straight text; and when a good translation is supplied, little editing is needed.

As noted earlier, it isn't only in fiction, art, and regional interests that a new openness is evident in university press title selection. Some titles, John Moore points out, are taken from trade publishers' lists and used as university press reprints. An example is Columbia's 1983 Morningside reprint of Ved Mehta's *The Fly in the Fly Bottle: Encounters with British Intellectuals* (originally Atlantic–Little, Brown).

How much a press should specialize and how it can best choose its special area in list building was the major theme of AAUP's annual meeting in June 1983. Presses of different sizes and kinds had different answers. A judiciously open attitude was reported by Leroy Barnes, who said the University of California Press had recently "decided that we would not and should not let first-rate manuscripts go because they don't fit one of our hand-picked areas."

An almost opposite point of view was voiced at a southern regional meeting in September by Kenney Withers, director at Southern Illinois, who held that the purpose of a university press is to pursue scholarship and to publish "the small, muted masterpiece that is commercially unappealing." This position may seem too limiting to other press people. On the other hand, many would agree with Herbert Bailey, who has been warning colleagues not to get entangled with "the big book," the tempting, glamorous project that can monopolize a staff's attention to the detriment of its other books: "We do better to concentrate on scholarly work that is produced to advance knowledge."

Computers and Word Processing

In any case, every title means a commitment of slim resources; accordingly, press managers are used to being careful. In the same careful spirit they are entering the world of computers and word processing. Princeton, experimenting over the past few years, has acquired 18 computers with an editor as overall supervisor. Half a dozen computers are in its plant and the rest are in use for some editorial work, marketing, and journals. The press has no plans, however, says Bailey, to do manuscript editing on computers. Some authors submit manuscripts on disks or tapes, and the press has purchased a translating machine to convert the sources from the authors' computer languages to Princeton's machines.

Yale, John Ryden reports, is "gearing up" for computers, using grant money and buying an on-line editorial system. The Yale Computer Service has been the press's teacher.

John Moore says Columbia "much prefers to get hard copy from authors"; this lets the press control coding and editing.

Early in 1983, 40 presses responded to an AAUP questionnaire about word processors. Of these, nearly half had the equipment, and a dozen had in-house composition. Detailed analysis by 28 presses showed a wide range of experience and an extreme range of opinions. The University of New Mexico Press offered a full report by its art and production chief, Emmy Ezzell, about its approaches to word processing. She stressed the need for patient, continuous dialogue with compositors and authors.

In sum, it appears that the university presses are nearly all in good health, lean but decently nourished, open to innovation but not venturing too far from their overriding reason for existence—to publish the best scholarly books they can find.

3

Professional and Business Books

ROBERT E. EWING

Before attempting to comment on 1983 results, or, even more brashly, to predict what we may see in the year ahead, I find it obligatory to try to define the category "Professional and Business Books."

The term is generally (although not universally) used to encompass both a broad spectrum of books and a broad and variegated range of markets. In the main, the term is used to cover all the disciplines of science and technology and all aspects of business. It is usually designed, as well, to include medical book publishing—particularly that aimed at the practitioner.

If the topic coverage seems broad, the marketplace is equally diffuse. It is quite unlike those areas of book publishing that seem to be, on the surface at least, self-explanatory. Publishers of school textbooks, college textbooks, and mass market paperbacks, and even general trade houses would all seem to have an understood publishing mission, a clear focus on their respective markets or audience, and even a fix on the market channel, or channels, needed to bring book and user together.

Not so, in the majority of cases, with the professional and business (or sci-tech for short) publishing houses. For many of them direct mail is the primary market channel—and for all of them it is a key ingredient. Most, but not all, work closely with the relative handful of specialized sci-tech bookstores (or through the sci-tech sections of larger retailers). The institutional, or library, market assumes enormous importance, with those in academia,

plus the special libraries in the for-profit sector, leading the way. Even here—or perhaps I should say particularly here—the fulfillment process is mostly tied to the wholesaler or book jobber, adding a further complicating factor to the equation.

On an ever-increasing basis, sci-tech books in many fields are finding their way into the classroom. Despite being written for practitioners (and, in numerous cases, by practitioners), titles in such disciplines as civil and mechanical engineering, architecture, data processing—to name but a few—are finding a lucrative peripheral market in academia, both as formal, adopted texts and on supplementary reading lists.

Sci-tech books, in increasing numbers, are being given special sales treatment outside traditional channels. Nowhere is this better demonstrated than in the business book area—a subject we will return to later on.

Finally, note that all the preceding remarks, designed to deal with the problem of identity in sci-tech publishing, have dealt with the domestic market scene. Beyond U.S. borders, this professional and business community of ours, the sci-tech houses, has a massive stake in the international marketplace. English is now commonly acknowledged to be the international language for science and technology. True, there are some specific disciplines—for example, business areas such as accounting, law, and taxation—that obviously do not "travel" well. But actual publishing decisions in the catholic areas of mathematics, physics, biology, and medicine are often governed by the publication's overseas distribution potential. So we see that regardless of definition, sci-tech publishing remains a hybrid complex in comparison with a great many of the areas that go to make up our total industry.

Having, it is hoped, dispensed with definitions, let me issue one caveat. The comments that follow are, clearly, generalities, and generalization is always difficult—even dangerous.

1983, in comparison with the two years immediately preceding it, had to be considered a favorable period for the professional and business book publisher. Both 1981 and 1982 have proved troublesome for the industry as a whole. In the sci-tech area itself sales showed a modest increase in 1982, basically reflecting (1) higher prices and (2) the rumblings of the computer-book boom.

Actually, 1983 got off to a somewhat sluggish start, with overall sci-tech book sales lagging behind the 1982 figures through the first half of the year. Then came the third quarter, and a major turnaround that carried through to the year's end. It is interesting and significant to note that the big unit increase occurred in the professional paperback category—one more manifestation of the impact of the computer-book bonanza.

There is little doubt that 1983 in the sci-tech area was dominated by two extraordinary occurrences: the computer revolution and the impact of the business book. Of the two, the more significant has to be the computer revolution. It turned from a large but previously somewhat controlled surge into a flood. Everyone published, everything sold—or so it seemed. It could, perhaps, be considered an irony that 1983 would have been judged by most as a flat year except for computer books. Stated another way, those companies with a healthy market share in computer titles look back at 1983 with approbation; those lacking a computer line most likely called the year a relative disappointment.

There seems to be no sign of any letup on the computer horizon, at least at the publishing end. The established houses continue, new companies enter the market almost daily, never-dreamed-of partnerships, ventures, and collaborations are constantly announced. A few random 1983 examples:

- Simon & Schuster (S&S) formed its Electronic Publishing Division for both software and books. In the spring of 1983 S&S outbid six other publishers and acquired, for $800,000, the rights to a multibook series on the IBM Personal Computer.
- Bantam announced the formation of its Electronic Publishing Division aimed at creating both software and books. Both Ballantine and Pocket Books followed suit.
- dilithium Press, already a leader in the computer field, has joined forces with Signet. Its basic line is being repackaged for mass marketing by the latter.
- Prentice-Hall, certainly one of the preeminent sci-tech publishers and one with a key position in professional computer books, has made a major marketing change. Using cardboard display units, Prentice-Hall is moving thousands of consumer-oriented titles designed for the home and game user through such mass-merchandise outlets as K-Mart.
- Microsoft Publishing, generally considered the leading software company in the business, has crossed over into computer books.
- Random House is distributing a book product developed by VisiCorp.
- Time-Life has jumped on the bandwagon, announcing the pending publication of its first computer titles.
- MicroText Publications, based in New York City, has been set up as a specialized packager, turning out tailor-made computer books on a six-to-eight-week schedule.
- At the New York Is Book Country fair, more than a dozen booths were mainly (and in some cases solely) devoted to computer books. Interest ran high enough to have a special area designated "Computer Country."
- At the American Booksellers Association (ABA) convention in Dallas, and at virtually every meeting held during the year, computers and computer books dominated conversation. This seemed to be the case whether the meeting was national, regional, or local; whether attendance was comprised of publishers, distributors, or both.
- Allyn & Bacon, Banbury Books, Dutton, Harper & Row, Methuen, New American Library, and Warner all announced entry plans during 1983. This list is, without doubt, incomplete, but a reasonable indication of 1983's trend.

We cannot leave the computer area without making the emphatic point that much of the computer-book explosion, in the strictest sense, should not really be equated with sci-tech publishing. The variety of computer books seems endless, with all sorts of introductory titles designed for the game addict and for the casual home user.

In an effort to zero in, for our purposes here, on the *professional* book, a "Better-Selling List" has been compiled. Note the deliberate avoidance of the bestseller terminology. Although access to sales records of firms is limited, this list represents (with reasonable fairness, I hope) at least some of the professional-level books that enjoyed success during 1983. The preponderance of computer titles is self-evident—as well as proof of the point. Of even greater interest are the publication dates. The majority of titles listed were published prior to calendar 1983—the strength of backlist books has long been a characteristic of all sci-tech publishing.

AISC. *Manual of Steel Construction.* 8th ed. Chicago: American Institute of Steel Construction, 1980. $38.

Blanchard and Johnson. *The One Minute Manager.* New York: Morrow, 1982. $15.

Bourne. *Unix System.* Reading, Mass.: Addison-Wesley, 1983. pap. $18.95.

Brooks. *Mythical Man-Month: Essays on Software Engineering.* Reading, Mass.: Addison-Wesley, 1978. pap. $12.95.

Brown. *System 370 Job Control Language.* New York: Wiley, 1978. pap. $19.95.

Feigenbaum. *Fifth Generation: Artificial Intelligence and Japan's Computer Challenge to the World.* Reading, Mass.: Addison-Wesley, 1983. $15.55.

Green. *D-Base User's Guide with Applications.* Englewood Cliffs, N.J.: Prentice-Hall, 1983. pap. $29.

Hogan. *CP/M Users Guide.* Berkeley, Calif.: Osborne, 1982. pap. $12.99.

Holtz. *How to Succeed as an Independent Consultant.* New York: Wiley, 1982. $19.95.

Kapp. *IMS Programming Techniques: A Guide to Using DL-1.* New York: Van Nostrand Reinhold, 1978. $17.95.

Kernighan. *A Programming Language, Digital Equipment Corporation Edition.* Englewood Cliffs, N.J.: Prentice-Hall, 1978. pap. $15.95.

Kruglinski. *Data Base Management Systems.* Berkeley, Calif.: Osborne, 1982. pap. $16.95.

Lim. *CICS/VS Command Level with ANS COBOL Examples.* New York: Van Nostrand Reinhold, 1982. $29.95.

McGilton. *Introducing the Unix System.* New York: McGraw-Hill, 1983. pap. $18.95.

Naisbitt. *Megatrends: Ten New Directions Transforming Our Lives.* New York: Warner, 1982. $15.50.

Peters and Waterman. *In Search of Excellence: Lessons from America's Best-Run Companies.* New York: Harper & Row, 1982. $19.95.

Porter. *Competitive Strategy: Techniques for Analyzing Industries and Competitors.* New York: Free Press, 1980. $19.95.

Sams. *Commodore Sixty-Four Programmers Reference Guide.* Indianapolis: Howard W. Sams, 1982. $19.95.

Sanders. *Computers Today.* New York: McGraw-Hill, 1982. $23.95.

Thomas. *A User Guide to the Unix System.* Berkeley, Calif.: Osborne, 1982. pap. $17.95.

In addition to these titles, some additional publications—all released in 1983 and some only a few months back—seem worthy of mention. Their early track record appears solid, their potential assured. Here again an effort has been made to single out professional titles rather than consumer-oriented works.

Bell Labs. *Unix—Volumes I and II.* New York: Holt, 1983. pap. $39.95 each.

Brooch. *Software Engineering with ADA.* Reading, Mass.: Addison-Wesley, 1983. pap. $18.95.

Christian. *The Unix Operating System.* New York: Wiley, 1983. pap. $18.95.

Glossbrenner. *The Complete Handbook of Personal Computer Communications.* New York: St. Martin's, 1983. pap. $14.95.

Hancock. *The Primer C.* New York: McGraw-Hill, 1983. pap. $12.95.

Hayes and Roth. *Building Expert Systems.* Reading, Mass.: Addison-Wesley, 1983. $32.50.

Hearn and Baker. *Computer Graphics for the IBM Personal Computer.* Englewood Cliffs, N.J.: Prentice-Hall, 1983. pap. $18.95.

Kudlick. *Assembly Language Programs: IBM 360-370.* Dubuque, Iowa: W. C. Brown, 1983. pap. $23.95.

Shooman. *Software Engineering.* New York: McGraw-Hill, 1983. $34.95.

A final word on this subject. All preceding remarks, one can easily note, have been restricted to conventional books. No reference has been made to software—either add-on or stand-alone. It is obvious to everyone that all sorts of software (and even hardware in some instances) must become an integral part of the total picture, and determining the role each of us plays is of paramount importance. It is, however, a topic left for someone else to address in a separate part of this annual.

While any review of sci-tech publishing in 1983 must begin with the saga of the still proliferating computer book, it must not, by any means, end there. If computer books ranked number one in significance, the business book took center stage in terms of dramatic impact. As the "Better-Selling List" shows, the final months of 1982 produced three blockbusters in the business area:

Blanchard and Johnson. *The One Minute Manager.* New York: Morrow, September 1982. $15.

Naisbitt. *Megatrends: Ten New Directions Transforming Our Lives.* New York: Warner, October 1982. $15.50.

Peters and Waterman. *In Search of Excellence: Lessons from America's Best-Run Companies.* New York: Harper & Row, November 1982. $19.95.

Their sales records and staying power, in all three cases, warrant the use of the word phenomenal. Using *Publishers Weekly* rankings in the hardcover nonfiction category we find that, in March 1983, they were running thus: (1) *Megatrends,* (2) *In Search of Excellence,* (3) *The One Minute Manager.* Six months later, in September, the first two had exchanged position, with the ranking then (1) *In Search of Excellence,* (2) *Megatrends,* (3) *The One Minute Manager.* Two months later, as we moved into November, there were—for the first time—some changes showing. At this point we find *In Search of Excellence* still in first place, but *Megatrends* had dropped to fifth and *The One Minute Manager* to thirteenth. The somewhat precipitous drop of *The One Minute Manager* is not hard to explain. On October 1, Berkley released its trade paperback version at $6.95, and within three weeks reported nearly 700,000 paperback copies in print. By the first of November it took over as the number-one trade paperback.

By year's end, *In Search of Excellence,* still showing remarkable resiliency, remained in the number-two hardcover spot; *Megatrends* held steady at number five, and

The One Minute Manager had dropped entirely off the hardcover list. The Berkley edition, however, rolled merrily along at the top of the paperback list. As of January 1984, the number of copies of each in print in hardcover were: *In Search of Excellence*, 1,320,000; *Megatrends*, 901,000; *The One Minute Manager*, 800,000.

Adding immeasurably to the drama surrounding the Peters and Waterman book, Harper & Row and Warner Books agreed in September to postpone the trade paperback from November to March 1, 1984. Since over a million hardcover copies were in print, the move and its timing were not totally surprising, considering the Christmas selling season upcoming. The postponement was not without cost—with Harper paying a reported $500,000 to Warner for the delay. While this scenario may not be unprecedented, veteran observers were hard pressed to recall a similar postponement arrangement involving these sums of money.

As a footnote, Warner has set an official *Feburary* publication date for its trade paperback edition of the Naisbitt book. Assuming no further postponements of the Peters and Waterman book, we can expect to see these same three titles jockeying for position on the trade paperback ranking reports even before spring officially arrives.

As for 1984, there seems to be just cause for optimism. In general terms the economy of the United States has undergone a rather remarkable recovery. Following one of the more painful slumps since the Great Depression, the immediate future of the information industry looks, on balance, bright. Unemployment is down, inflation has been virtually halted, corporate earnings are up, and the predictors think the prime rate will remain steady. As icing on the proverbial economic cake, 1984 is an election year. Much of this increased confidence showed up in the holiday period just concluded, with retailers enjoying their strongest season in over two years.

Of course, all of this good news hardly means that the problems in the professional and business publishing sector have dried up and blown away. A few of these of particular significance to the sci-tech community are outlined here:

• The spending power of the dollar overseas continues to surge. While this translates into good news for American tourists, it also leads to continued (or even increased) markups on U.S. book exports.

• A major concern of sci-tech publishers, and one that will be carefully watched in the coming months, is the new schedule proposed to the Postal Rate Commission by the Board of Governors of the U.S. Postal Service. Professional publishers with varying degrees of dependence on direct mail (at some firms it dominates the entire marketing program) will be among those most affected. Fortunately, the earliest date for implementation is October 1984, and strenuous efforts at deferral will be mounted.

• A vexing problem, and again one that has a disproportionately heavy impact on professional publishers, is the lack of any resolution to the Thor Power Tool Supreme Court case. This 1979 decision remains troublesome to more than one sci-tech house. Coupled with subsequent Internal Revenue Service (IRS) administrative rulings, the practical result of Thor has been to prohibit the depreciation of older and slow-moving titles that form the important backlists of many specialized houses. In November New York's Senator Daniel Moynihan introduced a bill designed to revise the tax law relating to publishers' inventories. While this is an encouraging sign, the bill has gone to committee and one would, I think, be charitable to call its fate "uncertain."

• Any real solution to the ever-tightening library budget dilemma seems, at best, remote. While public library monies would appear to show some signs of loosening, the same can hardly be said of academic and research library funding. Book prices, particularly in the sci-tech area, continue to rise at the same time that many conventional sci-tech books face ever-increasing competition, in the library area, from a variety of electronic publishing forms.

• The problem of piracy remains with us, in fact exacerbated by India's recent "legitimization" of reprinting by decree.

• Finally, returning one more time to the subject of computers, the industry's retailers in particular face a continuing flood tide of computer books, and now an equally sweeping array of software. Space is becoming—or has become—a major problem. Does the retailer cut back on the number of computer titles? Or will this, plus the almost inevitable commitment to software inventory and display, force him into a cutback in other, unrelated areas?

I will end this report with a peek at some of the potentially important titles assured of publication in 1984—a list drawn up through an informal survey of key sci-tech houses. The choices were made by the publishing houses, and the ranking is alphabetically by publisher. It can be assumed, at this point, that prices shown are approximate.

Addison-Wesley—Winston. *Artificial Intelligence*. 2nd ed. $29.95.

M. Dekker—Zelman. *What Every Engineer Should Know about Robots*. $24.95.

Facts On File. Blotnick. *The Corporate Steeplechase: Predictable Crises in a Business Career*. $17.95.

Gordon and Breach—Chinese Academy of Sciences. *History and Development of Ancient Chinese Architecture*. $1,500.

McGraw-Hill—Perry. *Chemical Engineer's Handbook*. 6th ed. $89.50.

Macmillan—Pascarella. *The New Achievers: Creating a Modern Work Ethic*. $17.95.

Morrow—Miller. *American Spirit: Visions of a New Corporate Culture*. $14.95.

Mosby. *Medical and Nursing Dictionary*.

Plenum—Zimmerman. *Biofuture: Confronting the Genetic Era.* $16.95.

Prentice-Hall—Seiden. *Product Safety Engineering.* $34.95.

H. Sams—Connolly and Leiberman. *Introducing the Apple Macintosh.* $12.95.

W. B. Saunders—Bennington. *Saunders Dictionary and Encyclopedia of Laboratory Medicine and Technology.* $45.

Van Nostrand Reinhold—Sax. *Dangerous Properties of Industrial Materials.* $198.

Wiley—Clarke. *Ascent to Orbit: A Scientific Autobiography, The Technical Writings of Arthur C. Clarke.* $19.95.

4

Religious Publishing

WILLIAM GRIFFIN

Bulls meant wealth in biblical times, and "bullish" is the only word to describe Bible and other religious book publishing in 1983. Sales rose, and convention attendance was up.

The Christian Booksellers Association (CBA) located in Colorado Springs has monitored the peaks and valleys—it's been mostly peaks—of religious publishing since the organization was founded in 1950. In 1982 it counted 3,198 members (retail stores) and 598 associate members (various suppliers); in 1983 it boasted 3,242 members and 640 associate members. The CBA convention held last July in Washington, D.C., had member attendance of 1,584 stores, up 6.6 percent over the previous year, and a total attendance of 8,830 people, up 17 percent. Gross revenues of the member stores and two religious book clubs were estimated by John Bass, executive director of CBA, to be in excess of $1.3 billion, topping the billion-dollar mark for the first time.

"Capitalism" may be a dirty word in the Third World, but in the First World where capitalism has been practiced by Christian publishers whose mission is to evangelize, spreading the Word and making money seem to coincide. Capitalism has even been defended by one scriptural exegete. Randolf O. Yeager, whose 20-volume *Renaissance New Testament* (Pelican Publishing Co., Gretna, La.) has been 40 years in the making, found John Maynard Keynes in Ephesians 4:28.

> Let him that stole steal no more [implies private ownership] but rather let him labor [there's the Puritan work ethic] working with his hands the thing which is good [good in the economic sense, which means profitable] that he may have to give to him that needeth [none other than the redistribution of wealth].

Both Thomas Nelson, Inc. (Nashville) and the Zondervan Corporation (Grand Rapids) were listed for the first time on the NASDAQ National Market System, and investors could follow the over-the-counter transactions of TNEL and ZOND in such newspapers as the *New York Times* and the *Los Angeles Times,* the *Washington Post* and the *Wall Street Journal.* Redistribution of wealth in the form of healthy dividends is expected by stock analysts.

Nelson's revenues for the fiscal year ending March 31, 1983, increased 17 percent over those of the preceding year; net income rose 22 percent; per-share earnings increased 18 percent. During that time the book division showed a 70 percent increase. The first book of an evangelical publisher to reach the *New York Times* bestseller list was Nelson's *Tough Times Never Last, But Tough People Do!* by Robert H. Schuller ($12.95); 243,000 copies had been sold by year's end.

Nelson made two major acquisitions in 1983: Ideals Publishing Co., of Milwaukee, which produces, among other things, cookbooks and children's books and magazines; and Interstate Book Manufacturing of Olathey, Kansas, which prints and binds both hard- and softcover books. The one will open new markets to Nelson; the other will complement the company's present bindery operations in Camden, New Jersey.

Zondervan published *Loving God* by Charles Colson in October and by year's end 140,000 copies had been shipped. It was a Judith Markham book, an imprint specializing in works of high literary and/or spiritual quality. Other successful imprints of the Zondervan book division are Daybreak Books, volumes of devotional significance; Lamplighter Books, which are comprised of Bible studies and aids; and Clarion Classics, stylish reissues of the best in devotional literature of the past.

A new imprint deserves mention only because it shows Zondervan's flexibility in addressing a significant portion of the contemporary market. Serenade Books are inspirational romances that deemphasize sex play and emphasize instead the interplay of faith and life. They are paperback originals, mass market format, 192 pages in length, and list for $1.95. Serenade/Saga books have historical settings; Serenade/Serenata, contemporary settings. Eight titles have been published; 34,000 copies of each have been sold.

During 1983 Zondervan carried on an aggressive acquisitions program. Among the companies acquired were:

- Francis Asbury Publishing Company of Wilmore, Kentucky, publishers of books for the substantial Wesleyan market.
- Fleming H. Revell Company of Old Tappan, New Jersey, publishers of evangelical and motivational books and a magazine for Christian women.
- The Benson Company, an evangelical Christian music company headquartered in Nashville.
- Marshall Pickering Holdings, Ltd., a British evangelical publishing group with international connections.

Zondervan also has a chain of family bookstores, which underwent substantial growth in 1983—from 78 stores grossing $25.6 million in 1982 to 87 stores grossing $32 million in 1983. And in 1984 10 more stores will be added to the chain with a corresponding growth in revenues expected.

The subject of *Newsweek*'s cover story for the Christmas 1982 issue was the Bible. President Reagan proclaimed 1983 "National Year of the Bible." And throughout the year, the "book of books," in a variety of bindings, stampings, and gildings as well as translations, continued to be the bestselling work in the Christian market.

Two Bibles introduced in 1982—Nelson's *New King James Version* (NKJV) and the Reader's Digest *Condensed Bible*—continued to meet their publishers' high expectations. Nelson published a massive concordance to NKJV as well as an edition of the *Topical Chain-Study Bible, New American Standard*. Zondervan published the *Thompson Chain-Reference Bible, New International Version*. By year's end 450,000 copies of the Zondervan book had been sold.

Jewish publishers made contributions to the Bible market. Schocken brought out *In the Beginning*, a rendition of Genesis by Everett Fox that emphasizes the oral quality of the original Hebrew text ($14.95). Hebrew Publishing came forth with *The Torah and the Haftarot*, translated into contemporary English by Philip Birnbaum; Hebrew and English texts are on facing pages ($19.50).

What happened between the end of the Old Testament and the beginning of the New Testament may be found in writings that were composed sometime between 300 B.C. and A.D. 200, that are Jewish or Jewish-Christian, that are often attributed to ideal figures in Israel's past, that may claim to contain God's word, and that sometimes build on ideas and narratives already appearing in the Old Testa-

ment. These writings have now been published by Doubleday as *The Old Testament Pseudepigrapha* under the general editorship of James J. Charlesworth; volume 1 costs $35.00; volume 2 will appear in 1984.

When Bibles appear, commentaries are sure to follow. Nelson published the *Liberty Bible Commentary*, of which Jerry Falwell is the executive editor, and it reflects the viewpoint of Liberty Bible College and Seminary, of which Dr. Falwell is chancellor ($29.95). Abingdon Press (Nashville) published the *Interpreter's Concise Commentary* in an 8-volume paperback series that also comes in a boxed set ($34.95). Word Books (Waco, Texas), is in the process of publishing 2 multivolume commentaries; the *Word Biblical Commentary* will have 52 volumes when completed—8 were published in 1983; the *Communicator's Commentary* will have 12 volumes when completed—7 were published in 1983; both series have sold far in excess of original expectations.

The most controversial religious book of the year was *An Inclusive Language Lectionary: Readings for Year A*, which was co-published by John Knox Press (Atlanta), Pilgrim Press (New York), and Westminster Press (Philadelphia). The lectionary is a collection of biblical readings normally used in the liturgy of a number of churches; the translation is the Revised Standard Version, but the Division of Education and Ministry of the National Council of Churches in the U.S.A. rerendered certain words and expressions so that females are included just about as many times as males.

"Father," "God the Father," and "God our Father" have become "God the Father [*and Mother*]." "Lord" has become "Sovereign" or "God the Sovereign." "King" and "Kingdom of God" have become "Realm of God." And women's names have been added, albeit bracketed and italicized, wherever possible. Matthew 3:9 is a good example: "And do not presume to say to yourselves, 'We have Abraham as our father [*and Sarah and Hagar as our mothers*]'; for I tell you, God is able from these stones to raise up children to Abraham [*Sarah and Hagar*]."

On publication, the work was reviewed in most secular and religious newspapers and magazines. "The council's effort to raise church consciousness is welcome," said a *New York Times* editorial on October 20, "even if some disturbed cadences are not." There were other editorials, and the lectionary was the subject of more than one editorial cartoon.

Once again the end of the world proved to be a popular and profitable subject for books. Hal Lindsey's *The Rapture: Truth or Consequences* (Bantam, paper, $6.95) deals with one specific moment in the end-time scenario; each of Lindsey's seven previous books about the end has had a rapturous sale of more than a million copies. *Approaching Hoofbeats* by Billy Graham (Word, $11.95) warns that the four horsemen of the Apocalypse—symbols of war, poverty, hunger, disease, and economic chaos— are riding hard and are just over the rise.

Coincidental with, if not causing, the end is the bomb. The American Catholic bishops issued "The Challenge of Peace," a pastoral letter on war and peace, and it immediately spawned comments and commentaries from just about every point on the Christian spectrum. Doubleday issued *The Bishops and the Bomb* edited by Jim Castelli (paper, $7.95). Crossroad came out with *Catholics and Nuclear War* edited by Philip Murnion (paper, $10.95). The argument in these is basically against the concept of nuclear weapons as deterrents. Arguing in favor of nuclear deterrence is Crossway's *Who Are the Peacemakers?* by Jerram Barris (paper, $2.95) and Nelson's *Moral Clarity in the Nuclear Age* by Michael Novak (paper, $3.95), which was also in the April 1, 1983, issue of *National Review.*

Arising from the evangelical camp, which is the largest among the Christian publishing community, were great hues and cries in 1983. Toes had been stepped on, or souls had been tromped on—it was hard to tell which, but one thing seems certain. *Metanoia,* the Greek word for the conversion process, was being superseded in some circles by *paranoia,* the fear some evangelicals have that they and/or others are being shadowed and brainwashed, assimilated and even eliminated.

Cal Thomas complained of censorship of Christian books in *Book Burning* (Crossway, paper, $5.95). John Whitehead lamented the loss of certain hard-won freedoms in *The Stealing of America* (Crossway, paper, $6.95). Franky Schaeffer predicted at the CBA convention and other forums that ten years down the line there will be no religious bookstores unless today bookstore owners promote and sell issue-oriented books like the ones written by himself, his father, Cal Thomas, and John Whitehead.

Schaeffer was given a standing ovation at CBA, but bookstore owners continued to put in their windows products that sell, like *The Christian Mother Goose,* Sparrow Records, Scripture Cookies and Scripture Tea, and Christian Hero Cards. Only time will tell how prophetic, or how paranoiac, these hues and cries may be. In the meantime, Crossway Books (Westchester, Illinois) continues to publish much of the critical, and indeed interesting, material of the new prophets.

As 1983 ended, so did the Seabury Press of New York City. Semi-official publishing arm of the Episcopal Church in the United States since its founding in 1951, it depended for its continued existence on subsidies approved by the executive council of the church; the subsidy for 1984 was voted down, and closure of publishing operations was immediate. Its backlist was offered for sale. Winston Press (Minneapolis) offered the highest bid. For Seabury's many authors, life was not ended; it was, as the liturgy for the dead suggests, only changed.

Some publishers, according to Ted Andrew, executive director of the Evangelical Christian Publishers Association, having enjoyed a successful year, are "wildly optimistic" about 1984. Others, having enjoyed an 11 to 12 percent growth in 1983, have budgeted for a 15 percent increase in 1984, and would not be surprised if the increase were even more than that. Still other publishers are laboring to keep their growth under control; too much growth in too short a time will mean destruction. What a way to go!

5

Higher Education Publishing

THOMAS W. GORNICK

Higher education publishing continued to show a modest increase in sales for 1983, reaching $1.22 billion, an increase of 9.4 percent over 1982. Total units sold rose slightly to 110.4 million, an increase of 1.6 percent over 1982's 108.7 million. The increase in units was good news after the previous year's decline.

The weak performance in unit sales over the past two years contributes to the feeling that much of the last two years' gains have come from price increases. Since 1977, unit prices have been increasing by approximately 9.5 percent per year or 90½ cents per unit. Prices of hardcover books have increased approximately $1.10 per unit, with paperbacks increasing an average of 90 cents per unit. These increases are less than those in trade publishing and on average in line with other price increases in higher education.

The total number of students increased slightly in 1983 with national enrollments up by 1.1 percent over the school year to approximately 13.9 million students in all institutions. Part-time students increased by 1.6 percent while full-time enrollments rose only eight-tenths of 1 percent. The trade or vocational-technical schools had the largest increase, with full-time students up by 13.4 percent. These changes clearly reflect the weak economy and government and institutional budget cuts during the Reagan administration.

Such career-oriented programs as business, computer science, and engineering continued to attract the most students. The social sciences and the liberal arts were hurt badly, causing some in the academic community to question national priorities. Higher education publishers had their strongest sales in the same career-oriented disciplines. Business continued to be the largest area, representing approximately 20 percent of sales. Computer science and engineering were the fastest growing disciplines.

Market Leaders

Textbook sales in the liberal arts continued to be stable with declines largest in the social sciences. In the largest college market, freshman English, such established books as the *Harbrace Handbook*, 9th edition, published by Harcourt Brace Jovanovich, and McCrimmon's *Writing with a Purpose*, 7th edition, published by Houghton Mifflin, dominated the market. Houghton Mifflin released the eighth edition of McCrimmon in October 1983. Little, Brown published the second edition of Fowler's *Little Brown Handbook* and it became one of the first new handbooks to take a significant share of the market. Houghton Mifflin's *Riverside Reader* by Harrison created a strong market for similar texts and paved the way for such books as St. Martin's *Bedford Reader*. In the introductory psychology course, McConnel's *Understanding Human Behavior*, 4th edition, published by Holt, Rinehart & Winston, continued to be the market leader. In Sociology, a declining market, McGraw Hill and Holt, Rinehart & Winston both published successful new introductory texts, McGraw's written by Schaffer and Holt's by Tischler. The trend in most liberal arts' markets was for established textbooks to retain their lead positions. Another example, Scott Foresman's *Introduction to Speech Communication*, 5th edition, by Monroe et al., continued to be the best selling text in the Speech Communication market. In history, Garrety, 5th edition, published by Harper & Row, and Current et al., 6th edition, published by Random House vied for the best-seller spot.*

In the sciences, instructors continued to use established titles. The Introduction to Biology market was dominated by Curtis, 4th edition, published by Worth; and Keeton, 3rd edition, published by W. W. Norton. William C. Brown Publishers offered a new title by Johnson et al. to capture some of the market. The Principles of Chemistry market continued to be led by Masterson and Slowinski, 5th edition, published by Saunders; and Brown and LeMay, 2nd edition, published by Prentice-Hall. Other strong titles for Introduction to Chemistry were Brady and Humiston, 3rd edition (John Wiley); Petrucci, 3rd edition (Macmillan), and Nebergall et al., 6th edition (D. C. Heath). The seventh edition of Nebergall will be published in 1984. The Introduction to Physics market was controlled by Halliday and Resnick, 2nd edition, published by John Wiley; Tipler, 2nd edition, published by Worth; and Sears and Zamanski, 6th edition, published by Addison-Wesley. In 1983, W. B. Saunders Publishing released a new anatomy and physiology text by Salmon and Davis. However, the Anatomy and Physiology market was led by the 3rd edition of Tortora and Anagnostakos, published by Harper & Row; and Hole, 3rd edition, published by William C. Brown Publishers. Both publishers will issue 4th editions of their Anatomy and Physiology texts in 1984.

The business schools continued to be a strong field for publishers in 1983. John Wiley published a successful Introduction to Business text by Gitman and McDaniels that rivaled previous market leaders by Rachman and Mescon, 2nd edition, published by Random House; and Boone and Kurtz, 3rd edition, published by Dryden Press. The Principles of Management course continued to be influenced by two books published in 1982, Certo (Brown) and Stoner (Prentice-Hall). The Introduction to Marketing course was dominated by new editions of Pride and Ferrell, 3rd edition, published by Houghton Mifflin; and Prentice-Hall's second edition of Kotler. Richard D. Irwin's 7th edition of McCarthy, published in 1981, continued to hold market share, as did Scott Foresman's 1982 *Principles of Marketing* by Kinnear and Bernhardt. Dryden Press continued to dominate the finance area with its books by Brigham and Weston. Publishing in accounting was light in 1983, but nine Principles of Accounting books are scheduled in 1984. Finally, McGraw-Hill's 1983 list included its third successful text for the Introduction to Economics by Fischer and Dornbusch. McGraw's previous texts for this course, Samuelson, 11th edition, and

McConnel, 9th edition, remain two of college publishing's most successful titles.

Computer Books and Software

Computer Science and Data Processing courses offered publishers the greatest new opportunity in 1983. McGraw-Hill's *Computers Today* by Donald Sanders became a market leader in the Introduction to Data Processing course. The text was one of the bestselling college titles published in 1983. Its success is attributed to the currentness of the material and the comprehensive teaching package, which includes instructor's manual, diskettes, student workbook, and so forth. *Computers Today* replaced books by Shelly and Cashman, Anaheim Publishing; and Capron and William, a Benjamin Cummings' book. This market will continue to be volatile with new editions of previous market leaders and new titles scheduled for publication in 1984. Heath's Introduction to Pascal by Dale et al. was one of the bestsellers in the computer language courses. Dale's teaching package included films to support the text.

On January 1, 1983, *Time* magazine declared the personal computer the "Machine of the Year" and sent the nation into what *Business Week* later labeled "computer shock." College publishing has been one of the beneficiaries of the microcomputer market by providing print support to potential and current users of microcomputers. In April, B. Dalton Bookseller reported that computer books accounted for over 10 percent of its trade business, outselling fiction; and Waldenbooks expected a threefold increase in computer-book sales. Many of the titles were purchased from publishers' college lists, because the supply of quality materials was limited. The market has been flooded throughout the year by new titles published by both new and established houses. The increased demand for computer science books caused many houses to increase their editorial and marketing staffs in this area. Addison-Wesley, Prentice-Hall, and John Wiley & Sons benefited greatly from already successful backlists.

The computer-book boom has blurred market divisions within larger established houses. College books sold well in trade markets. This raised the issue of discount structure and management responsibility for editorial and marketing functions. Smaller publishers handled this market shift better than did the larger houses. Another effect of the computer publishing programs was a larger demand for marketing dollars for the computer lists. It became necessary to advertise and promote at major trade shows, and in national computer magazines. These channels cost significantly more than those in traditional academic journals and conventions, putting strains on already limited marketing budgets. The computer science market offered publishers a new growth area. The market also had a higher base price range—$15 to $40 per unit, contributing to higher profit margins.

Most computer books could be classified into three

---

*College textbooks are titled after the appropriate course; therefore I have identified books by course, author's last name, edition, and publisher.

areas: (1) traditional textbooks with limited trade markets; (2) computer language books both generic and specific to a particular microcomputer—the latter with good trade potential; and (3) books about microcomputer applications, such as word processing, spreadsheets, or data-base management. The last group has the largest share of its market in trade, but the education market is growing, with more schools offering courses in computer skills or integrating computers into their traditional courses. The *Chronicle of Higher Education* reported in March 1983 that mathematical computation represents 60 percent of computer use and word processing 30 percent in higher education classrooms.

While computer books brought new sources of income to higher education publishers, computers themselves brought greater speed in manuscript preparation and general office tasks. Managing a manuscript electronically results in efficiency of revising and editing, speeding the book to market. Time can also be saved in typesetting; however, the lack of compatibility in hardware and software continues to be a major obstacle to using the technology in the editorial and production processes. Currently most savings are in time, not in cost of composition. This situation should improve as the personal-computer market stabilizes. The success of the IBM Personal Computer and IBM-compatible machines has already had a stabilizing effect on the hardware chosen by publishers and authors.

The Higher Education Division of the Association of American Publishers (AAP) assisted houses in coping with the new technology. It offered two-day Computer Literacy Workshops, conducted by consultant Stan Goldberg. The AAP Higher Education Editorial Committee planned, developed, and published (on June 16) *An Author's Primer to Word Processing*, which has sold over 8,500 copies. The 45-page pamphlet provides authors with the essentials to be informed consumers when they purchase word-processing equipment. The pamphlet also lists 30 mnemonic codes to use in preparing a manuscript, which will help the publisher in production and composition.

The euphoria among publishers over computer books may have some long-term negative effects as the general public becomes more knowledgeable about computers. Acquiring computer titles is very competitive, forcing royalties 3 to 5 percent above normal textbook contracts. The increased royalties, larger advances, higher grants-in-aid for manuscript development, and increased employee costs will have direct effects on the cash flow and profitability of computer science and college textbook lists. Finally, the academic computer science market will not remain so attractive as students discover the limited job market for computer science majors.

College publishers have also entered the computer-software market, offering educational material to accompany textbooks or stand-alone products. Most software supports textbooks, providing electronic test banks and computer-assisted instruction packages. Houses have created separate electronic publishing units to manage acquisition, development, production, and marketing.

Besides ancillary material, publishers are issuing tutorial software to accompany computer books on application software, such as VisiCorps's VisiCalc and Micropro's WordStar, and tests such as the Scholastic Aptitude Test (SAT).

It is too soon to answer the question of whether textbook publishers can afford to develop and market commercially successful software. Currently, software-development costs begin in the range of $50,000 with national marketing campaigns exceeding $1 million. It is becoming increasingly difficult to find the basement "hacker" willing to sell software at a price that minimizes risk. Another serious issue for software publishers is piracy. In a college environment it is virtually impossible to prevent students from stealing by copying the diskettes. Higher education publishers have just begun on the software learning curve; however, software will be a part of their business in the future.

Photocopying and Copyright Infringement

1983 gave higher education publishers a major victory over copying mills. On December 14, 1982, nine major publishers—Addison-Wesley, Alfred A. Knopf, Basic Books, Houghton Mifflin, Little, Brown and Co., Macmillan Publishing Co., the National Association of Social Workers, Random House, and Simon & Schuster—filed suit against New York University, nine professors, and the Unique Copy Center for copyright infringement. The litigation was coordinated by AAP and charged the parties with "unauthorized and unlawful reproduction, anthologizing, distribution, and sale of publishers' copyrighted works."

The case came as a result of an increase in illegal copying of materials by faculty for use in courses. The material is often photocopied at a nearby copy center, bound or gathered, and sold to students in direct violation of the 1976 Copyright law. The actions go beyond the reasonable limits allowed by the statute. On April 14, 1983, New York University and the professors settled the lawsuit by agreeing to impose 1976 guidelines that permitted teachers to make single copies without written permission and multiple copies limited to one copy per student after the material had been subjected to tests for brevity, spontaneity, rules governing anthologizing, and the effect of the copying on a course. In a second settlement, dated May 31, 1983, Unique Copy Center agreed to refrain from copying any of the plaintiffs' copyrighted works except under special conditions. The settlement requires certification by the customer that permission to copy material has been secured from the publisher. Unique Copy Center also agreed to pay the publishers involved an undisclosed amount equal to the copy center's profit from the copied material identified in the original complaint. The two settlements accomplished the objectives of the suit and notified faculty and institutions nationally of their responsibilities to honor the copyright of material. The *Chronicle of Higher Education* reported, in March 1983, a decline in copying, and Kinko's Graphics, a national chain with 170 outlets near colleges and universities, showed a 20 percent decline in activity.

The competitive college market caused the Executive Committee of the AAP Higher Education Division to reaffirm the industry's commitment to the highest ethical standards by adopting voluntarily the code of ethics for college sales representatives. The code is a result of growing concern over the questionable buying and selling practices of some individual faculty and sales representatives. The code asks that publishers "avoid making any improper inducement to any actual or potential customer . . . which can be described as a bribe . . . avoid methods of payments [of fees for services like book reviews] which could appear to represent improper inducement to college faculty or administrative personnel." The code goes on to encourage publishers to enforce individual house codes of ethics and to maintain the highest professional standards.

College Stores

The environment for college booksellers is changing rapidly, partly because of budget constraints in the institutions that own and operate the stores. Currently, 72 percent of all college bookstores are owned by the schools they serve. Store managers have responded to the changes by trying to increase profitability through improved nontextbook departments, creating computer departments that sell hardware and software, and increasing purchase and sales of used books. The stores currently earn approximately 50 to 80 percent of their income from textbook sales; they also represent approximately 3 percent of microcomputer sales.

The battle over used books continues to be a major issue among publishers. At the 1983 National Association of College Stores (NACS) Convention, it was reported that used-book sales increased by 27 percent in 1981/1982, representing 17 percent of a store's textbook business, while new-books sales increased by only 15 percent. One in five booksellers said they made a profit on new books with a 20 percent discount, while nine out of ten reported they made profit on used books. The increased used-book market has contributed to the decline in units sold, a need for shorter revision cycles, and a more aggressive pricing policy by publishers. Hardcover books have had the largest decline in units, and the greatest unit price increase. The majority of booksellers prefer raising the discount to 25 percent to having a net pricing plan. If booksellers receive a better discount, will they be willing to accept less favorable return policies? Bookstore managers often fail to mention that in many areas there are no general bookstores to give them competition.

The sample copy sent to a faculty member for consideration as a course text often is sold to a used-book dealer who then wholesales the book to a college bookstore. This allows the bookstore at least a 25 percent markup. Publishers have tried a variety of methods to curb the supply of complimentary copies to bookstores or used-book dealers. They have stamped the book with "Not for Resale," left out signatures, enclosed return envelopes, and sent notices to faculty explaining how selling a complimentary copy affects the price of books to their students. All of these methods and others have had only limited effect on the books' being sold. Authors' royalties and sales representative commissions are also negatively affected by the growing used-book business. Publishers and booksellers will eventually have to come to a mutual agreement to solve this problem.

Economic hard times have forced some schools to lease the campus bookstore, shifting the management and operation to an outside firm. Currently, approximately 10 percent of college bookstores are leased. Follett Corporation, a college bookstore operator, acquired United College Bookstore in the third quarter of 1983, making Follett the largest single college bookstore operator. United added 54 stores, located in 13 states, to the 72 operated by Follett. Follett is also one of the largest used-book wholesalers in the United States.

Forecast for the Remainder of the Decade

Higher education publishers will continue to acquire, develop, and produce texts for traditional college courses. Some will use the traditional areas to support publishing programs in such new areas as computer science, engineering, and vocational education. However, the houses will have to develop good research methods to determine market trends since career and technically oriented programs are subject to unpredictable enrollment shifts. Supporting broader publishing programs will place a heavy demand on lean budgets. Competition will continue to increase significantly among college publishers. In the next few years the industry will continue to see books with more elaborate designs and greater use of color. Already books that were printed in earlier editions in one color and with simple cover designs have two-color interiors and four-color covers. For many large-enrollment basic courses, texts are printed with four-color inserts or complete four-color interiors. The ancillary packages will become more comprehensive, resembling the elementary–high school materials, and more costly. Computer material will become necessary in basic course packages. New, more aggressive marketing plans will be needed just to maintain a company's position. The quality of marketing will make the difference.

The second half of the 1980s will see higher education publishers enter into intense marketing warfare. Editors can no longer publish experiments, but each new title must be carefully considered against books already in the market. Book-development staffs will have to be both competition- and customer-oriented. The number of introductory texts that are similar will force publishers to reconsider another "me-too" book for the same course. Editorial staffs will have to go beyond the generic product and even beyond the current expectations of faculty to a new level of imagination and creativity. The college sales representative will spend more time supporting and serving the faculty after the sale to establish a strong link with the customer. The successful companies in the 1980s will be ones that have established professional market research departments, developed a strong team spirit between editorial and marketing staff, and established sound financial planning for each title. The expertise of each department will be essential to the house's success. As Cosner et al. wrote in their study *Books: The Culture and Commerce of Publishing,* the very large and very small houses will have the advantage in this competitive marketplace. Publishers with large financial resources, provided by past success or membership in a conglomerate, will be able to meet the development, production, and marketing costs demanded by the intense competitive environment. Small publishers will have the creative resources and entrepreneur spirit to develop and produce high-quality, competitive texts. The small houses are less traditional, enabling them to produce new creative texts for markets dominated by a stack of me-too books. Finally, the medium-size houses will have hard decisions ahead to maintain current positions and achieve new growth. College publishing faces a mature market demanding management with imagination and focused on the customer and competition.

6

School Publishing

JAMES R. SQUIRE

The past year by no means has been a miraculous year for school publishers, but despite an increasingly competitive environment, industrywide revenue grew to an estimated $1.15 billion, an increase over 1982 of close to 10 percent. Final data on 1983 will not be fully analyzed until May, but present estimates suggest clearly that 1983 was the first year in many during which elhi publishers secured a revenue substantially in excess of the annual rate of inflation. Since unit sales appear to have remained relatively constant, the growth was essentially in price.

No particular phenomenon seems to account for this upswing. To be sure, California, the largest of the 23 adoption states, selected new elementary reading programs in 1983 and expended $20 million to support its choices. Given total elementary school revenues nationally of about $750 million, however, the one-time California thrust did little more than provide a slight one-year bulge in the largest single school market segment.

The conservative mood of the nation has long since been reflected in slowly rising expenditures for "basic subjects"—reading, mathematics, writing, spelling, and academic high school programs. 1983 was no exception. Sales of nonacademic textbooks and supplementary (nonessential) materials have been less than strong.

This year's increase in customer purchasing did not follow historical patterns for a nation emerging from recession. Local school tax levies are voted in the first quarter of the year preceding the academic year in which funds are spent. Taxpayers have tended not to approve substantial increases in school funding during periods of economic strain. Increases in school textbook purchases

thus have lagged at least a year or so behind the economic climate of the nation. During the first quarter of 1983, the country was only beginning to emerge from the recession, and evidence of substantial new support for school expenditures was not prevalent in voting patterns. It is surprising, therefore, to find schools able to fund increases in textbook purchases within only a few months. Concern with the quality of schooling and a felt need to change instructional materials presumably outweighed other considerations and gave textbook purchasing some degree of priority. These considerations are reflected in several key developments.

Funding

Indicative of the strengthened funding for instructional materials are developments in several pivotal states. In New York, Governor Mario Cuomo called for an increase of $5 per pupil for textbooks (to $20 per student) and as this is written is asking for additional support in 1984. Florida has appropriated around $40 million for the fiscal year, less than the $44 million called for by Governor Bob Graham but an increase of about 5 percent over the previous year. Texas moved from $51 million to $65.5 million, up more than 25 percent. Even more impressive action came in California when special legislative funding for one year supported purchases of $76 million for instructional materials, an increase of around 90 percent over the preceding year. And comforting indeed is the early 1984 call by Governor George Deukmejian to continue "full funding" in 1984.

Such regional developments are critical since textbook

funding is essentially a state and local responsibility. Federal support has never exceeded 8 percent of total schooling costs and recently has declined below this figure. Still, despite efforts to prune federal expenditures to the bone, Congress did vote slight increases. Expenditures for Chapter 2, for example, which funds programs for the disadvantaged, were approved at $3 billion, in contrast to $2.7 billion for the previous fiscal year. Also, as this is written, Senate and House committees must agree on funding for federally supported efforts to improve precollege mathematics and science at a level expected to range between $500 and $600 million annually. If historical patterns follow, about 5 percent of these funds will flow through to instructional materials.

However improved the outlook, school publishers cannot be sanguine. The average expenditure for school textbooks remains well under 1 percent of total school expenditures. If the average textbook expenditure per pupil had risen nationally to $22.20 in 1982, a 60 percent increase since 1977, the average cost of educating a pupil rose 79 percent during the same period, and among the states still expending less than the national average per pupil for instructional materials are several of the nation's wealthiest: New York, Pennsylvania, Texas, California, Maryland, Virginia, Massachusetts, Ohio, and North Carolina. The School Division of the Association of American Publishers (AAP), notably effective in its recent representation in California, Texas, Florida, and New York, must pursue its campaign to educate educational leaders with continued vigor.

Educational Reform

Pivotal in stimulating renewed interest in school funding are the well-publicized school-reform efforts that began in 1983 with President Reagan's personal introduction of *A Nation at Risk* (Government Printing Office). Since last spring's press conference, more than 160 separate studies, commissions, and task forces have been at work studying how to achieve excellence and equality in education. Reform legislation has been introduced in 47 state legislatures, and educational excellence ranks high among the current priorities of presidential candidates.

Aside from the report of the National Commission on Excellence in Education, the most influential reports thus far appear to be those prepared by Ernest Boyer for the Carnegie Foundation (*High School*, Harper & Row); *Action for Excellence* by the Task Force on Education for Economic Growth for the Education Commission of the States; the report on precollege mathematics and science of the National Science Board (National Science Foundation); John Goodlad's *A Place Called School* (McGraw-Hill), a body of 350 studies on effective teaching and effective schools that document much of what needs to be done; and Theodore Sizer's forthcoming recommendations on high school reform. Individually these and other reports might be forgotten. Collectively they seem likely to bring about a substantial transformation of the school curriculum, which will strongly impact the market for publishing.

The gist of the recommendations is now common knowledge: a longer school day and school year coupled with required homework to increase student time on academic tasks, better prepared teachers and higher teacher salaries, greatly strengthened academic schooling in the high school, stronger mathematics and science instruction, more courses, more challenging instruction, required study of and use of computers, four years of high school English, and strengthened reading and writing requirements. If improved instructional materials are not directly seen as fundamental to improved instruction as they were in school-reform movements of 20 years ago, the ferment for more academic instruction seems clearly leading toward a demand for new and better textbooks. In any period of strong curricular upheaval, school publishers inevitably find market opportunities.

Criticism of Textbooks

Paralleling and at times underscoring the school-reform efforts have been investigations of the quality of textbooks and the level of challenge they present to American students.

Beginning with the popularized criticisms of American history textbooks by Frances Fitzgerald during the late seventies, school textbooks have been increasingly subjected to intensive study. During recent years scholars at the Center for the Study of Reading (CSR)—notably Dolores Durkin, Thomas Anderson, Bonnie Armbruster, and Jean Osborn—have identified serious deficiencies in readers and in classroom use of the programs. During the 1982/1983 school year, CSR leaders met with school publishers to recommend appropriate action.

Less friendly and less carefully documented criticism came during the past year from Bruno Bettelheim, who found literary deficiencies in elementary reading programs. Educational and political leaders in Florida and elsewhere also charged that textbooks are being written "below grade level" and thus threatened the excellence of education. But as the year ended, a major investigation by Jeanne Chall reported that published reading programs at least have grown more difficult for a decade and that the level of challenge of science and social studies textbooks varies substantially from program to program. Chall also found today's schools seeking more challenging materials. Debate promises to continue with two national conferences this spring focusing on instructional materials. One will be cosponsored by the College Entrance Examination Board.

What significance do these developments have for publishers? On the one hand, they support the desire to purchase new material. On the other, they provide guidelines—for school customers no less than for publishers—on how to improve current texts. At Indiana University Roger Farr concluded a study of text-adoption practices and suggested important improvements. Educational research has not seen serious scholarly study of textbooks for many years, and current efforts almost certainly will lead to better books and better users of books. How appropriate then that the last two years have seen AAP's School Division launch a program to support selected graduate research in instructional materials. The fruits of such endeavor can be much more beneficial than the impact of would-be censors of school textbooks who throughout the seventies kept their own agenda in trying to improve school books. Indeed, 1983 may well have been a watershed year for such censorship activities, which, although continually present as they have been for the past half-century, seem to be declining in total influence. In Texas, for example, thanks in part to efforts of the People for the American Way in resisting self-appointed censors, the state board has adopted new selection procedures that eliminate the infamous and detailed bills of particulars as well as impose time restrictions on protestors. Concern with textbook-selection procedures continues but the alarming increase in complaints about books noted three or four years ago no longer seems characteristic of American education.

Microcomputers and Electronic Publishing

But if a sense of order and responsibility is emerging in the analysis and selection of printed materials, no such central tendency yet appears with respect to the uses of microcomputers. The report *Pre-College Mathematics and Science* (National Science Foundation, 1983) calls for education about, with, and through computers, but thus far no clear consensus has emerged on how computers seem likely to impact schools and school publishing, beyond a commonly shared belief that the influence will be profound.

At year's end Knowledge Industry Publications estimated that at least 400,000 microcomputers had been installed thus far in the nation's schools (an increase of 27 percent over the previous year), a number that some analysts see expanding to at least 2 million within five years. The market for software—estimated at $42 million in 1983—is estimated to increase to $60 million in 1984 and to as much as $150 million by 1987. But even informed estimates vary in such a rapidly changing environment. Suffice to say that 1983 has been a year in which the promise of the microcomputer has been balanced by the problems associated with the market in both hardware and software.

To the major school publishers establishing electronic divisions—Scott, Foresman, Houghton Mifflin, Holt, Addison-Wesley, Scholastic, Xerox, and Esquire Education—must be added new school marketers—Parker Brothers, Spinnaker, Bruderbond, Radio Shack, Millikan, Milton Bradley, Koala, and many others—each with educational software of its own. One study found 280 different designers of software for science and mathematics alone. Given such conditions, small wonder that schools and school publishers seem unable to predict the winds of change.

Yet a few directions are clear. Most school publishers see electronic publishing as offering opportunities. The majority of hardware installations thus far are in secondary schools; most of the software, particularly the more innovative programs, seems designed for elementary schools. This discrepancy occurs because courses in computer literacy have generally been installed above grades seven where teachers and students do much of their own programming.

School leaders on their part complain about the quality of available software and their inability to preview available software. It may take years before educational leaders can agree on criteria to evaluate software programs and methods of selection comparable to those that guide the book-selection business. Publishers on their part look nervously at the investment required for electronic publishing and worry about securing acceptable returns on software products, which tend to be marginally priced and easily copied.

One thing seems clear at the end of 1983. Electronic publishing not only will create change in basic and supplementary materials markets, but is creating new opportunities in and outside of formal education.

Industry Changes

Unlike the recent past, 1983 has been marked less by acquisition and mergers than by management changes: Gulf & Western did enter school publishing by acquiring Esquire Education, which in turn acquired Follett; Macmillan staked out a major claim in vocational and technical publishing for the schools through the acquisition of Bennett and McKnight; McDougal-Littel secured certain of the school titles no longer to be marketed by Science Research Associates; and at year's end Random House is reported to have purchased Reader's Digest skill-builder programs. But these changes may have less long-range impact on publishing strategies than will some of the executive changes: Richard Young, for instance, has just completed his first year as president of Houghton Mifflin; Robert Palmerton is now general manager of Holt, Rinehart & Winston; Richard T. Morgan assumed the presidency of Scott, Foresman and Company; and Bobby E. Jones now heads Macmillan School Publishing. New faces for new times.

Whatever the impact of increased funding, educational reform, criticisms of textbooks, and electronic publishing, one new strategy is becoming apparent throughout the industry. Convinced apparently that internal competition can lead to external market opportunities, at least four corporations are developing alternative and competitive school publishing companies. SFN Companies, for example, led the way with South-Western and Silver Burdett as well as the parent elhi company. Houghton Mifflin is strengthening Riverside in Chicago as a competitor to its Boston-based operation. Macmillan now has Bennett and McKnight to set alongside Glencoe. And Harcourt Brace Jovanovich appears to be investing heavily in Coronado. As a new year begins, new and strengthened imprints say much about the confidence that industry executives have in the future of school publishing.

7

Small Presses

JOHN HUENEFELD

1983 was essentially a year of shakeout for marginal small publishers, and recovery for stronger and more opportunistic ones. As with the rest of the book-publishing industry, small presses echoed the economic recession that peaked in 1982. Judging from the annual survey of small-press managers conducted by the *Huenefeld Report* newsletter, a soft economy with resulting sales declines was the single most troublesome problem those managers perceived for 1983. But overall, those same managers (a representative cross-section from 196 responding publishing enterprises) were predicting in January that 1983 sales would rebound to a 13.5 percent growth rate by year-end. While the statistics to substantiate or challenge that rosy forecast are just beginning to emerge, it is apparent from 1983 operating summaries of a variety of small presses monitored personally by the writer that the recession has indeed ended, and growth rates and profits are on the way back up.

What Do We Mean by "Small Presses"?

Perhaps some clarification of terminology is in order before we examine the statistics. The term *small press* means different things to different people. But the point at which size really makes a difference in the operating dynamics of a book-publishing house is essentially that point at which communication between the distinct publishing subfunctions (management, editorial development, marketing, production, fulfillment, financial and facilities administration) characteristically switches from oral to written (from face-to-face to remote). Size normally

generates departmental boundaries and physical inaccessibility between these functions in virtually all publishing houses whose sales volumes exceed $30 million a year—the "big publishers." From there down to about $3 million a year we find a range of "middle-size publishers" who may operate by either style of internal dynamics (face-to-face or remote/off-line). Below $3 million in annual sales volume (and below 30 or so employees), the instantaneous oral communication of face-to-face interaction is the natural and advantageous operating dynamic—and that basically defines the world of the small press.

There are, at best, no more than three or four hundred big and middle-size publishers in North America today. The rest of the 14,000 publishers of the books currently listed in *Books in Print,* and a thousand or more additional publishing entities that have not yet gotten their books "on the record," all operate in that small-press world. They tend to fall into four distinct categories (all with similar problems and operating dynamics, but with different economic-risk contexts, and different objectives):

- Entrepreneurial publishers—serious commercial ventures that are small only because they have not yet found the time, capital, authors, or managerial know-how to make them big—constitute perhaps 3,000 of the 15,000.
- Associational publishers—outreach and member-service programs of professional, trade, academic, religious, and other not-for-profit organizations using the book as a communications medium—constitute perhaps another 3,000.
- Self-publishers—authors or authoring organizations using book formats and distribution channels to exploit

their own manuscripts or data bases—constitute another 4,000 or 5,000.

Avocational publishers—people who (more-or-less) know how to use book formats to give access to book distribution channels to worthy literary, poetic, or ideological voices they wish to encourage—make up the remaining 4,000 or 5,000 members of the small-press population of North America.

Serious entrepreneurial publishers sometimes feel that the term *small press* popularly connotes the last, or last two, of the categories above, and consequently prefer for themselves the term *small publisher*. However, I will disregard such linguistic nuances here, and include all four in the scope of this review.

1981–1982 Recession Impacts

The effects of the recession on small presses, as well as the general economic realities of small press publishing, are shown in Table 1 in the results from the last four *Huenefeld Report* surveys (with about 200 publishers, averaging about $1 million in sales, reporting each year). Notice that as the growth rate slowed down in 1980—the first sign of the recession—profit margins dropped significantly. Publishers reacted first by beginning to reduce inventories; by the end of 1981 inventories declined from 33 percent of annual sales volume (a dangerous level) to 27 percent. This means that in one year the publishing houses represented in the survey got rid of (and did not replace) better than one of every six books they had been warehousing (and financing). And it did not seriously inhibit sales; the growth rate slowed by only one-tenth of a percent (statistically insignificant), and, as a result, profit margins started back up.

These inventory reductions had been achieved in two ways. First, average print quantities were reduced; the typical hardcover first printing went down from 5,490 books the year before to 4,000; average first printings of trade paperbacks declined from 6,512 to 5,366. Second, as the table shows, small publishers became much more restrained about publishing new titles—preferring instead

to lean on proven backlist titles. Also shown in the table, in 1979, the ratio of new titles to backlist reprintings was virtually one to one (1.01 to 1); by 1981, new titles appeared only half as often as backlist reprintings (0.52 to 1). In two years, the number of new titles released annually declined about 20 percent (in relation to total list size), while the number of backlist reprintings increased dramatically.

In 1982, unfortunately, small publishers apparently lost their nerve as the recession deepened. With sales depressed, they went back to the former level of new-title production. The rapid, dramatic decline in sales volume growth rates also suggests that small publishers significantly cut their marketing budgets. We know that by year's end they were spending only 18 percent of their resources on sales-and-promotion efforts (marketing). In view of their heavy dependence on mail-order marketing (which two-thirds cited as their most important marketing channel, and which normally requires reinvestment of 25 percent or more of a small publisher's sales volume to maintain growth), this level of marketing activity could only be expected to reinforce the negative effects of the recession.

Whether small publishers recovered their inventory discipline, their faith in their backlists, and their marketing nerve in 1983 remains to be seen as the statistical data accumulate. However, sales of a number of individual publishing programs that it was the writer's privilege to monitor during 1983 did show the same pronounced rebound in the closing months of the year as Association of American Publishers (AAP) and Book Industry Study Group (BISG) figures indicated for the larger houses. By year's end, the recession had clearly ended and a healthier bookselling climate prevailed.

The Changing Production Environment

In the aftermath of this recent shakeout—but in response as much to technological developments as economic ones—significant changes in the environment in which small presses operate can be seen. Some of those changes represent exploitation of small-press opportuni-

Table 1 The Effects of the Recession on Small Presses

	1979	*1980*	*1981*	*1982*
Annual sales growth	15.4%	12.6%	12.5%	8.2%
Before-tax profit on sales	8.9%	6.7%	7.3%	7.0%
Inventory as percent of sales	32.8%	33.0%	27.0%	30.0%
New titles as percent of total list	12.9%	n/a	10.45%	10.7%
Ratio of new titles to backlist reprintings	1.01	0.72	0.52	1.00
Portion of total backlist titles reprinted	12.9%	n/a	27.7%	10.7%

ties by other industries, or by larger publishers; others represent the innovative maneuvering of the small presses themselves.

Two of the most pronounced influences from other industries concern the way books are physically produced (from manuscripts). First, major book manufacturers have become increasingly interested in competing for short-run printing jobs, and more realistic about what constitutes true short-run printing, as a result of that dramatic (though temporary?) tightening of inventory investments during the recession. Second, the spectacular decline in computing costs that has accompanied the adaptation of personal computers to small-publishers' operations is rapidly changing the basic procedures for copy editing and typesetting.

With the continent's largest book manufacturer, R. R. Donnelly & Sons, dedicating one of its newest plants entirely to short-run printing, and aggressively courting small publishers through its sales force, it is clear that small presses no longer have to "take the leavings" by conforming their needs to leftover capacity and processes designed primarily for mass market, "bestseller," basal textbook, and other long-run requirements restricted largely to the bigger houses. Whereas manufacturers once tended to define short run as anything less than 10,000 books—and in recent years have certainly included any printing under 5,000 in the category—they have now become much more hospitable to the small-press need for print quantities below 3,000. In fact, one well-known national manufacturer (Thomson-Shore) now openly courts small press jobs in runs down to 50 copies.

This growing manufacturer interest in short-run jobs is good news for small presses only because it is accompanied by attractive pricing patterns. No longer must one pay an arm and a leg (per unit) to avoid overstuffing the warehouse. When 13 reputable national book manufacturers cooperated with the Huenefeld publishing consultants in late 1983 to produce a table of "reasonable" unit prices for short-run book manufacturing in quantities from 1,500 to 9,000 (*Huenefeld Report*, November 7, 1983), to help small presses evaluate their production purchasing, we found that the most substantial price break (per unit) came not in the larger quantities, but between 1,500 and 3,000 books.

Even more significant than the growing respectability of short-run production is the rapid adaptation of the microcomputer to manuscript editing and typesetting in small publishing houses. As recently as 1979, in-house typesetting (then utilized by 30 percent of small presses) seemed to be "the wave of the future" because it gave many the opportunity to substitute more elbow grease (plentiful in small publishing houses) for hard cash outlays (less plentiful) to compositors. But today we find this percentage unchanged, and many small publishers not renewing or replacing the equipment when the leases expire, while the "word-processor/typesetter interface" is rejuvenating the connection between the small publishing house and the trade compositor. Both a *Huenefeld Report* survey of leading book typesetters across the continent and consistent feedback from publishers themselves indi-

cate that typesetters who receive edited, formatted manuscripts on electronc media (floppy disks or magnetic tapes) are reducing their per-page charges to publishers by 20 to 30 percent, on average. This, publishers find, is enough saving to offset the leasing of word processors, and paying keypunchers to transfer manuscripts to the cathode-ray tube (CRT) before copy editors go to work on them. (In fact, several small publishers report compositors willing to "lend" them word processors without charge, to develop a typesetting account that is captive to their interface coding.)

Even when the extra keypunching eats up all or most of the eventual composition savings, editors and production managers find that the great improvement in control and substantial time-savings in prepress production stages make the new technology and revised procedures a godsend. And some have found it possible to persuade authors—many of whom are also now working on word processors—to submit their work in electronic form at the beginning, thus eliminating in-house keypunching and substantially cutting production costs.

In 1983, according to the annual *Huenefeld Report* survey, some 21.4 percent were using computerized word processors for manuscript editing, as compared with 69.8 percent doing computerized order processing, and 64.3 percent using computers for accounting. But the intriguing statistic is that while the latter two, more established computer functions were more common at the top size range of small presses ($1–$3 million in sales) —where 95.2 percent had computerized order processing and 78.6 percent used computers for accounting, compared with 40 percent on both counts among publishers with sales under $100,000—the reverse was true of computerized manuscript editing. Some 33 percent of the under-$100,000 publishers were editing on CRTs in 1983, compared with only 16.7 percent of the $1–$3 million houses.

Subtle New Trends in Capital Strategy

Two trends noticeable outside the production arena are also changing the environment in which small presses operate, because they have a bearing on the commodity that is in shortest supply in this portion of the industry—money. Especially pronounced in 1983 were the growth of co-publishing arrangements with larger houses, and the increasing acceptance of eventual acquisition by a publishing conglomerate as a worthy goal for the small publishing entrepreneur.

The co-publishing trend is clearly related to the growth of "packaging," whereby a publisher (usually a large one) meets part of its need for new product by contracting with external editorial operations, which assemble data or find authors, complete the substantive and copy editing, and usually provide interior design and typesetting (thus delivering camera-ready pages). For this, the editorial packager typically receives a substantial advance against a 35 percent share of eventual net receipts from the book, while the contracting co-publisher retains the remaining 65 percent for handling the manufacturing, marketing, fulfillment, and financial administration. (The packager, then, pays any contracted royalties to "its" author.)

Many small publishers are finding that playing the packager's role—at least with respect to licensing a big publisher for trade or other defined major markets—is a good way to minimize the capital needed to grow. The conventional division of the proceeds does turn out to be a fair, reasonable split within the context of normal industry costs for those functions performed by each partner. Such co-publishing deals can be both profitable and healthy for a small publisher—except when they give a potential competitor a toehold in a market niche that the small publisher may have previously dominated. A number of start-up publishing operations in larger companies in recent years have stressed co-publishing to build working capital reserves before shifting the eventual emphasis to their own imprints.

Perhaps the most exciting capital-strategy trend among small publishers during the 1980s, however, has been their new fervor for courting acquisition by one of the major publishing conglomerates. Traditionally, small presses have resented the conglomerate's ability to wait until the small publisher has completed the research and development necessary to establish a new publishing niche and also take the associated risks, and then to move in with acquisition money to exploit the breakthrough. But so many entrepreneurs made so much money pioneering the computer books of the last half-decade and then selling out, that the folklore of conglomerate courting has turned from sour grapes to glee, and publishing entrepreneurs now freely admit that their prime objective is not to pay double taxes on retained earnings, but rather to reap the capital-gains advantages offered by being acquired. And many have found that the conglomerates (perhaps underestimating how freely the imagination and innovation they seek flow in the small-press world) are considerably more generous in their price evaluations than bankers and brokers have traditionally been.

At any rate, rather than resenting the acquisition programs of the conglomerates as they once did, small publishers of the 1980s seem inclined to view them as "just another market."

Refinement of Small-Press Operating Styles

Innovation has long been the trademark of the small publisher; it is one of the compensating factors that enable small publishers to compete for their modest piece of the publishing pie. But as one who has been an intense and specialized observer of this segment of the publishing industry over the last 15 years, I sense a refinement of innovative forces, which is probably due to growing sophistication and growing knowledge of publishing processes on the part of small-press managers.

Outguessing intellectual and artistic fads to serve new social movements with book resources has long been a mainstay of the small presses: They led the way with the black-studies texts of the 1960s, the peace-movement ammunition of the Nixon era, and the pragmatic "field manuals" of the women's movement of the 1970s (from day-care guides to abortion counseling). But what was once haphazard coincidence between the fervors of publishing entrepreneurs and the resource needs of new social movements seems now to be a deliberate element in new-venture business plans. Small-publishers' meetings and seminar discussions are alive with talk of "publishing niches" as essential, highly valued components of both entrepreneurial strategy and not-for-profit mission.

The arrival of "special marketing" as a trendy buzzword in the jargon of the industry reflects another aspect of the growing sophistication and deliberateness of small-press innovation. As generally understood, the term refers to the pursuit of sales volume through channels other than those (bookstores, book wholesalers, newsstands, libraries, schools, subsidiary rights, and direct-to-reader mail order) traditionally employed by book publishers. Because they are so heavily outgunned by the big houses in those conventional channels, small presses have for years cultivated special outlets related to their subject areas rather than their physical product. Art books for museums, regional books for tourist gift shops, gardening books for nurseries, recreational guides for sporting-goods stores, fund-raising inventories for a host of local organizations, campaign ammunition for protest movements, premiums for a variety of sponsors, and salable baggage for traveling authors became even more commonplace in the small-press world in 1983.

With this growing sophistication in searching out unique editorial niches and special markets, increasing subtlety in compensating for capital shortages, and adaptability to new technology (whereby microcomputers are revolutionizing not only production procedures, but order processing and market planning), small presses seem to have more than held their own in book publishing and related media in 1983. With the recession behind us, prognostications are even more cheerful for 1984.

8

Trends in Hardcover Publishing

JOANN DAVIS

Economic recovery. Computer revolution. No buzz-words better reflected the movement of trade publishing in 1983 than these two subject areas. As the American economy began its long uphill climb out of the recession of the past several years, publishers responded with a burst of books about business and finance that were eagerly consumed by an American public caught up in the economic revival. And as the computer continued to make its presence felt in everyday American life, books about computers—buying them, programming them, operating them, and playing and living with them—swept through the industry like the latest dance craze.

Yet with the nation so preoccupied with money-making and high-tech adventurism, American fiction seemed to be entering a recession of its own. The year saw few novels of extraordinary stature or expected longevity. In fact, 1983 produced few novels of either overwhelming literary merit or commercial appeal that managed to capture the imagination of a public that was perhaps more concerned with getting back on its feet financially.

The best reflection of the supercharged American interest in business and financial affairs was the performance of three of the year's top-selling books, all of which either exceeded or neared the in-print figure of 1 million copies. *In Search of Excellence* by Thomas J. Peters and Robert H. Waterman, Jr. (Harper & Row), *Megatrends* by John Naisbitt (Warner), and *The One Minute Manager* by Kenneth Blanchard and Spencer Johnson (Morrow) were all published in the latter months of 1982 and each

remained on the hardcover bestseller lists for a year or longer. In a broad sense, these books were concerned with varying concepts of management. In the case of *In Search of Excellence*, the emphasis was on the management techniques utilized by the nation's best-run companies. As the title implied, *The One Minute Manager* dealt with personal managerial style, and its pithy advice, accompanied by a money-back guarantee from the publisher, struck a chord with a large readership. *Megatrends* emphasized managing the future, and author Naisbitt became a widely sought speaker on the broad changes that would be affecting American society and how business management must respond to those changes.

Business writer Robert Allen also struck double paydirt when his book *Creating Wealth* (Simon & Schuster) made the bestseller list and had a coattail effect, bringing back to bestsellerdom his earlier book *Nothing Down*. Other notable successes in the business and finance field include Vanita VanCaspel's *The Power of Money Dynamics* (Prentice-Hall) and *William E. Donoghue's No-Load Mutual Fund Guide* (Harper & Row).

The growing significance of the computer as a subject of interest to book publishers was demonstrated in two ways as the year went by. The first of these was the large number of publishers who were delving into the world of software by linking books they had already published or future publications to machine-usable software programs. Far more widespread was the introduction of books and book series aimed at computer users, both real and potential.

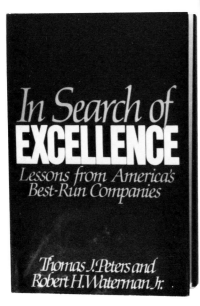

American interest in business and financial matters brought phenomenal success to three books in the business area and kept them at the top of bestseller lists throughout 1983.

The best expressions of the publishing industry's interest in publishing for the computer field came in two separate auctions in which major sums were spent for the acquisition of computer-related titles. The first of these was the $800,000 paid by Simon & Schuster for a ten-volume series for users of the IBM Personal Computer, the industry leader in the personal/professional computer field. In another major auction, Doubleday paid $1.3 million for the rights to *The Whole Software Catalog,* to be produced by the editors of *The Whole Earth Catalog.* (This amount

American cuisine made a strong showing in the cookbook field.

was reportedly a record advance for a trade paperback.) However, these and most other computer-related titles appeared to be paperback phenomena rather than a growth sector for hardcover publishers. Certainly, with the already large number of publishers getting into this subject area, including new publishing firms whose only books are computer-oriented, the likelihood of a glut of books in this market seemed assured with an eventual shakedown period almost certain to follow.

Diet and Health: Thinning Out?

The recent success of hardcover books in the diet, health, fitness, and beauty categories carried over into 1983, but these perennially popular categories seemed to be showing some signs of wearing thin. In the diet and health area, there were a number of successful new books led by *Mary Ellen's Help Yourself Diet Plan* by Mary Ellen

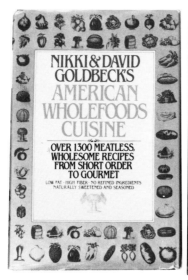

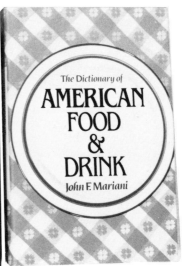

Pinkham (St. Martin's), *The F-Plan Diet* by Audrey Eyton (Crown), *The Diet Center Program* by Sybil Ferguson (Little, Brown), and *Dr. Abravnel's Body Type Diet and Lifetime Nutrition Plan* by Dr. Elliot Abravnel and Elizabeth King (Bantam). While these bestsellers provided evidence that Americans seem to have maintained their obsession with diet and health, none of the books created the sort of nationwide clamor that has gone along with other diets of the past.

While diet books flourished in numbers published if not in sales, their alter egos—cookbooks—continued as a staple of American publishers' output. Of course, there were the predictable number of ethnic cookbooks, but foreign food seemed to take backseat status to American cuisine in the cookbook field in 1983. Thus the presence and appeal of such titles as *Classic American Cooking* by Pearl Byrd Foster (Simon & Schuster), *The L. L. Bean Game and Fish Cookbook* by Angus Cameron and Judith Jones (Random House), *Back to Basics American Cooking* by Anita Pritchard (Putnam), *Masters of American Cooking* by Betty Fussell (Times Books), *Richard Nelson's American Cooking* (NAL Books), *The Dictionary of American Food and Drink* by John F. Mariani (Ticknor & Fields). The movement toward American cooking, coupled with the recent interest in natural foods, also produced a new bestselling cookbook in *Nikki and David Goldbeck's American Wholefoods Cuisine* (NAL).

In the beauty, fashion, and grooming fields, there were fewer discernible trends, such as the great number of *Dress for Success*–type books that appeared several years ago. However, there were several popular books aimed at men's grooming and fashion, signaling that this is a category to which more attention will be paid in the future. The most successful example of the male grooming and fitness books was *Working Out* by Charles Hix (Simon & Schuster), which detailed a variety of exercise regimens for men. Since men have rediscovered the benefits of fitness, and popular notions of masculinity have been altered during the past decade, the acceptance of male-grooming books can be expected to grow.

The major trend in fashion and beauty books in general continued to be the reliance on the celebrity diet or fitness program. Jane Fonda's 1981 bestseller, *Jane Fonda's Workout Book* (Simon & Schuster), continued its extraordinary sales pace in 1983 by topping the million-seller mark. While some publishers attempted to capitalize on the success of the Fonda book by producing a variety of clones with some star's name attached, there were no new books that approached Fonda's bestseller in terms of the sales and excitement it generated. Nonetheless, the celebrity-fitness craze did make bestsellers of *The Body Principal* by television star Victoria Principal (Simon & Schuster) and *Christie Brinkley's Outdoor Beauty and Fitness Book* by the well-known model and cover girl (Simon & Schuster). But neither book had quite the same nationwide impact as the Fonda book, which was sold concurrently with a popular videotape of the exercise program. Richard Simmons, another of the most successful celebrities of recent years, who became nationally

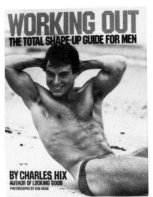

Successful 1983 contenders in the grooming and fitness field were Charles Hix's Working Out *and Victoria Principal's* The Body Principal.

famous for his television fitness show, was represented by *Richard Simmons's Better Body Book* (Warner). However, his new book failed to create the excitement achieved by his earlier diet books. Although not a media superstar like Fonda or Brinkley, the founder of the Mary Kay cosmetics line has become something of a household name in America. That status was no doubt a factor in the sales achieved by *The Mary Kay Guide to Beauty* (Addison-Wesley).

Past Lives

As celebrity-fitness programs gained the upper hand in the body makeover segment of the market, the perennial favorite celebrity-biography category failed to produce any large-scale bestsellers. In fact, only a few books that might be described as celebrity biographies made it onto the list of the year's most successful sellers. The first was Shirley MacLaine's autobiographical *Out on a Limb* (Bantam). MacLaine had written two earlier books and was a proven seller, but her new book marked a major departure for the actress in that it described her interest in the world of supernatural phenomena, including MacLaine's belief that she had experienced previous lives, while at the same time discussing her love affair with a married politician. The other major seller in the celebrity-biography area was *The Love You Make* by Peter Brown and Steven Gaines (McGraw-Hill), a biography of the Beatles. But the big-time Hollywood biography of years past was missing in 1983. The only books that came to close to this type of bestseller were Sir Laurence Olivier's *Confessions of an Actor* (Simon & Schuster), which made a brief appearance on the hardcover lists, and *How to Live to Be 100 or More* by George Burns (Putnam), which was also something of a surprise bestseller and a long way from the typical example of the Hollywood tell-all.

There were also few highly successful biographies of a more substantial sort selling in large quantities. The bestselling historical biography of the year was *The Last Lion* (Little, Brown), a biography of Winston Churchill by William Manchester, no stranger to the bestseller lists.

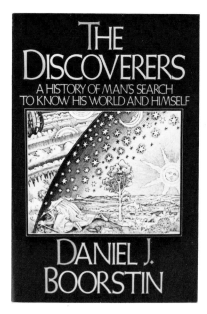

Librarian of Congress Daniel J. Boorstin's The Discoverers *was a popular success in the general history field.*

That was only one of Manchester's two successes in 1983. The other was *One Brief Shining Moment* (Little, Brown), a remembrance of President John F. Kennedy published on the twentieth anniversary of Kennedy's assassination. Manchester's book was only one of a rush of books that appeared on the occasion of this anniversary. Among these was one other bestseller, *A Hero for Our Time* by Ralph G. Martin (Macmillan), which took a somewhat more sensational view of the "private life" of Kennedy.

In terms of general history there were also few outstanding sellers in 1983, although one late entry, *The Discoverers* by Daniel Boorstin (Random House), a survey of the act of discovery throughout history, was a popular success. Another widely discussed book, *The Rosenberg File* by Ronald Radosh and Joyce Milton (Holt, Rinehart & Winston), aimed to present the final word on the guilt or innocence of the couple executed for passing atomic secrets to the Russians. The book reawakened the long-unsettled controversy, but probably made few converts.

The surprise of the year in general nonfiction was a book that fit into no simple category. *Blue Highways: A Journey into America* by William Least Heat Moon (Atlantic–Little, Brown) was the author's account of an odyssey through America's backroads. While books like *Megatrends* tried to show where America was headed, *Blue Highways* recaptured a sense of where it has been. In its depiction of ordinary Americans living and working, the book captured the spirit of the common man in America that has been almost forgotten in an increasingly complex electronic world.

Perhaps because there was so much emphasis among book buyers on the big-selling business books mentioned earlier, there was a noticeable falloff in major works of current events. Certainly no book had the broad-scale national impact felt in earlier years by Jonathan Schell's

The Fate of the Earth or Jacobo Timmerman's *Prisoner without a Name, Cell without a Number*. In terms of current American policies, the one book to briefly reach the bestseller lists was Joan Didion's *Salvador* (Simon & Schuster), a firsthand account of the civil war in that Central American country and the role being played by the United States there.

The major controversy of the year whirled around the long-awaited book about Henry Kissinger by former *New York Times* correspondent Seymour Hersh, which was published as *The Price of Power* (Summit Books). It immediately provoked a wave of charges and counter-charges regarding Hersh's motives and accuracy in depicting Kissinger and his decision-making process as national security advisor and secretary of state under presidents Nixon and Ford.

Vietnam: Fact and Fiction

Much of the emphasis in the Hersh book focused on Vietnam policy and the entire question of the conflict in Southeast Asia provided the backdrop for a number of successful books. *Vietnam: A History* by Stanley Karnow (Viking), which was tied into a Public Broadcasting System (PBS) documentary of the same name, became a major bestseller in 1983. *Chickenhawk* by Robert Mason (Viking) was a highly praised account of the experiences of a helicopter pilot during the war. Further evidence that the publishing world was eagerly exploring the leftover controversies and disquieting feelings that the war created were such titles as *Tim Page's Nam*, a photo collection (Knopf), and *Waiting for the Army to Die* by Fred Wilcox (Random House), a book about the effects of Agent Orange on veterans of the war in Vietnam. Unrelated to the conduct of the war itself but certainly a reminder of the period and the politics was *Fatal Vision* by Joe McGinniss (Putnam), which reexamined the murder case against Green Beret Captain Jeffrey MacDonald, who was convicted of murdering his pregnant wife and two daughters on an army base in North Carolina.

Vietnam also provided novelists with material that found its way into several highly praised works of fiction. Of these Vietnam novels, the three most prominent of the year were *Meditations in Green* by Stephen Wright (Scribner's), which was the winner of the Maxwell Perkins Prize given by the publisher to a first novel of exceptional promise; *Blue Dragon, White Tiger* by Tran Van Dinh (TriAm Press), which was also highly praised, as was *Tiger, the LURP Dog* by Kenn Miller (Little, Brown). Among the other novels with a Vietnam background were new books by writers who had earlier successes—Philip Caputo, author of *Delcorso's Gallery* (Holt, Rinehart & Winston), and James Webb, who wrote *A Country Such as This* (Doubleday). Although none of these novels made the bestseller list, as did *The Thirteenth Valley* by John Del Vecchio (Bantam), published a year earlier, their prominence was further evidence of the nation's ongoing examination of the war in Vietnam and its effects on America.

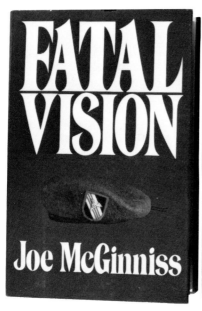
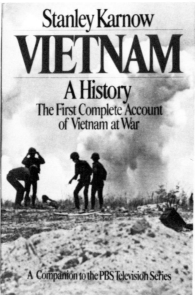
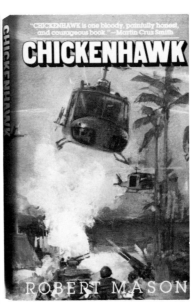

Vietnam was the backdrop for a variety of 1983 books, both fiction and nonfiction.

Fiction: A Fallow Year

Apart from these novels with their highly specific point of reference, few American novels published in 1983 were greeted with the sense of public excitement and critical acclaim that has recently been accorded books by such writers as D. M. Thomas, John Irving, and Alice Walker. the winner of both the Pulitzer Prize and the American Book Award last year for her novel *The Color Purple.* Two of the most enthusiastically received novels of the year were books originally published in England. *Shame* by Salman Rushdie (Knopf) was the successor to the

writer's award-winning *Midnight's Children.* Just as Rushdie had in that novel used the modern history of India to weave a mystical tale of the clash of politics and culture, he turned his sights on modern Pakistan in his new book and fictionally explored the political warfare there between two dictators. The other British-originated novel was South African writer J. M. Coetzee's *Life and Times of Michael K* (Viking), the new book by the author of the widely hailed *Waiting for the Barbarians* and winner of the 1983 Booker Prize, England's most prestigious literary award. A new novel by last year's Nobel Prize winner in Literature, Gabriel Garcia Marquez, was also published.

Three of the most enthusiastically received novels of 1983 came from abroad.

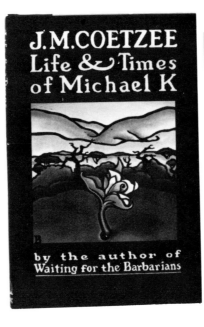

In *Chronicle of a Death Foretold* (Knopf), Marquez used a murder mystery in a small village to weave his unique brand of storytelling.

The Marquez book figured at the center of a rights controversy that dated back to summer 1982, when Knopf and Ballantine jointly acquired the book. Harper & Row, working with Avon, had hoped to acquire the rights and was so sure that acquisition would be no problem that it went ahead and listed *Chronicle* in its fall catalog. But Marquez's agent reputedly asked for stipulations that Harper & Row and Avon would not or could not meet. One was that all rights—hardcover as well as paperback—revert to Marquez after ten years. In addition to this unprecedented demand it was reported that contracts for Marquez's books already published by Harper & Row and Avon would have to be renegotiated. When Knopf and Ballantine jointly acquired rights to *Chronicle,* the terms of the agreement were not disclosed.

Another foreign novel provided the surprise literary bestseller of the year. A first novel set in a medieval Italian monastery, Umberto Eco's *The Name of the Rose* (A Helen & Kurt Wolff Book/Harcourt Brace Jovanovich) was a complex and even esoteric book that also used the conventions of the murder mystery to plumb deeper questions of faith, semiotics, and human nature. The book capped off a year of success in which it was even auctioned to a mass market house (Warner) for a substantial six-figure advance. While Eco's novel might have been one of the most unread bestsellers of the year, its unexpected degree of success served as a sharp counterpoint to the bulk of the rest of the fiction bestseller list, which was dominated for the most part by big-name writers, category novels, and little else that even approached its literary stature.

For American novelists, on the other hand, it was something of a fallow year. There were few new works by any of the major contemporary American writers and for those that were published, the critical response was guarded. Perhaps the most-talked-about novel by an American master was the long-awaited *Ancient Evenings* by Norman Mailer (Little, Brown). A broad, sprawling book set in Egypt thousands of years ago, Mailer's novel was greeted coolly by many critics and readers who found its panoramic view of sex and war in Ancient Egypt not up to expected standards. Others hailed it as a brave departure for Mailer, an ambitious undertaking in the area of historical fiction where few modern writers of seriousness operate any longer. Norman Mailer continued his career of controversy when he left his longtime publisher Little, Brown for a multimillion dollar, four-book contract with Random House. Industry observers linked the move to Mailer's displeasure at Little, Brown's handling of the paperback rights of *Ancient Evenings*. Little, Brown reportedly tried to sell the rights before the book was published and had a chance to establish a hardcover track record that would enhance its reprint value.

Similarly, a new novel by Philip Roth, *The Anatomy Lesson* (Farrar, Straus & Giroux), received mixed notices at best. It certainly caused none of the widespread discussion that accompanied earlier and more controversial Roth novels such as *Portnoy's Complaint,* although it was one of the books nominated by the National Book Critics Circle as best novel of the year. That honor went instead to William Kennedy for *Ironweed* (Viking), the third in a series of novels set in and around Albany, New York. (The previous books were *Legs* and *Billy Phelan's Greatest Game.*)

Of the other major names in modern American letters, John Updike presented a collection of essays and criticism, *Hugging the Shore* (Knopf), and Bernard Malamud was represented by *The Stories of Bernard Malamud* (Farrar, Straus & Giroux), a collection of stories rather than a new novel. There were also collections of short stories from Raymond Carver, whose *Cathedral* (Knopf) was another of the Book Critics Circle nominees; Gail Godwin, whose *Mrs. Bedford and the Muses* (Viking) failed to garner either the kind of reviews or sales that greeted her previous book, the novel *A Mother and Two Daughters* (Viking), which had been on the bestseller list in the preceding year; and Donald Barthelme, whose stories were collected in *Overnight to Many Distant Cities* (Putnam).

It would be unfair, however, to mark the year 1983 as one in which there was no distinguished fiction. One of the year's most highly praised books, and another of the nominees of the Book Critics Circle, was a first novel, *In the Reign of the Queen of Persia,* by Joan Chase (Harper & Row), a novel set in small-town Ohio during the 1950s and told from the point of view of four separate girls. The other major first novel was an experimental work by Ron Loewinsohn called *Magnetic Field(s)* (Knopf). Another of the most critically praised books of the year was Mark Helprin's *Winter's Tale* (Harcourt Brace Jovanovich), a

William Kennedy's Ironweed *was The National Book Critics Circle's choice for best novel of the year.*

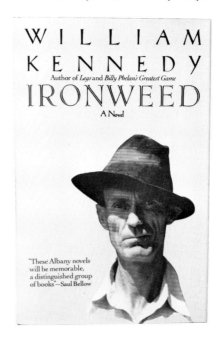

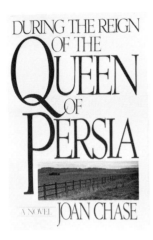

Two 1983 first novels that received critical acclaim.

modern fairy tale that straddled fantasy and reality and found its way onto the bestseller list toward the end of the year. A bestseller of considerable seriousness was Judith Rossner's *August* (Houghton Mifflin), which detailed the complex relationships between psychotherapist and patient and also made news as one of the few recent books to be auctioned to a paperback house for more than $1 million.

The Year of the Paperback

In a certain respect, it was really the year of the paperback on the hardcover bestseller list. Many of the most successful commercial writers who appeared on the hardcover bestseller list in 1983 were novelists who had previously achieved their greatest success in paperback and whose hardcover success derived from the existence of an audience created out of paperback readers. Among the most prominent of these were Sidney Sheldon, whose *Master of the Game* (Morrow) was a holdover from 1982; Stephen King, who has parlayed a devoted paperback following into a most loyal group of hardcover readers who made King a bestselling author twice with *Christine* (Viking) and *Pet Sematary* (Doubleday); and Louis L'Amour, the 100-million-plus paperback seller whose western novels only recently have been published in hardcover, including his 1983 winner, *The Lonesome Gods* (Bantam).

Three women novelists who broke into the business with successful paperback originals continued their successful crossover to hardcover bestsellerdom. Danielle Steel hit the lists with *Changes* (Delacorte), Jackie Collins offered *Hollywood Wives* (Simon & Schuster), and Jacqueline Briskin wrote *Everything and More* (Putnam).

Science Fiction in Hardcover

The paperback-crossover phenomenon also applied to one of the most notable category trends in hardcover fiction, the emergence of bestselling hardcover science fiction and fantasy. There were at least a dozen science

fiction/fantasy titles that appeared on the hardcover bestseller lists in 1983, a long way from the days when this category was considered a small specialty genre for paperback readers. Among the major successes were new hardcovers by science fiction writers whose audiences read their earlier work almost exclusively in paperback. Isaac Asimov, the prolific author of more than 200 books, returned to fiction writing for the first time in ten years and had two of his new novels make the bestseller lists, *Foundation's Edge* and *Robots of Dawn* (Doubleday). Arthur C. Clarke, whose story "The Sentinel" had formed the basis for the classic science fiction film *2001; A Space Odyssey*, pleased his fans by writing a sequel, *2010* (Del Rey), which appeared late in 1982 and stayed on the lists well into 1983.

Other science fiction and fantasy writers who fit this paperback-crossover mold included Stephen Donaldson, author of *White Gold Wielder* (Del Rey); Marion Zimmer Bradley, whose *Mists of Avalon* (Knopf) was a retelling of the Arthurian legends (a source of many bestsellers in the past) from the point of view of some of the women in the story; Anne McCaffrey, author of *Moreta, Dragonlady of Pern* (Del Rey), which brought hardcover success to a series that has been popular for years in paperback editions; L. Ron Hubbard, the mysterious founder of Dianetics and a long-time science fiction writer, whose first hardcover bestseller was *Battlefield Earth* (St. Martin's); and Douglas Adams, the author of *Life, the Universe and Everything* (Harmony/Crown), the third book in a trilogy that had built a cultish following in paperback that eventually translated into hardcover bestsellerdom.

Besides these former paperback successes making new waves in hardcover science fiction, there were a number of other hardcover science fiction titles that deserve note. *The E.T. Storybook* by William Kotzwinkle (Putnam) and *The Return of the Jedi Storybook* adapted by Joan D. Vinge (Random House) were spinoffs of two of the most successful movies ever made. Both were officially children's books, but both sold in quantities that merited bestseller status. Obviously, their extraordinary sales were directly attributable to the success of the films on which the books were based, but few movie tie-ins have ever approached this level of sales.

It would perhaps be unfair to characterize James Michener's novel *Space* (Random House) as science fiction. But the extraordinary appeal of Michener combined with the American appetite for the world of space travel made for an enormous success. *Space*, which had been published late in 1982, was only the first of Michener's two bestsellers in 1983. His more recent novel *Poland* (Random House), capitalizing on the heightened interest in Poland since the advent of Solidarity, became Michener's second hit of the year.

The interplay between current events and fiction that provided part of the appeal of *Poland* also played a role in the success and controversy of the most recent novel by John le Carré, another familiar name on the bestseller lists. His novel *The Little Drummer Girl* (Knopf) took le

Carré from the down-at-the-heels world of European spies to a controversial setting in the Middle East. Although the book was roundly criticized in some quarters as too critical of Israeli policy and too soft on Palestinian terrorists, the overlay of political implications did no harm to the book's sales. Critically and commercially, le Carré's novel of espionage and counterterrorism was one of the year's major successes.

While the good old-fashioned mystery genre failed to produce a blockbuster whodunit in 1983, there was a new-fashioned mystery that will undoubtedly create a new genre for publishers. Agent Bill Adler, who has had his share of bestsellers in the diet category and other nonfiction areas, got his name onto the fiction bestseller list by creating a mystery, written by veteran Thomas Chastain, that did not reveal the solution. Instead, the catch behind *Who Killed the Robins Family?* (Morrow) was the offer of a $10,000 reward to the first reader who correctly proposed the solution to the crime. A sort of *Choose Your Own Adventure* for adults, the book finally offered armchair detectives what they have been waiting for: a chance to really solve the murder. While the killer remained a mystery, it does not take a detective to see that there will be plenty of new mysteries inviting reader participation. In publishing, imitation has always been the sincerest form of flattery.

9

Trends in Paperback Publishing

SALLY A. LODGE

As murmurs of the end of trade publishing's economic slump became cries of joy in the later months of 1983, it became evident that paperback publishers were focusing on a number of subject areas in hopes of taking advantage of new technological, sociological, and economic developments. In many cases, they were right on target; looking back over 1983, one discerns several publishing trends that indicate that publishers indeed had the right ideas at the right time. As the sales figures for business and home computers soared, as the birth rate swelled to proportions it hadn't reached since the post–World War II baby explosion, as increased consumer awareness and interest in saving time and money in business and financial ventures grew, publishers were there with paperback books that approached these subjects from every conceivable angle, from the theoretical to the practical.

And there were too, of course, the humor, diet, and fitness books that have dominated the paperback best-seller lists for the past several years; 1983 had more than its share of books devoted to truly tasteless jokes, overweight cats, and promises of beauty, yet these are hardly the titles that will be remembered a decade hence. In addition to computer, business, and finance books, and books on pregnancy, childbirth, and childrearing, significant and hardly ephemeral paperback publishing trends were evident in the realm of fiction as well. Worthy of note are the new doors (and not just to the boudoir) that publishers of romance novels opened for their readers, some developments in fiction published for young adults,

the debuts of some high-quality fiction lines in mass market and trade paperback format, and the continued excellence of fiction released by several publishers.

Computer Books on Just About Every List and Bookshelf

No longer do manuals on how to master video games come to mind when one thinks of computer books. Publishers broadened their definition of this category enormously in 1983, as the percentage of American homes and businesses relying on small computers increased drastically and the market for instructional manuals, programming guides, and software mushroomed. No longer did the majority of the computer books published deal with the general concept of computers and background information. Many readers who had previously been interested in computers from a distance were now at the keyboards of their own machines. The new wave of books reflected their needs—from operator's manuals for specific models to ways to exploit their computers' functions.

By the end of 1983, it was difficult to find a publisher of trade paperbacks that didn't have at least one computer-related title on its list. The computer-book divisions and subsidiaries of numerous trade publishers continued to expand their publishing programs. Hefty lists of general computer books as well as books devoted to specific computer models were issued from such companies as Osborne/McGraw-Hill, which during the summer launched the DiskGuide™ Series, computer reference guides that explain vital commands, keys, tables and charts for five specific computer models; and Ballinger Publishing Company, a subsidiary of Harper & Row, which in March released the first of a series of guides that will be issued twice a year. The initial volume, *The Personal Computer Buyers Guide,* edited by Dennis Grimes and Brian Kelly, is a trade paperback instructing the reader on such areas as selecting and using a home computer, systems manufacturers, software products, and suppliers.

In addition to technical publishers and companies that had established track records in computer-book publishing (among them Sybex, Wiley, Addison-Wesley, McGraw-Hill, dilithium Press, Prentice-Hall's Reston, Brady, and other subsidiaries), a number of trade publishers either made the leap into computer-book publishing in 1983 or stepped up their computer-book programs.

News of new paperback lines and series appeared in many catalogs. In the spring, for example, Holt, Rinehart & Winston launched a line of books on programming the IBM Personal Computer, and at the same time Simon & Schuster announced that it had outbid six other publishers and paid $800,000 to issue a ten-volume series of paperbacks geared to users of IBM and IBM-compatible personal computers. The books, called the PC World Reference Library, are to be written, edited, and produced by the staff of *PC World* magazine, devoted to the IBM computer and compatible systems.

In November Macmillan got into the act with a new series designed for those who have little or no knowledge of how to make the most of a home computer. Among the first titles in the Easy Home Computer Series, edited by Roger C. Sharpe, were *The TI99/4A Start-Up Guide* and *The IBM PC Start-Up Guide.* Each was published with a first printing of 30,000 copies.

The Software Connection

Spring 1983 also brought the announcement of a new line of computer books from Warner, which, beginning in 1984, will issue two to four titles in the series each month. The new line of books marks the linking of Warner Software Inc. and Warner Books; together the two subsidiaries plan to issue book/software combinations. Developments during 1983 point to the fact that this will before long be a commonplace occurrence, as computer software becomes part of the product lines of an increasing number of publishers who realize that they have a gold mine in their backlists and new lists: books that lend themselves to adaptation to software.

Throughout 1983 came announcements of publishers forming electronic publishing divisions to produce and distribute software titles. Addison-Wesley's general books division formed a software publishing program in the fall and launched the venture with a $150,000 marketing campaign. Each of the five initial titles for home and business computers was available either in a book-and-software package or a software-only package.

In October Bantam established Bantam Electronic Publishing, a new division responsible for creating computer-software packages and related and independent computer-book publishing projects. The division's titles are to be aimed at the consumer home-computer market, as are those issued by Simon & Schuster's electronic publishing division, whose creation was also announced in October. This division was established to distribute home-computer software to bookstores, computer stores, and general merchandise outlets, as well as to develop its own line of home-computer software. In an effort to cover all distribution bases, the publisher will use the Simon & Schuster and Pocket Books sales forces as well as a network of some 100 commissioned reps who will call on computer and software outlets.

In addition to those publishers that created entire new electronic publishing divisions, a number of others launched lines of software products. Among them was Random House, which in May announced plans to publish at least 30 software titles for the home market over the following 18 months. Prentice-Hall, further spreading itself over the computer books/software field, made it known that its general publishing division was moving into the software marketplace with the introduction of the Profit Center: Business Software from Prentice-Hall, Inc.,™ a 21-module business application computer software series.

That the worlds of computers and books were becoming increasingly and inextricably linked was underscored by numerous business deals made in 1983. There was news of such agreements as that made between New American Library (NAL) and the Waite Group, a computer book packager, to produce together a new series of microcomputer how-to books to appear under the new Plume/Waite imprint. The books, which the publisher notes combine technical sophistication with accessible language, cover the operation of a range of computer products, from low-priced, consumer-oriented computers to more advanced machines.

In a similar development, computer-book publisher dilithium Press joined forces with Signet in an attempt to combine the former's success with computer-book publishing and NAL's knowledge of mass marketing. National magazine advertising, point-of-sale promotion, co-op advertising, and an author tour were part of the campaign to launch this mass market line, called dilithium books from Signet. Initial releases were *Computers for Everybody* by Jerry Willis and Merl Miller; *Bits, Bytes and Buzzwords: Understanding Small Business Computers* by Mark Garetz; and 12 books written for the user of specific computer models, called Things to Do With guides, developed under the direction of Merl Miller.

An interesting variation on the theme came with the announcement in the fall that a major software company was entering the computer book market. Microsoft Corporation ©, a leader in the development of personal computer software, established Microsoft Press, a trade book publishing division specializing in computer books. The focus of the line, which will be distributed to the trade by Simon & Schuster's new electronic publishing division,

Practical computer books of every sort dominated 1983 paperback lists. Bits, Bytes & Buzzwords *and* Computers for Everybody *were initial releases in a new mass market line, dilithium books from Signet. McGraw-Hill's* From Baker Street to Binary *injected humor into learning computer basics.*

will be books aimed at first-time users (including business professionals, hobbyists, and educators) of leading hardware and software. Initial titles, scheduled to be off press at the beginning of 1984, include *The New Papyrus: A Comprehensive Guide to Electronic Publishing*; *The Programmer's Trade Secrets Handbook*; and *The Silicon Valley Guide to Financial Success in Software*. The publisher estimates that 80 percent of the titles will be sold through bookstores.

A Closer Look at the Books

What, exactly, are these computer books all about? It is becoming quite a broad category, encompassing more and more types of books as new applications of the computer and additional needs of computer users emerge. For example, stacks of books came off press in 1983 aiming to instruct readers on the subjects of buying and using word processors, making the most of a personal computer for business and personal finances, deciphering various computer languages, programming computer games for home machines, introducing children to the applications of computers and guiding their baffled parents through the computer maze, exploring the possibilities in computer graphics, and, of course, operating specific computer models.

There was also evidence of some authors' attempts to

inject a sense of humor into learning computer basics, in an effort to ease the layperson's induction into the world of computer use. Books that fit this description include McGraw-Hill's *From Baker Street to Binary: An Introduction to Computers and Computer Programming with Sherlock Holmes*. Here, authors Patrick McQuaid and Andrew Singer examine general concepts of computers, using adventures of Sherlock Holmes (written in a nineteenth-century, Conan Doyle style) as starting points. Another eye-catcher was Ten Speed Press's *Computer Wimp* by John Bear, which purports to "lead the reader through the hype and technobabble" to an understanding of computers. The ad copy for the book said it all: "If you think that using a computer should be as simple as driving a car, then *Computer Wimp* is for you."

The number of 1983 titles that fall into the category of home-computer game books was particularly overwhelming; the signs point to a movement out of arcades and into the living room as book after book published describes yet further ways to use computers for recreational purposes. Addison-Wesley's September list reflected this interest: Four paperback titles issued that month introduced games adapted to specific computers, among them *Tantalizing Games for the Timex/Sinclair 2000* and *Cosmic Games for the Commodore Vic 20*, both by Hal Renko and Sam Edwards. The following month, Addison-Wesley issued *Dr. Wacko's Miracle Guide to Designing and Programming Your Own Atari Computer Arcade Games* by David Heller, John Johnson, and Robert Kurcina, a book (available with a software package) that provides instructions on playing games in BASIC on any Atari home computer. Also released by the publisher in October was Tim Hartnell's *70 Games for the Timex/Sinclair 1500*.

That paperback publishers believe that there is a future in computer game books was made evident by several announcements in 1983 of the creation of series of books in this category. In May, Dell entered the arena with the Dell Computer Games Series, books that present game programs designed for specific computer systems. The first four titles, released in November, were *Games for Your Vic 20* by Alastair Gourlay, *Games for Your Timex-Sinclair 1000* by Mark Charlton, *Games for Your Timex-Sinclair 2000* by Peter Shaw, and *Games for Your Atari 400/600/800* by Paul Bunn. Included in each volume are programs for moving graphics games, brain stretchers, word games, and puzzles, as well as dictionaries of computer terms and hints for players who want to write their own programs or to extend those explained in the books.

On the basis of its success with its first computer book for children, *BASIC Fun* by Susan Drake Lipscomb and Margaret Ann Zuanich (a 1982 release), Avon/Camelot launched a series of computer game books designed specifically for junior computer whizzes. Also by Lipscomb and Zuanich, *BASIC Beginnings* (a "prequel" to *BASIC Fun*) was released in July, and was followed in November by the authors' *BASIC Fun with Graphics*, published in three variations: *The Apple Way, The Atari Way* and *The IBM/PC Way*. In December, Avon gave young readers yet another excuse to spend time at their home computers with a series with a different twist: the Bytes Brothers books, each of which contains five mysteries that can be solved with the use of a computer.

Another imaginative link between fiction and computers was made with Tor Books's December publication of a novelization of Zork, a fantasy/adventure computer game produced by Infocom, a computer software manufacturer. Written by S. Eric Meretzky, the novelization was published as a trilogy: *Zork: The Forces of Krill (#1), Zork: The Malifestro Quest (#2),* and *Zork: The Cavern of Doom (#3).*

Business and Finance: On the Computer and Off

The November 4, 1983, issue of *Publishers Weekly* quoted a recent *Wall Street Journal* article that decreed that "business is hotter than sex, at least in the publishing industry." The year's plethora of books on the subjects of business and personal finance leads one to surmise that perhaps this was not much of an exaggeration. Not surprisingly, the computer played a large role in 1983's list of books related to business and personal finance. Technical and trade publishers alike issued numerous books focusing on the use of small computers in business and on such financial applications of computers as their use for investment analysis and portfolio management.

Digital Press, in fact, made its first venture into trade publishing with its First Time Users series, the inaugural volume in which was *Your First Business Computer*, which strives to teach businesspeople how to survey their businesses to discover what their computer needs are. Subsequent books planned for the series will be aimed at

small-business owners as well as department managers, teachers, and students.

Books on using computers not only to facilitate one's business transactions but also to expand career opportunities were seen on many publishers' lists. An example of the former is *Contemporary Business Letters with Wordstar* by Jane E. Robbins and Dennis P. Curtin, a Curtin & London/Van Nostrand Reinhold release that offers the reader a chance to combine business savvy with computer know-how. Exemplifying the latter category of book is Peggy Glenn's *Word Processing Profits at Home*, published by Aames-Allen, which gives potential entrepreneurs ideas on cashing in on the capabilities of their word processors.

Making and managing money were indeed hot topics in 1983. Aware of this and of the fact that the last of the postwar baby boomers were entering the job market, intent on making their fortunes fast, Dell Trade Paperbacks announced the debut of a new series, packaged by Cloverdale Press, entitled The Clear and Simple Books: Rapid Access Business Primers for Young Professionals. Among the first titles in the series are *How to Write a Million Dollar Memo* and *Becoming a Boss* by Cheryl Reimold, *Running a Business Meeting* by Judson Mead, and *Getting the Most out of Your Benefits* by Don Patla.

Also aimed at the young person entering the world of business were books with an eccentric note, such as *The Harvard Entrepreneurs Society's Guide to Making Money: Or the Tycoon's Handbook* by Edward A. Gazvoda, Jr., and William M. Haney III, with John Greenya, a Little, Brown release; and books offering straightforward advice, among them *Sylvia Porter's Your Own Money*, published by Avon in May—another encyclopedic financial planning guide from this expert, this volume is aimed at young people in their "first independent years."

And this was just the beginning of the business and finance books that crowded 1983's bookshelves. A sweeping glance at the roundup of new books in this area reveals financial planning guides for virtually everyone— singles, women, those about to retire; management guides for individuals in various business spheres; books on starting a range of small businesses; guides to making a variety of real estate purchases; and books to help one decipher just about any money-related phenomena, from social security to IRAs. As in previous years, there were tax guides and workbooks galore, including some very alluring titles on how to beat the tax man: *How to Pay Zero Taxes*, an Addison-Wesley trade paperback by Jeff A. Schnepper, and *How to C*H*E*A*T on Your Taxes*, by "X," C.P.A. (1040 Press).

A Boom in Books Related to Babies

Given the fact that this country's annual birth rate is approaching the 4 million figure, one can safely say that there will be no shortage of future readers for these books on computers, business, and finance. But first things first: Before concerning themselves with the reading needs of this new generation, publishers seem determined to lead parents through pregnancy, childbirth, and the child-rearing years. And it certainly appears that these new parents (whom statistics show are older, better-educated, and wealthier than the average parent two decades ago) are book buyers.

There seemed no end to 1983's list of books on preparing for and bringing up baby, and no end to the angles from which authors approached the issues. There were general, encyclopedic child-care tomes as well as books that focused on very specific topics: yoga during pregnancy; pregnancy and delivery through Shiatsu; preventing Cesarean births; the postpartum months; raising twins; parent "burn-out"; premature babies; single parenting; the mental and social lives of babies; breastfeeding; infant nutrition; watersafing a baby; colic; toys and playtime; and baby exercise and massage.

Given that an estimated 40 percent of recent births were first births, these babies' parents will have to begin building their child-care libraries from scratch, and most will include among their first purchases Dr. Spock's classic *Baby and Child Care*, the 30 million-copy seller from Pocket Books. But the past decade has witnessed the making of other bestsellers that have also come to deserve the label "classic," and 1983 saw several of these books either reissued in revised, updated editions or published in this country for the first time.

Perhaps foremost among these is *Infants and Mothers* by T. Berry Brazleton, M.D., which went through nine hardcover printings and sold 300,000 copies in trade paper since its original publication 14 years ago. In 1983, Delacorte and Delta brought out a revised edition of the book as a Merloyd Lawrence title issued under the Seymour Lawrence imprint. The well-respected Brazleton, an associate professor of pediatrics at the Harvard Medical School, has revised his book to address issues of particu-

A boom in books on bringing up baby was another 1983 trend. Among the proliferation of titles in this field was a revised edition of T. Berry Brazelton's bestseller, Infants and Mothers, *brought out in paperback by Delta, and* 2001 Hints for Working Mothers, *by Gloria Gilbert Mayer (Morrow Quill).*

lar concern to parents in the eighties, including the situations of single mothers, returning to work after the birth of a baby, and the father's vital role in raising a child.

Another book that has been heavily relied on since its original publication in 1958 is *The Womanly Art of Breastfeeding* by the La Leche League International, with a foreword by Herbert Ratner, M.D., and Niles Newton. The La Leche League has sold 1.5 million copies of this breastfeeding and infant-care guide through mail order, and in September of 1983 the volume made its bookstore debut when NAL released it in both hardcover and Plume trade paperback editions, the latter with a 200,000-copy first printing. Also on its way to becoming a classic is Louise Lambert-Legace's *Feeding Your Child: From Infancy to Six Years Old*, which Beaufort Books introduced to this country in April. The book has sold steadily since 1974, when it was first published in Canada in both English and French.

Reflecting the needs of this decade's mothers, general books on child care published during 1983 were more likely than not to have at least a chapter on the subject of returning to work and balancing parenting with working outside the home, and a number of paperbacks were devoted exclusively to this topic. Between May and October, in fact, at least four such titles were published: Gloria Gilbert Mayer's *2001 Hints for Working Mothers* (Morrow Quill); *Mothers Who Work: Strategies for Coping* by Jeanne Bodin and Bonnie Mitelman (Ballantine); *Handbook for Latchkey Children and Their Parents* by Lynette and Thomas Long, a dual from Arbor House; and *The Working Parents' Survival Guide* by Sally Wendkos Olds (Bantam).

A final measure of the boom in baby books are two series of books produced by two leading magazines for parents. From Ballantine in mass market editions came the *Parents*™ Magazine Baby and Child Care series; among the first releases were Maja Bernath's *Parents*™ *Book for Your Baby's First Year* and Susan Trien's *Parents*™ *Complete Book of Breastfeeding*. *American Baby* magazine added to its series of books on pregnancy and child care, distributed by Ideals Publishing, with several 1983 titles, including *Breast Is Best: A Commonsense Approach to Breastfeeding* by Drs. Penny and Andrew Stanway. First published in London in 1978, the book was completely revised for the contemporary American market.

A Romantic Year in Mass Market Fiction

There were story collections, westerns, science fiction novels, adventure stories, mysteries and tales of suspense, thrillers and chillers, contemporary and historical romances. Indeed, 1983's mass market and trade paperback fiction releases spanned the usual assortment of genres, more or less in predictable numbers. Of these categories, the last mentioned deserves special attention, since 1983 brought a startling number of new ventures in this area, despite warnings that the romance market was saturated and despite the failure of several loudly touted new romance lines launched in 1982.

In the first six months of the year alone, five new romance imprints entered the marketplace, and three more followed in the summer and fall months. The keynotes of the new generation of romance lines appeared to be increased sensuality, more complex plot and character development, and a sharper focus on realism.

In April Harlequin launched, with the support of a $5 million advertising and promotion campaign, a new series entitled Harlequin American Romances. The books in the series (four appear each month) feature American settings, characters, and contemporary life-styles, rather than exotic locales and idealized heroes and heroines. At an average of 256 pages, the books in the series are longer than the traditional Harlequin releases. According to the publisher, they are more realistic and sensual, with greater emphasis on characterization and plot development. First titles in the series included *Tomorrow's Promise* by Sandra Brown and *The Same Last Name* by Kathleen Gilles Seidel.

The failure of Bantam's Circle of Love line did not dash the publisher's hopes for success in the romance market. In April, the new Loveswept series made its debut with six titles, among them *Surrender* by Helen Mittermeyer, *The Joining Stone* by Noelle Berry McCue, and Dorothy Garlock's *A Love for All Time*. Bantam targeted the line at what it described as "hard-core" romance readers, those who read at least one romance a day. The plots are highly sexual, and attempt to focus on believable emotions.

In January, a point-of-sale contest (first prize was a trip to Paradise Island in the Bahamas) helped launched Rapture Romances, NAL's first romance line. This series is also aimed at the serious romance fan, and promises more romance and passion and a heroine who is a strong and capable woman. *Love So Fearful* by Nina Coombs and *River of Love* by Lisa McConnell were among the first titles off press.

The publisher evidently was pleased with its foray into romance publishing, for in August came the inaugural novel of Signet's Scarlet Ribbons line of historical romances. Insisting that the series will not adhere to a formula, Signet promised books with strong, impetuous heroines who will face many trials and finally find true love.

"Heightened sexuality, more story, more depth of development" were among Silhouette's selling points for its Silhouette Intimate Moments line, which was started in May with a $1 million advertising campaign and a 50-cents off introductory offer for consumers who bought the initial releases. Nora Roberts (*Once More with Feeling*) and Pat Wallace (*Sweetheart Contract*) are among the authors on the first month's list. In July, the publisher made an announcement that hinted at tamer things to come. Planned for the new year was Silhouette's sixth line of romances: Silhouette Inspirations, stories featuring wholesome people who have made a commitment or recommitment to God in their lives.

Again, pledges of longer, more complex plots and more

fully developed characters accompanied the debut in July of another romance imprint, Dell's Candlelight Ecstasy Supremes. Four titles a month will be added to the series; among the first are Heather Graham's *Tempestuous Eden* and *Emerald Fire* by Barbara Andrews.

Recognizing a success when it has one, Berkely/Jove in the fall launched a subcategory of its Second Chance at Love series. The new To Have and To Hold line features novels with contemporary settings that concern married couples who have a problem that is eventually resolved. Among the titles released during the first few months were Melanie Randolph's *Heart Full of Rainbows* and Vivian Connolly's *I Know My Love*.

A heroine who has achieved some level of success in life, faces a crisis, is forced to make a choice between two men, and eventually finds "Mr. Right" was at the center of each book in Avon's Finding Mr. Right series, which was launched in February with *Paper Tiger* by Elizabeth Neff Walker. The new romance line did not fulfill the publisher's expectations, however, and was discontinued after ten months.

Realism in Romance for Younger Readers

Adult romance readers weren't the only ones filling their bookshelves with realistic romances in 1983. One of the most discernible trends in young-adult (YA) fiction was a continued focus on romances and fiction with down-to-earth, frank concerns. It is worthy of note that an increasing number of these titles were issued originally in trade or mass market paperbacks, rather than appearing first in hardcover.

"There are no topics we will not touch," declared Fawcett when introducing the newly revived Juniper young-adult imprint in May. The line is described as "The YA line that explores what life's *all* about," a statement that is underscored by the topics dealt with in the initial releases: the death of a parent (*A Formal Feeling*) by Zibby Oneal; an adopted girl's search for her natural mother (*The Searching Heart* by Patricia Aks); and the aftermath of a young girl's first affair (*After the First Love* by Isabelle Holland).

Romance bloomed on other publishers' lists as well. In July, Tempo's Caprice line was launched with Judith Enderie's *Programmed for Love* and Katherine Manning's *The Boy Next Store*. In October, Warner introduced a new YA romance series with an interesting twist. Each of the books in the Two by Two™ Romance series contains two 96-page novels in a flipover format: The books must be turned upside down to get the second story right-side up. The novels recount a romance related from both the girl's and the boy's perspectives. According to the publisher, these are not "problem books per se, but they handle real situations." The series, which is aimed at the 12- to 15-year-old reader, offered among its first releases *Cassie and Chris* by Sam Casey and *Change of Heart* by Patricia Aks. Within a month of this line's debut, Warner, due to what it called "popular demand in the trade," announced plans to step up it's publishing schedule and

Initial releases in Fawcett's newly revived Juniper young adult imprint included The Searching Heart, *by Patricia Aks and* A Formal Feeling, *by Zibby Oneal.*

add two rather than one title to the series each month starting in early 1984.

As a further sign of the healthy state of romance publishing for this age group, Warner announced in November also a plan to expand further into this area with a new teenage romance series, Make Your Dream Come True, scheduled to make its first appearance at the beginning of the new year. The new series combines the romance genre with another successful concept, the "choose-your-own-plot" format. Inaugural titles include *Angie's Choice* by Mary Ellen Bradford and Amanda McNicol's *Winning at Love.*

There was, certainly, room for escapism on the young-adult fiction lists of 1983. Young readers not tempted by realistic romances had several new mystery series to keep them busy. Meadowbrook Press issued a total of eight titles in 1983 in its new Can You Solve the Mystery™ series, which boasts appealing heroes, visual clues, and solutions printed in "mirror type" at the back of the book. Each book contains ten cases running a maximum of eight pages in length.

From Grosset & Dunlap/Putnam came three Jenny Dean Sci-Fi Mysteries, created by Dale Carlson. These were published in the fall, as was a new series from NAL, Diana Winthrop Mysteries; the first four titles in the series are by Kate Chambers. Atheneum began publishing the Escapade mystery series, promising six titles each fall and spring, issued in paper over boards.

Noteworthy Paperback Fiction Lines

A wrap-up of 1983's trends in paperback publishing cannot ignore several high-quality fiction lines that were either launched or added to during the year. Although the titles in these lines do not boast sales figures that can begin to compare with those of mass market romances and other commercial fiction, their importance as a phenomenon in paperback publishing today is undeniable. Thanks to the publishers committed to these paperback programs, very worthy fiction was in 1983 either introduced into this country for the first time or rescued from oblivion and brought back into print.

Suggesting renewed life and long life, the phoenix inspired the name of the University of Chicago Press's PhoenixFiction line, originated in the spring to reprint fiction originally published by commercial houses. An-

Among the high quality fiction lines launched during the year was Vintage's Aventura line, designed to highlight the variety of work by modern writers in Europe, Asia, Africa, Australia, the Caribbean, and North, Central, and South America.

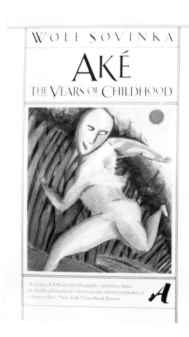 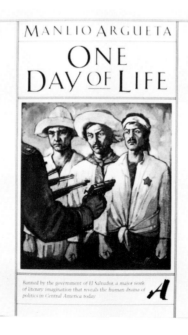 

nouncing the new paperback series, the publisher noted that it brings together the best of both worlds—past and future—by letting those familiar with the novels rediscover them and at the same time introducing new generations of readers to works of merit. The first five PhoenixFiction titles were originally published between 1929 and 1968; none has ever been released in paperback in the United States. The novels are *Angel Pavement, The Good Companions,* and *Bright Day* by J. B. Priestly; *A Use of Riches* by J. I. M. Stewart; and *The Department* by Gerald Warner Brace.

September brought the first volumes in another praiseworthy paperback publishing venture, Aventura: The Vintage Library of Contemporary World Literature. This line includes both reprints and original paperbacks, some available for the first time in English. The publisher designed Aventura to highlight the variety of work written by modern writers in Europe, Asia, Africa, Australia, the Caribbean, and North, Central and South America. The international quality of the line was reflected in its initial list, which included *One Day of Life* by Manlio Argueta, a novel, banned by the government of El Salvador, which describes a day in the life of a peasant family caught up in the turmoil of the Salvadoran civil war; *Aké: The Years of Childhood* by Wole Soyinka, a memoir of childhood before and during World War II by a Nigerian novelist and playwright; and *The Questionnaire* by Jiri Grusa, a novel about a boy growing up in a Czechoslovakian town.

Also deserving mention is Dell's rejuvenation of its Laurel imprint at the beginning of 1983 to reprint or reissue on a regular basis contemporary fiction and nonfiction. The publisher describes the new Laurel line as a "quality rack size formatted imprint aimed at bookstore sales with potential for academic adoption." Dell plans to reprint titles originally issued by other publishers, as well as to reissue titles on the Dell and Delta backlists. Among the first new Laurel releases were *Irwin Shaw Short Stories: Five Decades,* Jayne Ann Phillips's *Black Tickets,* and *Sounding the Territory* by Laurel Goldman.

Finally, applause must be sounded for the continuing programs of several houses dedicated to publishing excellent fiction in paperback. The Dial Press added a number of new novels to its Virago Modern Classics Series, bringing back into print novels by and about nineteenth- and twentieth-century women; Dutton's Obelisk line and Pocket Book's Washington Square Press continued to reprint and reissue outstanding fiction, as well as nonfiction; and Avon's Bard imprint introduced the first English-language editions of novels that have been well received in their countries of origin— notably Ignacio de Loyola Brandão's *Zero,* a novel that was banned in the author's native Brazil until 1979, when it became a bestseller there, and *The Dead Girls* by Jorge Ibargüengoitia, by the winner of the National Prize for a Novel in Mexico.

In recognition of its publication of consistently excellent fiction, Penguin in 1983 received the Carey-Thomas

Programs dedicated to publishing excellent fiction in paperback continued throughout the year. Notable from Avon's Bard imprint was Ignácio de Loyola Brandão's Zero, *among the first in a program of English language editions of novels that have been well-received in their countries of origin. Penguin introduced several novels by prize-winning Australian novelists never before published in this country, among them,* A Boat Load of Home Folk, *by Thea Astley.*

Award for its Penguin Contemporary American Fiction Series and the Penguin Originals Series. Penguin thus became only the third publisher to win the principal Carey-Thomas Award for a paperback series in the 41-year history of the awards, which are given annually by *Publishers Weekly* for creative book publishing. In addition to publishing new volumes in both of these quality series, Penguin gave further dimension to its fiction list in 1983 with the introduction of several Australian novels never before published in this country. Announcing that it was joining "Australia's cultural explosion," Penguin released several novels by prize-winning Australian novelists: the haunting *Tirra Lirra by the River* by Jessica Anderson and Theo Astley's *A Boat Load of Home Folk,* as well as short story collections: *Dirty Friends* by Morris Lurie and *Whoring Around* by John Bryson.

And thus it is a balance of nonfiction and fiction trends and of commercial and literary developments that emerges as one examines what went on in paperback publishing in 1983. It seems safe to assume that technology, the ever-changing economy, and the still escalating birth rate will keep publishers scrambling well into the eighties. There will undoubtedly be new heartaches and heartthrobs conceived to keep romance heroines trembling and triumphing. And, one hopes, the presses will continue to roll in those houses responsible for the superior fiction that makes tracking developments in paperback publishing so rewarding.

10

Bestsellers

Hardcover Top Sellers

DAISY MARYLES

Hardcover book sales in 1983, at least for bestsellers, continued to rack up impressive numbers, always matching last year's record-breaking figures and in some cases establishing new sales records.

Once again all of the top 25 novels boasted sales of over 100,000 and a few fiction titles with sales just into the six-figure area didn't even make the list of top sellers.

In nonfiction, each of the top 10 titles sold over 300,000 copies, the first time this has ever happened. A new record of sorts was also set by the #1 bestseller of the year, *In Search of Excellence*, with its sales of over 1 million copies in 1983; the only other bestseller to achieve that distinction on these end-of-the-year lists was *The Living Bible* in 1972 and 1973. Also, at least ten nonfiction books that sold well over 100,000 this past year did not grab one of the 25 nonfiction spots.

In fiction, name authors with track records continued to dominate the list. Once again, as in 1982, 17 of the top 25 fiction titles were by authors who have previously appeared on the year's bestseller charts. While two of the three first novels were written by well-known figures in the book or entertainment fields, the third, *The Name of*

the Rose, could be dubbed one of the most unlikely bestselling novels ever—it was written by an Italian professor of semiotics, set in a fourteenth-century monastery, and filled with numerous untranslated Latin passages.

The bestselling nonfiction fare in 1983 was more predictable. But here, too, there were some surprises. While business, self-improvement, humor, and religious titles dominated, a book about travel along America's back roads made the list of top 15. By far, the strongest category in 1983 was business books, and the top three books in this group—*In Search of Excellence, Megatrends,* and *The One Minute Manager*—were also the longest-running bestsellers on *PW*'s 1983 lists.

The books on *PW*'s annual bestseller lists, including runners-up, are based on sales figures supplied by publishers. These figures, according to the respective firms, reflect only 1983 U.S. trade sales—that is, sales to bookstores, wholesalers, and libraries only. Not included, claim publishers, are book club, overseas, and direct mail transactions. Some books appear in the listings without accompanying sales figures. These were submitted to *PW* in confidence, for use only in placing the titles in their correct positions on a specific list.

"Sales," as used on these lists, refers to books shipped and billed in calendar year 1983. Publishers were asked to reflect returns made through January 15, 1984. Still, in many cases, the 1983 sales figures include books still on bookstore and wholesaler shelves and/or books on the

Publishers Weekly's 1983 Hardcover Bestsellers

Fiction

1. **Return of the Jedi™ Storybook** adapted by Joan D. Vinge. Random House (published May 1983); *882,124* copies sold in 1983
2. **Poland** by James A. Michener. Random House (August 1983); *786,235*
3. **Pet Sematary** by Stephen King. Doubleday (Nov. 14, 1983); *657,741*
4. **The Little Drummer Girl** by John le Carré. Knopf (Mar. 21, 1983); *400,444*
5. **Christine** by Stephen King. Viking (Apr. 29, 1983); *303,589*
6. **Changes** by Danielle Steel. Delacorte (Sept. 2, 1983); *295,000*
7. **The Name of the Rose** by Umberto Eco. A Helen and Kurt Wolff Book/Harcourt Brace Jovanovich (June 9, 1983); *275,000*
8. **White Gold Wielder: Book Three of The Second Chronicles of Thomas Covenant** by Stephen R. Donaldson. Del Rey/Ballantine (April 1983); *267,000*
9. **Hollywood Wives** by Jackie Collins. Simon & Schuster (July 29, 1983); *226,505*
10. **The Lonesome Gods** by Louis L'Amour. Bantam (April 1983); *205,000*
*11. **Who Killed the Robins Family?** by Bill Adler and Thomas Chastain. Morrow (August 1983)
12. **The Robots of Dawn** by Isaac Asimov. Doubleday (Oct. 21, 1983); *171,322*
13. **August** by Judith Rossner. Houghton Mifflin (Aug. 15, 1983); *157,535*
*14. **Ancient Evenings** by Norman Mailer. Little, Brown (April 1983)
15. **Moreta: Dragonlady of Pern** by Anne McCaffrey. Del Rey/ Ballantine (November 1983); *151,000*

NOTE: Rankings on this list are determined by sales figures provided by publishers; the numbers reflect reports of copies "shipped and billed" only and should not be regarded as net sales figures since publishers do not yet know what their final returns will be.

*Sales figures were submitted to *PW* in confidence, for use only in placing the titles in their correct positions on a specific list.

way back to the publishers' warehouses, as well as books already stacking up on returns piles.

The Fiction Bestsellers

At $6.95, and with about 60 illustrated pages, the novelization *Return of the Jedi Storybook* could very easily be considered a children's title. Yet it enjoyed a 22-week run on *PW*'s and the *New York Times* hardcover adult bestseller charts, several times in the #1 spot. A title similar in appeal and scope to last year's leading fiction bestseller, *E.T. The Extra-Terrestrial Storybook*, it shares an even more significant feature with its outer-space cousin. Both books managed to knock a new James Michener book off a customary spot on top of the year's annual fiction bestselling chart.

Michener's *Poland* sold 786,235 copies to *Jedi*'s 882,124. But at $17.95 and 560 pages—covering that Eastern European country's history from the thirteenth century to the present day—Michener's book clearly ranks as #1 in terms of dollar sales for a 1983 novel. And although *Space* was the #2 fiction bestseller in 1982, many of the author's previous works were leading novels when they were published, including *The Source* (1965), *Centennial* (1974), and *Chesapeake* (1978).

A distinction that occurs rarely on these annual lists is for an author to have two novels among the top 10 of the

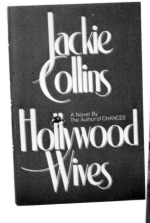

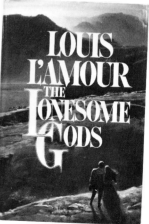

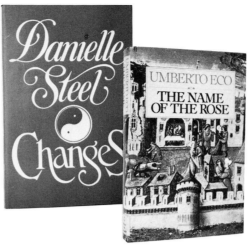
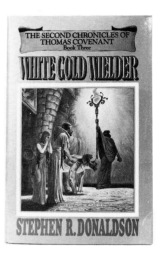

year. Stephen King captured the #3 and #5 spots with two new books, *Pet Sematary* and *Christine,* with 657,741 (his highest ever year-end sales figure) and 303,589 copies respectively. Three other novelists who achieved similar laurels were Frederick Forsyth in 1972, John O'Hara in 1960, and James Hilton in 1935. Two books on the same list by a nonfiction writer is a bit more common; in 1982, Leo Buscaglia and Andrew A. Rooney each had two titles on the end-of-the-year hardcover list. This year William Manchester has two major biographies in the top 25.

The #4 position on these annual lists seems to be a favorite spot for John le Carré. His latest thriller, *The Little Drummer Girl,* sold over 400,000 copies in 1983 and was the year's longest-running fiction hardcover bestseller on *PW*'s weekly list; it was on the list for 35 weeks, 18 weeks in the #1 spot. Four previous le Carré titles also made the year-end #4 spot—*The Honourable Schoolboy* (1977), *Tinker, Tailor, Soldier, Spy* (1974), *A Small Town in Germany* (1968), and *The Looking Glass War* (1965); in 1979, *Smiley's People* was the #10 fiction bestseller.

Three science fiction/fantasy novels, in addition to *Return of the Jedi Storybook,* were among the top 15 fiction bestsellers for the year—the same number as last year. Again, this points to the continued strong showing of this category on hardcover bestseller lists; just a few years ago the appearance of just one book in this genre was a noteworthy event.

Isaac Asimov takes the #12 spot with sales of more than 171,300 for *The Robots of Dawn*. Last year, the prolific author made it to the end-of-the-year hardcover list for the first time with the fourth novel in his famous Foundation series, *Foundation's Edge*. Another 1982 bestselling author in the genre returning in 1983 is Stephen R. Donaldson, with sales of about 267,000 in 1983 for *White Gold Wielder: Book Three of The Second Chronicles of Thomas Covenant*, enough to give it the #8 spot on the fiction list. Rounding off the science fiction/fantasy category and the top 15 fiction list is a newcomer to these annual bestseller charts, Anne McCaffrey, with the continuing saga of Pern in *Moreta: Dragonlady of Pern;* sales of about 151,000 gives it the #15 spot on the 1983 fiction list.

Another category, usually reserved for paperback bestsellerdom, is westerns. But Louis L'Amour crosses into the hardcover top-seller frontier with *The Lonesome Gods,* #10 with 1983 sales of 205,000. This is the first time Bantam has published an original L'Amour in hardcover. It has been about 60 years since western hardcovers have made these annual charts; at that time one could count on a Zane Grey title showing up on an annual list. L'Amour is hardly a stranger to the bestseller world; according to his publisher, he is one of the world's four bestselling living novelists, with over 130 million copies of his fiction works in print. In 1982, he became the first novelist in

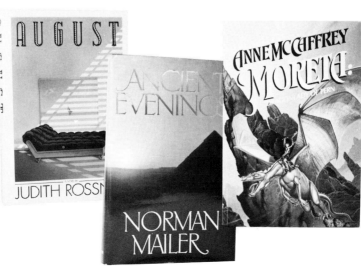

Publishers Weekly's 1983 Hardcover Bestsellers

Nonfiction

1. **In Search of Excellence: Lessons from America's Best-Run Companies** by Thomas J. Peters and Robert H. Waterman, Jr. Harper & Row (Oct. 21, 1982); *1,160,491*
2. **Megatrends: Ten New Directions Transforming Our Lives** by John Naisbitt. Warner (Oct. 18, 1982); *788,260*
3. **Motherhood: The Second Oldest Profession** by Erma Bombeck. McGraw-Hill (Oct. 3, 1983); *725,372*
*4. **The One Minute Manager** by Kenneth Blanchard and Spencer Johnson. Morrow (Sept. 1, 1982)
5. **Jane Fonda's Workout Book** by Jane Fonda. Simon & Schuster (Nov. 16, 1981); *420,617*
6. **The Best of James Herriot** by James Herriot. St. Martin's (September 1983); *388,905*
7. **The Mary Kay Guide to Beauty: Discovering Your Special Look** by the Beauty Experts at Mary Kay Cosmetics. Addison-Wesley (Sept. 26, 1983); *334,580*
*8. **On Wings of Eagles** by Ken Follett. Morrow (September 1983)
9. **Creating Wealth** by Robert G. Allen. Simon & Schuster (Apr. 28, 1983); *315,193*
10. **The Body Principal: The Exercise Program for Life** by Victoria Principal. Simon & Schuster (Sept. 19, 1983); *307,976*
11. **Approaching Hoofbeats: The Four Horsemen of the Apocalypse** by Billy Graham. Word (November 1983); *259,000*
12. **Tough Times Never Last but Tough People Do** by Robert H. Schuller. Thomas Nelson (May 1, 1983); *257,641*
*13. **Blue Highways: A Journey into America** by William Least Heat Moon. Atlantic Monthly Press/Little, Brown (January 1983)
14. **The Secret Kingdom** by Pat Robertson with Bob Slosser. Thomas Nelson (Oct. 1, 1982); *214,899*
15. **While Reagan Slept** by Art Buchwald. Putnam (Oct. 14, 1983); *185,417*

> NOTE: Rankings on this list are determined by sales figures provided by publishers; the numbers reflect reports of copies "shipped and billed" only and should not be regarded as net sales figures since publishers do not yet know what their final returns will be.
>
> *Sales figures were submitted to *PW* in confidence, for use only in placing the titles in their correct positions on a specific list.

American history to be voted a special National Gold Medal by the U.S. Congress for "his distinguished career as an author and his contribution to the nation through his historically based works."

There was an extra incentive for consumers to pay $9.95 for this year's #11 fiction bestseller, *Who Killed the Robins Family?* In what Morrow called "an unprecedented publishing event," the publisher was offering a $10,000 cash reward to the reader who came up with the best solution to the mystery posed by the novel. Created by agent/packager Bill Adler and written by veteran mystery writer Thomas Chastain, *PW* called it "a most ingenious puzzle that would have had even Sherlock Holmes guessing." As of this writing, that continues to hold true for readers in search of the jackpot.

Ten years in the writing, Norman Mailer's opus on Egypt, *Ancient Evenings*, was published to mixed reviews; still, enough fans (over 151,000) bought the book to place it #14 on the 1983 fiction list. Mailer is no stranger to these lists, making his first appearance in 1948 with a first novel, *The Naked and the Dead*; it was #2 that year with over 137,000 copies sold. In 1979, his true-life novel of the life and death of Gary Gilmore was among the top 25 fiction bestsellers.

As noted earlier, a most unusual first novel made it to the top 15; with sales of 275,000, Umberto Eco's *The Name of the Rose* placed #7 on this year's list of fiction

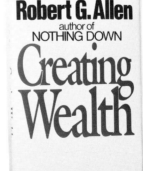

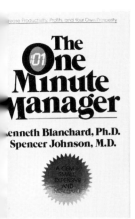

top sellers. The book was a bestseller in Italy, France, and Germany and had won some prestigious literary prizes, including two major Italian honors and France's Prix Medicis for best foreign novel. Still, its success here was a surprise to almost all, including its publisher, who reportedly bought the manuscript for somewhere between $4,000 and $5,000. Warner Books paid $550,000 for paperback reprint rights. The book was on *PW*'s bestseller list for 26 weeks, five weeks in the #1 spot (it got bumped by Michener's *Poland)*.

Judith Rossner returned to a New York setting for *August,* #13 with sales of over 157,500. The city was also the setting for her previous title that made it onto these annual lists—*Looking for Mr. Goodbar,* #4 in 1975 with sales of over 163,000.

Another veteran of these lists, Danielle Steel, outdid her previous hardcover record, attained only last year with *Crossings* (it garnered the #13 position with sales close to 199,000). Her 1983 bestseller, *Changes,* gained the #6 position with sales of 295,000.

A newcomer to these lists is Jackie Collins (Joan's younger sister). Her book *Hollywood Wives* racked up sales of 226,505 in 1983, enough to give it the #9 fiction spot for the year. She has written eight other novels, currently published in more than 30 languages; according to her publisher, each of her books has sold more than 1 million copies worldwide.

The Fiction Runners-Up

The second tier of bestsellers is also dominated by authors whose previous books have been major bestsellers. Len Deighton has written 15 thrillers, many of which have made it onto these end-of-the-year lists. In fact, this year's only newcomers at this level are Bette Midler and Nora Ephron. Midler, who toured extensively on behalf of this work, certainly is no new name. While *Heartburn* is Ephron's first novel, her nonfiction books have enjoyed excellent sales—and the fact that many reviewers and journalists drew parallels between Ephron's marriage to Carl Bernstein and what happens to *Heartburn*'s heroine didn't hurt the book's sales.

New hardcover novels selling over 100,000 copies in 1983 that did not make the top 25 fiction list include *Banker* by Dick Francis (Putnam), *Delta Star* by Joseph Wambaugh (Morrow), and *Monimbo* by Robert Moss and Arnaud de Borchgrave (Simon & Schuster).

In ranked order, the 10 fiction runners-up are: *The Seduction of Peter S.* by Lawrence Sanders (Putnam, 8/83; 145,117 copies sold in 1983); *Voice of the Heart* by Barbara Taylor Bradford (Doubleday, 3/83; 144,356); *The Saga of Baby Divine* by Bette Midler (Crown, 11/83; 140,798); *Ascent into Hell* by Andrew M. Greeley (Warner, 6/83; 139,681); *Berlin Game* by Len Deighton (Knopf, 1/84, books were shipped in 12/83; 138,909); *The Wicked Day*

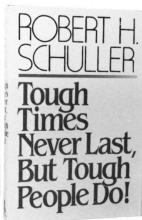
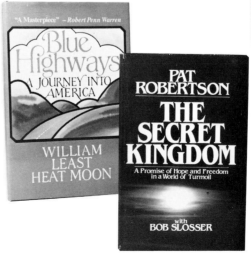

by Mary Stewart (Morrow, 10/83); *Summer of Katya* by Trevanian (Crown, 6/83; 130,597); *Heartburn* by Nora Ephron (Knopf, 4/83; 123,751); *The Auerbach Will* by Stephen Birmingham (Little, Brown, 8/83); and *Godplayer* by Robin Cook (Putnam, 7/83; 117,530).

The Nonfiction Leaders

Without question, business was the hottest bestselling subject in 1983; there were a couple of months during 1983 when the top four spots on *PW*'s weekly list were commanded by the four leaders in this category—*In Search of Excellence, Megatrends, The One Minute Manager,* and *Creating Wealth.* They ranked #1, #2, #4, and #9, respectively, on the final 1983 nonfiction list. Except for *Creating Wealth,* the other three titles also made the top 25 1982 bestseller list, but in much lower spots.

Perhaps the most remarkable performance by any bestseller in many years was achieved by *In Search of Excellence.* The book reached 1 million copies in sales within 10 months of publication, making it one of the fastest-selling books of all time. The sales figure is even more astounding when compared with the publisher's sales advance of 8,100 copies prior to its November 1982 publication date. It was one of the most sought-after books of Christmas 1982 and dominated the top of the 1983 bestseller charts for almost three-quarters of the year. With sales of 1,160,491 in 1983, added to about 122,000 copies in 1982, this title was the best-selling book in Harper & Row's 166-year history.

The #2 nonfiction bestseller, *Megatrends,* sold 788,260 copies in 1983. Its 1982 sales of 210,708 made it #15 on last year's annual list. Both *Megatrends* and *In Search of Excellence* did not miss a week on *PW*'s weekly charts.

Offering advice on the quickest way to increase productivity, *The One Minute Manager,* the #3 nonfiction seller, scored high on the weekly charts until the trade paperback edition was published in late fall (that quickly became the #1 trade paperback seller). Sales of more than 200,000 in 1982 earned it the #16 spot that year.

In *Creating Wealth,* the author shares some of the steps in the wealth-building program that made him a multimillionaire before the age of 35. (Writing bestsellers was certainly a contributing factor to his new financial status.) The popularity of *Creating Wealth,* with sales of over 315,000 books in 1983, also propelled his first book, *Nothing Down,* back onto the national bestseller charts. That title captured the #9 spot in 1980 with sales of 197,000 copies; in mid-February 1984, it was the #1 hardcover bestseller at Waldenbooks and the #2 hardcover bestseller at B. Dalton.

Body and face tone-up were also the theme of several major bestsellers. Last year's nonfiction leader, *Jane Fonda's Workout Book,* sold an additional 420,617 in 1983, enough to capture the #5 spot. For the lead position in 1982, the Fonda book sold over 692,000. Fonda's very attractive colleague in show business, Victoria Principal, also scored with her first book: an exercise program based on isometric exercises designed to take about 30 minutes a day. Close to 308,000 consumers picked up the book, enough to make it the #10 nonfiction bestseller in 1983.

Once the figure is shipshape, the face comes next (or maybe the order is reversed). A well-coordinated marketing campaign by the publishers and the Mary Kay Cosmetic Company quickly launched Mary Kay's bestselling title, #6 for 1983 with sales totals for the year of more than 334,500; one week after shipping, it captured the #1 spot on B. Dalton's bestseller list.

Three veterans of these hardcover lists made it again to the top 15 with their latest works. In the #3 spot, Erma Bombeck, one of the most popular funny ladies, managed to sell 725,372 copies of *Motherhood.* Obviously, many customers took the publisher's advice seriously, that "this book is not for everyone—only for those who are mothers or who had one." Bombeck has been on the year-end lists a number of times, most recently in the #1 spot in 1979 for *Aunt Erma's Cope Book* with sales of 692,000.

Well-known British veterinarian James Herriot has been a bestselling author ever since his first book, *All Creatures Great and Small,* appeared in 1972. The author's latest work is an illustrated anthology of the best of all his previous writings, chosen by Herriot himself. Sales of over 388,905 made it the #6 bestselling nonfiction hardcover of the year.

A regular on these end-of-the-year charts on the fiction list is Ken Follett. His nonfiction debut with *On Wings of Eagles* earned him one of the most impressive sales records of his career—sales of more than 315,000, for the #8 nonfiction spot in 1983. His last appearance on an annual list was in 1982, when *A Man from St. Petersburg* placed #10 on the fiction list with sales of over 225,000. Ken Follett's American debut in hardcover fiction was in 1978 with *Eye of the Needle;* it was the #10 fiction bestseller of the year with 122,000 copies sold.

Three religious titles made it to the top 15, an impressive number for the annual list. All were by well-known religious personalities with extensive television exposure. In the #11 spot is Billy Graham's *Approaching Hoofbeats;* sales of 259,000 gave it the #11 spot for the year-end nonfiction list. Graham's first appearance on a *PW* annual list was in 1955 with *The Secret of Happiness;* sales of 115,697 made it #7 that year. Exactly 20 years later, his book *Angels: God's Secret Agents* took the #1 spot for the year with sales of 810,000. Two titles from Thomas Nelson finished in the #12 and #14 spots. Robert H. Schuller's *Tough Times Never Last, But Tough People Do* sold 257,641 copies in 1983, and Pat Robertson's *The Secret Kingdom* sold 214,899 books.

William Least Heat Moon scored with his first published book, *Blue Highways,* #13 on *PW*'s annual 1983 hardcover list. According to Little, Brown, it is one of the most successful books ever published by Atlantic Monthly Press.

Another newcomer to these annual lists, but certainly not to weekly national charts, is Art Buchwald. His satirical look at the president enjoyed sales of over 185,417 books, enough to get it the #15 spot in 1983. Buchwald's syndicated column appears in 550 newspapers worldwide.

The Nonfiction Runners-Up

This year's 10 runners-up in nonfiction were all books that enjoyed long runs on weekly national bestseller charts. William Manchester scored with two impressive biographical works. A 13-part PBS-TV special based on Stanley Karnow's *Vietnam* helped that book's bestseller run. Other books making up this second tier of nonfiction bestsellers are a first collection of essays by *Ms. Magazine* editor Gloria Steinem; books from two well-known people from the entertainment field, and still more books on diet and fitness.

1983 nonfiction bestsellers that did not make a top-25 list include such titles as *No More Hot Flashes and Other Good News* by Penny Budoff (Putnam), *The Love You Make: An Insider's Story of the Beatles* by Peter Brown and Steven Gaines (McGraw-Hill), *A Hero for Our Time: An Intimate Story of the Kennedy Years* by Ralph G. Martin (Macmillan), *Richard Simmons' Better Body Book* by Richard Simmons (Warner), and *The Price of Power: Kissinger in the Nixon White House* by Seymour M. Hersh (Summit). All sold 119,000 copies or more in 1983.

In ranked order, the 10 nonfiction runners-up are: *Vietnam: A History* by Stanley Karnow (Viking, 10/83; 176,635 books sold in 1983); *Out On a Limb* by Shirley MacLaine (Bantam, 6/83; 175,000); *Fatal Vision* by Joe McGinniss (Putnam, 9/83; 168,342); *Working Out* by Charles Hix (Simon & Schuster, 2/83; 165,285); *Outrageous Acts and Everyday Rebellions* by Gloria Steinem (Holt, Rinehart and Winston, 9/83; 158,107); *The Peter Pan Syndrome* by Dr. Dan Kiley (Dodd, Mead, 9/83; 141,000); *One Brief Shining Moment: Remembering Kennedy* by William Manchester (Little, Brown, 11/83); *The Diet Center Program* by Sybil Ferguson (Little, Brown, 4/83); *How to Live to be 100. . . or More* by George Burns (Putnam, 5/83; 135,806); and *The Last Lion: Winston Spencer Churchill* by William Manchester (Little, Brown, 5/83).

Paperback Top Sellers

SALLY A. LODGE

The *Publishers Weekly*'s annual trade paperback bestseller list continues to mushroom: for the first time ever, more than 200 trade paperbacks qualified for the top-seller list. With a tally of 208 titles (including annuals, atlases, and almanacs) published in 1982 or 1983 that sold 50,000 copies or more in 1983, the list sets a new record, topping last year's total of 174 titles. To put this in perspective, the trade paperback list covering books published in 1977 (the first such list *PW* ran) contained only 65 titles; six

years later there are more than three times that number of books on the list.

Examining 1982's list, we found that of the top 20 titles all but two fit conveniently into three categories: humor, fitness/beauty, and romance. Although no such clear-cut definition exists on 1983's list, these three categories once again make very strong showings. For yet another year, Garfield has reason to celebrate. Jim Davis's furry feline is featured in a grand total of seven books on 1983's bestseller list, one more than last year. *Garfield Eats His Heart Out* and *Garfield Sits Around the House*, both released in 1983, hold the number 2 and number 5 spots on the list; the seven Garfield titles had a combined sales figure of 3,039,000 copies in 1983.

That Garfield had the lion's share of sales in 1983's humor market becomes all the more apparent when one considers that three additional Garfield collections, whose 1980 and 1981 publication dates disqualified them from inclusion on the 1983 list, had sales approaching 200,000 copies each in 1983 alone, pushing sales of Garfield titles well over 3.5 million copies for the year.

Parodies also moved quickly off bookstore shelves in 1983. Linda Sunshine cashed in on the Jane Fonda exercise craze with a less demanding method for working out. Those not up to the Fonda pace found an alternative in *Plain Jane Works Out*, which had sales of 455,000 copies in 1983. And the success of Alfred Gingold's parody of the L.L. Bean catalogue, *Items from Our Catalog*, seemed to have inspired several other similar take-offs. Two of these made our list: Philip Leif's *Bumpee Gardening Catalog* and Stephen M. Kirschner's *Not the Frederick's of Hollywood Catalog*. Gingold published a sequel to his 1982 bestseller, *More Items from Our Catalog*, which sold 427,000 copies between its October pub date and the end of 1983. The original version also appears on this year's list, having sold 138,000 copies in 1983 alone.

And yet another trend in humor books can't be ignored. Bruce Feirstein's *Real Men Don't Eat Quiche*, a 1982 publication whose 1983 sales totaled 130,500 copies, led to a number of spinoffs that appear on this year's list. Two were published at the end of 1982: *Real Women Don't Pump Gas* by Joyce Jillson, and *Real Men Don't Cook Quiche* by Scott Redman, edited by Bruce Feirstein; their 1983 sales figures are 198,000 and 50,000 copies, respectively. And one successful *Real Men* takeoff goes so far as to encompass another species: Lee Lorenz's *Real Dogs Don't Eat Leftovers* sold 96,000 copies between its September pub date and year's end.

Beauty, Fitness, and Romance All Flourish

A glance at the 1983 trade paperback bestseller list discloses that beauty and fitness are still big business in the bookstores. Authors continue to promise near-miraculous physical transformations in very little time: a total of seven books on the list lure the reader with vows of changes that can be made in 30 days—anything from healthy hair to sexual satisfaction.

And in the realm of big promises...those who can't wait 30 days will find that a great deal can be accomplished in 60 seconds, which is apparently long enough to become a manager, a lover, or a good employee. *The One Minute Manager* by Spencer Johnson, M.D., and Kenneth Blanchard holds the number 3 spot on the list, with sales of 1 million copies; *The One Minute Lover* by M. Wiener and Zaza Petz sold 163,000 copies; and, released in December, *The :59 Second Employee* by Rae Andre and Peter Ward registered sales of 50,000 copies.

In the romance genre, Danielle Steel reigns as leading lady of the year, with her *Thurston House* crowning the list with sales of 1,100,000 copies in 1983. (It is interesting to note that another original romance, Kathleen E. Woodiwiss's *A Rose in Winter*, also held the number 1 spot on the 1982 trade paperback list.) In addition to *Thurston House*, Steel is also represented on this year's list by *Once in a Lifetime*, a holdover from 1982 that sold 623,000 copies in 1983. And four of her titles (two of which were released in 1982) appear on this year's mass market top-seller list; combined, their 1983 in-print figures total 7,308,550 copies.

And another author familiar to bestseller lists, Janet Dailey, makes an impressive showing on this year's trade paperback list with three titles from her Calder saga, two published this year and one in 1982. The three had combined 1983 sales of 1,281,000 copies.

Not All of 1982's Trends Still Going Strong

In 1981, both the trade paperback and the mass market bestseller lists compiled by *PW* at year's end were headed by books aimed at helping readers crack Rubik's cube. At the end of 1982, we noted that books on mastering the cube had been overshadowed by books promising to teach readers another skill: getting the best of computer games. Pac Man and company seemed doomed to human domination with four trade paperback and two mass market titles appearing on the 1982 lists. This year, not a single title devoted to solving the cube sold sufficiently to make either list; the two titles on outsmarting Pac Man that appear on the 1983 mass market list were both published at the beginning of 1982.

Glancing over the lists, no analogous trend seems to have surplanted these two waning ones. Although the computer book market appears to be turning away from titles focusing on computer games to those devoted to more serious applications of computers and computer software, this trend has yet to result in a profusion of titles selling in bookstores in quantities great enough to qualify for our list. Only three computer-related trade paperback books sold more than 50,000 copies or more in 1983 (*The Beginner's Guide to Computers* by Robin Bradbeer, Peter De Bono, and Peter Laurie; *A Guide to Programming in Applesoft* by Bruce Presley; and *Kids and Computers: The Parents Micro-Computer Handbook* by Eugene Galanter), and the first two mentioned were published in 1982.

The Size of the Mass Market List Holds Its Own

The 1983 mass market bestseller list contains 99 titles (including media tie-ins), published in 1982 or 1983, with in-print figures of 1 million copies or more, which is but two titles more than last year's list. Not an impressive growth, yet this is the first time in two years that the list has not declined in size, as 1982's list of 97 titles followed 1981's list of 109 titles, down from 1980's all-time high of 113.

This year, as last year, there was no need to include a 3 million-plus category, since only two titles had in-print figures that topped this mark. In previous years, since *Publishers Weekly*'s annual bestseller list first appeared in this format in 1977, a number of titles qualified for this category; in 1978, it was even necessary to include 4 million-plus and 6 million-plus categories.

The single book whose 1983 in-print figure exceeded 4 million copies is Sidney Sheldon's *Master of the Game*. Sheldon is hardly new to bestseller lists; his *Rage of Angels*, released in 1981, held the number 2 spot on last year's mass market list. With 4,377,000 copies in print, *Master of the Game* looms high above the title on the 1982 list that had the largest in-print figure for a book published in that year: Harold Robbins's *Goodbye Janette* (2,537,000). In fact, four titles on this year's list released in 1983 (plus one holdover from 1982) have in-print figures that exceed 2,537,000 copies. Also worthy of note is that, unlike other recent years' annual mass market bestseller lists, every one of 1983's top 12 titles is a reprint.

Two other veterans of bestseller lists have triple entries on this year's mass market list. Stephen King has the rare distinction of authoring three of the top nine titles (*Cujo*, published in 1982, and *Christine* and *Different Seasons*, 1983 releases). The combined 1983 in-print figures for these titles is 8,784,000 copies. Also appearing three times on this year's list is Louis L'Amour, whose *Bowdrie*, *Ride the River,* and *Law of the Desert Born* (with a combined 1983 in-print figure of 3,915,000 copies) were all published in 1983.

And while on the subject of big numbers, two in-print figures in particular caught the eye while looking over figures submitted by publishers for the 1983 list. Avon's 2,075,000-copy printing for the TV tie-in edition of *The Thorn Birds* by Colleen McCullough brings the total number of copies in print in Avon editions to a grand total of 10,340,000. And even more staggering is NAL's announcement that with 1,125,000 copies issued of *1984 Commemorative Edition*, there are now 11,500,000 copies in print of various Signet editions of George Orwell's classic.

What the Publishers Are Saying

Only a handful of publishers responded to *Publishers Weekly*'s questions about the future directions of their trade paperback or mass market publishing programs, but several notable observations were made.

In the mass market area, both Walter Meade of Avon and William R. Grose of Pocket Books noted that they had marked success with original novels in 1983, and this will continue to be a point of focus for both. (It should be noted, however, that Grose believes that it is increasingly difficult to launch a new or not well-known writer at the top of the list.) Both Grose and Mead also remarked on their success in 1983 with TV tie-ins (*The Thorn Birds* for Avon, *The Winds of War* for Pocket Books), and the high potential for novels of merit that are reissued as tie-ins.

Virtually every publisher of trade paperbacks who responded registered enormous optimism about the future of the genre. Traditionally hardcover houses as well as mass market publishers reported that trade paperbacks are accounting for an increasingly large percentage of their total sales (at both Van Nostrand Reinhold and Avon, for example, trade paperbacks represented 15 percent of total sales in 1983).

A number of publishers are on the lookout for out-of-print titles that will have new lives as trade paperbacks. Bridget Marmion of Farrar, Straus and Giroux noted that this house is not only constantly reviewing its own backlist for titles to reissue in trade paperback, but is also acquiring the rights to backlist titles held by other publishers and is retaining rights to titles that a few years ago it would have sold to a mass market publisher.

There were also numerous reports of publishers expanding their trade paperback originals programs, particularly in the areas of reference (World Almanac Publications, Avon, Andrews and McMeel) and humor. On the subject of humor books, Donna Martin of Andrews and McMeel wrote that, since six of her house's cartoon humor books qualified for the 1983 trade paperback bestseller list, "we must be doing something right," and the publisher will continue to focus on this area. George Young of Ten Speed Press noted that this publisher also plans to release more humor books, particularly those "that originate here in California." And Martin Asher of Long Shadow Books has a different kind of qualification for books in this genre: "Even though it's war on the humor shelves these days, we will publish it, but we *have* to break our legs from laughing."

And, finally, there is indication that publishers are anticipating a continued burgeoning of the computer book market in trade paperback, as announcements are made of new electronic publishing divisions, new imprints, and new titles in this genre. But an alien and somehow refreshing cry is heard from Ten Speed Press, where George Young insists that "we would cut back on computer books if we had more than the one we have."

Trade Paperbacks

500,000 PLUS

Titles listed here are trade paperbacks (originals, reprints, reissues, or books issued in dual editions) published in 1982 or 1983 of which publishers have billed and shipped at least 50,000 copies to bookstores in 1983. It should be noted that publishers' sales figures are not necessarily the final net sales for the books, as they do not always reflect returns. Those titles that were released in 1982 are marked with an asterisk. Almanacs, atlases, and annuals are listed on page 59.

Thurston House. Danielle Steel. Original. Dell. (1,100,000)

Garfield Eats His Heart Out. Jim Davis. Original. Ballantine. (1,012,000)

The One Minute Manager. Spencer Johnson, M.D., and Kenneth Blanchard. Reprint. Berkley. (1,000,000)

Living, Loving, Learning. Leo Buscaglia. Original. Fawcett/Columbine. (868,000)

Garfield Sits Around the House. Jim Davis. Original. Ballantine. (783,000)

Life Extension: Adding Years to Your Life and Life to Your Years—A Practical Scientific Approach. Durk Pearson and Sandy Shaw. Reprint. Warner. (650,070)

*Once in a Lifetime. Danielle Steel. Original. Dell. (623,000)

The Color Purple. Alice Walker. Reprint. Washington Square Press/Pocket Books. (564,000)

The Star Wars® Intergalactic Passport. Lucasfilm Ltd. Original. Ballantine. (545,000)

Stands a Calder Man. Janet Dailey. Original. Pocket Books. (506,000)

Garfield on the Town. Jim Davis. Original. Ballantine. (500,000)

200,000 PLUS

Calder Born, Calder Bred. Janet Dailey. Original. Pocket Books. (489,000)

Plain Jane Works Out. Linda Sunshine. Original. Bantam. (455,000)

More Items from Our Catalog. Alfred Gingold. Original. Avon. (427,000)

30 Days to a Flatter Stomach for Women. Nancy Burstein. Original. Bantam. (425,000)

Wild Bells to the Wild Sky. Laurie McBain. Original. Avon. (424,286)

*Garfield Takes the Cake. Jim Davis. Original. Ballantine. (415,000)

The Official Cambridge Diet Plan. Eugene Boe. Original. Bantam. (375,000)

*The Read-Aloud Handbook. Jim Trelease. Original. Penguin. (365,000)

Diet Simply with Soup. Gail Becker. Original. Pocket Books. (363,500)

30 Days to a Flatter Stomach for Men. Ray Matthews and Nancy Burstein. Original. Bantam. (345,000)

Flames of Glory. Patricia Matthews. Original. Bantam. (320,000)

The Second Garfield Treasury. Jim Davis. Original. Ballantine. (319,000)

Growing Up. Russell Baker. Reprint. NAL/Plume. (300,000)

The Rapture. Hal Lindsey. Original. Bantam. (295,000)

***This Calder Range.** Janet Dailey. Original. Pocket Books. (286,000)

***Thin Thighs in 30 Days.** Wendy Stehling. Original. Bantam. (285,000)

Bloom Country: Loose Tails. Berke Breathed. Original. Little, Brown. (250,000)

Getting to Yes. Roger Fisher and William Ury. Reprint. Penguin. (225,000)

***The Silver Palate Cookbook.** Julee Rosso and Sheila Lukins with Michael McLaughlin. Dual. Workman. (213,348)

30 Days to Healthy Hair. Julie Davis. Original. Bantam. (205,000)

Royal Seduction. Jennifer Blake. Original. Fawcett/Columbine. (202,000)

***How to Beat the IRS (Legally).** Andrew Ciaramataro. Original. Berkley. (200,000)

100,000 PLUS

***Real Women Don't Pump Gas.** Joyce Jillson. Original. Pocket Books. (198,000)

Beloved. Bertrice Small. Original. Ballantine. (192,000)

Linda Evans Beauty and Exercise Book. Linda Evans. Original. Simon & Schuster/Wallaby. (188,000)

***Garfield Weighs In.** Jim Davis. Original. Ballantine. (186,000)

Jane Fonda's Workout Book. Jane Fonda. Reprint. Simon & Schuster. (179,734)

Return of the Jedi™ Illustrated Edition. James Kahn. Original. Ballantine. (170,000)

***Personhood.** Leo Buscaglia. Reprint. Fawcett/Columbine. (166,000)

The One Minute Lover. M. Wiener and Zaza Petz. Original. NAL/Plume. (163,000)

Beyond the Far Side. Gary Larson. Original. Andrews and McMeel. (157,498)

Return of the Jedi™ Portfolio. Ralph McQuarrie. Original. Ballantine. (156,000)

Miss Manners® Guide to Excruciatingly Correct Behavior. Judith Martin. Reprint. Warner. (152,817)

Menudo! Keith Elliot Greenberg. Original. Pocket Books. (150,000)

Not Quite TV Guide. Gerald Sussman. Original. Prince/Crown. (149,708)

Flatten Your Stomach for Men and Women. Editors of Consumer Guide. Original. Pocket Books. (142,500)

Slimming Your Hips and Thighs. Editors of Consumer Guide. Original. Pocket Books. (142,000)

Wrap Me in Splendor. Ellen Tanner Marsh. Original. Berkley. (140,000)

***Items from Our Catalog.** Alfred Gingold. Original. Avon. (138,000)

Flatten Your Stomach, Book II. Jim Everroad. Original. Price/Stern/Sloan. (136,000)

Morning Star. Kerry Newcomb. Original. Bantam. (135,000)

***Garfield Treasury.** Jim Davis. Original. Ballantine. (133,000)

***Real Men Don't Eat Quiche.** Bruce Feirstein. Original. Pocket Books. (130,500)

Information U.S.A. Matthew Lesko. Original. Penguin. (130,000)

The Curse of Lono. Hunter S. Thompson, illustrated by Ralph Steadman. Original. Bantam. (125,000)

Happy to Be Here. Garrison Keillor. Reprint. Penguin. (125,000)

The Fires of July. Sharon Salvato. Original. Dell. (123,000)

How to Regain Your Virginity. Patricia Marx and Charlotte Stewart. Original. Workman. (122,693)

***At Dawn We Slept.** Gordon Prange. Reprint. Penguin. (120,000)

Miracle at Midway. Gordon Prange. Reprint. Penguin. (120,000)

Weight Watchers 365 Day Menu Planner. Weight Watchers International. Reprint. NAL/Plume. (120,000)

The Impatient Gardener. Henry Baker. Original. Ballantine. (116,000)

Dare to Be Dull. Joseph L. Troise. Original. Bantam. (115,000)

Sons and Lovers. D. H. Lawrence. Reissue; TV tie-in. Penguin. (115,000)

Fishing. Henry Beard and Roy McKie. Original. Workman. (114,394)

The Official Lawyer's Handbook. D. Robert White, Esq. Original. Simon & Schuster/Wallaby. (114,000)

Microwave Cookbook. Pat Jester. Reprint. HP Books. (113,417)

The Immortals. Natasha Peters. Original. Fawcett/Columbine. (113,000)

***Phoenix Rising.** Frances Patton Statham. Original. Fawcett/Columbine. (110,000)

***30 Days to a Beautiful Bottom.** Julie Davis. Original. Bantam. (110,000)

Roseanne Roseannadanna's "Hey Get Back to Work" Book. Roseanne Roseannadanna with lots o' help from Alan Zweibel and Gilda Radner. Original. Long Shadow Books/Pocket Books. (109,000)

*Here Comes Garfield. Jim Davis. Original. Ballantine. (106,000)

Firm Skin in 10 Minutes a Day. R. Minear and W. Proctor. Original. NAL/Plume. (105,000)

Tao of Pooh. Benjamin Hoff. Reprint. Penguin. (105,000)

*The Enchanted Broccoli Forest. Mollie Katzen. Original. Ten Speed Press. (103,443)

Bumpee Gardening Catalog. Philip Leif & Associates. Original. NAL/Plume. (102,000)

The Sidetracked Sisters Catch-Up on the Kitchen. Pam Young and Peggy Jones. Original. Warner. (101,150)

Deadeye Dick. Kurt Vonnegut, Jr. Reprint. Dell. (101,000)

How to Clear Up Your Face in 30 Days. Jonathan Zizmor. Reissue. Bantam. (100,000)

Lavender Blue. Parris Afton Bonds. Original. Fawcett/Columbine. (100,000)

75,000 PLUS

*Baby & Child Medical Care. Terril Hart, M.D. Original. Meadowbrook Press. (98,589)

A Whack on the Side of the Head: How to Unlock Your Mind for Innovation. Roger von Oech. Original. Warner. (96,296)

Real Dogs Don't Eat Leftovers. Lee Lorenz. Original. Long Shadow Books/Pocket Books. (96,000)

Millennium. John Varley. Original. Berkley. (95,000)

How to Attract Birds. Michael McKinley. Original. Ortho Books. (94,500)

The Cave Dreamers. Jeanne Williams. Original. Avon. (92,339)

The Underground Shopper. Sue Goldstein. Original. Andrews and McMeel. (87,496)

The Joy of Pigging Out. David Hoffman. Original. Warner. (86,525)

*Hardcore Bodybuilding. Robert Kennedy. Original. Sterling. (86,000)

Unicornis. Annotated by Michael Green. Original. Running Press. (86,000)

America in Search of Itself: The Making of the President 1956–1980. Theodore S. White. Reprint. Warner. (83,568)

You Give Great Meeting, Sid. G. B. Trudeau. Original. Holt, Rinehart and Winston/Owl. (83,210)

*The Far Side. Gary Larson. Original. Andrews and McMeel. (81,648)

My Jedi™ Journal. Lucasfilm Ltd. Original. Ballantine. (81,000)

*A Rose in Winter. Kathleen E. Woodiwiss. Original. Avon. (80,000)

Schindler's List. Thomas Keneally. Reprint. Penguin. (80,000)

Teach Only Love: The Seven Principles of Attitudinal Healing. Gerald Jampolsky, M.D. Original. Bantam. (80,000)

*30 Days to a Better Bust. Regina Larkin and Julie Davis. Original. Bantam. (80,000)

*The Twilight Zone Companion. Marc Scott Zicree. Original. Bantam. (80,000)

Sea Star. Pamela Jekel. Original. Crown. (78,956)

How to Get Married. Julie Davis and Herman Weiss. Original. Ballantine. (78,000)

The Citadel. A. J. Cronin. Dual. Little, Brown. (75,000)

30 Days to Sexual Satisfaction. Alan Schneider and Deirdre Laiken. Original. Bantam. (75,000)

50,000 PLUS

Y.A.P.: The Official Young Aspiring Professional's Fast-Track Handbook. C. E. Crimmins. Original. Running Press. (74,800)

*The Beginner's Guide to Computers. Robin Bradbeer, Peter De Bono, and Peter Laurie. Original. Addison-Wesley. (73,298)

*Murphy's Law, Book Three. Arthur Bloch. Original. Prince/Stern/Sloan. (73,000)

A Woman's Notebook III. Illustrated by Amira Dvorah. Original. Running Press. (72,900)

Salvador. Joan Didion. Reprint. Washington Square Press/Pocket Books. (72,000)

The Drums of December. Sharon Salvato. Original. Dell. (71,000)

Beef It!: Upping the Muscle Mass. Robert Kennedy. Original. Sterling. (70,050)

Luminous Animals. B. Kliban. Original. Penguin. (70,000)

The Doors: An Illustrated History. Danny Sugarman. Dual. Morrow. (69,211)

*Herman You Were a Much Stronger Man... Jim Unger. Original. Andrews and McMeel. (68,216)

Canning. Sue and Bill Deeming. Original. HP Books. (67,005)

*A Guide to Programming in Applesoft. Bruce Presley. Original. Van Nostrand Reinhold. (67,000)

Teddy Bear Journal. Illustrated by Patricia Perleburg. Original. Running Press. (67,000)

It Must Be Nice to Be Little. Lynn Johnson. Original. Andrews and McMeel. (66,848)

The Wreck of the "Rusty Nail." G. B. Trudeau. Original. Holt, Rinehart and Winston/Owl. (66,045)

Star Wars Return of the Jedi™: Marvel Books, The Official Comics Version. Adapted by Archie Goodwin. Original. Crown. (65,101)

Keeping Faith: Memoirs of a President. Jimmy Carter. Reprint. Bantam. (65,000)

Lyonesse. Jack Vance. Original. Berkley. (65,000)

9 to 5: The Working Woman's Guide to Office Survival. Ellen Cassedy and Karen Nussbaum. Original. Penguin. (65,000)

The Puzzle Palace. James Bamford. Reprint. Penguin. (65,000)

Signing: How to Speak with Your Hands. Elaine Costello. Original. Bantam. (65,000)

The New York Times More 60-Minute Gourmet. Pierre Franey. Reprint. Fawcett/Columbine. (64,000)

You Can Write a Romance. Yvonne MacManus. Original. Pocket Books. (64,000)

Writing the Natural Way. Gabriele Rico. Original. J. P. Tarcher. (63,983)

Naughty Nineties. Produced by Intervisual. Original. Price/Stern/Sloan. (62,000)

Sylvia Porter's Your Own Money. Sylvia Porter. Original. Avon. (61,956)

The 60-Day Diet Diary. Karen Kreps. Original. Dell. (61,000)

***How to Master the Art of Selling.** Tom Hopkins. Reprint. Warner. (60,020)

***Jane Brody's Nutrition Book.** Jane Brody. Reprint. Bantam. (60,000)

Looking, Working, Living Terrific 24 Hours a Day. Emily Cho. Reprint. Ballantine. (60,000)

The Sentinel. Arthur C. Clarke. Original. Berkley. (60,000)

Short Chic. Allison Kyle Leopold and Anne Marie Cloutier. Reprint. Bantam. (60,000)

***Herman the Third Treasury.** Jim Unger. Original. Andrews and McMeel. (58,931)

***Making Wood Decoys.** Patrick Spielman. Original. Sterling. (58,498)

Twelve Steps to a Pain-Free Back. R. Mulry and A. White, M.D. Original. NAL/Plume. (58,000)

***A Book of Five Rings.** Miyamoto Musashi. Reprint. The Overlook Press. (57,870)

Buzzwords. Jim Fisk and Robert Barron. Original. Simon & Schuster/Wallaby. (57,000)

Hope: Facing the Music on Nuclear War and the 1984 Elections. Ground Zero. Original. Long Shadow Books/Pocket Books. (56,500)

Chicken. Ceil Dyer. Original. HP Books. (56,303)

John Lennon: Summer of 1980. Yoko Ono with Eight Photographers. Original. Perigee/Putnam. (56,000)

Mister Rogers Talks with Parents. Fred Rogers and Barry Head. Original. Berkley. (55,000)

The Women of Brewster Place. Gloria Naylor. Reprint. Penguin. (55,000)

Cookies. Natalie Haughton. Original. HP Books. (54,917)

The Joy of Photographing People. The Editors of Eastman Kodak Co. Original. Addison-Wesley. (54,539)

What Did You Learn in School Today?: A Comprehensive Guide to Getting the Best Possible Education for Your Child. Bruce Baron, Christine Baron, and Bonnie MacDonald. Original. Warner. (53,677)

Concise Columbia Encyclopedia. Edited by Judith S. Levey and Agnes Greenhall. Dual. Avon. (52,352)

***Go for It!** Judy Zerafa. Original. Workman. (52,107)

The Official M.D. Handbook. E. Ricks. Original. NAL/Plume. (52,000)

***Pain Erasure: The Bonnie Prudden Way.** Bonnie Prudden. Reprint. Ballantine. (52,000)

Salads & Buffets. Christian Teubner and Annette Wolter. Reprint. HP Books. (51,720)

The Complete Air Guitar Handbook. John McKenna and Michael Moffitt. Original. Long Shadow Books/Pocket Books. (51,500)

A Mouthful of Breath Mints and No One to Kiss. Cathy Guisewite. Original. Andrews and McMeel. (51,333)

Catch a Fire: The Life of Bob Marley. Timothy White. Dual. Holt, Rinehart and Winston/Owl. (51,231)

The Gardener's Notebook. Illustrated by Marie Garafano. Original. Running Press. (51,200)

The Art of Return of the Jedi™. Lucasfilm Ltd. Original. Ballantine. (51,000)

***Funny Insults & Snappy Put-Downs.** Joseph Rosenbloom. Original. Sterling. (51,000)

Jane Brody's Guide to Personal Health. Jane Brody. Reprint. Avon. (51,000)

Kids and Computers: The Parents Micro-Computer Handbook. Eugene Galanter. Original. Perigee/Putnam. (51,000)

***The Hurried Child: Growing Up Too Fast Too Soon.** David Elkind. Original. Addison-Wesley. (50,539)

The Aerobics Program for Total Well-Being. Kenneth Cooper, M.D. Reprint. Bantam. (50,000)

And Then There Was Duck. John Ward. Original. Pocket Books. (50,000)

Don't Get Mad...Get Even!: A Manual for Retaliation. Alan Abel. Dual. Norton. (50,000)

Don't Get Taken Everytime. Remar Sutton. Reprint. Penguin. (50,000)

The :59 Second Employee. Rae Andre and Peter Ward. Original. Houghton Mifflin. (50,000)

Getting In! Paulo de Oliveira and Steve Cohen. Original. Workman. (50,000)

The Gold's Gym Book of Bodybuilding. Ken Sprague with Bill Reynolds. Dual. Contemporary Books. (50,000)

Lovejoy's College Guide, Revised and Updated Edition. Charles Straughn and Barbarasue Lovejoy Straughn. Dual. Simon & Schuster/Monarch. (50,000)

The Mismeasure of Man. Stephen Jay Gould. Reprint. Norton. (50,000)

***The Nautilus Bodybuilding Book.** Ellington Darden. Dual. Contemporary Books. (50,000)

Not the Frederick's of Hollywood Catalog. Stephen M. Kirschner. Original. Simon & Schuster/Wallaby. (50,000)

***Real Men Don't Cook Quiche.** Scott Redman. Original. Pocket Books. (50,000)

The Turning Point. Fritjof Capra. Reprint. Bantam. (50,000)

The Weider System of Bodybuilding. Joe Weider with Bill Reynolds. Dual. Contemporary Books. (50,000)

The Womanly Art of Breastfeeding. La Leche League, International. Original. NAL/Plume. (50,000)

Almanacs, Atlases, and Annuals

Rand McNally Road Atlas: United States/Canada/Mexico. Edited by Jon Leverenz. Rand McNally & Co. (2,088,364)

The World Almanac and Book of Facts 1984. Edited by Hana Lane. World Almanac Publications. (1,800,000)

The Guinness Book of World Records 1983. Edited by Norris McWhirter. Mass market reprint. Bantam. (1,160,000)

J. K. Lasser's Your Income Tax 1984. J. K. Lasser. Simon & Schuster/Fireside. (832,000)

Mobil Travel Guide, 27th Annual Ed. Rand McNally & Co. (829,533)

The Teacher Brothers' Modern-Day Almanac 1984. Lawrence and Stuart Teacher. Running Press. (755,000)

Pay Less Tax Legally 1984. Barry Steiner. NAL/Signet. (300,000)

Rand McNally Campground & Trailer Park Guide. Edited by Mary Niles. Rand McNally & Co. (252,165)

Rand McNally Interstate Road Atlas: United States/Canada/Mexico. Edited by Jon Leverenz. Rand McNally & Co. (246,881)

What Color Is Your Parachute?, 1983 Edition. Richard N. Bolles. Ten Speed Press. (245,975)

Rand McNally City & Highway Road Atlas. Edited by Jon Leverenz. Rand McNally & Co. (212,929)

Goushā North American Road Atlas. Goushā. NAL/Signet. (150,000)

Sylvia Porter's 1984 Tax Book. Sylvia Porter. Avon. (130,810)

The Daily Planet Almanac 1984. Edited by Terry Reim. Avon. (123,144)

1984 H & R Block Income Tax Workbook. H & R Block. Macmillan. (114,973)

Laura Ashley Home Furnishings Catalog 1983. The Laura Ashley Studio. Crown. (101,526).

Goushā U.S. Road Atlas. Goushā. NAL/Signet. (100,000)

Europe on $20 a Day. Arthur Frommer. Simon & Schuster/Frommer. (95,000)

The Bill James Baseball Abstract 1983. Bill James. Ballantine. (87,000)

Laura Ashley Home Furnishings Catalog 1984. The Laura Ashley Studio. Crown. (81,398)

Rand McNally Quick Reference World Atlas. Edited by Jon Leverenz. Rand McNally & Co. (77,425)

Rand McNally Student's World Atlas. Edited by Jon Leverenz. Rand McNally & Co. (68,124)

Rand McNally Motor Carrier's Road Atlas. Philip Ranney. Rand McNally & Co. (64,413)

Kovels' Antiques and Collectibles Price List, 16th Edition. Ralph and Terry Kovel. Crown. (61,041)

Warman's Antiques and Their Prices, 17th Edition. Edited by Harry L. Rinker. Warman Publishing. (58,000)

Walt Disney World, 1984. Steve Birnbaum. Houghton Mifflin. (51,400)

The Civil War Almanac. Edited by John S. Bowman. World Almanac Publications. (50,000)

Omni Future Almanac. Edited by Robert Weil. World Almanac Publications. (50,000)

Mass Market

Here is a listing of those mass market titles published in 1982 or 1983 whose 1983 in-print figures exceed 1 million copies. Figures represent publishers' claims of copies in print and, as such, do not necessarily indicate how well the books actually sold. Titles marked with an asterisk were published in 1982. Books issued or reissued as movie or TV tie-ins are listed on page 61.

2 MILLION PLUS

Master of the Game. Sidney Sheldon. Reprint. Warner. (4,377,000)

*Gorky Park. Martin Cruz Smith. Reprint. Ballantine. (3,227,000, of which 700,000 copies are the movie tie-in edition)

*Cujo. Stephen King. Reprint. NAL/Signet. (3,154,000)

Christine. Stephen King. Reprint. NAL/Signet. (3,125,000)

The Parsifal Mosaic. Robert Ludlum. Reprint. Bantam. (2,655,000)

*Goodbye Janette. Harold Robbins. Reprint. Pocket Books. (2,579,625)

Mistral's Daughter. Judith Krantz. Reprint. Bantam. (2,575,000)

*Noble House. James Clavell. Reprint. Dell. (2,515,000)

Different Seasons. Stephen King. Reprint. NAL/Signet. (2,505,000)

The Man From St. Petersburg. Ken Follett. Reprint. NAL/Signet. (2,500,000)

Space. James Michener. Reprint. Fawcett Crest. (2,493,000)

The Valley of Horses. Jean Auel. Reprint. Bantam. (2,320,000)

*A Perfect Stranger. Danielle Steel. Original. Dell. (2,260,000)

My Sweet Audrina. V. C. Andrews. Reprint. Pocket Books. (2,258,809)

*The Cardinal Sins. Andrew M. Greeley. Reprint. Warner. (2,200,000)

Remembrance. Danielle Steel. Reprint. Dell. (2,132,375)

North and South. John Jakes. Reprint. Dell/Harcourt Brace Jovanovich. (2,100,000)

The Case of Lucy Bending. Lawrence Sanders. Reprint. Berkley. (2,005,000)

*Brain. Robin Cook. Reprint. Warner. (2,000,000)

1.5 MILLION PLUS

Spellbinder. Harold Robbins. Reprint. Pocket Books. (1,998,593)

Lace. Shirley Conran. Reprint. Pocket Books. (1,987,165)

The Prodigal Daughter. Jeffrey Archer. Reprint. Pocket Books. (1,908,639)

*The Third Deadly Sin. Lawrence Sanders. Reprint. Berkley. (1,885,750)

*The Hotel New Hampshire. John Irving. Reprint. Pocket Books. (1,878,959)

Fever. Robin Cook. Reprint. NAL/Signet. (1,871,000)

Thy Brother's Wife. Andrew M. Greeley. Reprint. Warner. (1,804,600)

*A Few Minutes with Andy Rooney. Andrew A. Rooney. Reprint. Warner. (1,794,000)

Celebrity. Thomas Thompson. Reprint. Warner. (1,715,000)

Eden Burning. Belva Plain. Reprint. Dell. (1,644,000)

*Bread Upon the Waters. Irwin Shaw. Reprint. Dell. (1,616,700)

*The Beverly Hills Diet. Judith Mazel with Susan Schultz. Reprint. Berkley. (1,600,000)

Once in a Lifetime. Danielle Steel. Reprint. Dell. (1,600,000)

*Truly Tasteless Jokes. Blanche Knott. Original. Ballantine. (1,600,000)

*Mastering Pac Man. Ken Uston. Original. NAL/Signet. (1,500,000)

1 MILLION PLUS

Bowdrie. Louis L'Amour. Original. Bantam. (1,480,000)

*The Legacy. Howard Fast. Reprint. Dell. (1,452,700)

Cinnamon Skin. John D. MacDonald. Reprint. Fawcett Gold Medal. (1,434,000)

Ride the River. Louis L'Amour. Original. Bantam. (1,430,000)

And More by Andy Rooney. Andrew A. Rooney. Reprint. Warner. (1,408,000)

A Mother and Two Daughters. Gail Godwin. Reprint. Avon. (1,405,000)

Second Heaven. Judith Guest. Reprint. NAL/Signet. (1,400,000)

A Cry in the Night. Mary Higgins Clark. Reprint. Dell. (1,361,000)

Max. Howard Fast. Reprint. Dell. (1,353,000)

Acceptable Losses. Irwin Shaw. Reprint. Avon. (1,352,000)

When Bad Things Happen to Good People. Harold S. Kushner. Reprint. Avon. (1,343,000)

*The White Hotel. D. M. Thomas. Reprint. Pocket Books. (1,325,631)

*Palomino. Danielle Steel. Reprint. Dell. (1,316,175)

Gross Jokes. Julius Alvin. Original. Zebra. (1,300,000)

A Rose in Winter. Kathleen E. Woodiwiss. Original. Avon. (1,291,000)

Public Smiles, Private Tears. Helen van Slyke with James Elward. Reprint. Bantam. (1,270,000)

*Women's Work. Anne Tolstoi Wallach. Reprint. NAL/Signet. (1,252,000)

*Midwife. Gay Courter. Reprint. NAL/Signet. (1,225,000)

War and Remembrance. Herman Wouk. Reissue. Pocket Books. (1,215,000)

*Fonda: My Life as Told to Howard Teichmann. Howard Teichmann. Reprint. NAL/Signet. (1,165,000)

Life Sentences. Elizabeth Forsythe Hailey. Reprint. Dell. (1,153,000)

The God Project. John Saul. Reprint. Bantam. (1,146,000)

So Speaks the Heart. Johanna Lindsey. Original. Avon. (1,140,000)

*Century. Fred Mustard Stewart. Reprint. NAL/Signet. (1,138,000)

Deceptions. Judith Michaels. Reprint. Pocket Books. (1,137,445)

Pacific Vortex. Clive Cussler. Original. Bantam. (1,135,000)

*A Green Desire. Anton Myrer. Reprint. Avon. (1,125,000)

1984 Commemorative Edition. George Orwell. Reissue. NAL/Signet. (1,125,000)

*How to Win at Pac Man. Editors of Consumer Guide. Original. Pocket Books. (1,114,900)

*How to Make Love to a Man. Alexandra Penney. Reprint. Dell. (1,110,000)

Touch the Devil. Jack Higgins. Reprint. NAL/Signet. (1,103,000)

*The Cinderella Complex. Colette Dowling. Reprint. Pocket Books. (1,085,583)

Life, the Universe and Everything. Douglas Adams. Reprint. Pocket Books. (1,071,384)

*XPD. Len Deighton. Reprint. Ballantine. (1,070,000)

*License Renewed. John Gardner. Reprint. Berkley. (1,065,000)

Family Trade. James Carroll. Reprint. NAL/Signet. (1,049,000)

Heart of Thunder. Johanna Lindsey. Original. Avon. (1,047,000)

No Comebacks. Frederick Forsyth. Reprint. Bantam. (1,045,000)

Truly Tasteless Jokes Two. Blanche Knott. Original. Ballantine. (1,035,000)

Jade. Pat Barr. Reprint. Warner. (1,030,000)

*Original Sins. Lisa Alther. Reprint. NAL/Signet. (1,022,000)

For Special Services. John Gardner. Reprint. Berkley. (1,015,000)

Lovely Lying Lips. Valerie Sherwood. Original. Warner. (1,015,000)

Rich, Radiant Love. Valerie Sherwood. Original. Warner. (1,015,000)

Foundation's Edge. Isaac Asimov. Reprint. Ballantine. (1,010,000)

Montana. Dana Fuller Ross. Original. Bantam. (1,010,000)

*666. Jay Anson. Reprint. Pocket Books. (1,007,556)

Dakota. Dana Fuller Ross. Original. Bantam. (1,005,000)

Law of the Desert Born. Louis L'Amour. Original. Bantam. (1,005,000)

*Delta Decision. Wilbur Smith. Reprint. NAL/Signet. (1,000,000)

Emerald. Phyllis A. Whitney. Reprint. Fawcett Crest. (1,000,000)

God Emperor of Dune. Frank Herbert. Reprint. Berkley. (1,000,000)

*The Keep. F. Paul Wilson. Reprint. Berkley. (1,000,000)

*Kiss Mommy Goodbye. Joy Fielding. Reprint. NAL/Signet. (1,000,000)

19 Purchase Street. Gerald A. Browne. Reprint. Berkley. (1,000,000)

The Other Woman. Joy Fielding. Reprint. NAL/Signet. (1,000,000)

*Webster's New World Dictionary of the American Language. Reissue. Warner. (1,000,000)

Mass Market Media Tie-Ins

Listed below are those titles reissued in 1982 or 1983 as movie or TV tie-ins, for which the publisher reports an in-print figure of more than 1 million copies for the tie-in edition.

Return of the Jedi™. James Kahn. Ballantine. (3,177,000)

E.T.: The Extra-Terrestrial in His Adventure on Earth. William Kotzwinkle. Berkley. (3,045,000)

The Winds of War. Herman Wouk. Pocket Books. (2,550,000)

The Thorn Birds. Colleen McCullough. Avon. (2,075,000)

The World According to Garp. John Irving. Pocket Books. (1,151,000)

The Right Stuff. Tom Wolfe. Bantam. (1,100,000)

Princess Daisy. Judith Krantz. Bantam. (1,000,000)

Scarface. Paul Monette, based on the screenplay by Oliver Stone. Berkley. (1,000,000)

Longest-Running Hardcover Bestsellers for 1983

The books on these special PW hardcover and paperback bestseller lists are those that lasted longest on our regular weekly bestseller lists in 1983.

This list of fiction and nonfiction titles does not necessarily reflect the year's bestselling hardcover books in terms of actual sales. Often titles that achieve bestsellerdom in the last quarter of the year will have the highest rate of sales for the year, because of Christmas numbers. The 1982 list of longest-running hardcover bestsellers included 19 fiction titles and 19 nonfiction titles that made the weekly charts 15 or more times.

Fiction

		Weeks on 1983 List	Weeks on 1982 List	Date publ.
*1.	The Little Drummer Girl. John le Carré. Knopf, $15.95	35		3/83
2.	Christine. Stephen King. Viking, $16.95	31		4/83
3.	The Valley of Horses. Jean M. Auel. Crown, $15.95	29	16	9/82
4.	White Gold Wielder. Stephen R. Donaldson. Del Rey/Ballantine, $14.95	26		4/83
*	The Name of the Rose. Umberto Eco. A Helen & Kurt Wolff Book/Harcourt Brace Jovanovich, $15.95	26		6/83
5.	Heartburn. Nora Ephron. Knopf, $11.95	25		4/83
6.	Master of the Game. Sidney Sheldon. Morrow, $15.95	23	16	10/82
*7.	Space. James A. Michener. Random House, $17.95	22	12	10/82
*	Return of the Jedi. Adapted by Joan D. Vinge. Random House, $6.95	22		6/83
8.	The Lonesome Gods. Louis L'Amour. Bantam, $14.95	21		4/83
9.	Voice of the Heart. Barbara Taylor Bradford. Doubleday, $17.95	20		3/83
	Hollywood Wives. Jackie Collins. Simon & Schuster, $16.95	20		7/83
10.	August. Judith Rossner. Houghton Mifflin, $15.95	19		8/83
11.	The Summer of Katya. Trevanian. Crown, $12.95	18		6/83
12.	2010: Odyssey Two. Arthur C. Clarke. Del Rey/Ballantine, $14.95	17	5	12/82
13.	Who Killed the Robins Family? Bill Adler and Thomas Chastain. Morrow, $9.95	16		8/83
*	Poland. James A. Michener. Random House, $17.95	16		9/83
	Changes. Danielle Steel. Delacorte, $15.95	16		9/83
14.	Mistral's Daughter. Judith Krantz. Crown, $15.95	15	5	1/83
	Banker. Dick Francis. Putnam, $14.95	15		4/83
	Ancient Evenings. Norman Mailer. Little, Brown, $19.95	15		4/83
	Monimbó. Robert Moss and Arnaud de Borchgrave. Simon & Schuster, $15.95	15		8/83

Nonfiction

		Weeks on 1983 List	Weeks on 1982 List	Date publ.
*1.	Megatrends. John Naisbitt. Warner, $17.50	51	8	10/82
*	In Search of Excellence. Thomas J. Peters and Robert H. Waterman, Jr. Harper & Row, $19.95	51		11/82
2.	The One Minute Manager. Kenneth Blanchard and Spencer Johnson. Morrow, $15	44	11	9/82
3.	Jane Fonda's Workout Book. Jane Fonda. Simon & Schuster, $19.95	41	48	11/81
4.	Blue Highways. William Least Heat Moon. Atlantic/Little Brown, $17.95	33		1/83
5.	Creating Wealth. Robert Allen. Simon & Schuster, $14.95	29		4/83
6.	Growing Up. Russell Baker. Congdon & Weed, $15	28	4	10/82
7.	Working Out. Charles Hix. Simon & Schuster, $16.95	24		2/83
*8.	And More by Andy Rooney. Andrew A. Rooney. Atheneum, $12.95	19	9	10/82
	The Love You Make. Peter Brown and Steven Gaines. McGraw-Hill, $14.95	19		4/83
9.	Living, Loving and Learning. Leo Buscaglia. Charles B. Slack/Holt, Rinehart and Winston, $13.50	18	37	4/82
10.	The Last Lion. William Manchester. Little, Brown, $25	17		5/83
	On Wings of Eagles. Ken Follett. Morrow, $16.95	17		9/83
11.	Mary Ellen's Help Yourself Diet Plan. Mary Ellen Pinkham. St. Martin's/Marek, $10.95	15		2/83
	The Youngest Science: Notes of a Medicine Watcher. Lewis Thomas. Viking, $14.75	15		2/83
	The F-Plan Diet. Audrey Eyton. Crown, $12.95	15		2/83
	Out on a Limb. Shirley MacLaine. Bantam, $15.95	15		8/83

*These titles achieved the No. 1 spot during their 1983 tenure on PW's Bestseller List

Longest-Running Paperback Bestsellers for 1983

Once again, reprints of hardcover bestsellers, humor and cartoon books dominate this yearend paperback bestseller list. Only four of the 24 mass market yearend bestsellers were paperback originals and two of these were joke books.

In trade originals fared much better. Fifteen of 20 were originals, but here also satire and humor were strong—seven of the 15 were in the lighter vein.

Color Me Beautiful is certainly among the longest-running continuous trade paperback bestsellers; in addition to not missing a single week on PW's 1983 and 1982 lists, it was on the 1981 list 31 weeks.

Mass Market

	Weeks on 1983 List	Weeks on 1982 List	Date publ.
1. Truly Tasteless Jokes. Blanche Knott. Ballantine, $2.25	26		8/82
2. When Bad Things Happen to Good People. Harold S. Kushner. Avon, $3.95	24		2/83
*3. Master of the Game. Sidney Sheldon. Warner, $3.95	21		8/83
*4. The Parsifal Mosaic. Robert Ludlum. Bantam, $4.50	18		2/83
* The Man from St. Petersburg. Ken Follett. NAL/Signet, $3.95	18		5/83
*5. My Sweet Audrina. V. C. Andrews. Pocket Books, $3.95	15		4/83
* The Valley of Horses. Jean M. Auel. Bantam, $3.95	15		8/83
*†6. Sophie's Choice. William Styron. Bantam, $3.95	14		12/82
* The Prodigal Daughter. Jeffrey Archer. Pocket Books, $3.95	14		6/83
7. Truly Tasteless Jokes Two. Blanche Knott. Ballantine, $2.25	13		7/83
† Clan of the Cave Bear. Jean M. Auel. Bantam, $3.95	13		9/83
8. Dinner at the Homesick Restaurant. Anne Tyler. Berkley, $3.50	12		3/83
* Remembrance. Danielle Steel. Dell, $3.95	12		4/83
Lace. Shirley Conran. Pocket Books, $3.95	12		7/83
*9. A Mother and Two Daughters. Gail Godwin. Avon, $3.95	11		1/83
Different Seasons. Stephen King. NAL/Signet, $3.95	11		8/83
10. Fever. Robin Cook. NAL/Signet, $3.95	10		1/83
Thy Brother's Wife. Andrew M. Greeley. Warner/Bernard Geis Associates, $3.95	10		2/83
† War and Remembrance. Herman Wouk. Pocket Books, $5.95	10		2/83
* Return of the Jedi. James Kahn. Del Rey/Ballantine, $2.95	10		6/83
Cinnamon Skin. John D. MacDonald. Fawcett/Gold Medal, $3.50	10		7/83
* The Case of Lucy Bending. Lawrence Sanders. Berkley, $3.95	10		7/83
Second Heaven. Judith Guest. NAL/Signet, $3.95	10		10/83
A Cry in the Night. Mary Higgins Clark. Dell, $3.95	10		10/83

Trade

	Weeks on 1983 List	Weeks on 1982 List	Date publ.
1. Color Me Beautiful. Carole Jackson. Ballantine, $8.95	51	51	4/81
*2. Living, Loving and Learning. Leo Buscaglia. Fawcett/Columbine, $5.95	33		4/83
3. Thin Thighs in 30 Days. Wendy Stehling. Bantam, $2.95	32	27	5/82
4. The Color Purple. Alice Walker. Washington Square Press, $5.95	28		6/83
*5. Garfield Eats His Heart Out. Jim Davis. Ballantine, $4.95	26		3/83
6. Bloom County: Loose Tails. Berke Breathed. Little, Brown, $5.95	23		5/83
*7. Items from Our Catalog. Alfred Gingold. Avon, $4.95	22	2	12/82
*Thurston House. Danielle Steel. Dell, $7.95	22		7/83
*8. Life Extension. Durk Pearson and Sandy Shaw. Warner, $10.95	20		6/83
9. Real Women Don't Pump Gas. Joyce Jillson. Pocket Books, $3.95	19		12/82
10. A Rose in Winter. Kathleen E. Woodiwiss. Avon, $6.95	17	4	12/82
11. Real Men Don't Eat Quiche. Bruce Feirstein. Pocket Books, $3.95	15	30	5/82
What Color Is Your Parachute? 1983 Ed. Richard N. Bolles. Ten Speed Press, $7.95	15		4/83
12. Getting to Yes. Roger Fisher and William Ury. Penguin, $4.95	14		1/83
13. The Read-Aloud Handbook. Jim Trelease. Penguin, $5.95	12		9/82
Plain Jane Works Out. Linda Sunshine. Bantam, $3.95	12		5/83
*14. Garfield Sits Around the House. Jim Davis. Ballantine, $4.95	11		10/83
15. Garfield Takes the Cake. Jim Davis. Ballantine, $4.95	10	11	10/82
At Dawn We Slept. Gordon W. Prange. Penguin Books, $9.95	10	2	11/82
*The One Minute Manager. Kenneth Blanchard and Spencer Johnson. Berkley, $6.95	10		10/83

*These titles achieved the No. 1 spot during their 1983 tenure on PW's Bestseller List.   †These titles were published earlier and reissued in 1983.

All-time Hardcover Bestsellers, Adult and Children's Books

DAISY MARYLES & BETTE-LEE FOX

Three "all-time" bestseller lists are offered in the following pages—hardcover, trade, and mass market. Adult and children's titles are intermingled on the appropriate lists.

Qualifications for getting on these lists were specific. For the hardcover list, a title had to have accumulated net sales of 750,000 copies from publication through the end of 1982. The sales figures reflect U.S trade sales only, that is, sales made by the publishers to libraries, wholesalers, and booksellers; book club sales are not included. Annuals, almanacs, and yearbooks were not eligible. The list also omits encyclopedias, hymnals, prayer books, dictionaries, textbooks, and new Bible translations.

The criteria for the mass market list was similar except that the titles had to have sold over one million copies. Also, dictionaries were included.

The lists are neither all-inclusive nor definitive. A number of reasons account for this. Publishers find that getting some of the numbers an arduous if not impossible task. Many report that their sales records were such that information on U.S. trade sales from publication date to the end of 1982 was not available. Others could not extrapolate domestic, trade hardcover sales from total sales figures, which also include book club, paperback, and/or foreign sales. Also, there are many bestselling titles that have come into public domain and are now published under several imprints so that it was not possible to arrive at a final hardcover total for these old-timers.

Mass market publishers faced additional challenges. New American Library (NAL) insisted they could only supply print figures. Most of the other firms were able to give estimated sales figures and even exact sales. The one million eligibility also proved to be a problem. All the publishers agreed that it would have been better to have made the eligibility requirement a minimum of two million copies sold from pub date to end of 1982. In fact, NAL and Dell only gave us figures for books that have sold or have in print two million copies or more.

Despite the above difficulties, the lists offer all kinds of interesting as well as valuable information on books. Any information on bestselling books is useful for what it tells about public taste and trends in bookselling. Also, the titles listed on these three lists do rank among the all-time bestsellers and deserve to be acknowledged. Finally, because lists like these do rouse to action the publishers, agents, and authors with eligible books that are not included, we urge members of these groups to alert us to any missing information. In this way, we can offer better data in next year's annual. (Please direct any such submissions to Daisy Maryles, *Publishers Weekly,* 205 East 42nd Street, New York, NY 10017.)

In almost all cases, books on the lists are still in print.

Those that are out of print have the letters "OP" after the sales figures. The letters "C," "F," and "P" that appear before the titles indicate children's, fiction, and poetry books respectively. Books are arranged by order of sales.

Better Homes & Gardens New Cook Book (Meredith, 1930) 20,331,815

Betty Crocker's Cookbook (Golden Press, 1969) 20,000,000+

The Joy of Cooking by Irma S. Rombauer and Marion Rombauer Becker (Bobbs-Merrill, 1931) 10,000,000

Mr. Boston Bartender's Guide edited by Leo Cotton (Warner Books, 1935) 8,659,686

C **The Tale of Peter Rabbit** by Beatrix Potter (Frederick Warne, 1902) 8,000,000

F **Gone with the Wind** by Margaret Mitchell (Macmillan, 1936) 6,008,257

The Prophet by Kahlil Gibran (Knopf, 1923) 5,462,902

C **The Littlest Angel** by Charles Tazewell (Children's Press, 1946) 4,341,729

Halley's Bible Handbook (Zondervan, 1960) 4,112,873

C **The Children's Bible** (Golden Press, 1965) 3,571,302

Better Homes and Gardens Baby Book (Meredith, 1943) 3,278,676

F **Jonathan Livingston Seagull** by Richard Bach (Macmillan, 1970) 3,007,893

Streams in the Desert by Mrs. Charles Cowman (Zondervan, 1925) 2,958,896

C **Real Mother Goose** (Rand McNally, 1916) 2,751,838

The Power of Positive Thinking by Norman Vincent Peale (Prentice-Hall, 1952) 2,600,000

Better Homes and Gardens New Garden Book (Meredith, 1959) 2,527,133 (OP)

Better Homes and Gardens Handyman's Book (Meredith, 1951) 2,456,705 (OP)

C **Richard Scarry's Best Word Book Ever** by Richard Scarry (Golden Press, 1963) 2,156,000

C **Winnie-the-Pooh** by A. A. Milne (Dutton, 1926) 2,135,178

C **The Cat in the Hat** by Dr. Seuss (Random House, 1957) 2,093,280

C **Green Eggs and Ham** by Dr. Seuss (Random House, 1960) 2,035,935

DIANETICS The Modern Science of Mental Health by L. Ron Hubbard (Bridge Publications, 1950) 1,974,000

C **Hop on Pop** by Dr. Seuss (Random House, 1963) 1,813,299

C **Dr. Seuss's ABC** by Dr. Seuss (Random House, 1963) 1,713,285

C **One Fish, Two Fish, Red Fish, Blue Fish** by Dr. Seuss (Random House, 1960) 1,704,350

The Prophet by Kahlil Gibran, pocket edition (Knopf, 1927) 1,679,530

C **Pat the Bunny** by Dorothy Kunhardt (Golden Press, 1940) 1,632,369

Better Homes and Gardens Junior Cook Book (Meredith, 1975) 1,583,682

F **The Robe** by Lloyd C. Douglas (Houghton Mifflin, 1942) 1,569,563

Better Homes and Gardens Cooking for Two (Meredith, 1968) 1,547,553

C **Cat in the Hat Beginner Book Dictionary** by P.D. Eastman (Random House, 1964) 1,523,909

C **Charlotte's Web** by E.B. White (Harper & Row, 1952) 1,505,879

The Joy of Sex by Alex Comfort (Crown, 1972) 1,500,000

Better Homes and Gardens Fondue Cook Book (Meredith, 1970) 1,484,887 (OP)

A Field Guide to the Birds of Eastern and Central North America by Roger Tory Peterson (Houghton Mifflin, 1934) 1,408,605

C **My Book About Me (by Me, Myself)** by Dr. Seuss (Random House, 1969) 1,356,208

C **Richard Scarry's Best Story Book Ever** by Richard Scarry (Golden Press, 1968) 1,356,145

C **The Cat in the Hat Comes Back** by Dr. Seuss (Random House, 1958) 1,354,789

How To Win Friends and Influence People by Dale Carnegie (Simon & Schuster, 1937) 1,331,487 (OP)

C **The Giving Tree** by Shel Silverstein (Harper & Row, 1964) 1,329,445

Eastman's Expectant Motherhood by Keith P. Russell (Little, Brown, 1940) 1,285,546

P **101 Famous Poems** compiled by Roy J. Cook (Contemporary Books, 1916) 1,250,000

Better Homes and Gardens Story Book (Meredith, 1951) 1,243,570

C **Fox in Sox** by Dr. Seuss (Random House, 1965) 1,241,083

Jane Fonda's Workout Book by Jane Fonda (Simon & Schuster, 1981) 1,222,033

How To Stop Worrying and Start Living by Dale Carnegie (Simon & Schuster, 1948) 1,207,838 (OP)

Better Homes and Gardens Meals in Minutes (Meredith, 1963) 1,177,719 (OP)

Roots by Alex Haley (Doubleday, 1976) 1,176,784

Better Homes and Gardens Barbecue Cook Book (Meredith, 1956) 1,148,960 (OP)

Better Homes and Gardens Home Canning (Meredith, 1973) 1,127,985 (OP)

P **Listen to the Warm** by Rod McKuen (Random House, 1967) 1,125,471

I'm O.K.—You're O.K.: A Practical Guide to Transactional Analysis by Thomas Harris (Harper & Row, 1969) 1,122,104

C **Richard Scarry's Story Book Dictionary** by Richard Scarry (Golden Press, 1966) 1,107,136

Better Homes and Gardens Eat and Stay Slim (Meredith, 1968) 1,103,554

C **Are You My Mother?** by Phillip Eastman (Random House, 1960) 1,102,428

Better Homes and Gardens Meat Cook Book (Meredith, 1959) 1,029,738 (OP)

C **The Little Prince** by Antoine de Saint-Exupery (Harcourt Brace Jovanovich, 1943) 1,023,679

Fannie Farmer Cookbook by Fannie Farmer (Little, Brown, 1896) 1,009,849 (OP)

Better Homes and Gardens Houseplants (Meredith, 1959) 1,003,747 (OP)

C **The Golden Book of 365 Stories** by Kathryn Jackson, illus. by Richard Scarry (Golden Press, 1955) 989,718

Weight Watchers® International Cookbook by Weight Watchers International (NAL Books, 1980) 983,000

C **The Tall Book of Nursery Tales** illustrated by Feodor Rojankovsky (Harper & Row, 1944) 974,640

C **Where the Sidewalk Ends: Poems and Drawings** by Shel Silverstein (Harper & Row, 1974) 966,047

F **The Silmarillion** by J. R. R. Tolkien (Houghton Mifflin, 1977) 960,058

Better Homes and Gardens Salad Book (Meredith, 1957) 954,054 (OP)

Reader's Digest Complete Do-It-Yourself Manual by Editors of Reader's Digest Association (Reader's Digest, 1973) 953,840

The New Roget's Thesaurus in Dictionary Form by Norman Lewis (Putnam, 1948) 952,000

P **Best-Loved Poems of the American People** edited by Hazel Felleman (Doubleday, 1936) 949,363

Better Homes and Gardens Decorating Book (Meredith, 1956) 910,066

C **Go, Dog, Go!** by Phillip Eastman (Random House, 1961) 898,494

Better Homes and Gardens Casserole Cook Book (Meredith, 1961) 896,059 (OP)

Weight Watchers® New Program Cookbook by Jean Nidetch (NAL Books, 1980) 894,000

Webster's New World Dictionary, 2nd College Edition edited by David Guralnik (Simon & Schuster, 1980) 893,358

C **Album of Horses** by Marguerite Henry (Rand McNally, 1950) 892,551

F **Chesapeake** by James A. Michener (Random House, 1978) 889,297

C **Return of the Jedi** by Joan D. Vinge (Random House, 1983) 882,124

Better Homes and Gardens Sewing Book (Meredith, 1961) 877,946

Cosmos by Carl Sagan (Random House, 1980) 872,915

Weight Watchers® New Program by Jean Nidetch (NAL Books, 1978) 850,000

C **How the Grinch Stole Christmas** by Dr. Seuss (Random House, 1957) 849,715

Better Homes and Gardens Flower Arranging (Meredith, 1957) 846,005 (OP)

See You at the Top by Zig Ziglar (Pelican, 1976) 845,760

Peace of Mind by Joshua Loth Liebman (Simon & Schuster, 1946) 842,634 (OP)

C **Santa Mouse** by Michael Brown (Grosset & Dunlap, 1966) 828,727

Gnomes by Rien Poortvliet and Wil Huygen (Abrams, 1977) 828,000

Bartlett's Familiar Quotations (Little, Brown, 1859) 824,771

Angels: God's Secret Agents by Billy Graham (Doubleday, 1975) 818,544 (OP)

Random House College Dictionary, indexed (Random House, 1975) 815,951

My Utmost for His Highest by Oswald Chambers (Dodd, Mead, 1935) 811,733

Audubon Society Guide to North American Birds–East by J. Bull and J. Farrand (Random House, 1977) 809,720

Someone Cares by Helen Steiner Rice (Revell, 1972) 802,463

The Complete Dog Book by The American Kennel Club (Howell Book House, 1929) 800,000

Better Homes and Gardens Our Baby (Meredith, 1959) 798,796 (OP)

C **Charlie and the Chocolate Factory** by Roald Dahl (Knopf, 1964) 796,000

Your Erroneous Zones by Wayne W. Dyer (A Funk & Wagnalls Book/T. Y. Crowell and Harper & Row, 1976) 792,400

Better Homes and Gardens Crockery Cook Book (Meredith, 1976) 780,281

C **What Do People Do All Day** by Richard Scarry (Random House, 1968) 778,784

C **The Golden Songbook** (Golden Press, 1965) 778,000

Better Homes and Gardens Best Buffets (Meredith, 1963) 775,704 (OP)

C **Little House in the Big Woods** by Laura Ingalls Wilder (Harper & Row, 1933) 772,383

C **Where the Wild Things Are** by Maurice Sendak (Harper & Row, 1964) 772,383

Better Homes and Gardens Blender Cook Book (Meredith, 1971) 768,606

The Family of Man by Edward Steichen (Simon & Schuster, 1955) 761,837

C **The Velveteen Rabbit** by Margery Bianco Williams (Doubleday, 1922) 754,449

The Complete Scarsdale Medical Diet by Herman Tarnower, M.D. and Samm Sinclair Baker (Rawson Associates, 1978) 752,800

Better Homes and Gardens Family Medical Guide (Meredith, 1964) 751,292

Let's Eat Right to Keep Fit by Adelle Davis (Harcourt Brace Jovanovich, 1954) 750,000

Let's Get Well by Adelle Davis (Harcourt Brace Jovanovich, 1965) 750,000

All-time Trade Paperback Bestsellers

DAISY MARYLES & BETTE-LEE FOX

F **Lord of the Flies** by William Golding (Perigee, 1959) 7,068,345

The Joy of Sex by Alex Comfort (Fireside/Simon & Schuster, 1974) 5,052,085

F **The Great Gatsby** by F. Scott Fitzgerald (Scribners, 1960) 4,352,653

F **Shanna** by Kathleen Woodiwiss (Avon, 1978) 4,190,000

Houseplants by Editors of Sunset Books (Sunset Books/Lane Publishing Co., 1968) 3,723,145

The Possible Dream by Charles Paul Conn (Revell, 1978) 3,601,096

F **Death of a Salesman** by Arthur Miller (Viking Penguin, 1958) 3,268,000

DIANETICS The Modern Science of Mental Health by L. Ron Hubbard (Bridge Publications, 1968) 3,256,000

F **The Old Man and the Sea** by Ernest Hemingway (Scribners, 1961) 3,237,595

F **The Stranger** by Albert Camus (Vintage, 1954) 3,108,360

A Manual for Writers of Term Papers, Theses, and Dissertations by Kate Turabian (University of Chicago Press, 1967) 2,982,140

Mad Libs #3 by Roger Price and Leonard Stern (Price/Stern/Sloan, 1962) 2,960,000

New Western Garden Book by Editors of Sunset Books (Sunset Books/Lane Publishing Co., 1933) 2,950,122

F **The Little Prince** by Antoine de Saint-Exupery (Harcourt Brace Jovanovich, 1968) 2,890,980

Droodles by Roger Price (Price/Stern/Sloan, 1954) 2,805,000

The World's Worst Elephant Jokes (The Elephant Book) by Roger Price, Leonard Stern, and Lawrence Sloan (Price/Stern/Sloan, 1963) 2,725,000

The Total Woman by Marabel Morgan (Revell, 1976) 2,687,103

The Late Great Planet Earth by Hal Lindsey (Zondervan, 1970) 2,673,567

Mad Libs #4 by Roger Price and Leonard Stern (Price/Stern/Sloan, 1965) 2,660,000

F **Ashes in the Wind** by Kathleen Woodiwiss (Avon, 1979) 2,625,000

Why Am I Afraid to Tell You Who I Am? by John Powell (Argus, 1969) 2,583,866

Mad Libs #2 by Roger Price and Leonard Stern (Price/Stern/Sloan, 1959) 2,540,000

The Hiding Place by Corrie ten Boom (Revell, 1974) 2,476,133

Mad Libs #1 by Roger Price and Leonard Stern (Price/Stern/Sloan, 1958) 2,440,000 ·

F **Portrait of the Artist as a Young Man** by James Joyce (Viking Penguin, 1964) 2,308,000

F **Hamlet** by William Shakespeare (Washington Square Press, 1958) 2,296,000

Our Bodies, Ourselves by The Boston Women's Health Book Collective (Simon & Schuster, 1976) 2,266,029

Crockery Cookery by Mable Hoffman (HP Books, 1975) 2,248,672

F **The Sun Also Rises** by Ernest Hemingway (Scribners, 1960) 2,247,602

On Death and Dying by Elisabeth Kübler-Ross (Macmillan, 1970) 2,180,910

How to Flatten Your Stomach by Jim Everroad (Price/Stern/Sloan, 1977) 2,015,000

F **The Crowd Pleasers** by Rosemary Rogers (Avon, 1980) 2,007,000

The Nutrition Almanac by John Kirschmann (McGraw-Hill, 1979) 2,000,000

Basic Gardening by Editors of Sunset Books (Sunset Books/Lane Publishing Co., 1963) 1,865,567

Born Again by Charles Colson (Revell, 1977) 1,849,494

Mad Libs #5 by Roger Price and Leonard Stern (Price/Stern/Sloan, 1968) 1,810,000

Born to Win by Muriel James (Addison-Wesley, 1971) 1,794,603

Landscaping & Garden Remodeling by Editors of Sunset Books (Sunset Books/Lane Publishing Co., 1950) 1,775,990

Mexican Cook Book by Editors of Sunset Books (Sunset Books/Lane Publishing Co., 1969) 1,733,592

Mere Christianity by C.S. Lewis (Macmillan, 1962) 1,723,980

Barbecue Cook Book by Editors of Sunset Books (Sunset Books/Lane Publishing Co., 1938) 1,690,682

Mad Libs #6 by Roger Price and Leonard Stern (Price/Stern/Sloan, 1970) 1,650,000

The Magic of Thinking Big by David Schwartz (Simon & Schuster, 1977) 1,635,621

Joni by Joni Eareckson with Joe Musser (Zondervan, 1976) 1,628,377

F **Tropic of Cancer** by Henry Miller (Grove Press, 1961) 1,610,000

F **The Odyssey** by Homer (Viking Penguin, 1946) 1,600,000

Thin Thighs in 30 Days by Wendy Stehling (Bantam, 1982) 1,600,000

What the Bible Is All About by Henrietta C. Mears (Regal Books, 1977) 1,565,335

Easy to Make Furniture by Editors of Sunset Books (Sunset Books/Lane Publishing Co., 1953) 1,564,035

Joy of Cooking by Irma Rombauer and Marion Rombauer Becker (NAL, 1973) 1,556,300

C **Velveteen Rabbit** by Margery Williams (Avon, 1982) 1,542,000

F **The Screwtape Letters** by C.S. Lewis (Macmillan, 1962) 1,539,230

Fireplaces by Editors of Sunset Books (Sunset Books/Lane Publishing Co., 1951) 1,522,041

F **Macbeth** by William Shakespeare (Washington Square Press, 1958) 1,511,000

Mary Ellen's Best of Helpful Hints by Mary Ellen Pinkham (Warner, 1979) 1,500,000

None of These Diseases by S.I. McMillen (Revell, 1967) 1,483,234

F **The Grapes of Wrath** by John Steinbeck (Viking Penguin, 1958) 1,460,000

The Worldly Philosphers by Robert Heilbroner (Touchstone/Simon & Schuster, 1953) 1,443,000

Kitchens by Editors of Sunset Books (Sunset Books/Lane Publishing Co., 1955) 1,430,957

Mastering Rubik's Cube by Don Taylor (Owl/Holt, Rinehart & Winston, 1981) 1,428,322

How to Keep Your Volkswagen Alive: A Manual of Step-by-Step Procedures for the Complete Idiot by John Muir (John Muir Publications, 1969) 1,401,959

The Gospel According to Peanuts by Robert L. Short (John Knox Press, 1964) 1,400,662

F **Waiting for Godot** by Samuel Beckett (Grove Press, 1954) 1,400,000

Murphy's Law #1 by Arthur Bloch (Price/Stern/Sloan, 1978) 1,396,000

C **500 Words to Grow On** by Harry McNaught (Random House, 1973) 1,388,236

Gardening in Containers by Editors of Sunset Books (Sunset Books/Lane Publishing Co., 1952) 1,376,676

F **Cry, the Beloved Country** by Alan Paton (Scribners, 1961) 1,357,379

The Will of God by Leslie Weatherhead (Abingdon Press, 1945) 1,345,136

Walks, Walls & Patio Floors by Editors of Sunset Books (Sunset Books/Lane Publishing Co., 1952) 1,342,280

The Big Dummy's Guide to C.B. Radio by Albert Houston, Mark Long, and Jeffrey Keating (The Book Publishing Co., 1976) 1,340,000

C **Grover Everything World Museum** by Stiles & Wilcox (Random House, 1974) 1,328,611

The Christian's Secret of a Happy Life by Hannah Whitall Smith (Revell, 1966) 1,326,126

Storage by Editors of Sunset Books (Sunset Books/Lane Publishing Co., 1958) 1,305,147

Soul on Ice by Eldrige Cleaver (Delta Books, 1970) 1,301,844

Garfield at Large by Jim Davis (Ballantine, 1980) 1,295,840

Patios & Decks by Editors of Sunset Books (Sunset Books/Lane Publishing Co., 1952) 1,295,471

C **Richard Scarry's Please & Thank You** by Richard Scarry (Random House, 1973) 1,294,095

Pruning by Editors of Sunset Books (Sunset Books/Lane Publishing Co., 1952) 1,285,642

Color Me Beautiful by Carole Jackson (Ballantine, 1981) 1,268,965

The Secret of Staying in Love by John Powell (Argus, 1974) 1,249,987

Breads by Editors of Sunset Books (Sunset Books/Lane Publishing Co., 1963) 1,249,786

The Last Whole Earth Catalog by Stewart Brand (Random House, 1971) 1,220,567

F **The Sound and the Fury** by William Faulkner (Vintage, 1954) 1,214,699

The Official Preppy Handbook edited by Lisa Birnbach (Workman, 1980) 1,214,000

Why Am I Afraid to Love? by John Powell (Argus, 1967) 1,209,970

The Woman at the Well by Dale Evans Rogers (Revell, 1973) 1,197,923

C **Little Duck** by Judy Dunn (Random House, 1976) 1,197,018

Twelve Angels from Hell by David Wilkerson (Revell, 1967) 1,188,860

More Joy of Sex by Alex Comfort (Fireside/Simon & Schuster, 1975) 1,184,598

Bathrooms by Editors of Sunset Books (Sunset Books/Lane Publishing Co., 1963) 1,175,104

C **Night Before Christmas** by Clement C. Moore (Random House, 1975) 1,174,678

Student's Guide for Writing College Papers by Kate Turabian (University of Chicago Press, 1963) 1,174,262

Decks by Editors of Sunset Books (Sunset Books/Lane Publishing Co., 1963) 1,172,23

Two from Galilee by Marjorie Holmes (Revell, 1974) 1,171,498

Real Men Don't Eat Quiche by Bruce Feirstein (Pocket Books, 1982) 1,169,000

More World's Worst Elephant Jokes (Price/Stern/Sloan, 1965) 1,160,000

Favorite Recipes I by Editors of Sunset Books (Sunset Books/Lane Publishing Co., 1949) 1,158,030

Contract Bridge for Beginners by Charles H. Goren (Simon & Schuster, 1971) 1,152,290 (OP)

Garden & Patio Building by Editors of Sunset Books (Sunset Books/Lane Publishing Co., 1969) 1,151,929

Mad Libs #9 by Roger Price and Leonard Stern (Price/Stern/Sloan, 1979) 1,145,000

Satan Is Alive and Well on Planet Earth by Hal Lindsey (Zondervan, 1972) 1,142,055

Roses by Editors of Sunset Books (Sunset Books/Lane Publishing Co., 1940) 1,138,776

Bonsai by Editors of Sunset Books (Sunset Books/Lane Publishing Co., 1965) 1,136,637

How to Be a Jewish Mother by Dan Greenburg (Price/Stern/Sloan, 1964) 1,134,000

F **Love Play** by Rosemary Rogers (Avon, 1982) 1,125,000

Garfield Gains Weight by Jim Davis (Ballantine, 1981) 1,124,412

F **Romeo and Juliet** by William Shakespeare (Washington Square Press, 1958) 1,115,000

Garfield Bigger Than Life by Jim Davis (Ballantine, 1981) 1,110,187

F **The Canterbury Tales** by Geoffrey Chaucer (Viking Penguin, 1951) 1,100,000

The American Political Tradition by Richard Hofstadter (Vintage, 1954) 1,094,108

Furniture Finishing by Editors of Sunset Books (Sunset Books/Lane Publishing Co., 1969) 1,086,760

Oriental Cook Book by Editors of Sunset Books (Sunset Books/Lane Publishing Co., 1970) 1,080,028

C **Richard Scarry's Find Your ABC's** by Richard Scarry (Random House, 1973) 1,073,863

Teachings of Don Juan by Carlos Castenada (Washington Square Press, 1974) 1,072,000

Mad Libs #10 by Roger Price and Leonard Stern (Price/Stern/Sloan, 1979) 1,065,000

C **Leo the Lop** by Stephen Cosgrove (Serendipity Books/Price/Stern/Sloan, 1976) 1,049,000

F **Sons and Lovers** by D.H. Lawrence (Viking Penguin, 1958) 1,042,000

Hidden Persuaders by Vance Packard (Washington Square Press, 1981) 1,041,000

Hors D'Oeuvres by Editors of Sunset Books (Sunset Books/Lane Publishing Co., 1976) 1,039,584

C **Best Rainy Day Book Ever** by Richard Scarry (Random House, 1974) 1,035,463

Canning by Editors of Sunset Books (Sunset Books/Lane Publishing Co., 1975) 1,031,407

C **Flutterby** by Stephen Cosgrove (Serendipity Books/Price/Stern/Sloan, 1976) 1,031,000

C **Alphabet Book** by P.D. Eastman (Random House, 1974) 1,029,600

Abundant Living by E. Stanley Jones (Abingdon Press, 1942) 1,025,111

P.E.T. by Dr. Thomas Gordon (NAL, 1975) 1,011,700

Field Guide to Eastern Birds by Roger Tory Peterson (Houghton Mifflin, 1968) 1,010,279

C **Serendipity** by Stephen Cosgrove (Serendipity Books/Price/Stern/Sloan, 1974) 1,007,000

Lawns & Groundcovers by Editors of Sunset Books (Sunset Books/Lane Publishing Co., 1955) 1,000,704

F **Tropic of Capricorn** by Henry Miller (Grove Press, 1963) 1,000,000

All-time Mass Market Paperback Bestsellers

DAISY MARYLES & BETTE-LEE FOX

Baby and Child Care by Dr. Benjamin Spock (Pocket Books, 1946) 32,000,000

How to Win Friends and Influence People by Dale Carnegie (Pocket Books, 1940) 15,000,000

New American Roget's College Thesaurus (Signet/NAL, 1957) 14,430,000

F **The Hobbit** by J.R.R. Tolkien (Ballantine, 1972) 13,163,494

Merriam Webster Dictionary (Pocket Books, 1974) 13,000,000

F **The Exorcist** by William Peter Blatty (Bantam, 1972) 12,074,000

F **1984** by George Orwell (Signet Classic/NAL, 1950) 12,000,000

The American Heritage Dictionary (Dell, 1970) 11,167,751

The New American Webster's Handy College Dictionary (Signet/NAL, 1956) 10,500,000

F **The Thorn Birds** by Colleen McCullough (Avon, 1978) 10,340,000

F **Love Story** by Erich Segal (Signet/NAL, 1970) 9,500,000 (OP)

F **Valley of the Dolls** by Jacqueline Susann (Bantam, 1967) 9,450.000

F **Animal Farm** by George Orwell (Signet Classic/NAL, 1956) 8,950,000

Mythology by Edith Hamilton (Mentor/NAL, 1953) 8,950,000

The Sensuous Woman by ''J'' (Dell, 1971) 8,733,000

F **The Pearl** by John Steinbeck (Bantam, 1948) 8,296,000

F **Jaws** by Peter Benchley (Bantam, 1975) 8,286,000

Everything You Always Wanted to Know About Sex—but Were Afraid to Ask by David R. Reuben, M.D. (Bantam, 1971) 8,243,000

F **God's Little Acre** by Erskine Caldwell (Signet Classic/NAL, 1946) 8,225,000

Spanish-English Dictionary (Pocket Books, 1950) 8,085,000

F **Jonathan Livingston Seagull** by Richard Bach (Avon, 1973) 7,750,000

F **Catcher in the Rye** by J.D. Salinger (Bantam, 1964) 7,658,000

I'm OK, You're OK by Thomas Harris (Avon, 1973) 7,580,113

F **Fellowship of the Ring** by J.R.R. Tolkien (Ballantine, 1972) 7,429,012

The Happy Hooker by Xaviera Hollander (Dell, 1972) 7,360,000

F **The Other Side of Midnight** by Sidney Sheldon (Dell, 1975) 7,184,000

Simple Solution to Rubik's Cube by James Nourse (Bantam, 1981) 7,053,000

F **One Flew Over the Cuckoo's Nest** by Ken Kesey (Signet/NAL, 1963) 7,000,000

Hoyle's Rules of the Game edited by Albert Morehead and G. Mott-Smith (Signet/NAL, 1946) 6,925,000

F **I Never Promised You a Rose Garden** by Joanne Greenberg (Signet/NAL, 1965) 6,925,000

F **Exodus** by Leon Uris (Bantam, 1959) 6,838,000

F **Catch-22** by Joseph Heller (Dell, 1961) 6,800,000

F **Rich Man, Poor Man** by Irwin Shaw (Dell, 1971) 6,696,000

F **Shogun** by James Clavell (Dell, 1976) 6,690,000

F **I the Jury** by Mickey Spillane (Signet/NAL, 1948) 6,575,000

Helter Skelter by Vincent Bugliosi and Curt Gentry (Bantam, 1975) 6,465,000

The Amityville Horror by Jay Anson (Bantam, 1978) 6,422,000

F **The Two Towers** by J.R.R. Tolkien (Ballantine, 1972) 6,329,491

Complete Scarsdale Medical Diet by Herman Tarnower, M.D. & Samm Sinclair Baker (Bantam, 1980) 6,212,000

Chariots of the Gods by Erich Von Däniken (Bantam, 1971) 6,198,000

F **Airport** by Arthur Hailey (Bantam, 1969) 6,105,000

F **Return of the King** by J.R.R. Tolkien (Ballantine, 1972) 6,012,595

F **Fear of Flying** by Erica Jong (Signet/NAL, 1974) 6,000,000

F **Of Mice and Men** by John Steinbeck (Bantam, 1955) 5,903,000

Diary of a Young Girl by Anne Frank (Pocket Books, 1958) 5,900,000

Dr. Atkins' Diet Revolution: The High Calorie Way to Stay Thin by Dr. Robert Atkins (Bantam, 1973) 5,852,000

F **The Big Kill** by Mickey Spillane (Signet/NAL, 1951) 5,800,000

F **Lady Chatterley's Lover** by D.H. Lawrence (Signet Classic/NAL, 1946) 5,500,000

F **One Lonely Night** by Mickey Spillane (Signet/NAL, 1951) 5,500,000

Your Erroneous Zones by Wayne Dyer (Avon, 1977) 5,450,000

F **The Long Wait** by Mickey Spillane (Signet/NAL, 1952) 5,400,000

F **My Gun Is Quick** by Mickey Spillane (Signet/NAL, 1950) 5,400,000

Future Shock by Alfin Toffler (Bantam, 1971) 5,244,000

F **The Love Machine** by Jacqueline Susann (Bantam, 1970) 5,221,000

F **Shane** by Jack Schaefer (Bantam, 1950) 5,204,000

Black Like Me by John H. Griffin (Signet/NAL, 1962) 5,200,000

F **Kiss Me Deadly** by Mickey Spillane (Signet/NAL, 1953) 5,200,000

Sybil by Flora Rheta Schreiber (Warner, 1974) 5,200,000

F **Vengeance Is Mine** by Mickey Spillane (Signet/NAL, 1951) 5,200,000

F **Once Is Not Enough** by Jacqueline Susann (Bantam, 1974) 5,089,000

Joy of Cooking by Irma Rombauer and Marion Rombauer Becker (Signet/NAL, 1973) 5,000,000

F **The Shining** by Stephen King (Signet/NAL, 1978) 4,950,000

F **Hotel** by Arthur Hailey (Bantam, 1966) 4,941,000

All Creatures Great and Small by James Herriot (Bantam, 1973) 4,907,000

Passages by Gail Sheehy (Bantam, 1977) 4,860,000

F **Princess Daisy** by Judith Krantz (Bantam, 1981) 4,850,000

F **Hiroshima** by John Hersey (Bantam, 1948) 4,844,000

The Sensuous Man by ''M'' (Dell, 1972) 4,726,000

F **Coma** by Robin Cook (Signet/NAL, 1977) 4,700,000

F **The Crucible** by Arthur Miller (Bantam, 1959) 4,689,000

F **Hawaii** by James Michener (Bantam, 1961) 4,506,000

Let's Eat Right to Keep Fit by Adelle Davis (Signet/NAL, 1970) 4,500,000

French-English Dictionary (Pocket Books, 1950) 4,448,000

F **Tragic Ground** by Erskine Caldwell (Signet/NAL, 1948) 4,400,000 (OP)

F **The Grapes of Wrath** by John Steinbeck (Bantam, 1946) 4,358,000

F **In Cold Blood** by Truman Capote (Signet/NAL, 1967) 4,300,000

F **Light in the Forest** by Conrad Richter (Bantam, 1958) 4,298,000

F **The Red Pony** by John Steinbeck (Bantam, 1948) 4,265,000

F **Eye of the Needle** by Ken Follett (Signet/NAL, 1979) 4,250,000

F **Scruples** by Judith Krantz (Warner, 1979) 4,250,000

F **Thunderball** by Ian Fleming (Signet/NAL, 1962) 4,250,000 (OP)

Linda Goodman's Sun Signs by Linda Goodman (Bantam, 1971) 4,235,000

F **The Moneychangers** by Arthur Hailey (Bantam, 1976) 4,187,000

F **Brave New World** by Aldous Huxley (Bantam, 1955) 4,167,000

F **The Betsy** by Harold Robbins (Pocket Books, 1972) 4,161,000

F **Christy** by Catherine Marshall (Avon, 1968) 4,133,000

How to Buy Stocks by Louis Engel (Bantam, 1955) 4,132,000

F **Atlas Shrugged** by Ayn Rand (Signet/NAL, 1959) 4,100,000

F **Dr. Zhivago** by Boris Pasternak (Signet/NAL, 1960) 4,100,000 (OP)

Psycho Cybernetics by Maxwell Maltz, M.D. (Pocket Books, 1969) 4,092,000

Coffee, Tea or Me? by T. Baker and R. Jones (Bantam, 1968) 4,052,000

Better Homes and Gardens Baby Book by Editors of Better Homes & Gardens (Bantam, 1965) 4,015,000

F **Carrie** by Stephen King (Signet/NAL, 1975) 4,000,000

F **Journeyman** by Erskine Caldwell (Signet/NAL, 1947) 4,000,000 (OP)

F **The Flame & the Flower** by Kathleen Woodiwiss (Avon, 1975) 3,948,000

F **The Day of the Jackal** by Frederick Forsyth (Bantam, 1972) 3,915,000

F **Up the Down Staircase** by Bel Kaufman (Avon, 1966) 3,914,000

F **Portnoy's Complaint** by Philip Roth (Bantam, 1970) 3,902,000

F **The Odyssey** by Homer (Mentor/NAL, 1946) 3,900,000

F **Tobacco Road** by Erskine Caldwell (Signet Classic/NAL, 1947) 3,900,000

F **Battle Cry** by Leon Uris (Bantam, 1954) 3,882,000

Late Great Planet Earth by Hal Lindsey (Bantam, 1975) 3,862,000

All Things Bright and Beautiful by James Herriot (Bantam, 1975) 3,852,000

F **The Dead Zone** by Stephen King (Signet/NAL, 1980) 3,850,000

F **Salem's Lot** by Stephen King (Signet/NAL, 1976) 3,850,000

F **Taipan** by James Clavell (Dell, 1967) 3,828,000

F **Bloodline** by Sidney Sheldon (Warner, 1979) 3,800,000

F **The French Lieutenant's Woman** by John Fowles (Signet/NAL, 1971) 3,800,000

F **The Omen** by David Seltzer (Signet/NAL, 1976) 3,800,000

F **The Bastard** by John Jakes (Jove, 1974) 3,798,539

Bury My Heart at Wounded Knee by Dee Brown (Bantam, 1972) 3,787,000

Roots by Alex Haley (Dell, 1977) 3,776,000

F **Wicked Loving Lies** by Rosemary Rogers (Avon, 1976) 3,775,000

F **Goldfinger** by Ian Fleming (Signet/NAL, 1960) 3,750,000

F **The Martian Chronicles** by Ray Bradbury (Bantam, 1951) 3,680,000

F **Jaws 2** by Hank Searls (Bantam, 1978) 3,658,000

Incredible Journey by Sheila Burnford (Bantam, 1962) 3,655,000

Roget's Pocket Thesaurus (Pocket Books, 1946) 3,654,000

F **On Her Majesty's Secret Service** by Ian Fleming (Signet/NAL, 1963) 3,650,000

F **Watership Down** by Richard Adams (Avon, 1975) 3,635,000

F **Sweet Savage Love** by Rosemary Rogers (Avon, 1974) 3,619,000

F **Dark Fires** by Rosemary Rogers (Avon, 1975) 3,602,000

Love Without Fear by Eustace Chesser (Signet/NAL, 1949) 3,600,000 (OP)

F **The Stand** by Stephen King (Signet/NAL, 1980), 3,600,000

Xaveria! by Xaviera Hollander (Warner, 1973) 3,600,000

The Art of Loving by Erich Fromm (Bantam, 1963) 3,562,000

F **The World According to Garp** by John Irving (Pocket Books, 1979) 3,554,000

Alive by Piers Paul Read (Avon, 1975) 3,539,604

F **The Fountainhead** by Ayn Rand (Signet/NAL, 1952) 3,510,000

All the President's Men by Carl Bernstein and Bob Woodward (Warner, 1975) 3,500,000

F **The Lonely Lady** by Harold Robbins (Pocket Books, 1976) 3,497,000

F **Cannery Row** by John Steinbeck (Bantam, 1947) 3,495,000

F **The Choirboys** by Joseph Wambaugh (Dell, 1976) 3,488,000

F **Looking for Mr. Goodbar** by Judith Rossner (Pocket Books, 1976) 3,466,000

F **Wheels** by Arthur Hailey (Bantam, 1973) 3,462,000

F **The Wolf & the Dove** by Kathleen Woodiwiss (Avon, 1974) 3,455,500

F **Petals on the Wind** by V.C. Andrews (Pocket Books, 1980) 3,449,000

F **Close Encounters of the Third Kind** by Steven Spielberg (Dell, 1977) 3,438,000

F **Star Wars®: From the Adventures of Luke Skywalker** by George Lucas (Ballantine/Del Rey, 1977) 3,436,110

F **Stiletto** by Harold Robbins (Dell, 1961) 3,435,000

F **If There Be Thorns** by V.C. Andrews (Pocket Books, 1981) 3,417,000

Calories & Carbohydrates by Barbara Kraus (Signet/NAL, 1973) 3,400,000

F **The Catcher in the Rye** by J.D. Salinger (Signet/NAL, 1953) 3,400,000 (OP)

F **You Only Live Twice** by Ian Fleming (Signet/NAL, 1964) 3,400,000

F **Flowers for Algernon** by Daniel Keyes (Bantam, 1967) 3,398,000

F **The Winds of War** by Herman Wouk (Pocket Books, 1973) 3,387,000

Travels with Charley by John Steinbeck (Bantam, 1966) 3,382,000

F **Sophie's Choice** by William Styron (Bantam, 1980) 3,377,000

F **Evergreen** by Belva Plain (Dell, 1979) 3,369,500

Name Your Baby by LaReina Rule (Bantam, 1966) 3,365,000

F **From Russia with Love** by Ian Fleming (Signet/ NAL, 1958) 3,360,000 (OP)

F **The Deep** by Peter Benchley (Bantam, 1977) 3,347,000

Life After Life by Dr. Raymond Moody (Bantam, 1976) 3,342,000

My Mother, My Self by Nancy Friday (Dell, 1978) 3,333,000

F **From Here to Eternity** by James Jones (Signet/ NAL, 1953) 3,325,000 (OP)

F **Ragtime** by E.L. Doctorow (Bantam, 1976) 3,317,000

F **Never Leave Me** by Harold Robbins (Avon, 1953) 3,315,800

F **Trinity** by Leon Uris (Bantam, 1977) 3,293,000

F **A Woman of Substance** by Barbara Taylor Bradford (Avon, 1980) 3,287,478

F **50 Great Short Stories** edited by M. Crane (Bantam, 1952) 3,278,000

F **Adventures of Huckleberry Finn** by Mark Twain (Signet Classic/NAL, 1959) 3,260,000

F **Doctor No** by Ian Fleming (Signet/NAL, 1959) 3,260,000 (OP)

F **The Final Diagnosis** by Arthur Hailey (Bantam, 1960) 3,255,000

Analysis of the Kinsey Report edited by Donald Porter Geddes (Signet/NAL, 1954) 3,250,000 (OP)

F **Casino Royale** by Ian Fleming (Signet/NAL, 1960) 3,250,000 (OP)

F **Kramer vs. Kramer** by Avery Corman (Signet/ NAL, 1978) 3,250,000

F **Flowers in the Attic** by V.C. Andrews (Pocket Books, 1979) 3,245,000

F **Oliver's Story** by Erich Segal (Avon, 1977) 3,243,365

F **The Promise** by Danielle Steel (Dell, 1978) 3,225,500

F **The Arrangement** by Elia Kazan (Avon, 1968) 3,222,500

Between Parent & Child by Haim Ginott (Avon, 1969) 3,218,000

The All New Fannie Farmer Cookbook by W.L. Perkins (Bantam, 1957) 3,206,000

F **House in the Uplands** by Erskine Caldwell (Signet/ NAL, 1948) 3,200,000 (OP)

F **Trouble in July** by Erskine Caldwell (Signet/NAL, 1945) 3,200,000 (OP)

F **East of Eden** by John Steinbeck (Bantam, 1955) 3,143,000

F **The Insiders** by Rosemary Rogers (Avon, 1978) 3,125,000

F **Anthem** by Ayn Rand (Signet/NAL, 1961) 3,110,000

F **Wifey** by Judy Blume (Pocket Books, 1979) 3,109,000

F **Cujo** by Stephen King (Signet/NAL, 1982) 3,100,000

F **Firestarter** by Stephen King (Signet/NAL, 1981) 3,100,000

F **Rage of Angels** by Sidney Sheldon (Warner, 1981) 3,100,000

F **Go Ask Alice** by Anonymous (Avon, 1972) 3,085,605

A Gift of Prophecy by Ruth Montgomery (Bantam, 1966) 3,063,000

If Life Is a Bowl of Cherries, What Am I Doing with the Pits? by Erma Bombeck (Ballantine/Fawcett, 1979) 3,040,000

F **QB VII** by Leon Uris (Bantam, 1972) 3,032,000

Mommie Dearest by Christina Crawford (Berkley, 1979) 3,031,053

F **The Naked and the Dead** by Norman Mailer (Signet/ NAL, 1951) 3,000,000 (OP)

F **The Women's Room** by Marilyn French (Jove, 1978) 2,974,820

Royal Canadian Air Force Exercise Plans for Physical Fitness (Pocket Books, 1972) 2,963,000

F **The Furies** by John Jakes (Jove, 1976) 2,961,368

F **2001: A Space Odyssey** by Arthur C. Clarke (Signet/ NAL, 1968) 2,950,000

F **Where Are the Children?** by Mary Higgins Clark (Dell, 1976) 2,950,000

F **The Lawless** by John Jakes (Jove, 1978) 2,935,619

How to Be Your Own Best Friend by Mildred Newman and Bernard Berkowitz (Ballantine, 1974) 2,935,545

F **The Chapman Report** by Irving Wallace (Signet/ NAL, 1961) 2,900,000

F **Live and Let Die** by Ian Fleming (Signet/NAL, 1959) 2,900,000 (OP)

F **Moonraker** by Ian Fleming (Signet/NAL, 1960) 2,900,000 (OP)

F **The Sure Hand of God** by Erskine Caldwell (Signet/ NAL, 1949) 2,900,000 (OP)

The New Roget's Thesaurus edited by Norman Lewis (Berkley, 1972) 2,859,409

F **The Pirate** by Harold Robbins (Pocket Books, 1975) 2,857,000

F **For Your Eyes Only** by Ian Fleming (Signet/NAL, 1961) 2,850,000 (OP)

F **Lost Love, Last Love** by Rosemary Rogers (Avon, 1980) 2,850,000

The Grass Is Always Greener Over the Septic Tank by Erma Bombeck (Ballantine/Fawcett, 1977) 2,846,000

Let's Get Well by Adelle Davis (Signet/NAL, 1972) 2,820,000

F **The Materese Circle** by Robert Ludlum (Bantam, 1980) 2,819,000

F **Clan of the Cave Bear** by Jean Auel (Bantam, 1981) 2,818,000

F **The Rhinemann Exchange** by Robert Ludlum (Dell, 1975) 2,803,000

F **Fools Die** by Mario Puzo (Signet/NAL, 1979) 2,800,000

Pregnancy, Birth & Family Planning by Alan F. Guttmacher, M.D. (Signet/NAL, 1958) 2,800,000

F **The Spy Who Loved Me** by Ian Fleming (Signet/NAL, 1963) 2,800,000 (OP)

The Final Days by Bob Woodward & Carl Bernstein (Avon, 1977) 2,787,500

F **The Onion Field** by Joseph Wambaugh (Dell, 1974) 2,773,000

F **The Titans** by John Jakes (Jove, 1976) 2,772,330

F **The Key to Rebecca** by Ken Follett (Signet/NAL, 1981) 2,750,000

F **The Ox-Bow Incident** by W.V.T. Clark (Signet Classic/NAL, 1943) 2,750,000

F **A Raisin in the Sun** by Lorraine Hansberry (Signet/NAL, 1961) 2,750,000

F **Bridge Over the River Kwai** by Pierre Boulle (Bantam, 1957) 2,733,000

F **The Bramble Bush** by Charles Mergendahl (Bantam, 1959) 2,732,000

F **The Bourne Identity** by Robert Ludlum (Bantam, 1981) 2,731,000

F **The Inheritors** by Harold Robbins (Pocket Books, 1971) 2,730,000

Elvis: What Happened? by Red West, Sonny West and Dave Hebler (Ballantine, 1977) 2,713,219

F **Diamonds Are Forever** by Ian Fleming (Signet/NAL, 1961) 2,700,000 (OP)

F **The Odessa File** by Frederick Forsyth (Bantam, 1974) 2,691,000

F **The Immigrants** by Howard Fast (Dell, 1978) 2,690,000

Serpico by Peter Maas (Bantam, 1974) 2,689,000

Charlie Brown's All Stars by Charles Schulz (Signet/NAL, 1967) 2,675,000

F **Triple** by Ken Follett (Signet/NAL, 1980) 2,675,000

F **The Wildest Heart** by Rosemary Rogers (Avon, 1974) 2,674,000

F **The Jungle** by Upton Sinclair (Signet Classic/NAL, 1960) 2,670,000

F **The Parsifal Mosaic** by Robert Ludlum (Bantam, 1983) 2,657,000

Body Language by Julius Fast (Pocket Books, 1971) 2,656,000

F **Night Shift** by Stephen King (Signet/NAL, 1979) 2,650,000

F **The New Centurions** by Joseph Wambaugh (Dell, 1972) 2,640,000

F **Chesapeake** by James Michener (Ballantine/Fawcett, 1979) 2,603,287

F **Lisa, Bright and Dark** by John Neufeld (Signet/NAL, 1970) 2,600,000

F **The Man with the Golden Gun** by Ian Fleming (Signet/NAL, 1966) 2,600,000

Greening of America by Charles Reich (Bantam, 1971) 2,583,000

Pulling Your Own Strings by Wayne Dyer (Avon, 1981) 2,574,000

How to Get Control of Your Time & Your Life by Alan Lakein (Signet/NAL, 1974) 2,550,000

F **The Crazy Ladies** by Joyce Elbert (Signet/NAL, 1970) 2,540,000

F **The Americans** by John Jakes (Jove, 1980) 2,532,551

F **This Very Earth** by Erskine Caldwell (Signet/NAL, 1951) 2,525,000 (OP)

F **Dreams Die First** by Harold Robbins (Pocket Books, 1978) 2,524,000

F **The Agony and the Ecstasy** by Irving Stone (Signet/NAL, 1963) 2,520,000

F **Surrender to Love** by Rosemary Rogers (Avon, 1982) 2,520,000

F **Dune** by Frank Herbert (Berkley, 1975) 2,516,937

F **Noble House** by James Clavell (Dell, 1982) 2,515,000

A Charlie Brown Christmas by Charles Schulz (Signet/NAL, 1967) 2,500,000

F **Inferno** by Dante (Mentor/NAL, 1954) 2,500,000

Manchild in the Promised Land by Claude Brown (Signet/NAL, 1966) 2,500,000

New American Medical Dictionary & Health Manual by Robert Rothenberg, M.D. (Signet/NAL, 1962) 2,500,000

F **The Warriors** by John Jakes (Jove, 1977) 2,482,473

Let's Cook It Right by Adelle Davis (Signet/NAL, 1970) 2,480,000

F **Stanger in a Strange Land** by Robert Heinlein (Berkley, 1972) 2,478,677

Total Woman by Marabel Morgan (Pocket Books, 1975) 2,475,000

F **Heart of Darkness and The Secret Sharer** by Joseph Conrad (Signet Classic/NAL, 1950) 2,460,000

The Hite Report by Shere Hite (Dell, 1977) 2,454,500

F **The Establishment** by Howard Fast (Dell, 1980) 2,402,000

F **Sphinx** by Robin Cook (Signet/NAL, 1980) 2,400,000

F **A Stranger in the Mirror** by Sidney Sheldon (Warner, 1977) 2,400,000

Walden & Civil Disobedience by Henry Thoreau (Signet Classic/NAL, 1942) 2,400,000

F **Illusions** by Richard Bach (Dell, 1979) 2,379,000

F **Beggarman, Thief** by Irwin Shaw (Dell, 1978) 2,376,000

Bermuda Triangle by Charles Berlitz (Avon, 1975) 2,376,000

F **An Indecent Obsession** by Colleen McCullough (Avon, 1982) 2,376,000

F **The Scarlet Letter** by Nathaniel Hawthorne (Signet Classic/NAL, 1959) 2,360,000

F **The Dream Merchants** by Harold Robbins (Pocket Books, 1961) 2,356,000

F **Love's Tender Fury** by Jennifer Wilde (Warner, 1976) 2,350,000

The Possible Dream by Charles Paul Conn (Berkley, 1978) 2,349,862

F **Mr. & Mrs. Bo Jo Jones** by Ann Head (Signet/NAL, 1968) 2,330,000

F **The Fan Club** by Irving Wallace (Bantam, 1975) 2,318,000

F **Second Generation** by Howard Fast (Dell, 1979) 2,317,000

F **Marathon Man** by William Goldman (Dell, 1975) 2,304,000

F **The Caretakers** by Dariel Telfer (Signet/NAL, 1960) 2,300,000

F **The Iliad** by Homer (Mentor/NAL, 1950) 2,300,000

F **The Black Marble** by Joseph Wambaugh (Dell, 1979) 2,294,000

Great Dialogues of Plato (Mentor/NAL, 1956) 2,275,000

F **Sackett** by Louis L'Amour (Bantam, 1961) 2,275,000

F **The First Deadly Sin** by Lawrence Sanders (Berkley, 1974) 2,272,241

F **Moonstruck Madness** by Laurie McBain (Avon, 1977) 2,270,000

F **A Perfect Stranger** by Danielle Steel (Dell, 1982) 2,265,000

F **The Boys from Brazil** by Ira Levin (Dell, 1977) 2,242,000

F **A Stone for Danny Fisher** by Harold Robbins (Pocket Books, 1953) 2,236,000

F **The Deep** by Mickey Spillane (Signet/NAL, 1962) 2,220,000

F **Random Winds** by Belva Plain (Dell, 1981) 2,216,000

F **The Ring** by Danielle Steel (Dell, 1981) 2,215,000

F **Audrey Rose** by Frank DeFelitta (Warner, 1976) 2,200,000

F **The Naked Face** by Sidney Sheldon (Dell, 1975) 2,199,000

F **The Gemini Contenders** by Robert Ludlum (Dell, 1977) 2,190,000

F **A Streetcar Named Desire** by Tennessee Williams (Signet/NAL, 1951) 2,175,000

F **The Seven Minutes** by Irving Wallace (Pocket Books, 1970) 2,163,000

The Boston Strangler by Gerold Frank (Signet/NAL, 1967) 2,160,000

F **Semi-Tough** by Dan Jenkins (Signet/NAL, 1973) 2,160,000

F **Class Reunion** by Rona Jaffe (Dell, 1980) 2,158,500

F **Tinker, Tailor, Soldier, Spy** by John Le Carré (Bantam, 1975) 2,155,000

F **The Young Lions** by Irwin Shaw (Signet/NAL, 1950) 2,150,000 (OP)

F **Gone with the Wind** by Margaret Mitchell (Avon, 1973) 2,147,000

F **Remembrance** by Danielle Steel (Dell, 1983) 2,132,000

F **War and Remembrance** by Herman Wouk (Pocket Books, 1980) 2,110,000

F **We the Living** by Ayn Rand (Signet/NAL, 1960) 2,110,000

F **Babbitt** by Sinclair Lewis (Signet Classic/NAL, 1961) 2,100,000

F **The Revolt of Mamie Stover** by William Bradford Huie (Signet/NAL, 1952) 2,100,000 (OP)

Rascal by Sterling North (Avon, 1964) 2,075,000

F **Flint** by Louis L'Amour (Bantam, 1960) 2,070,000

F **A World Full of Strangers** by Cynthia Freeman (Bantam, 1976) 2,070,000

F **Ghost Story** by Peter Straub (Pocket Books, 1980) 2,064,000

F **Gorky Park** by Martin Cruz Smith (Ballantine, 1982) 2,058,590

F **George Boy** by Erskine Caldwell (Signet/NAL, 1950) 2,050,000 (OP)

F **Sanctuary** by William Faulkner (Signet/NAL, 1947) 2,050,000 (OP)

F **A Stranger Is Watching** by Mary Higgins Clark (Dell, 1979) 2,034,000

F **Shibumi** by Trevanian (Ballantine, 1980) 2,025,958

Man's Search for Meaning by Victor Frankl (Pocket Books, 1953) 2,002,000

Open Marriage by Nena O'Neill and George O'Neill (Avon, 1973) 2,013,000

F **Kane & Abel** by Jeffrey Archer (Ballantine/Fawcett, 1981) 2,008,879

F **Ordinary People** by Judith Guest (Ballantine, 1977) 2,006,704

F **The Girl Hunters** by Mickey Spillane (Signet/NAL, 1963) 2,000,000

F **The King** by Morton Cooper (Signet/NAL, 1968) 2,000,000 (OP)

The New World Spanish/English, English/Spanish Dictionary edited by Salvatore Ramondino (Signet/NAL, 1969) 2,000,000

The Other Side of the Mountain by E.G. Valens (Warner, 1975) 2,000,000

F **The Prize** by Irving Wallace (Signet/NAL, 1963) 2,000,000

F **Second Lady** by Irving Wallace (Signet/NAL, 1981) 2,000,000

30 Days to a More Powerful Vocabulary by Wildred Funk and Norman Lewis (Pocket Books, 1971) 1,999,000

F **79 Park Avenue** by Harold Robbins (Pocket Books, 1956) 1,988,000

F **Brain** by Robin Cook (Signet/NAL, 1982) 1,950,000

F **Memories of Another Day** by Harold Robbins (Pocket Books, 1980) 1,926,000

Mastering Rubik's Cube by Don Taylor (Owl/Holt, Rinehart & Winston, 1981) 1,924,864

F **Tears of Gold** by Laurie McBain (Avon, 1979) 1,915,000

F **Curtain** by Agatha Christie (Pocket Books, 1976) 1,914,000

F **Goodbye Janette** by Harold Robbins (Pocket Books, 1982) 1,913,000

F **Sunshine** by Norma Klein (Avon, 1974) 1,906,500

F **Forever** by Judy Blume (Pocket Books, 1976) 1,884,000

F **The Rich Are Different** by Susan Howatch (Ballantine/Fawcett, 1978) 1,884,000

F **The Word** by Irving Wallace (Pocket Books, 1973) 1,856,000

Born Again by Charles Colson (Revell, 1977) 1,849,494

German-English Dictionary (Pocket Books, 1953) 1,848,000

F **The Rebels** by John Jakes (Jove, 1975) 1,836,402

Born to Win by Muriel James (Addison-Wesley, 1971) 1,794,603

Zelda by Nancy Milford (Avon, 1978) 1,778,000

F **Devil's Desire** by Laurie McBain (Avon, 1975) 1,768,000

F **Chance the Winds of Fortune** by Laurie McBain (Avon, 1980) 1,725,000

Mere Christianity by C.S. Lewis (Macmillan, 1962) 1,723,980

F **The Crystal Cave** by Mary Stewart (Ballantine/Fawcett, 1971) 1,712,000

How to Flatten Your Stomach by Jim Everroad (Price/Stern/Sloan, 1977) 1,680,000

F **M*A*S*H** by Richard Hooker (Pocket Books, 1969) 1,676,000

F **The Seekers** by John Jakes (Jove, 1975) 1,665,327

F **Ashes in the Wind** by Kathleen Woodiwiss (Avon, 1979) 1,660,000

Letters to Karen by Charlie Shedd (Avon, 1968) 1,656,900

Between Parent & Teenager by Haim Ginott (Avon, 1971) 1,642,000

The Magic of Thinking Big by David Schwartz (Simon & Schuster, 1977) 1,635,621

Joni by Joni Ereckson with Joe Musser (Zondervan, 1976) 1,628,377

F **Penmarric** by Susan Howatch (Ballantine/Fawcett, 1972) 1,624,000

F **E.T.: The Extraterrestrial** by William Kotzwinkle (Berkley, 1982) 1,612,892

F **The Human Factor** by Graham Greene (Avon, 1978) 1,610,000

F **The Adventurers** by Harold Robbins (Pocket Books, 1966) 1,609,000

F **Children of Dune** by Frank Herbert (Berkley, 1977) 1,608,414

F **The Odyssey** by Homer (Viking Penguin, 1946) 1,600,000

Word Power Made Easy by Norman Lewis (Pocket Books, 1979) 1,585,000

Beyond Ourselves by Catherine Marshall (Avon, 1968) 1,575,800

F **The Third Deadly Sin** by Lawrence Sanders (Berkley, 1982) 1,560,889

Bless the Beasts and the Children by Glendon Swarthout (Pocket Books, 1970) 1,555,000 (OP)

F **The Covenant** by James Michener (Ballantine/Fawcett, 1982) 1,538,573

F **The Second Deadly Sin** by Lawrence Sanders (Berkley, 1978) 1,535,455

Nurse by Peggy Anderson (Berkley, 1979) 1,509,739

F **Foundation** by Isaac Asimov (Avon, 1966) 1,475,000

F **Spring Moon** by Bette Bao Lord (Avon, 1982) 1,475,000

Aunt Erma's Cope Book by Erma Bombeck (Ballantine/Fawcett, 1980) 1,460,000

F **The Grapes of Wrath** by John Steinbeck (Viking Penguin, 1958) 1,460,000

F **Wildfire at Midnight** by Mary Stewart (Ballantine/Fawcett, 1962) 1,455,000

F **Second Foundation** by Isaac Asimov (Avon, 1964) 1,433,000

F **The Silmarillion** by J.R.R. Tolkien (Ballantine, 1979) 1,429,814

F **The Empire Strikes Back**™ by Donald F. Glut (Ballantine/Del Rey, 1980) 1,428,203

F **Dune Messiah** by Frank Herbert (Berkley, 1974) 1,427,961

When Bad Things Happen to Good People by Harold Kushner (Avon, 1983) 1,415,000

I Lost Everything in the Post-Natal Depression by Erma Bombeck (Ballantine/Fawcett, 1974) 1,405,000

F **A Mother & Two Daughters** by Gail Godwin (Avon, 1982) 1,405,000

Just Wait Till You Have Children of Your Own by Erma Bombeck (Ballantine/Fawcett, 1972) 1,403,000

F **The Bermuda Triangle** by Adi-Kent Thomas Jeffrey (Warner, 1975) 1,400,000 (OP)

F **The Cardinal Sins** by Andrew M. Greeley (Warner, 1982) 1,400,000

F **Good as Gold** by Joseph Heller (Pocket Books, 1979) 1,400,000

How to Prosper During the Coming Bad Years by Howard Ruff (Warner, 1980) 1,400,000

F **Voyage** by Sterling Hayden (Avon, 1977) 1,397,888

A Separate Reality by Carlos Castenada (Pocket Books, 1971) 1,394,000

Relaxation Response by Herbert Benson (Avon, 1976) 1,381,000

F **The Ivy Tree** by Mary Stewart (Ballantine/Fawcett, 1963) 1,376,000

F **Eiger Sanction** by Trevanian (Avon, 1973) 1,373,300

F **Endless Love** by Scott Spencer (Avon, 1980) 1,370,000

F **Rally Round the Flag, Boys** by Max Shulman (Bantam, 1958) 1,360,000

Nigger by Dick Gregory (Pocket Books, 1965) 1,356,000

F **Acceptable Loses** by Irwin Shaw (Avon, 1983) 1,352,000

F **A Woman of Independent Means** by Elizabeth Hailey (Avon, 1979) 1,350,000

F **Chances** by Jackie Collins (Warner, 1982) 1,300,000

F **The Hollow Hills** by Mary Stewart (Ballantine/Fawcett, 1974) 1,296,000

F **The Plot** by Irving Wallace (Pocket Books, 1968) 1,294,000

F **Cashelmara** by Susan Howatch (Ballantine/Fawcett, 1975) 1,292,000

F **Captive Bride** by Johanna Lindsey (Avon, 1977) 1,287,000

F **Moonspinners** by Mary Stewart (Ballantine/Fawcett, 1965) 1,286,000

F **Never Love a Stranger** by Harold Robbins (Pocket Books, 1962) 1,253,000

Coal Miner's Daughter by Loretta Lynn with George Vecsey (Warner, 1977) 1,250,000

My Secret Garden by Nancy Friday (Pocket Books, 1974) 1,250,000

F **Where Love Has Gone** by Harold Robbins (Pocket Books, 1963) 1,248,000

F **The Investigation** by Dorothy Uhnak (Pocket Books, 1978) 1,247,000

F **Murder on the Orient Express** by Agatha Christie (Pocket Books, 1980) 1,233,000

At Wit's End by Erma Bombeck (Ballantine/Fawcett, 1975) 1,232,000

F **The Hotel New Hampshire** by John Irving (Pocket Books, 1982) 1,229,000

F **The Camerons** by Robert Crichton (Warner, 1974) 1,200,000 (OP)

F **Nemesis** by Agatha Christie (Pocket Books, 1972) 1,180,000

F **The Sixth Commandment** by Lawrence Sanders (Berkley, 1980) 1,177,299

F **The Carpetbaggers** by Harold Robbins (Pocket Books, 1962) 1,175,000

F **This Rough Magic** by Mary Stewart (Ballantine/Fawcett, 1965) 1,147,000

F **Sins of the Fathers** by Susan Howatch (Ballantine/Fawcett, 1981) 1,142,000

How to Read a Person Like a Book by Gerard I. Nierenberg and Henry H. Calero (Pocket Books, 1973) 1,140,000

F **The Last Convertible** by Anton Myrer (Berkley, 1979) 1,105,682

F **The Ninja** by Eric Van Lustbader (Ballantine/Fawcett, 1981) 1,101,625

F **Dare to Love** by Jennifer Wilde (Warner, 1978) 1,100,000

F **This Loving Torment** by Valerie Sherwood (Warner, 1977) 1,100,000

Toilet Training in Less Than a Day by Nathan H. Azrin and Richard M. Foxx (Pocket Books, 1976) 1,097,000

How to Stop Worrying and Start Living by Dale Carnegie (Pocket Books, 1953) 1,091,000

F **Passenger to Frankfort** by Agatha Christie (Pocket Books, 1966) 1,089,000

F **Love** by Leo Buscaglia (Ballantine/Fawcett, 1981) 1,085,492

F **Touch Not the Cat** by Mary Stewart (Ballantine/Fawcett, 1977) 1,054,000

F **The Third World War** by Sir John Hackett (Berkley, 1980) 1,038,019

F **The Tenth Commandment** by Lawrence Sanders (Berkley, 1981) 1,033,732

F **The Legacy** by John Coyne (Berkley, 1979) 1,030,866

F **Nightway** by Janet Dailey (Pocket Books, 1981) 1,010,000

F **Once an Eagle** by Anton Myrer (Berkley, 1976) 1,008,058

F **The Tomorrow File** by Lawrence Sanders (Berkley, 1976) 1,005,436

F **Alien** by Alan Dean Foster (Warner, 1979) 1,000,000

Dress for Success by John T. Molloy (Warner, 1976) 1,000,000

F **The Entity** by Frank DeFelitta (Warner, 1979) 1,000,000

Letters to the Happy Hooker edited by Xaviera Hollander (Warner, 1973) 1,000,000 (OP)

Xaviera Goes Wild by Xaviera Hollander (Warner, 1973) 1,000,000

11

Awards and Prizes

MIRIAM E. PHELPS

Adult Awards (U.S.A.)

ASCAP-Deems Taylor Awards

Established 1967. To honor outstanding books about music, in memory of the composer-critic-commentator and president of ASCAP (1942–1948).

Samuel Adler. *The Study of Orchestration.* Norton.

David Beach and Jurgen Thym, tr. *The Art of Strict Musical Composition* by Johann Phillip Kirnberger. Yale University Press.

Samuel Charters. *The Roots of the Blues.* Perigee.

B. Lee Cooper. *Images of American Society in Popular Music.* Nelson-Hall.

Joseph Horowitz. *Conversations with Arrau.* Knopf.

Carol J. Oja. *Stravinsky in Modern Music.* Da Capo.

Sally Placksin. *American Women in Jazz.* Wideview.

Mark Slobin. *Tenement Songs.* University of Illinois.

Emanuel Winternitz. *Leonardo da Vinci as a Musician.* Yale University Press.

Academy of American Poets

ACADEMY OF AMERICAN POETS FELLOWSHIP. Established 1946. To recognize and reward poets of proven merit.

James Schuyler

Philip Booth

LAMONT POETRY SELECTION. Established 1954 as a first-book award; since 1975 given to encourage the publication of a poet's second book.

Sharon Olds. *The Dead and the Living.* Knopf.

PETER I. B. LAVAN YOUNGER POETS AWARDS

Edward Hirsch

Brad Leithauser

Gjertrud Schnackenberg

WALT WHITMAN AWARD. Established 1974. To honor an American poet who has not yet published a book of poems and to ensure the publication of that poet's first book.

Christopher Gilbert. *Across the Mutual Landscape.* Graywolf Press.

American Academy and Institute of Arts and Letters

Established 1941. For creative achievement.

AMERICAN ACADEMY IN ROME FELLOWSHIP IN CREATIVE WRITING

Gjertrud Schnackenberg

AWARD OF MERIT MEDAL FOR THE SHORT STORY

Elizabeth Spencer

AWARDS IN LITERATURE

Alfred Corn

Stephen Dixon

Robert Mezey

Mary Oliver

David Plante

George Starbuck

Leo Steinberg

Edmund White

WITTER BYNNER PRIZE FOR POETRY

Douglas Crase

SUE KAUFMAN PRIZE FOR FIRST FICTION

Susanna Moore. *My Old Sweetheart*. Houghton Mifflin/Pocket Books.

LOINES AWARD FOR POETRY

Geoffrey Hill

RICHARD AND HINDA ROSENTHAL FOUNDATION AWARD FOR FICTION

A. G. Mojtabai. *Autumn*. Houghton Mifflin.

MILDRED AND HAROLD STRAUSS LIVINGS

Raymond Carver and Cynthia Ozick

HAROLD D. VURSELL MEMORIAL AWARD

Jonathan D. Spence. *The Gate of Heavenly Peace*. Viking/Penguin.

American Book Awards

Established 1980 (successor to National Book Awards). To honor living American authors for the year's best books.

AUTOBIOGRAPHY/BIOGRAPHY

Hardcover: Judith Thurman. *Isak Dinesen: The Life of a Storyteller*. St. Martin's Press.

Paperback: James R. Mellow. *Nathaniel Hawthorne in His Times*. Houghton Mifflin.

FICTION

Hardcover: Alice Walker. *The Color Purple*. Harcourt Brace Jovanovich.

Paperback: Eudora Welty. *The Collected Stories of Eudora Welty*. Harvest/HBJ.

FIRST NOVEL

Gloria Naylor. *The Women of Brewster Place*. Viking.

GENERAL NONFICTION

Hardcover: Fox Butterfield. *China: Alive in the Bitter Sea*. Times Books.

Paperback: James Fallows. *National Defense*. Vintage.

GRAPHICS

Book Design—Pictorial: Barry Moser, designer/illustrator; Steve Renick, art director. *Alice's Adventures in Wonderland* by Lewis Carroll. University of California Press.

Book Design—Typographical: David Lance Goines, designer/illustrator; William F. Luckey, art director. *A Constructed Roman Alphabet*. Godine.

Book Illustration—Collected Art: Howard Morris, designer; Nancy Grubb, editor; Dana Cole, production manager. *John Singer Sargent* by Carter Ratcliff. Abbeville Press.

Book Illustration—Original Art: Erick Ingraham, illustrator; Cynthia Basil, designer/art director. *Porcupine Stew* by Beverly Major. William Morrow Junior Books.

Book Illustration—Photographs: Eleanor Morris Caponigro, designer. *Alfred Stieglitz: Photographs and Writings* by Sarah Greenough and Juan Hamilton. National Gallery of Art/Callaway Editions.

Cover Design—Mass Market Paperback: Martha Sedgwick, designer; Matt Tepper, art director. *Key Exchange* by Kevin Wade. Avon.

Cover Design—Trade Paperback: Doris Ettlinger, illustrator; Neil Stuart, designer/art director. *Bogmail* by Patrick McGinley. Penguin.

Jacket Design: Fred Marcellino, designer; Frank Metz, art director. *Souls on Fire* by Elie Wiesel. Summit Books/Simon & Schuster.

HISTORY

Hardcover: Alan Brinkley. *Voices of Protest: Huey Long, Father Coughlin and the Great Depression*. Knopf.

Paperback: Frank E. Manuel and Fritzie P. Manuel. *Utopian Thought in the Western World*. Belknap Press of Harvard University Press.

ORIGINAL PAPERBACK

Lisa Goldstein. *The Red Magician*. Timescape/Pocket Books.

POETRY

Galway Kinnell. *Selected Poems*. Houghton Mifflin.

Charles Wright. *Country Music*. Wesleyan University Press.

SCIENCE

Hardcover: Abraham Pais. *Subtle Is the Lord: The Science and Life of Albert Einstein*. Oxford University Press.

Paperback: Philip J. Davis and Reuben Hersh. *The Mathematical Experience*. Houghton Mifflin.

TRANSLATION

Richard Howard. *Les Fleurs du Mal* by Charles Baudelaire. Godine.

American Literary Translators Association/University of Missouri Awards

Established 1983. To honor book-length translations for literary and technical merit, as well as the significance of the works in their original languages. Winning books to be published by the University of Missouri Press.

GREGORY RABASSA PRIZE (prose)

Margaret Kidder Ewing. *A Night in the Forest* by Blaise Cendrars.

RICHARD WILBUR PRIZE (poetry)

Sandra Reyes. *Sermons and Homilies of the Christ of Elqui* by Nicanor Parra.

American Printing History Association Award

Established 1976. For a distinguished contribution to the study of the history of publishing and printing.

Leona Rostenberg and Madeleine B. Stern of Leona Rostenberg—Rare Books

American Society of Mechanical Engineers Ralph Coats Roe Medal

Established 1972. To recognize outstanding contributions toward better public understanding and appreciation of the engineer's worth to contemporary society.

Tracy Kidder. *The Soul of a New Machine*. Little, Brown.

Jim Andrews Communicator Award

Established 1982 by Universal Press Syndicate/Andrews and McMeel, Inc. To honor an outstanding work on contemporary journalism. Winning manuscript to be published by Andrews and McMeel.

Peter Benjaminson. *Death in the Afternoon: Big City Newspapers Struggle for Survival*.

Associated Writing Programs Award Series

Competition for book-length manuscripts to be published by university presses.

NOVEL. Established 1979.

Douglas Finn. *Heart of a Family*. State University of New York Press.

POETRY. Established 1974.

Lisa Ress. *Flight Patterns*. University Press of Virginia.

SHORT FICTION. Established 1977.

Charles Baxter. *Harmony of the World*. University of Missouri Press.

Association of Logos Bookstores Book Awards

Established 1981. To honor excellence in religious publishing.

BEST CREATIVE BOOK
Not awarded in 1983.

BEST INSPIRATIONAL BOOK
Not awarded in 1983.

BEST SCHOLARLY BOOK
Not awarded in 1983.

MOST SIGNIFICANT AUTHOR
Not awarded in 1983.

MOST SIGNIFICANT NEW PUBLISHER
Not awarded in 1983.

PUBLISHER WITH BEST OVERALL CONTENT
Not awarded in 1983.

Bancroft Prizes

Established 1948 by Columbia University. To honor two distinguished works in either American history (including biography) or American diplomacy, or both.

John P. Demos. *Entertaining Satan: Witchcraft and the Culture of Early New England*. Oxford University Press.

Nick Salvatore. *Eugene V. Debs: Citizen and Socialist*. University of Illinois Press.

Banta Award

Established 1974 by Wisconsin Library Association. To honor literary achievement by a Wisconsin author.

Susan Engberg. *Pastorale*. University of Illinois Press.

Beefeater Club Prize for Literature

Established 1980 by the Beefeater Club of the Incorporated Ancient Order of the Beefeater. For works of true literary merit, having significance for both England and the United States.

Not awarded in 1983.

Before Columbus Foundation American Book Awards

Established 1980. To promote multicultural art and recognize literary achievement by people of various ethnic backgrounds.

Nash Candelaria. *Not by the Sword*. Bilingual Press.

Barbara Christian. *Black Women Novelists*. Greenwood Press.

Judy Grahn. *Queen of Wands*. The Crossing Press.

Peter Guralnick. *Lost Highway: Journeys and Arrivals of American Musicians*. Godine.

Jessica Hagedorn. *Pet Food and Tropical Apparitions*. Momo's Press.

James D. Houston. *Californians*. Knopf.

Joy Kogawa. *Obasan*. Godine.

Cecilia Liang, tr. *Chinese Folk Poetry*. Beyond Baroque.

Sean O'Tuma and Thomas Kinsella, eds. *An Duainne: Poems of the Dispossessed*. University of Pennsylvania Press.

Harriet Rohmer. *The Legend of Food Mountain*. Children's Book Press.

Evangelina Vigil. *Thirty an' Seen a Lot*. Arte Publico Press.

John Williams. *!Click Song*. Houghton Mifflin.

SPECIAL LIFETIME ACHIEVEMENT AWARD
Kay Boyle

Curtis G. Benjamin Award for Creative Publishing

Established 1974. To honor individuals for exceptional contributions to innovation and creativity in publishing.
W. Bradford Wiley

Bennett Award

Established 1976 by the Hudson Review. Awarded biennially to a writer whose work has not received full recognition, or a writer who is at a critical stage where a substantial grant would be particularly beneficial in furthering creative development.
Not awarded in 1983.

Elmer Holmes Bobst Awards for Arts and Letters

Established 1983 by New York University; funded by the Elmer and Mamdouha Bobst Foundation. To honor individuals for distinguished lifetime literary achievement.
Russell Baker
Kenneth Burke
Alfred Knopf
Denise Levertov
Bernard Malamud
Arthur Miller

Bollingen Prize for Poetry

Established 1950 by Yale University Library. Awarded biennially to American poets whose work represents the highest achievement in the preceding two-year period.
Anthony Hecht
John Hollander

Brandeis University Creative Arts Award

Established 1956. To recognize a lifetime of distinguished achievement.
Robert Penn Warren

John Burroughs Medal

Established 1926 by the John Burroughs Memorial Association. For distinguished American nature writing.
Alexander S. Skutch. *A Naturalist on a Tropical Farm.* University of California Press.

Carey-Thomas Awards

Established 1942 by the R. R. Bowker Company, in honor of two notable pioneers of American publishing. For a distinguished project of book publishing.

Penguin Books. Penguin Contemporary American Fiction Series and Penguin Originals Series.

HONOR CITATION
Literary Classics of the United States. *Library of America.*

SPECIAL CITATIONS
Callaway Editions/National Gallery of Art. *Alfred Stieglitz: Photographs and Writings.*
Sierra Club Books. For books on environmental issues.
Philomel Books. For books for blind children.

Gilbert Chinard Prize

Awarded jointly by the Institut Français de Washington and the Society for French Historical Studies. For a distinguished scholarly book or manuscript in the history of Franco-American relations by a Canadian or U.S. author.
Orville T. Murphy. *Charles Gravier, Comte de Vergennes: French Diplomacy in the Age of Revolution, 1719–1787.* State University of New York Press.

Christopher Book Awards

Established 1949 by the Christophers. To honor books that affirm the highest values of the human spirit, exhibit artistic and technical proficiency, and attain a significant degree of public acceptance.
James MacGregor Burns. *The Vineyard of Liberty.* Knopf.
James Tunstead Burtchaell. *Rachel Weeping.* Andrews & McMeel.
Yaffa Eliach. *Hasidic Tales of the Holocaust.* Oxford University Press.
Stephen B. Oates. *Let the Trumpet Sound: The Life of Martin Luther King, Jr.* Harper & Row.
Richard Reeves. *American Journey.* Simon & Schuster.
Barbara and Barry Rosen, with George Feifer. *The Destined Hour.* Doubleday.
Jonathan Schell. *The Fate of the Earth.* Knopf.

Columbia University Translation Center

TRANSLATION AWARDS. Established 1973. To encourage and recognize excellence in translation.
Roger Greenwald. *The Silence Afterwards: Selected Poems* by Rolf Jacobson (from the Norwegian).
Carol Rubenstein. Traditional works of the Sarawak Dayaks.
Lawrence Venuti. *The Colomber* by Dino Buzzati (from the Italian).
Craig Williamson. *A Feast of Creatures: Anglo-Saxon Riddle Songs* (from the Old English).
Jeno Brogyanyi. *The Line* by Geza Paskandi (from the Hungarian).
Stanley F. Lombardo. *Hesiod's Works and Days* (from the Greek).

Moss Roberts. *The Three Kingdoms* by Lo Guanzhong (from the Chinese).

Lisa Sapinkopf. *For the Lure of the Threshold* by Yves Bonnefoy (from the French).

MAX HAYWARD AWARD

Michael Katz. *Who Is to Blame?* by Alexander Herzen (from the Russian).

VAN DE BOVENKAMP–ARMAND G. ERPF AWARD

Frederick H. Fornoff. *The Endless Voyage* by Laureano Alban (from the Spanish).

THORNTON NIVEN WILDER PRIZE. Established 1979–1980. To honor distinguished translation of contemporary American literature into foreign languages.

Rita Rait. For translations into the Russian of many American authors.

Common Wealth Award for Distinguished Service in Literature

Established 1980. To recognize and foster excellence and outstanding achievements in various fields of human endeavor.

Christopher Isherwood

Commonwealth Club of California Book Awards

Established 1930. To honor the finest works of literature by California authors.

GOLD MEDALS

Fiction: Gina Berriault. *The Infinite Passion of Expectation: Twenty-five Stories.* North Point Press.

Nonfiction: Robert Middlekauff. *The Glorious Cause: The American Revolution, 1763–1789.* Oxford University Press.

SILVER MEDALS

General: James Cahill. *The Compelling Image: Nature and Style in Seventeenth-Century Chinese Painting.* Harvard University Press.

General: Thomas Perry. *The Butcher's Boy.* Scribners.

First Novel: Clayton Bess. *Story for a Black Night.* Parnassus Press/Houghton Mifflin.

Poetry: Barry Spacks. *Spacks Street: New & Selected Poems.* Johns Hopkins University Press.

Californiana: Ruth Teiser and Catherine Harroun. *Winemaking in California.* McGraw-Hill.

Dance Perspectives Foundation de la Torre Bueno Prize

Established 1973. To honor an outstanding work in the field of dance.

SPECIAL CITATION

Roger Copeland and Marshall Cohen, eds. *What Is Dance? Readings in Theory and Criticism.* Oxford University Press.

Editors' Book Award

Established 1982 by Bill Henderson of Pushcart Press. To recognize unpublished books of exceptional quality.

Frank Stiffel. *The Tale of the Ring: A Kaddish.* Pushcart Press.

English-Speaking Union Books-Across-the-Sea Ambassador of Honor Books

Established 1942. For books of outstanding merit sent to English-speaking countries abroad to serve as interpreters of American life and culture.

Thomas Boylston Adams. *A New Nation.* Globe Pequot Press.

Susan Mary Alsop. *Yankees at the Court: The First Americans in Paris.* Doubleday.

Jervis Anderson. *This Was Harlem.* Farrar, Straus & Giroux.

Jackson R. Bryer. *The Letters of Eugene O'Neill to Kenneth MacGowan.* Yale University Press.

Justin Kaplan. *Whitman: Poetry and Prose.* Library of America.

Henry Kissinger. *Years of Upheaval.* Little, Brown.

Olga Maynard. *Judith Jamison: Aspects of a Dancer.* Doubleday.

Robert Middlekauff. *The Glorious Cause: The American Revolution.* Oxford University Press.

Hal Morgan and Andreas Brown. *Prairie Fires and Paper Moons: The American Photographic Post Card.* Godine.

Roy Harvey Pearce. *Hawthorne: Tales and Sketches.* Library of America.

Kate Simon. *Bronx Primitive.* Viking.

Kathryn Kish Sklar. *Harriet Beecher Stowe: Three Novels.* Library of America.

Jane S. Smith. *Elsie De Wolfe: A Life in the High Style.* Atheneum.

Thomas G. Tanselle. *Herman Melville: Typee, Omoo, Mardi.* Library of America.

Edward Weeks. *Writers and Friends.* Atlantic-Little, Brown.

Theodore White. *America in Search of Itself.* Harper & Row.

Roy Wilkins with Tom Mathews. *Standing Fast: The Autobiography of Roy Wilkins.* Viking.

R. T. French Tastemaker Awards

Established 1966 by the R. T. French Company. To give recognition to the outstanding cookbooks of the year.

AMERICAN

Melinda M. Vance, ed. *Connecticut à la Carte.* Connecticut à la Carte of West Hartford.

BASIC/GENERAL

Anne Willan. *The Varenne Cooking Course.* Morrow.

BEST COOKBOOK
Evan Jones and Judith Jones. *The Book of Bread.* Harper & Row.

INTERNATIONAL
Giuliano Bugialli. *Giuliano Bugialli's Classic Techniques of Italian Cooking.* Simon & Schuster.

NATURAL FOODS/SPECIAL DIET
Joyce Trollope, ed. *Better Homes & Gardens Dieter's Cookbook.* Meredith Corporation.

ORIGINAL SOFTCOVER—BASIC/GENERAL
Janeth Nix, Elaine Woodard, and other editors of Sunset Books and *Sunset* Magazine. *Easy Basics for Good Cooking.* Lane.

ORIGINAL SOFTCOVER—INTERNATIONAL/AMERICAN REGIONAL
Rose Dosti. *Middle Eastern Cooking.* HP Books.

ORIGINAL SOFTCOVER—MEAT/FISH/EGGS
Yvonne Young Tarr. *The Great East Coast Seafood Book.* Random House.

ORIGINAL SOFTCOVER—SPECIALTY
Lou Seibert Pappas. *Vegetable Cookery.* HP Books.

SPECIALTY
John Clancy. *John Clancy's Christmas Cookbook.* Hearst Books.

Friends of American Writers Awards

Established 1928 by a group in the Chicago area. To encourage and promote high standards and ideals among American writers.
Will D. Campbell. *The Glad River.* Holt, Rinehart and Winston.
John Madson. *Where the Sky Began.* Houghton Mifflin.

Friends of the Chicago Public Library Carl Sandburg Awards

Established 1979. To recognize exceptional achievement in literature by Chicago-area writers.

FICTION
Harry Mark Petrakis. *Days of Vengeance.* Doubleday.

NONFICTION
Louise B. Young. *The Blue Planet.* Little, Brown.

POETRY
Sterling Plumpp. *The Mojo Hands Call, I Must Go.* Thunder Mouth Press.

Tony Godwin Award

Established 1977 in honor of the late Tony Godwin, British publisher and bookseller, co-publisher at Harcourt Brace Jovanovich. Awarded in alternate years to an American and a British editor, enabling each to spend six weeks working at a publishing house in the other's country.
Patricia Mulcahy, Penguin Books.

Great Lakes Colleges Association New Writers Awards

Established 1969. To honor literary merit in a first book of fiction and a first book of poetry.

FICTION
Michael Joyce. *The War Outside Ireland.* Tinkers Dam Press.

POETRY
Maria Flook. *Reckless Wedding.* Houghton Mifflin.

Sarah Josepha Hale Award

Established 1956 by the Friends of the Richards Library, Newport, NH. To give recognition to a writer whose work has achieved distinction and reflects the literary tradition of New England.
Donald Hall

Alice and Edith Hamilton Prize

Established 1978, sponsored by the University of Michigan Rackham School of Graduate Studies, winning book to be published by the University of Michigan Press in the Women and Culture Series. For the best original, scholarly, book-length manuscript on women.
Leslie W. Rabine. *Reading the Romantic Heroine: Text, History, Ideology.*

John L. Haney Fund Prizes in the Humanities and Social Sciences

Established 1980 (biennial, first given in 1982) by the University of Pennsylvania Press to honor distinguished works of scholarship accepted for publication by the Press.

HUMANITIES
Not awarded in 1983.

SOCIAL SCIENCES
Not awarded in 1983.

Harcourt Awards

Established 1982 with a grant from the Harcourt Foundation, administered by Columbia University.

ALFRED HARCOURT AWARD FOR OUTSTANDING WORKS OF BIOGRAPHY AND MEMOIRS
Elisabeth Young-Bruehl. *Hannah Arendt: For Love of the World.* Yale University Press.
ELLEN KNOWLES HARCOURT AWARD FOR AN OUTSTANDING DOCTORAL DISSERTATION ON THE LIFE, DIARIES, LETTERS OR MEMOIRS OF AN AMERICAN WOMAN

Sharon N. White. *Mabel Loomis Todd: Gender, Language, and Power in Victorian America.* To be published by Columbia University Press.

Hugh Hefner First Amendment Award

Established 1980 by the Playboy Foundation. To recognize the efforts of individuals working to protect the First Amendment.

No book award given in 1983.

Drue Heinz Literature Prize

Established 1980 by the University of Pittsburgh Press and the Howard Heinz Endowment. To honor an outstanding collection of short fiction, winning manuscript to be published by the Press.

Jonathan Penner. *Private Parties.*

Sidney Hillman Foundation Prize Awards

Established 1950 by the Sidney Hillman Foundation of the Amalgamated Clothing & Textile Workers Union. To honor outstanding books on such themes as civil liberties, race relations, social and economic welfare, and world understanding and related problems.

Jonathan Schell. *The Fate of the Earth.* Knopf.

Clarence L. Holte Prize

Established 1979 by the Twenty-First Century Foundation. Awarded biennially in recognition of a significant and lasting contribution by a living writer to the public understanding of the cultural heritage of Africa and the African diaspora.

Vincent Harding. *There Is a River: The Black Struggle for Freedom in America.* Harcourt Brace Jovanovich/ Vintage Books.

Hugo Awards. *See* World Science Fiction Convention Awards

Iowa School of Letters Award for Short Fiction

Established 1969 (first given 1970) in cooperation with the Iowa Arts Council, Writers Workshop, and the University of Iowa Press. To encourage writing in a typically American literary genre, winning manuscript to be published by the Press.

Ivy Goodman. *Heart Failure.*

Juniper Prize

Established 1975 by the University of Massachusetts Press. To honor an outstanding manuscript of original English poetry, winning manuscript to be published by the Press.

Marc Hudson. *Afterlight.*

Janet Heidinger Kafka Prize in Fiction by an American Woman

Established 1976 by the English Department and the Writers' Workshop of the University of Rochester. Awarded to a woman citizen of the United States for an outstanding work of fiction, whether novel, short story collection, or experimental writing, but excluding children's books.

Mary Lee Settle. *The Killing Ground* (conclusion to the Beulah Quintet). Farrar, Straus & Giroux.

Robert F. Kennedy Book Awards

Established 1981 with endowment by Arthur M. Schlesinger, Jr., from proceeds of his biography *Robert Kennedy and His Times.* To honor authors whose works most faithfully and forcefully reflect Robert Kennedy's purposes.

Stephen B. Oates. *Let the Trumpet Sound: The Life of Martin Luther King, Jr.* Harper & Row.
Jonathan Schell. *The Fate of the Earth.* Knopf.

Jules F. Landry Award

Established 1968. To recognize the best manuscript accepted for publication by Louisiana State University Press in southern history, biography, or literature.

Fred Hobson. *Tell About the South: The Southern Rage to Explain.*

Locus Awards

Established 1971 by Locus Publications. To honor the year's best novel, short fiction, collection, anthology, artist, magazine, illustrated or art book, reference work, and publisher in the field of science fiction and fantasy.

ANTHOLOGY
Terry Carr, ed. *The Best Science Fiction of the Year #11.* Timescape.

ARTIST
Michael Whelan

FANTASY NOVEL
Gene Wolfe. *The Sword of the Lictor.* Timescape.

FIRST NOVEL
Donald Kingsbury. *Courtship Rite.* Timescape.

MAGAZINE
Locus

NONFICTION/REFERENCE
Barry Malzberg. *The Engines of the Night.* Doubleday.

NOVELETTE
Harlan Ellison. *Djinn, No Chaser.* TZ 4/82.

NOVELLA
Joanna Russ. "Souls." *F&SF* 1/82.

PUBLISHER
Pocket/Timescape

SCIENCE FICTION NOVEL
Isaac Asimov. *Foundation's Edge*. Doubleday.

SHORT STORY
Ursula K. Le Guin. ''Sur'' from *The Compass Rose*. Harper & Row.

SINGLE-AUTHOR COLLECTION
Ursula K. Le Guin. *The Compass Rose*. Harper & Row.

Los Angeles Times Book Awards

Established 1980. To honor literary excellence.

BIOGRAPHY
Seymour M. Hersh. *The Price of Power: Kissinger in the Nixon White House*. Summit Books.

CURRENT INTEREST
Walker Percy. *Lost in the Cosmos: The Last Self-Help Book*. Farrar, Straus & Giroux.

FICTION
Thomas Keneally. *Schindler's List*. Simon & Schuster.

HISTORY
Fernand Braudel. *The Wheels of Commerce: Civilization and Capitalism, 15th–18th Century*. Harper & Row.

POETRY
James Merrill. *The Changing Light at Sandover*. Atheneum.

ROBERT KIRSCH AWARD FOR A BODY OF WORK BY AN AUTHOR FROM THE WEST OR FEATURING THE WEST. To honor the memory of the longtime literary critic of the *Los Angeles Times*.
M. F. K. Fisher

Lenore Marshall/Nation Poetry Prize

Established 1974. To honor the outstanding book of poems published in the United States.

[The Lenore Marshall Poetry Prize, sponsored by The New Hope Foundation and formerly administered by *Saturday Review*, has since 1982 been sponsored jointly by the *Nation* and The New Hope Foundation and known as the Lenore Marshall/Nation Poetry Prize.]
George Starbuck. *The Argot Merchant Disaster: Poems New and Selected*. Atlantic-Little, Brown.

Medieval Academy of America

JOHN NICHOLAS BROWN PRIZE. Established 1978. For a first book or monograph on a medieval subject judged to be of outstanding quality.
David Berger. *The Jewish-Christian Debate in the High Middle Ages: A Critical Edition of the Nizzahon Vetus with an Introduction, Translation and Commentary*. Jewish Publication Society of America.

ELLIOTT PRIZE. Established 1971. For a first article in the field of medieval studies.
Lance W. Brunner. ''A Perspective on the Southern Italian Sequence: The Second Tonary of the Manuscript Monte Cassino 318'' from *Early Music History* 1 (1981) 117–164.

HASKINS MEDAL. Established 1940. For a distinguished book in the field of medieval studies by a scholar having professional residence in the United States or Canada.
Jean Bony. *The English Decorated Style: Gothic Architecture Transformed 1250–1350*. Oxford University Press.

Frederic G. Melcher Book Award

Established 1964 by the Unitarian Universalist Association. To honor a new work judged to make a significant contribution to religious liberalism.
Jonathan Schell. *The Fate of the Earth*. Knopf.

Mitchell Prizes for the History of Art

Established 1977 and 1982 for, respectively, the outstanding book and the most promising first book on the subject. Presented alternately in New York and London.
Hugh Honour and John Fleming. *A World History of Art*. Macmillan (Great Britain). Published in the United States as *The Visual Arts: A History* by Prentice-Hall.
Keith Christiansen. *Gentile da Fabriano*. Chatto (Great Britain). Published in the United States by Cornell University Press.

Modern Language Association of America

JAMES RUSSELL LOWELL PRIZE. Established 1968. To honor an outstanding literary or linguistic study, a critical edition, or a critical biography by a member of MLA.
Thomas M. Greene. *The Light in Troy: Imitation and Discovery in Renaissance Poetry*. Yale University Press.

HOWARD R. MARRARO PRIZE. Established 1973. Awarded biennially for a distinguished scholarly study on any phase of Italian literature or comparative literature involving Italian.
Not awarded in 1983.

KENNETH W. MILDENBERGER MEDAL. Established 1980. To honor an outstanding research publication in the field of teaching foreign languages and literatures.
Not awarded in 1983.

MINA P. SHAUGHNESSY MEDAL. Established 1980. To honor an outstanding research publication in the field of teaching English language and literature.

Marie Ponsot and Rosemary Deen. *Beat Not the Poor Desk: Writing—What to Teach, How to Teach It, and Why*. Boynton/Cook.

Frank Luther Mott-Kappa Tau Alpha Research Award in Journalism

Established 1944 by the National Journalism Scholarship Society. To honor the best-researched book dealing with the media.

John Naisbitt. *Megatrends*. Warner Books.

Mystery Writers of America Edgar Allan Poe Awards

Established 1945. To recognize outstanding mystery, crime, and suspense writing.

BIOGRAPHICAL/CRITICAL
Roy Hoopes. *Cain*. Holt, Rinehart and Winston.

FACT CRIME
Richard Hammer. *The Vatican Connection*. Holt, Rinehart and Winston.

FIRST NOVEL
Thomas Perry. *The Butcher's Boy*. Scribners.

NOVEL
Rick Boyer. *Billingsgate Shoal*. Houghton Mifflin.

PAPERBACK
Teri White. *Triangle*. Ace/Charter.

SHORT STORY
Frederick Forsyth. "There Are No Snakes in Ireland" from *No Comebacks*. Viking.

GRAND MASTER AWARD
Margaret Millar

National Arts Club Medal of Honor for Literature

Established 1968. To honor a distinguished literary career.

James Laughlin

National Book Critics Circle Book Awards

Established 1975. To encourage excellence in criticism, fiction, nonfiction, and poetry.

BIOGRAPHY/AUTOBIOGRAPHY
Joyce Johnson. *Minor Characters*. Houghton Mifflin.

CRITICISM
John Updike. *Hugging the Shore*. Knopf.

FICTION
William Kennedy. *Ironweed*. Viking.

GENERAL NONFICTION
Seymour Hersh. *The Price of Power: Kissinger in the Nixon White House*. Simon & Schuster.

POETRY
James Merrill. *The Changing Light at Sandover*. Atheneum.

National Catholic Book Awards

Established 1976 (then called Religious Book Awards); cosponsored by Catholic Press Association and Associated Church Press as an outgrowth of the National Catholic Book Awards, administered 1964–1975 by Catholic Press Association. Discontinued 1978. Reinstated 1983. To honor outstanding religious book publishing and stimulate the reading of religious books.

GENERAL BOOKS
John Welch. *Spiritual Pilgrims, Carl Jung and Teresa of Avila*. Paulist Press.

PROFESSIONAL/EDUCATIONAL BOOKS
Adam J. Maida, ed. *Issues in the Labor-Management Dialogue: Church Perspectives*. Catholic Health Association.

QUALITY OF DESIGN AND PRODUCTION
Regis J. Armstrong and Ignatius Brady, tr. *Francis and Clare, The Complete Works*. Paulist Press.
Simon Tugwell, ed. *Early Dominicans: Selected Writings*. Paulist Press.

National Council of Teachers of English

ALAN AWARD. Established 1974 by the NCTE Assembly on Literature for Adolescents. For significant contributions to the field of adolescent literature.

Kenneth Donelson. Research and writing on the use, effect, and history of adolescent literature in a special issue of the *Arizona English Bulletin*.

AWARDS FOR EXCELLENCE IN SCIENTIFIC AND TECHNICAL WRITING. Established 1981 by the NCTE Committee on Technical and Scientific Communication. For excellence in scientific and technical writing.

Carolyn J. Mullins. *The Complete Manuscript Preparation Style Guide*. Prentice-Hall.

GEORGE ORWELL AWARD. Established 1975 by the NCTE Committee on Public Doublespeak. To recognize an outstanding piece of writing combating the use of deceptive language by spokespersons in the United States.

Haig A. Bosmajian. *The Language of Oppression*. Public Affairs Press, 1976; University Press of America, 1983.

DAVID H. RUSSELL AWARD. Established 1963. For distinguished research in the teaching of English.
Margaret Donaldson. *Children's Minds*. Norton.

National Jewish Book Awards

Established 1948 by the Jewish Book Council. To promote American Jewish literary creativity and an appreciation of Jewish literature.

GERRARD AND ELLA BERMAN AWARD FOR A BOOK OF JEWISH HISTORY
Yosef Hayim Yerushalmi. *Zakhor: Jewish History and Jewish Memory*. University of Washington Press.

FRANK AND ETHEL COHEN AWARD FOR A BOOK OF JEWISH THOUGHT
Bernard Septimus. *Hispano-Jewish Culture in Transition: The Career and Controversies of Ramah*. Harvard University Press.

WILLIAM AND JANICE EPSTEIN AWARD FOR A BOOK OF JEWISH FICTION
Robert Greenfield. *Temple*. Summit Books.

LEON L. GILDESGAME AWARD FOR VISUAL ARTS
Andrew S. Ackerman and Susan L. Braunstein. *Israel in Antiquity*. Jewish Museum.

LEON JOLSON AWARD FOR A BOOK ON THE HOLOCAUST
Irving Abella and Harold Troper. *None Is Too Many: Canada and the Jews of Europe 1933–1948*. Lester and Orpen Dennys; Random House, U.S. dist.

MORRIS J. KAPLUN MEMORIAL AWARD FOR A BOOK ON ISRAEL
J. Robert Moskin. *Among Lions*. Arbor House.

SARAH H. KUSHNER MEMORIAL AWARD FOR SCHOLARSHIP
Jeremy Cohen. *Friars and Jews*. Cornell University Press.

WORKMEN'S CIRCLE AWARD FOR YIDDISH LITERATURE
Chaim Spilberg and Yaacov Zipper. *Canadian Jewish Anthology*. National Committee on Yiddish of the Canadian Jewish Congress.

Nebula Awards. *See* Science Fiction Writers of America Nebula Awards

Frederic W. Ness Book Award

Established 1979 by the Association of American Colleges. To honor a significant contribution to studies on liberal education.
Howard R. Bowen. *The State of the Nation and the Agenda for Higher Education*. Jossey-Bass.

Flannery O'Connor Short Fiction Awards

Established 1981 by the University of Georgia Press. Awarded in honor of the late writer, winning manuscripts to be published by the Press.
Sandra Thompson. *Close-Ups*.

Ohioana Book Awards

Established 1929 by Ohioana Library Association. To honor Ohio writers, to acquaint the public with their books, and to collect these books in one place, thereby preserving the culture and traditions of the state.

FICTION
Helen Hooven Santmyer. *"...And Ladies of the Club."* Ohio State University Press, 1982; Putnam, 1984.

HISTORY
Lawrence J. Friedman. *Gregarious Saints*. Cambridge University Press.

OHIO SUBJECTS
James Westwater. *Ohio*. Graphic Arts Center Publishing Co.

FLORENCE ROBERTS HEAD MEMORIAL AWARD. Established 1963. To honor the first director of the association and to recognize a book about the Ohio scene.
Jack Bickham. *I Still Dream about Columbus*. St. Martin's Press.

SCIENCE
Milton B. Trautman. Six books on biological subjects, including *The Fishes of Ohio*. Ohio State University Press.

PEN American Center Awards

AMERICAN-SCANDINAVIAN FOUNDATION/PEN TRANSLATION PRIZES. Established 1981. To honor previously unpublished translations of poetry and fiction by Danish, Finnish, Icelandic, Norwegian, and Swedish writers born in the last century.

FICTION
Not awarded in 1983.

POETRY
Not awarded in 1983.

ERNEST HEMINGWAY FOUNDATION AWARD. Established 1976, donated by Mary Hemingway in honor of her husband. For a first work of fiction by an American.
Bobbie Ann Mason. *Shiloh and Other Stories*. Harper & Row.

PEN/ROGER KLEIN AWARD FOR EDITING. Established 1970, sponsored by PEN American Center beginning 1982. Given biennially to an editor who has an outstanding record of recognizing writing talent, and of helping authors of serious literature to realize their full potential through a sensitivity for, and commitment to, the work of editing.

Not awarded in 1983.

PEN MEDAL FOR TRANSLATION. Established 1982. To honor translators who have demonstrated in their careers exceptional commitment to excellence through the body of their work.

Not awarded in 1983.

PEN PUBLISHER CITATION. Established 1976. For distinctive and continuous service to international letters, to the freedom and dignity of writers, and to the free transmission of the printed word across the barriers of poverty, ignorance, censorship, and repression.

Not awarded in 1983.

PEN TRANSLATION COMMITTEE RENATO POGGIOLI TRANSLATION AWARDS. Established 1978, sponsored in 1983 for the first time by Arnaldo Mondadori Editore (Milan) and the Ingram Merrill Foundation. To a young translator for an unpublished manuscript of a work of Italian literature.

Sarah Henry. *Uomini e No (Men and No Others)* by Elio Vittorini.

Janice Thresher. *Early Novellas of Giovanni Verga.*

PEN TRANSLATION PRIZE. Established 1963 by Book-of-the-Month Club. For a superior book-length translation into English published in the preceding year.

Richard Wilbur. *Four Comedies* (Molière). Harcourt Brace Jovanovich.

PEN WRITING AWARDS FOR PRISONERS. Established 1972 by the Prison Writing Committee. To promote literacy and literature in America's prisons.

FICTION (MALCOLM BRALY PRIZE)
Steven Pannell. *A Simple Game of Chance.*

NONFICTION
Nicholas Wolf. *Tour San Quentin.*

POETRY (MURIEL RUKEYSER PRIZE)
W. M. Aberg. *Reductions.*

PEN American Center and PEN South PEN/Faulkner Award for Fiction

Established 1981. For a book of fiction by an American.
Toby Olson. *Seaview.* New Directions.

PEN Los Angeles Center

Established 1982. For writing that exemplifies the principles of freedom of expression.

DISTINGUISHED BODY OF WORK AWARD
Christopher Isherwood

FIRST PUBLISHED WORK OF FICTION AWARD
Henry Bean. *False Match.* Poseidon Press.

FIRST PUBLISHED WORK OF POETRY AWARD
Thom Dunn. *Passages of Joy.* Farrar, Straus & Giroux.

MAXWELL PERKINS EDITORS AWARD
Barry Gifford

THOMAS THOMPSON NONFICTION BOOK AWARD
Tom Reiterman. *Raven: The Untold Story of the Reverend Jim Jones and His People.* Dutton.

PSP Awards (Professional and Scholarly Publishing Division, AAP)

Established 1976 by the Technical, Scientific, and Medical Division (TSM) of the Association of American Publishers. To honor those publishing companies who have published the year's most outstanding books in the fields of science, medicine, technology, and business; in addition, the R. R. Hawkins Award is presented to the publisher of the single most outstanding book of the year, selected from among the year's winners. Names of the division and the awards were changed in 1980.

ARCHITECTURE AND URBAN PLANNING
Adolf K. Placzek. *Macmillan Encyclopedia of Architects.* Macmillan/Free Press.

BOOK DESIGN AND PRODUCTION
Edward C. Papenfuse and Joseph M. Coale III. *The Hammond-Harwood House Atlas of Historical Maps of Maryland, 1608–1908.* Johns Hopkins University Press.

BUSINESS, MANAGEMENT, AND ECONOMICS
William O. Cleverley, ed. *Handbook of Health Care Accounting and Finance.* Aspen Systems Corporation.

ENGINEERING
Gabriel Salvendy, ed. *Handbook of Industrial Engineering.* John Wiley & Sons.

R. R. HAWKINS AWARD
Sybil P. Parker, ed. *Synopsis and Classification of Living Organisms*, Vols. 1 and 2. McGraw-Hill.

HEALTH SCIENCES
Marvin Wagner and Thomas L. Lawson. *Segmental Anatomy: Applications to Clinical Medicine.* Macmillan.

HUMANITIES
Charlotte Streifer Rubinstein. *American Women Artists: From Early Indian Times to the Present.* G. K. Hall.

LAW
Richard A. Givens, ed. *Legal Strategies for Industrial Innovation.* Shepard's/McGraw-Hill.

LIFE SCIENCES

Ernst Mayr. *The Growth of Biological Thought: Diversity, Evolution, and Inheritance.* Harvard University Press.

MOST CREATIVE AND INNOVATIVE NEW PROJECT

Linda Schele. *Maya Glyphs: The Verbs.* University of Texas Press.

PHYSICAL AND EARTH SCIENCES

Gerard R. Case. *A Pictorial Guide to Fossils.* Van Nostrand Reinhold.

SOCIAL AND BEHAVIORAL SCIENCES

Stanley H. Cath, Alan R. Gurwitt, and John Munder Ross. *Father and Child: Developmental and Clinical Perspectives.* Little, Brown.

TECHNOLOGY

Carl H. Meyer and Stephen M. Matyas. *Cryptography: A New Dimension in Computer Data Security.* John Wiley & Sons.

Pegasus Prize for Literature

Established 1977 by Mobil Corporation. To introduce American readers to important works from countries whose literature is rarely translated into English, winning books to be published by Louisiana State University Press.

Not awarded in 1983.

Pfizer Award

Established 1959 by the History of Science Society. To honor the best book on the history of science published in the preceding three years.

Richard S. Westfall. *Never at Rest: A Biography of Isaac Newton.* Cambridge University Press.

Phi Beta Kappa Book Awards

RALPH WALDO EMERSON AWARD. Established 1960. For a study of the intellectual and cultural condition of man.

Daniel Joseph Singal. *The War Within.* University of North Carolina Press.

CHRISTIAN GAUSS AWARD. Established 1950. For a book in the field of literary scholarship or criticism.

W. R. Johnson. *The Idea of Lyric.* University of California Press.

SCIENCE AWARD. Established 1959. For an outstanding contribution by a scientist to the literature of science.

Stephen Jay Gould. *Hen's Teeth and Horses' Toes.* Norton.

Edgar Allan Poe Awards. *See* Mystery Writers of America Edgar Allan Poe Awards

Poetry Society of America

MELVILLE CANE AWARD. Established 1960 by Harcourt Brace Jovanovich. To honor, in alternate years, an outstanding book of poems and a book on poetry or a poet.

Ian Hamilton. *Robert Lowell: A Biography.* Random House.

ALICE FAY DI CASTAGNOLA AWARD. Established 1965. Awarded to a work in progress (prose, verse, or verse drama) by a member of the Poetry Society of America, in honor of a benefactor of the society.

Thomas Lux. *Fireplace Full of Crutches.*

SHELLEY MEMORIAL AWARD. Established 1929. For a poet or poets judged most deserving on the basis of published work and financial need.

Jon Anderson
Leo Connellan

WILLIAM CARLOS WILLIAMS AWARD. Established 1978. For a book of poetry published by a small press, a nonprofit press, or a university press.

David Wojahn. *Icehouse Lights.* Yale University Press.

George Polk Memorial Awards in Journalism

Established 1948 by the Long Island University department of journalism. To honor outstanding achievement in journalism, in books, and other media.

No book award in 1983.

Pulitzer Prizes in Letters

Established 1917. To honor distinguished works by American writers, dealing preferably with American themes.

BIOGRAPHY

Russell Baker. *Growing Up.* Congdon & Weed.

FICTION

Alice Walker. *The Color Purple.* Harcourt Brace Jovanovich.

GENERAL NONFICTION

Susan Sheehan. *Is There No Place on Earth for Me?* Houghton Mifflin.

HISTORY

Rhys L. Isaac. *The Transformation of Virginia, 1740–1790.* University of North Carolina Press.

POETRY

Galway Kinnell. *Selected Poems.* Houghton Mifflin.

Harold U. Ribalow Prize

Established 1982 by Hadassah, administered by *Hadassah Magazine.* To honor the best work of fiction on a Jewish theme.

Chaim Grade (posthumous). *Rabbis and Wives.* Knopf.

San Francisco Foundation Awards

JOSEPH HENRY JACKSON AWARD. Established 1957 as a grant-in-aid to the author of an unpublished work of fiction, nonfiction prose, or poetry.

Michael Covino. *Full Particulars* (short stories).

JAMES D. PHELAN AWARD. Established 1935 as an award to the author of an unpublished work of fiction, nonfictional prose, poetry, or drama.

Gary Young. *A Dream of a Moral Life* (poetry).

Delmore Schwartz Memorial Poetry Award

Established 1970 by friends of the late poet, administered by the New York University College of Arts and Science. Awarded periodically (not annually) to a young poet of exceptional promise or to a more mature poet who, in the opinion of the selection committee, has received insufficient acclaim.

Sherod Santos. *Accidental Weather*. Doubleday.

Science Fiction Research Association

JOHN W. CAMPBELL MEMORIAL AWARD. Established 1972. To honor an outstanding science fiction novel.

Brian Aldiss. *Helliconia Spring*. Atheneum.

PILGRIM AWARD. Established 1971. To honor outstanding contributions to science fiction and fantasy scholarship.

H. Bruce Franklin

Science Fiction Writers of America Nebula Awards

Established 1965. To honor outstanding works of science fiction.

NOVEL

Michael Bishop. *No Enemy but Time*. Timescape.

NOVELETTE

Connie Willis. "Fire Watch." *Isaac Asimov's SF Magazine* 2/15/82.

NOVELLA

John Kessel. "Another Orphan." *Fantasy & Science Fiction* 9/82.

SHORT STORY

Connie Willis. "A Letter from the Clearys." *Isaac Asimov's SF Magazine* 7/82.

Charles Scribner's Sons Book Awards

MAXWELL PERKINS PRIZE. Established 1982. For a first work of fiction about the American experience, winning book to be published by Scribners.

Stephen Wright. *Meditations in Green*.

SCRIBNER CRIME NOVEL AWARD. Established 1982. For a first mystery, winning book to be published by Scribners.

Ted Wood. *Dead in the Water*.

Kenneth B. Smilen/Present Tense Literary Awards

Established 1980 by the American Jewish Committee and Kenneth B. Smilen. To honor authors and translators of works that have intrinsic value and lasting quality, and reflect humane Jewish values.

BIOGRAPHY/AUTOBIOGRAPHY

Elisabeth Young-Bruehl. *Hannah Arendt: For Love of the World*. Yale University Press.

FICTION

Aharon Megged. *Asahel*. Taplinger.

GENERAL NONFICTION

Thérèse and Mendel Metzger. *Jewish Life in the Middle Ages*. Alpine Fine Arts Editions.

HISTORY

David Vital. *Zionism: The Formative Years*. Oxford University Press.

OUTSTANDING CONTRIBUTION TO JEWISH LITERATURE

Gabriel Preil

SOCIAL AND POLITICAL ANALYSIS

Stephen Sharot. *Messianism, Mysticism and Magic*. University of North Carolina Press.

TRANSLATION

Stephen Mitchell. *Points of Departure*. Yale University Press.
Special Citation: Chaim Potok, representing the committee, on completion of the new translation of the Hebrew Bible.

John Ben Snow Prize

Established 1978 by Syracuse University Press. For an outstanding nonfiction manuscript dealing with some aspect of New York State, especially the upstate area, winner to be published by the Press.

Mary Ann Smith. *Gustav Stickley, the Craftsman*.

Society of Midland Authors Awards

Established in the late 1950s. To recognize outstanding books about the Midwest or by midwestern authors.

BIOGRAPHY

Richard Dunlop. *Donovan: America's Master Spy*. Rand McNally.

FICTION

Susan Engberg. *Pastorale*. University of Illinois Press.

NONFICTION

Robert Pisor. *The End of the Line—The Siege of Khe Sanh.* Norton.

POETRY

Carolyn Forché. *The Country Between Us.* Harper & Row.

SPECIAL 1983 BEST WRITER AWARD FOR A LONG-TIME CAREER OF LITERARY EXCELLENCE

Studs Terkel

Agnes Lynch Starrett Poetry Prize

Established 1981 by the University of Pittsburgh Press in honor of a former director. For an outstanding book of poetry, the winning book to be published by the Press.

Kate Daniels. *The White Wave.*

Texas Institute of Letters

COLLECTORS' INSTITUTE AWARD FOR BEST BOOK DESIGN

Barbara Whitehead and Fred Whitehead, designers. *Journey to Pleasant Hill: The Civil War Letters of Captain Elijah P. Petty, Walker's Texas Division, C.S.A.* University of Texas Institute of Texan Cultures.

CARR P. COLLINS AWARD FOR NONFICTION. Established 1946. For an outstanding book of nonfiction.

Robert A. Caro. *The Path to Power: The Years of Lyndon Johnson,* Vol I. Knopf.

FRIENDS OF THE DALLAS PUBLIC LIBRARY AWARD. Established 1960. To honor a book that makes an important contribution to knowledge.

David J. Weber. *The Mexican Frontier, 1821–1846: The American Southwest under Mexico.* University of New Mexico Press.

JESSE JONES AWARD FOR FICTION. Established 1960. To honor an outstanding book of fiction.

Allen Hannay. *Love & Other Natural Disasters.* Atlantic-Little, Brown.

SPECIAL AWARDS FOR CONTINUING EXCELLENCE IN TEXAS LETTERS

John Graves

Glen Rose

VOERTMAN'S POETRY AWARD. Established 1945 as the Daedalian Poetry Award; sponsored by Paul Voertman since 1965. For an outstanding volume of poetry.

Naomi Shihab Nye. *Hugging the Jukebox.* Dutton.

Thomas Whitbread. *Whomp and Moonshiver.* Boa Editions.

Union League Club Abraham Lincoln Literary Award

Established 1977. To honor an author's contribution to American literature.

William Manchester. *The Last Lion, Winston Spencer Churchill: Visions of Glory 1874–1932.* Little, Brown.

Western Heritage Awards

Established 1960 by the National Cowboy Hall of Fame and Western Heritage Center. To encourage writing about the West with accuracy and artistic quality.

ART BOOK

William Albert Allard, author/photographer. *Vanishing Breed: Photographs of the Cowboy and the West.* New York Graphic Society/Little, Brown.

MAGAZINE ARTICLE

Patricia Nell Warren. "Saga of an American Ranch." *Reader's Digest.*

NONFICTION BOOK

Margaret F. Maxwell. *A Passion for Freedom: The Life of Sharlot Hall.* University of Arizona Press.

Laurence L. Winship Book Award

Established 1975 by the *Boston Globe* in honor of its late editor. For a book having some relation to New England, in author, theme, plot, or locale.

Cynthia Zaitzevsky. *Frederick Law Olmstead and the Boston Park System.* Harvard University Press.

Nero Wolfe Award for Mystery Fiction

Established 1979 by the Wolfe Pack. For the best of the year in this genre.

Martha Grimes. *The Anodyne Necklace.* Little, Brown.

World Fantasy Convention Awards

Established 1975 by a committee of fantasy writers, editors, publishers, and fans. To honor excellence and achievement in the categories listed.

ANTHOLOGY

Charles L. Grant, ed. *Nightmare Seasons.* Doubleday.

LIFE ACHIEVEMENT AWARD

Roald Dahl

NOVEL

Michael Shea. *Nifft the Lean.* DAW Books.

NOVELLA

Karl Edward Wagner. "Beyond All Measure." *Whispers* 15/16.

SHORT STORY

Tanith Lee. "The Gorgon." *Shadows* 5.

World Science Fiction Convention Awards

JOHN W. CAMPBELL AWARD. Established 1955. To an author whose first professional story was published during the two years preceding presentation of the award.
Paul O. Williams

HUGO AWARDS. Established 1955. For outstanding science fiction writing in the categories listed.

NONFICTION BOOK
James Gunn. *Isaac Asimov: The Foundations of Science Fiction.* Oxford University Press.

NOVEL
Isaac Asimov. *Foundation's Edge.* Doubleday.

NOVELLA
Joanna Russ. "Souls." *Fantasy & Science Fiction* 1/82.

NOVELETTE
Connie Willis. "Fire Watch." *Isaac Asimov's SF Magazine* 2/15/82.

SHORT STORY
Spider Robinson. "Melancholy Elephants." *Analog* 6/82.

Yale Series of Younger Poets

Established 1919 by Yale University Press. To provide a medium for publication of a first volume of poetry by poets under forty who have not previously published a volume of verse, winning manuscript to be published by the Press.
Richard Kenney. *The Evolution of the Flightless Bird.*

Children's Awards (U.S.A.)

Jane Addams Peace Association Children's Book Award

Established 1953. For the book that most effectively promotes peace, social justice, and world community.
Toshi Maruki. *Hiroshima No Pika.* Lothrop, Lee & Shepard.

American Book Awards

Established 1980 (successor to National Book Awards). To honor living American authors for the best books of the year.

FICTION
Hardcover: Jean Fritz. *Homesick: My Own Story.* Putnam.
Paperback: Paula Fox. *A Place Apart.* Signet/New American Library.
Paperback: Joyce Carol Thomas. *Marked by Fire.* Avon Flare.

NONFICTION
James Cross Giblin; illustrated by Margot Tomes. *Chimney Sweeps.* T. Y. Crowell.

PICTURE BOOKS
Hardcover: Barbara Cooney. *Miss Rumphius.* Viking.
Hardcover: William Steig. *Doctor De Soto.* Farrar, Straus & Giroux.
Paperback: Mary Ann Hoberman; illustrated by Betty Fraser. *A House Is a House for Me.* Puffin Books/Viking.

Association for Library Service to Children of the American Library Association, administrator

MILDRED L. BATCHELDER AWARD. Established 1966. To honor an American publisher for a children's book considered to be most outstanding of those books originally published in a foreign language in a foreign country and subsequently published in English in the United States.
Toshi Maruki. *Hiroshima No Pika.* Lothrop, Lee & Shepard.

CALDECOTT MEDAL. Established 1942 by Frederic G. Melcher, R. R. Bowker Company. To honor the artist of the most distinguished picture book.
Marcia Brown. *Shadow.* Scribners.

NEWBERY MEDAL. Established 1922 by Frederic G. Melcher, R. R. Bowker Company. To honor the author of the most distinguished contribution to American literature for children.
Cynthia Voight. *Dicey's Song.* Atheneum.

LAURA INGALLS WILDER MEDAL. Established 1954. Given triennially to an author or illustrator whose books, published in the United States, have made a substantial and lasting contribution to literature for children.
Maurice Sendak

Association of Jewish Libraries Children's Book Awards

Established 1968. To honor the books and writers deemed to have made the most outstanding contribution in the field of Jewish literature for children and young people.

CHILDREN'S BOOK AWARD
Linda Heller. *Castle on Hester Street.* Jewish Publication Society of America.

CHILDREN'S BOOK AWARD FOR OLDER CHILDREN
Marilyn Sachs. *Call Me Ruth.* Doubleday.

Association of Logos Bookstores Book Award

Established 1981. To honor excellence in religious publishing.
Not awarded in 1983.

Batchelder Award. *See* Association for Library Service to Children of the American Library Association, administrator

Irma Simonton Black Award

Established 1972 by the Bank Street College of Education. For unified excellence of story line, language, and illustration in a published work for young children.

Charlotte Graeber; illustrated by Donna Diamond. *Mustard*. Doubleday.

Boston Globe-Horn Book Awards

Established 1967. To foster and reward excellence in text and illustration.

FICTION

Virginia Hamilton. *Sweet Whispers, Brother Rush*. Philomel.

ILLUSTRATION

Vera B. Williams. *A Chair for My Mother*. Greenwillow.

NONFICTION

Daniel S. Davis. *Behind Barbed Wire: The Imprisonment of Japanese Americans during World War II*. Dutton.

Caldecott Medal. *See* Association for Library Service to Children of the American Library Association, administrator

Catholic Library Association Regina Medal

Established 1959. To honor excellence in the writing of literature for children.

Tomie De Paola

Christopher Awards

Established 1949 by the Christophers. To honor books that affirm the highest values of the human spirit, exhibit artistic and technical proficiency, and attain a significant degree of public acceptance.

Jim Arnosky. *Drawing from Nature*. Lothrop, Lee & Shepard.
Jean Fritz; illustrated by Margot Tomes. *Homesick: My Own Story*. Putnam.
Zibby Oneal. *A Formal Feeling*. Viking.
James Stevenson. *We Can't Sleep*. Greenwillow.

Commonwealth Club of California Book Awards

Established 1930. To honor the finest works of literature by California authors.

SILVER MEDAL

Children's Book: Margot Zemach. *Jake and Honeybunch Go to Heaven*. Farrar, Straus & Giroux.

Delacorte Press First Young Adult Novel Prize

Established 1982. To encourage the writing of contemporary young adult fiction.

Joyce Sweeney. *The Center Line*. Delacorte Press.

English-Speaking Union Books-Across-the-Sea Ambassador of Honor Books

Established 1942. For books of outstanding merit sent to English-speaking countries abroad to serve as interpreters of American life and culture.

Diana H. Cross and Jan Brett. *Some Birds Have Funny Names*. Crown.
Jean Lipman with Margaret Aspinwall. *Alexander Calder and His Magical Mobiles*. Hudson Hills Press.
John F. Loeper. *The House on Spruce Street*. Atheneum.
Lorus J. Milne and Margery Milne. *Dreams of a Perfect Earth*. Atheneum.
Helen Plotz. *Gladly Learn and Gladly Teach: Poems of the School Experience*. Greenwillow.
Cynthia Rylant and Diane Goode. *When I Was Young in the Mountains*. Dutton.

Dorothy Canfield Fisher Children's Book Award

Established 1957, sponsored by Vermont Department of Libraries and Vermont Congress of Parents and Teachers, winning book voted on by schoolchildren. To encourage the state's children to read and to honor a distinguished Vermont author.

Judy Blume. *Tiger Eyes*. Bradbury.

Friends of American Writers

Established 1960 by a group in the Chicago area. To encourage and promote high standards and ideals among American writers.

Kathy Callaway. *Bloodroot Flower*. Knopf.
Huynh Quang Nhuong. *The Land I Lost*. Harper & Row.

Friends of the Chicago Public Library Carl Sandburg Award

Established 1979. To recognize exceptional achievement in literature by Chicago-area writers.

Mildred Johnson. *Wait, Skates!* Childrens Press.

Garden State Children's Book Awards

Established 1977, winners chosen by a committee of the Children's Services Section of the New Jersey Library Association. To honor literary merit and popularity with readers.

EASY-TO-READ BOOKS

James Stevenson. *Clams Can't Sing*. Greenwillow.

Jane Yolen. *Commander Toad in Space*. Coward, McCann & Geoghegan.

YOUNGER FICTION

Judy Blume. *Superfudge*. Dutton.

YOUNGER NONFICTION

Mary Beth Sullivan and Linda Bourke; illustrated by Linda Bourke. *A Show of Hands: Say It in Sign Language*. Addison-Wesley.

Georgia Children's Book Awards

Established 1968 and 1976 by the College of Education, University of Georgia, winning books voted on by schoolchildren. To encourage reading.

GEORGIA CHILDREN'S BOOK AWARD (1968)

Judy Blume. *Superfudge*. Dutton.

GEORGIA CHILDREN'S PICTURE STORYBOOK AWARD (1976)

Carol Chapman; illustrated by Kelly Oechsli. *Herbie's Troubles*. Dutton.

Golden Kite Awards

Established 1973, expanded 1977, by the Society of Children's Book Writers, to give separate recognition to fiction and nonfiction. To honor excellence in writing and genuine appeal to the interests and concerns of children.

FICTION

Beverly Cleary. *Ralph S. Mouse*. Morrow.

ILLUSTRATION

Tomie De Paola. *Marianna May and Nursey*. Holiday House.

NONFICTION

James Giblin. *Chimney Sweeps*. Clarion Books.

International Reading Association Children's Book Award

Established 1975 by the Institute for Reading Research. For a first or second book, either fiction or nonfiction, by an author from any country and writing in any language, who shows unusual promise.

Meredith Ann Pierce. *The Darkangel*. Atlantic/Little, Brown.

Irvin Kerlan Award

Established 1975 by the Kerlan Collection Committee, University of Minnesota. For singular attainments in the creation of children's literature.

Katherine Paterson

Coretta Scott King Award

Established 1970 by American Library Association. To honor Coretta Scott King and the late Martin Luther King, Jr.; to encourage writers and artists to promote the cause of peace and brotherhood through their works; and to inspire children and youth to dedicate their talents and energies to help achieve these goals.

Virginia Hamilton. *Sweet Whispers, Brother Rush*. Philomel.

Evelyn Sibley Lampman Award

Established 1982 by the Oregon Library Association. To honor an author who has made a significant contribution to the Pacific Northwest area in children's literature.

Patricia Feehan

Mystery Writers of America Edgar Allan Poe Award

Established 1945. To recognize outstanding contributions to mystery, crime, and suspense writing.

Robbie Branscum. *The Murder of Hound Dog Bates*. Viking.

National Catholic Book Awards

Established 1976 (then called Religious Book Awards); cosponsored by Catholic Press Association and Associated Church Press as an outgrowth of the National Catholic Book Awards, administered 1964–1975 by Catholic Press Association. Discontinued 1978. Reinstated 1983. To honor outstanding religious book publishing and stimulate the reading of religious books.

CHILDREN'S AND YOUTH BOOKS

David R. Collins; Mary Beth Froehlich, illustrator. *Thomas Merton: Monk with a Mission*. St. Anthony Messenger Press.

National Council of Teachers of English Award for Excellence in Poetry for Children

Not awarded in 1983.

National Jewish Book Award

Established 1948 by the Jewish Book Council. To promote American Jewish literary creativity and an appreciation of Jewish literature.

WILLIAM FRANK MEMORIAL AWARD FOR CHILDREN'S LITERATURE

Barbara Cohen. *King of the Seventh Grade*. Lothrop, Lee & Shepard.

MARCIA AND LOUIS POSNER AWARD FOR CHILDREN'S PICTURE BOOKS

Barbara Cohen; illustrated by Michael Deraney. *Yussel's Prayer: A Yom Kippur Story*. Lothrop, Lee & Shepard.

Nene Award

Established 1964 by the Hawaii Association of School Librarians and the Children's and Youth Section, Hawaii Library Association, winning book voted on by the state's schoolchildren.

Deborah Howe and James Howe. *Bunnicula: A Rabbit Tale of Mystery*. Atheneum.

New York Academy of Sciences Children's Science Book Awards

Established 1971. To encourage the writing of more high-quality books about science for children.

OLDER CATEGORY

Judith St. George. *The Brooklyn Bridge*. Putnam.

YOUNGER CATEGORY

Joanne Rider; illustrated by Lynne Cherry. *The Snail's Spell*. Frederick Warne.

SPECIAL AWARD FOR A BEAUTIFULLY PHOTOGRAPHED SERIES OF REFERENCE BOOKS FOR YOUNGER CHILDREN

Lerner Natural Science Books.

New York Times Best Illustrated Children's Book Awards

Established 1952. To encourage better-quality art in children's books.

Leonard Baskin. *Leonard Baskin's Miniature Natural History: First Series*. Pantheon.

Henrik Drescher. *Simon's Book*. Lothrop, Lee & Shepard.

Roy Gerrard. *The Favershams*. Farrar, Straus & Giroux.

Ann Jonas. *Round Trip*. Greenwillow.

Martin Leman. *Twelve Cats for Christmas*. Pelham/Merrimack Publishers' Circle.

Ken Robbins. *Tools*. Four Winds.

Chris Van Allsburg. *The Wreck of the Zephyr*. Houghton Mifflin.

Ed Young. *Up a Tree*. Harper & Row.

Lisbeth Zwerger. *Little Red Cap* by the Brothers Grimm. William Morrow.

Newbery Medal. *See* Association for Library Service to Children of the American Library Association, administrator

PEN–Los Angeles Center

Established 1982. For children's books that exemplify the principles of freedom of expression.

Clare Bell. *Ratha's Creature*. Atheneum.

Zilpha Keatley Snider. *The Birds of Summer*. Atheneum.

Edgar Allan Poe Award. *See* Mystery Writers of America Edgar Allan Poe Award

Regina Medal. *See* Catholic Library Association Regina Medal

Kenneth Smilen/Present Tense Literary Award

Established 1980 by the American Jewish Committee and Kenneth B. Smilen. To honor authors and translators of works that have intrinsic value and lasting quality, and reflect humane Jewish values.

Barbara Cohen. *King of the Seventh Grade*. Lothrop, Lee & Shepard.

Society of Midland Authors Awards

Established late 1950s. To recognize outstanding books about the Midwest or by midwestern authors.

Patricia DeMuth. *Joel Growing Up a Farm Man*. Dodd, Mead.

Southern California Council on Literature for Children and Young People

Established 1961. To acknowledge outstanding books, illustrations, and bodies of work by Southern California authors and illustrators; in addition, the Dorothy C. McKenzie Award, named for the council's founder, honors an individual for significant endeavors on behalf of children and books.

CONTRIBUTION OF CULTURAL SIGNIFICANCE

Clayton Bess. *Story for a Black Night*. Houghton Mifflin.

DISTINGUISHED WORK OF FICTION

Patricia Beatty. *Jonathan Down Under*. Morrow.

DISTINGUISHED WORK OF NONFICTION

Ann Elwood and Linda Wood. *Windows in Space*. Walker.

EXCELLENCE IN A SERIES

Tom Bethancourt. Doris Fein Mysteries. Holiday House.

DOROTHY McKENZIE AWARD FOR SERVICE ON BEHALF OF CHILDREN AND LITERATURE

Michael Cart

Texas Bluebonnet Award

Established 1980 by Texas Association of School Librarians and Children's Round Table (two units of the Texas Library Association), winning book chosen by vote of schoolchildren. To recognize children's reading interests and preferences, to encourage discriminating reading among children, and to recognize writers of creative and enjoyable books.

Bill Wallace. *A Dog Called Kitty*. Holiday House.

University of Southern Mississippi School of Library Service Silver Medallion

Established 1969. To honor an author or illustrator

whose entire body of work constitutes an outstanding contribution to the field of children's literature.
Katherine Paterson

Washington Post/Children's Book Guild Nonfiction Award

Established 1977. Awarded to an author of nonfiction in recognition of a total body of work. Formerly known as Children's Book Guild Nonfiction Book Award.
Patricia Lauber

William Allen White Children's Book Award

Established 1952 by Emporia Kansas State University and Ruth Garver Gagliardo, winning book voted on by schoolchildren. To honor the memory of one of the state's most distinguished citizens by encouraging the children of Kansas to read and enjoy good books.
Barbara Brooks Wallace. *Peppermints in the Parlor.* Atheneum.

Young Hoosier Book Award

Established 1975 by the Association for Indiana Media Educators, winning book voted on by schoolchildren. To encourage recreational reading by upper elementary children.
Judy Blume. *Superfudge.* Dutton.

Adult Awards (Foreign)

Alice Hunt Bartlett Award (Great Britain)

Established 1966 by the Poetry Society. Awarded to poets the society wishes to honor and encourage.
Medbh McGuckian. *The Flower Master.* Oxford University Press.

James Tait Black Memorial Prizes
(Great Britain)

Established 1919 by the University of Edinburgh in honor of a partner in the publishing house of A. & C. Black Ltd. For the best biography and the best novel, respectively, of the year.

BIOGRAPHY
Richard Ellman. *James Joyce.* Oxford University Press.

NOVEL
Bruce Chatwin. *On the Black Hill.* Cape.

Book Publishers Association of New Zealand Wattie Book of the Year
(New Zealand)

Established 1967. To honor literary excellence.
Janet Frame. *To the Is-Land.* Hutchinson.

Booker McConnell Prize for Fiction.

See National Book League (Great Britain), administrator

Books in Canada Award for First Novels
(Canada)

Established 1977 by *Books in Canada.* To recognize literary achievement by a first novelist and to promote the publication of Canadian books.
W. P. Kinsella. *Shoeless Joe.* Houghton Mifflin.

Canada-Australia Literary Prize (Australia and Canada)

Established 1977 by the Department of External Affairs, the Canada Council, and the Australia Council. To make Australians and Canadians familiar with each other's writers; awarded in alternate years to an English-language Australian or Canadian writer for the author's complete works.
Barry Oaklay

Canada Council (Canada)

GOVERNOR GENERAL'S LITERARY AWARDS. Established 1937 by the Canadian Authors Association; administered since 1959 by the Canada Council; honors literary excellence.

ENGLISH-LANGUAGE WORKS
Fiction: Guy Vanderhaeghe. *Man Descending.* Macmillan.
Poetry: Phyllis Webb. *The Vision Tree: Selected Poems.* Talonbooks.
Drama: John Gray. *Billy Bishop Goes to War.* Talonbooks.
Nonfiction: Christopher Moore. *Louisbourg Portraits: Life in an Eighteenth-Century Garrison Town.* Macmillan.

FRENCH-LANGUAGE WORKS
Fiction: Roger Fournier. *Le cercle des arènes.* Albin Michel.
Poetry: Michel Savard. *Forages.* Editions du Noroît.
Theatre: Réjean Ducharme. *H A ha!...* Editions Lacombe.
Nonfiction: Maurice Lagueux. *Le marxisme des années soixante: une saison dans l'histoire de la pensée critique.* Hurtubise HMH.

TRANSLATION PRIZES. Established 1974. To honor the best translations (one in English and one in French), in recognition of the increasingly important role played by this discipline in communications, the arts, and culture in Canada.
English into French: Claude Aubry. *Je t'attends à Peggy's Cove* by Brian Doyle. Exile Editions.
French into English: Raymond Y. Chamberlain, Jr. *Jos Connaissant* by Victor-Lévy Beaulieu. Cercle du Livre de France.

Canadian Authors Association Literary Awards (Canada)

Established 1937, reinstituted 1975. To honor writing that achieves literary excellence without sacrificing popular appeal.

DRAMA
W. O. Mitchell. *Back to Beulah*. Macmillan.

NONFICTION
Christina McCall-Newman. *Grits*. Macmillan.

NOVEL
W. P. Kinsella. *Shoeless Joe*. Houghton Mifflin.

POETRY
George Amabile. *"the presence of fire."* McClelland & Stewart.

Duff Cooper Memorial Prize (Great Britain)

Established 1956. For a distinguished book written in English or French on a subject of history, biography, politics, or poetry.
Richard Ellman. *James Joyce*. Oxford University Press.

Geoffrey Faber Memorial Prize (Great Britain)

Established 1963 by Faber & Faber Ltd. as a memorial to the founder and first chairman of the firm. To honor, in alternate years, a volume of verse and a volume of prose fiction.
Graham Swift. *Shuttlecock*. Faber & Faber.

Prix Femina (France)

Established 1904 by a group of women writers in connection with the reviews *Femina* and *Vie Heureuse*; originally called the Prix Vie Heureuse, and given to either poetry or prose, now established as a novel prize.
Florence Delay. *Riche et légère*. Gallimard.

Prix Goncourt (France)

Established 1903 by the Académie Goncourt. For a work of imagination in prose, preferably a novel, exemplifying youth, originality, *esprit*, and form.
Frederick Tristan. *Les Egarés*. Balland.

Guardian Fiction Prize (Great Britain)

Established 1965 by the Manchester *Guardian*. To honor a novel of originality and promise by a British or Commonwealth writer.
Graham Swift. *Waterland*. Heinemann.

Prix Interallié (France)

Established 1930 by a group of journalists. For a distinguished novel.
Jacques Duquesne. *Maria Vandamme*. Grasset.

Jerusalem Prize (Israel)

Established 1963 by the Jerusalem Municipality at the first Jerusalem International Book Fair. Given biennially to honor an author who has contributed to the understanding of the freedom of the individual in society.
V. S. Naipaul

Prix Médicis (France)

Established 1958. To honor experimental fiction written in French.
Jean Echenoz. *Cherokee*. Editions de Minuit.

Prix Médicis Etranger (France)

Established 1970. For the best foreign novel translated into French.
Kenneth White. *La Route bleue*. Grasset.

National Book League (Great Britain), administrator

BOOKER McCONNELL PRIZE FOR FICTION. Established 1969. For a full-length novel in English by a citizen of Britain or the British Commonwealth, Republic of Ireland, or South Africa.
J. M. Coetzee. *The Life and Times of Michael K*. Secker & Warburg.

COMMONWEALTH POETRY PRIZE. Established 1972. For a first published book of poetry in English by an author from a Commonwealth country other than Britain. Co-sponsored by the Commonwealth Institute.
Grace Nichols. *I Is a Long-Memoried Woman*. Caribbean Cultural International.

THOMAS COOK TRAVEL BOOK AWARDS. Established 1980. For the best travel book and the best guide book.
Vikram Seth. *From Heaven Lake*. Chatto & Windus.
Michael Leapman. *The Companion Guide to New York*. Collins.

MIND BOOK OF THE YEAR—THE ALLEN LANE AWARD. Established 1981. For the book, fiction or nonfiction, that furthers public understanding of the prevention, causes, treatment, or experience of mental illness and/or mental handicap.
Dorothy Rowe. *Depression: The Way Out of Your Prison*. Routledge & Kegan Paul.

H. H. WINGATE PRIZE. Established 1982 in association with the Balfour Diamond Jubilee Trust. To honor the book that best stimulates an interest in and awareness of themes of Jewish concern among a wider reading public. Successor to the *Jewish Chronicle*/H. H. Wingate Literary Award.
Chaim Herzog. *The Arab-Israeli Wars*. Arms & Armour Press.
Chaim Raphael. *The Springs of Jewish Life*. Chatto & Windus.

Neustadt International Prize for Literature
(United States)

Established 1969 by *World Literature Today* (University of Oklahoma) and endowed by the Neustadt family in 1972. Awarded biennially for distinguished and continuing artistic achievement in poetry, drama, or fiction.
Not awarded in 1983.

Nobel Prize for Literature

Established 1901 by the will of Alfred Nobel, administered by the Swedish Academy in Stockholm. To honor the total literary output of a distinguished writer.
William Golding, English novelist

Noma Award for Publishing in Africa (Japan)

Established 1980 by Shoichi Noma of Kodansha, administered by the quarterly *African Book Publishing Record,* Oxford, England. To encourage publication in Africa of books by African writers.
A. N. E. Amissah. *Criminal Procedure in Ghana.* Sedco Publishing Ltd., Accra, Ghana.

Trevor Reese Memorial Prize (Great Britain)

Established 1980 by the University of London Institute of Commonwealth Studies in honor of the late Reader in Commonwealth History at the institute. Awarded biennially to the best scholarly book published in Great Britain in the field of British Imperial and Commonwealth history.
Not awarded in 1983.

Prix Renaudot (France)

Established 1926 by Gaston Picard and a group of journalists, named for Théophraste Renaudot (1558–1653), founder of the first French newspaper. For a distinguished novel.
Jean-Marie Rouart. *Avant-guerre.* Grasset.

Grand Prix du Roman (France)

Established 1912 by the Académie Française. Awarded to a young novelist usually for a work of "higher inspiration."
Liliane Guignabodet. *Natalia.* Albin Michel.

Royal Society of Literature (Great Britain),
administrator

HEINEMANN AWARD. Established 1944. For a genuine contribution to literature.
Derek Walcott. *The Fortunate Traveller.* Faber & Faber.

WINIFRED HOLTBY PRIZE. Established 1966. For the best regional novel.

Kazuo Ishiguro. *Pale View of the Hills.* Faber & Faber.

Seal Books First Novel Award (Canada)

Established 1978. For an outstanding first novel by a Canadian writer.
David Kendall. *Lázaro.* McClelland & Stewart; Seal Books.
Jonathan Webb. *Pluck.* McClelland & Stewart; Seal Books.

Society of Authors (Great Britain), administrator

CHOLMONDELEY AWARD. Established 1965. For contributions to poetry.
John Fuller
Craig Raine
Anthony Thwaite

ERIC GREGORY TRUST AWARDS. Established 1959. For poets under the age of thirty.
Martin Stokes
Hilary Davis
Michael O'Neill
Lisa St. Aubin de Teran
Deirdre Shanahan

HAWTHORNDEN PRIZE. Established 1919. For a work of imaginative literature by an English writer under the age of forty-one.
Timothy Mo. *Sour Sweet.* André Deutsch.

SOMERSET MAUGHAM AWARDS. Established 1946. To enable young British authors to enrich their writing by experience in foreign countries.
Lisa St. Aubin de Teran. *Keepers of the House.* Cape.

TRAVELLING SCHOLARSHIPS. Established 1944 by an anonymous donor. To enable British creative writers to travel and to keep in touch with their colleagues abroad.
Rosemary Dinnage
Richard Holmes

Whitbread Literary Awards (Great Britain)

Established 1971 by Whitbreads, administered by the Booksellers Association of Great Britain and Ireland. To recognize literature of merit that is readable on a wide scale.

BIOGRAPHY
Victoria Glendinning. *Vita: The Life of V. Sackville-West.* Weidenfeld.
Kenneth Rose. *King George V.* Weidenfeld.

FIRST NOVEL
John Fuller. *Flying to Nowhere.* Salamander Press.

NOVEL
William Trevor. *Fools of Fortune.* Bodley Head.

Children's Awards (Foreign)

Hans Christian Andersen Medals

Established 1956 by the International Board on Books for Young People. Awarded biennially to one author and one illustrator for the entire body of his or her work.

Not awarded in 1983.

Australian Children's Book Awards (Australia)

BOOK OF THE YEAR. Established 1956. Awarded primarily for literary merit, but with attention to the quality and design of the book as a whole.

Victor Kelleher. *Master of the Grove*. Penguin.

MEDAL FOR JUNIOR READERS. Established 1982. For excellence of text and pictures.

Robin Klein; illustrated by Alison Lester. *Thing*. Oxford University Press.

PICTURE BOOK OF THE YEAR. Established 1952, first award made in 1956. Awarded primarily for the quality of the pictures, but with attention also to the text.

Pamela Allen. *Who Sank the Boat?* Nelson Australia.

Bologna Children's Book Fair Prizes (Italy)

Established 1963 by the Bologna Trade Fair Promotion Agency. For the best books in three categories.

GRAPHICS

Younger Children: Roy Gerrard. *The Favershams*. Gollancz (Great Britain).
Young Adults: *Il était une fois les mots*. La Farandole (France).
Junior Critics: Ingrid Selberg; illustrated by Andrew Miller. *Our Changing World*. Collins (Great Britain).

British Library Association (Great Britain), administrator

CARNEGIE MEDAL. Established 1937. For an outstanding book for children.

Margaret Mahy. *The Haunting*. Dent.

KATE GREENAWAY MEDAL. Established 1957. For the most distinguished work in the illustration of a book for children.

Michael Foreman. *Long Neck and Thunder Foot* by Helen Piers. Kestrel/Penguin.
Sleeping Beauty and Other Favourite Fairy Tales, trans. by Angela Carter. Gollancz.

Canada Council (Canada)

CHILDREN'S LITERATURE PRIZES. Established 1975. To honor outstanding authors and illustrators.

ENGLISH-LANGUAGE BOOKS

Monica Hughes. *Hunter in the Dark*. Clarke Irwin.
Vlasta van Kampen, illustrator. *ABC, 123, The Canadian Alphabet and Counting Book*. Hurtig.

FRENCH-LANGUAGE BOOKS

Ginette Anfousse. *Fabien 1* and *Fabien 2*. Leméac.
Darcia Labrosse, illustrator. *Agnès et le singulier bestiaire*. Editions Pierre Tisseyre.

Canadian Association of Children's Librarians (Canada)

BOOK OF THE YEAR. Established 1947; through 1953, one award each year for an English-language book; 1954-1973, one award each year for an English-language book and a French-language book. To honor outstanding books.

Brian Doyle. *Up to Low*. Douglas & McIntyre.

AMELIA FRANCES HOWARD-GIBBON ILLUSTRATOR'S AWARD. Established 1971. To honor the illustrator of an outstanding book.

Lindee Climo. *Chester's Barn*. Tundra Books.

Carnegie Medal. *See* British Library Association (Great Britain), administrator

Emil Award. *See* Kurt Maschler Emil Award (Great Britain)

Eleanor Farjeon Award (Great Britain)

Established 1966 by the Children's Book Circle in memory of the noted children's writer. For distinguished service to children's books.

Jean Russell

Kate Greenaway Medal. *See* British Library Association (Great Britain), administrator

Kurt Maschler Emil Award (Great Britain)

Established 1982 by Kurt Maschler in memory of Erich Kästner and Walter Trier, author and illustrator of *Emil and the Detectives*, published in Germany in 1929 by Atrium Verlag. For a work of the imagination in which text and illustration are of excellence and so presented that each enhances yet balances the other.

Anthony Browne. *Gorilla*. Julia MacRae.

Mother Goose Award

Established 1980 by Books for Your Children/Booksellers, Haxey, South Yorkshire. To recognize and encourage newcomers to children's book illustration.

Satoshi Kitamura. *Angry Arthur*. Andersen.

Whitbread Literary Award (Great Britain)

Established 1971 by Whitbreads, administered by the Booksellers Association of Great Britain and Ireland. To recognize literature of merit that is readable on a wide scale.

CHILDREN'S NOVEL

Roald Dahl. *The Witches*. Cape.

The Business of Books

12

Book Industry Economics in 1983

JOHN P. DESSAUER

Overview

Along with the rest of the American economy, the book industry moved out of the recession during 1983. However, its recovery was slower than that of most other sectors, probably because book prices continued to inflate at above-average rates.

After a mixed first quarter and a disappointing second quarter, publishers' and retailers' sales improved dramatically in the third quarter and maintained a healthy pace in the fourth. The rebound during the second half of the year was strong enough to make 1983 a generally good year—certainly one much improved over 1982.

Retailers were the major factor in the recovery. Institutional markets remained weak, and direct-to-consumer sales by publishers and book clubs proved disappointing. A third-quarter surge by mail order publishers was insufficient to overcome the first half decline experienced by this category, especially as the rebound lost some of its momentum in the final quarter. The recovery also came too late to offset a noticeable slowing in the expansion of the bookstore universe. Although net gains in the number of retailers continued, the pace of addition, which had begun to lose some momentum even in 1982, was decidedly more sedate in 1983.

Nevertheless the industry's performance, particularly by its consumer sector, was sufficiently improved so that one could hope for increases in the profit levels of trade and mass market publishers. In 1982 net income for these houses had been less than satisfactory. The momentum generated late in 1983, furthermore, brightened industry prospects for 1984 and succeeding years. Consumers

were apparently ready to continue, or even to extend, their commitment to books, and a growing network of producers and suppliers promised to make it increasingly convenient for their patrons to indulge their book-buying interests.

Slower Expansion

Before embarking on an examination of key industry statistics, I must once again point out the limitations of all such data. Because many books are published by very small houses, or by divisions of not-for-profit organizations that do not participate in any of the surveys of industry activity, a significant proportion of book volume consistently goes unrecorded. Rosters of publishers and retailers are invariably incomplete. Estimates, such as mine for *Book Industry Trends* (BISG), which are based on U.S. Census and industry-sponsored surveys, inevitably understate sales. Because our statistical analyses, though incomplete, are consistent, it is possible to discern vital trends from examining the data. Readers should bear in mind, however, that the data represent only samples, and that there is substantial variation among the samples in materiality and reliability.

The expansion of the publishing and retail universes continued during 1983, albeit at a more modest pace. The number of publishers contributing to *Books in Print* (R. R. Bowker) grew by 9.4%—only a minor decline from the 10% rate established during the previous decade. The number of booksellers, on the other hand, grew by only 3.6%, a significant decrease from the 7.4% established in 1982, which itself represented a noticeable retreat from the more than 10% growth rate that had characterized recent years.

Most of the new publishers are what have come to be called "small presses": modestly capitalized ventures favoring specialized publishing programs, often developing their own, direct distribution methods to gain circulation for their titles. By contrast, the majority of new retail outlets are branches of major chains. In 1983, 423 of the 749 new stores opened were chain operated; only 388 out of the 1,448 that were begun in 1982 had been part of chains.

With economic conditions much improved, it is probable that bookstore openings will soon regain their former pace and that the number of chain branches and independent dealers will become better balanced once again. It is significant, however, that countervailing trends are at work in the growth of the numbers of publishers and booksellers. Among publishers a proliferation of independent imprints prevails, which, despite mergers and acquisitions by a few giants, is decentralizing the field. Among booksellers, the chains are expanding more rapidly than the independents. Do these phenomena hold any significance for the industry's future?

Probably not. The consumer audience for books promises to continue to grow, with additional book buyers entering the market. This development augurs well for all types of book distributors—independent and chain bookstores, specialty stores, mass market outlets, book clubs, and publishers selling directly to consumers. In the process, a diverse and multifaceted marketing environment will be created in which it will be easier to sell a wider range of titles, from the broadly popular to the narrowly specialized, than is currently the case. This development will not only make good economic sense, but will fall in line with the needs and interests of our culturally maturing and pluralistic population.

Markets and Revenues

As in the past, the sales estimates incorporated in this article are based on my annual report, *Book Industry Trends,* and its monthly supplement, *Trends Update.* Sponsored by the Book Industry Study Group and distributed by R. R. Bowker, this report estimates and forecasts industry sales of publishers and wholesalers, and furnishes consumer expenditures, for 28 product categories, 6 domestic market areas, and export. It utilizes U.S. Census reports, National Center for Educational Statistics (NCES) data, and industry statistical surveys—notably those of Association of American Publishers (AAP), Evangelical Christian Publishers Association (ECPA), National Association of College Stores (NACS), and Association of Research Libraries (ARL).

At the time this article was prepared, I had compiled a preliminary summary estimate for 1983, and completed final data for 1982 (except for details on library acquisitions where the final year was 1981). The preliminary figures for 1983 appear in Tables 1 and 2. Publishers' net sales (Table 1) showed a marked improvement over the deep recession year of 1982, with a healthy gain of 11.8% in dollars and 5.2% in units. Categories displaying particular strength included trade, mass market paperback, and professional books, with adult trade titles, both hardcover and paperbound, leading the field.

Domestic consumer expenditures (Table 2) showed similar dollar gains but displayed greater unit weakness due largely to the impact of continued high inflation on the limited purchasing power of institutions. Retailers fared better, with general outlets posting strong gains of 19.4% in dollars and 11.3% in units.

A puzzling development has been the persistent price inflation afflicting books at a time when inflation has been moderating elsewhere in the economy. Not only do industry reports reveal that book inflation has hardly been dampened, but book-inclusive categories are among the most rapidly inflating on the Consumer Price Index (CPI). Comparing data for September 1983 with those of a year earlier, we note the following rates of increase for the CPI: All Items 3.1%, Food 1.7%, Housing 2.0%, Apparel 3.2%, Energy 0.9%, Medical Care 7.8%, Entertainment 5.4%, Schoolbooks and Supplies 8.3%, and Magazines, Periodicals, and Books 5.9%.

A number of factors could account for the failure of book prices to moderate. Publishers are often insufficiently sensitive to the marketing implications of their pricing policies; many employ formulas tying those prices to manufacturing costs, and as manufacturing and paper costs have continued to rise so has the formulated price structure. Another consideration may be the determination of some publishers to protect profits from erosion due to declining subsidiary rights revenue and increasing write-offs of unearned big-title guarantees.

A special reason for quite drastic increases in the average prices of trade paperbounds has been a tendency by many publishers to employ the paperback format too liberally and optimistically. In recent years the selection of trade titles being paperbacked has grown increasingly specialized and complex. Many of these titles have had to command extravagant prices because of their high manufacturing costs and limited appeal, suffering a serious disadvantage in the market as a result. (See "Trade Paperbacks: No Panacea," by John P. Dessauer, *PW*, January 13, 1984.)

The preceding, certainly, had been factors contributing to the price inflation in 1982, which is reflected in the data in Table 6. Here unit revenues of publishers for 1982 and 1981 are compared by product category. Although 1982 was a seriously depressed year, with inflation of many consumer commodities moderating dramatically, most book categories inflated at double-digit rates. (Note that adult trade paperbounds were among the worst offenders. Note also that the revenue averages in Table 6 differ significantly from the price data discussed by Chandler Grannis in Chapter 13. Table 6 figures, which represent receipts per unit and not list prices, are affected by publishers' discounts and weighted by sales. The data in Chapter 13, on the other hand, consist of unweighted list price averages only.)

TABLE 1 Estimated Publishers' Net Book Sales (Millions of Dollars and Units)

	1983		1982		% Change	
	$	Units	$	Units	$	Units
Trade	1,774.3	514.03	1447.7	449.68	22.6	14.3
Adult hardbound	995.4	179.78	798.2	157.01	24.7	14.5
Adult paperbound	487.2	126.87	387.3	117.58	25.8	7.9
Juvenile hardbound	215.9	95.64	199.5	85.70	8.2	11.6
Juvenile paperbound	75.8	111.74	62.7	89.39	20.9	25.0
Religious	425.6	111.65	383.1	106.62	11.1	4.7
Hardbound	303.8	46.11	271.5	43.42	11.9	6.2
Paperbound	121.8	65.54	111.6	63.20	9.1	3.7
Professional	1,398.1	71.64	1,245.1	67.22	12.3	6.6
Hardbound	1,107.4	46.11	992.3	35.96	11.6	2.4
Paperbound	290.7	34.82	252.8	31.26	15.0	11.4
Book club	637.7	174.37	577.1	184.43	10.5	−5.5
Hardbound	502.2	57.78	448.4	58.25	12.0	−.8
Paperbound	135.5	116.59	128.7	126.18	5.3	−7.6
Mail order publications	566.1	51.85	599.7	55.63	−5.6	−6.8
Mass market paperbacks	1,133.7	699.76	990.1	663.28	14.5	5.5
University presses	92.6	12.04	87.4	11.75	5.9	2.5
Hardbound	66.5	5.31	64.1	5.26	3.7	1.0
Paperbound	26.1	6.73	23.3	6.49	12.1	3.7
Elhi text	1,204.5	252.49	1,091.4	251.95	10.4	.2
Hardbound	666.1	107.30	614.5	106.03	8.4	1.2
Paperbound	538.4	145.19	476.9	145.92	12.9	−.5
College text	1,294.8	109.69	1,179.5	108.96	9.8	.7
Hardbound	962.6	69.46	884.7	70.02	8.8	−.8
Paperbound	332.2	40.23	294.8	38.94	12.7	3.3
Subscription reference	372.0	1.14	360.1	1.08	3.3	5.5
Total	8,899.4	1,998.66	7,961.2	1,900.60	11.8	5.2

TABLE 2 Estimated Domestic Consumer Expenditures on Books (Millions of Dollars and Units)

	1983		1982		% Change	
	$	Units	$	Units	$	Units
General retailers	4,482.4	906.52	3,754.1	814.48	19.4	11.3
College stores	1,996.2	214.13	1,791.9	204.32	11.4	4.8
Libraries & institutions	802.3	60.05	751.2	62.42	6.8	−3.8
Schools	1,409.4	277.52	1,329.6	282.61	6.0	−1.8
Direct to consumer	2,039.3	289.34	1,938.5	293.15	5.2	−1.3
Other	158.8	86.66	141.4	78.79	12.3	10.0
Total	10,888.4	1,834.22	9,706.7	1,735.70	12.2	5.7

High prices were probably the principal reason for the industry's poor unit performance in 1982, revealed in Table 4. Even general retailers managed to advance their unit sales by only 3.7%, while libraries, schools, and direct-to-consumer sales suffered unit declines from 3.7% to 10.0%. Trade books, both adult and juvenile, accounted for some of the largest unit erosion in the institutional markets. The industry's dollar gains hovered only around 6.0%.

Total and per capita general consumer expenditures for

TABLE 3 Estimated Total and Per Capita Expenditures on Books by U.S. General Consumers, 1982

	Population (000,000)	$ (000,000)	1967 $ (000,000)	Units (000,000)	Per Capita $	Per Capita 1967 $	Per Capita Units
Adult trade hardbound	177.3	920.8	318.5	84.59	5.19	1.79	.47
Adult trade paperbound	177.3	440.6	152.4	70.01	2.48	.85	.39
Juvenile trade hardbound	37.3	178.6	61.7	56.45	4.78	1.65	1.51
Juvenile trade paperbound	37.3	104.5	36.1	86.48	2.80	.96	1.83
Religious	214.6	529.7	183.2	80.41	2.46	.85	.37
Book clubs	214.6	564.5	195.3	180.40	2.63	.91	.84
Mail order publications	214.6	596.4	206.3	51.00	2.77	.96	.23
Mass market paperbacks	214.6	1,270.9	439.7	471.48	5.92	2.04	2.19
Subscription reference	214.6	295.2	102.1	.92	1.37	.47	*
Total expenditures	*214.6*	*4,901.2*	*1,695.3*	*1,063.74*	*22.83*	*7.89*	*4.95*
Sales through retailers	214.6	3,349.5	1,158.7	790.31	15.60	5.39	3.68
Direct-to-consumer	214.6	1,551.7	536.6	273.43	7.23	2.50	1.27
Total hardbound sales	214.6	2,796.9	967.3	281.28	13.03	4.50	1.31
Total paperbound sales	214.6	2,104.3	727.7	782.46	9.80	3.39	3.64

Source: Population data from U.S. Census. Sales data from *Book Industry Trends 1983*.
*Less than one hundredth.

1982, reported in Table 3, also reflected the negative impact of recession and inflation. (The data base here is limited to trade, religious, book club, mail order publications, mass market paperback, and subscription reference books, channeled through general retailers or sold directly to consumers by publishers and book clubs.) On comparing the 1982 data shown with equivalent figures for 1980, we find that, while per capita expenditures rose in current dollars during the two-year interval, they declined in constant 1967 dollars and in units in nearly all categories except sales through retailers and total paperbound sales. Even in those brackets, however, increases were modest compared to the spectacular gains to which the industry had become accustomed in former years.

Library acquisitions, as reported in Table 5, were on a decidedly downward course in 1981. In 1980 these libraries had shown gains of 9.4% in dollars and 3.4% in units—a far healthier result than the marginal 1.0% dollar gain and 8.0% unit loss they experienced in 1981. The summary data for 1982 in Table 4, and the preliminary estimates for 1983 in Table 2, suggest that 1981 may have been a low point and that dollar acquisition levels have risen again since then. However, unit acquisitions still declined in 1982 and 1983.

The industry's title output, according to data covered by Chandler B. Grannis in Chapter 13, experienced a drop in 1982, one of few such years in recent memory. The decline affected both hardbound and paperbound titles overall, although trade paperbounds still posted gains. (Since these data, like other industry statistics, are incomplete, the reflected trend may have been countervailed to some extent in the output of small presses not represented in the data base.)

Operating Data

The operating report samples in the *Association of American Publishers 1982 Industry Statistics* represent publishers with some $3.2 billion in revenues, or 40% of my estimated $8 billion industry total. Collectively, the group posted an operating income of 13.1% of net sales (by definition operating income excludes interest earned or expended, corporate fees, or income taxes). A glance at Figure 1 makes clear, however, that, as usual, this broad average incorporated a wide range of experiences. The net income of trade publishers was 4.1%, of professional publishers 9.1%, of rack-sized mass market paperback publishers 2.4%, of book clubs 9.7%, of mail order publications 11.1%, of elhi publishers 16.5%, and of college publishers 23.1%.

Substantial variations occurred within the categories as well. Adult hardcover and softcover trade publishers recorded incomes of 2.5% and 2.1% respectively, while juvenile trade publishers reached a 10.1% level. Trade houses with sales below $10 million achieved only a 0.2% loss, while those with sales from $10 million to $35 million reported a 5.2% income, and those with sales above $35 million a 4.4% income. The incomes of professional publishers ranged from 1.9% for firms with sales up to $5 million to 11.8% for houses selling above $15 million. Among school publishers the net income range extended from 4.4% for the smallest to 20.4% for the largest, and among college publishers it ranged from 4.0% to 26.9%. Equally diverse were the differences between the 1982 and 1981 performances posted by these categories (in some measure because of variations in the sample populations for the two years). The net income of trade publishers reporting to the AAP survey in 1981 had been 8.4%, that of professional publishers 14.5%, that of rack-sized mass market paperback publishers 5.2%, of book clubs 9.7%, of mail order publications 17.0%, of elhi publishers 18.6%, and of college publishers 22.4%.

Table 7 provides detailed operating data for 27 trade publishers who reported 1982 figures to AAP. Before reviewing the information in this table, a few general observations on the manner in which operating data are presented in industry surveys appears appropriate.

To facilitate analysis and provide a basis for comparison, industry operating reports usually provide ratios to net sales for the income and cost items listed. Higher profits normally mean lower proportionate costs and/or higher "other" (mostly subsidiary rights) income, while the opposite applies when profits shrink. What is not always clear, however, are the reasons why cost ratios have increased or decreased in a particular report. Expense ratios will grow, for example, when costs rise more rapidly than sales. On the other hand, the same ratios will grow even without significant cost increases whenever sales drop off. Thus, the deterioration of an effective marketing program, which results in a decrease in sales, will cause marketing and other expense ratios to rise in proportion.

I place some emphasis on this point because too often in analyzing operating reports, management becomes exclusively preoccupied with cost controls, ignoring the more immediate and more debilitating effects of below-par sales. To disregard marketing failures, however, be they caused by poor editorial choices, rampaging inflation, or inadequate promotion, in order to concentrate on cost cutting, could well weaken a weak imprint further, making it even less competitive than before.

The 28 trade publishers who reported 1981 data to AAP showed generally better profit levels than the 27 publishers who participated in the 1982 survey reported in Table 7. In 1981 the operating income for adult trade hardbound publishers had been 8.8%, that of adult trade paperbound houses 6.0%, and that of juvenile imprints 14.9%. The indications are that, particularly in the adult hardbound area, profits shrank not because of galloping costs but because of collapsing sales. The samples reporting adult hardcover data for the two years were of course not matched, but they were sufficiently similar to suggest a good deal of overlap between them.

Operating cost ratios in this category in 1982 rose across the board, to a total of 52.7%. (The total operating expense ratio reported in 1981 had been 45.1%.) Since price inflation in adult trade hardbounds substantially exceeded general inflation, we must assume that operating ratios would have declined if sales had held steady or had increased over the year before. Knowing, however, that adult trade hardcover sales decreased by 6.9% in dollars and 15.8% in units in 1982, we must attribute the rising cost ratios to poor sales rather than to reckless spending. In a similar vein, we would be mistaken if we assumed from Table 7 that "other" income in this category increased in 1982 (to 15.7%, whereas the 1981 sample had reported 14.3%). Judging from the sales background, "other" income remained steady or perhaps even declined somewhat in 1982.

FIGURE 1. 1982 Net Income Before Taxes from Operations (divisional averages based on operating data reported by participating publishers).

Source: *Association of American Publishers 1982 Industry Statistics.* © 1983 by Association of American Publishers, Inc. Reprinted with permission.

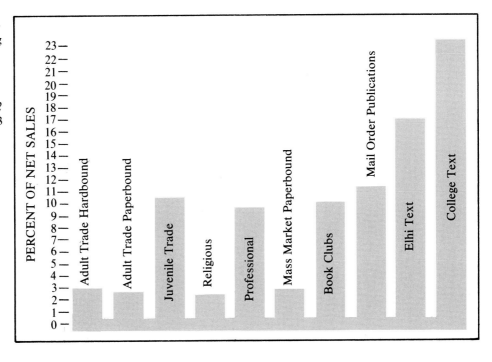

TABLE 4 Estimated Publishers' Book Sales and Domestic Consumer Expenditures on Books by Type of Book and Market, 1982
(Millions of Dollars and Units)

	General Retailers						College Stores					
	Publishers' Sales		Consumer Exp.		Units		Publishers' Sales		Consumer Exp.		Units	
	$	% Change from 1981	$	% Change from 1981	No.	% Change from 1981	$	% Change from 1981	$	% Change from 1981	No.	% Change from 1981
Trade	843.4	2.0	1,602.9	2.2	273.46	5.0	112.5	13.1	219.4	16.7	33.37	.3
Adult hardbound	480.7	−9.3	896.9	−9.9	81.98	−21.3	31.9	−.6	60.0	−1.5	5.28	−18.0
Adult paperbound	219.2	18.8	424.3	20.3	66.98	1.5	76.8	20.4	151.9	25.6	24.93	3.5
Children's hardbound	91.4	34.8	177.2	36.5	56.05	22.8	2.8	3.7	5.5	3.8	1.66	−4.6
Children's paperbound	52.1	16.0	104.5	16.6	68.45	53.6	1.0	11.1	2.0	17.6	1.50	48.5
Religious	250.4	8.8	492.4	10.9	75.07	2.8	23.9	6.7	47.5	8.7	8.02	.1
Hardbound	171.0	8.3	337.8	10.4	28.57	1.3	14.4	6.7	28.4	8.8	2.33	−.9
Paperbound	79.4	10.0	154.6	12.1	46.50	3.7	9.5	6.7	19.1	8.5	5.69	.5
Professional	202.9	18.4	298.9	19.2	15.42	15.0	174.9	−.3	236.1	.4	12.29	.5
Hardbound	140.5	16.6	204.3	17.5	6.27	8.3	117.0	−7.0	159.6	−6.0	4.82	−15.1
Paperbound	62.4	22.8	94.6	23.0	9.15	20.1	57.9	16.5	76.5	16.8	7.47	14.0
Book club	.0	.0	.0	.0	.00	.0	.0	.0	.0	.0	.00	.0
Hardbound	.0	.0	.0	.0	.00	.0	.0	.0	.0	.0	.00	.0
Paperbound	.0	.0	.0	.0	.00	.0	.0	.0	.0	.0	.00	.0
Mail order publications	28.8	−1.4	50.5	−1.6	4.22	−3.7	3.6	−7.7	6.4	−7.2	.60	−1.6
Mass market paperbacks	634.2	10.5	1,203.7	10.6	437.56	2.8	91.2	11.4	168.4	11.3	62.07	3.5
University presses	16.9	10.5	25.3	9.5	3.04	2.7	18.7	12.7	25.9	12.6	3.16	3.6
Hardbound	9.8	11.4	14.2	10.1	.89	7.2	10.0	16.3	14.1	15.6	.84	12.0
Paperbound	7.1	9.2	11.1	8.8	2.15	.9	8.7	8.8	11.8	9.3	2.32	.9
Elhi text	.0	.0	.0	.0	.00	.0	31.5	5.4	39.5	5.3	9.08	−4.1
Hardbound	.0	.0	.0	.0	.00	.0	17.2	2.4	21.6	2.4	3.67	−4.7
Paperbound	.0	.0	.0	.0	.00	.0	14.3	9.2	17.9	9.1	5.41	−3.7
College text	61.1	10.7	80.4	10.6	5.71	.0	797.0	11.8	1,048.7	11.8	75.73	1.2
Hardbound	45.9	10.1	60.4	10.0	3.71	−.8	580.0	10.8	763.2	10.8	46.85	−.2
Paperbound	15.2	12.6	20.0	12.4	2.00	1.5	217.0	14.5	285.5	14.5	28.88	3.5
Subscription reference	.0	.0	.0	.0	.00	.0	.0	.0	.0	.0	.00	.0
Total	2,037.7	7.2	3,754.1	7.3	814.48	3.7	1,253.3	9.7	1,791.9	10.3	204.32	1.4

TABLE 4 Estimated Publishers' Book Sales and Domestic Consumer Expenditures on Books by Type of Book and Market, 1982 (cont.)
(Millions of Dollars and Units)

	Libraries & Institutions						Schools					
	Publishers' Sales		Consumer Exp.		Units		Publishers' Sales		Consumer Exp.		Units	
	$	% Change from 1981	$	% Change from 1981	No.	% Change from 1981	$	% Change from 1981	$	% Change from 1981	No.	% Change from 1981
Trade	179.2	-4.6	237.3	-3.6	31.80	-8.6	80.6	-19.4	99.7	-19.0	13.90	-23.5
Adult hardbound	116.7	-6.4	158.5	-5.3	17.43	-13.4	25.5	-4.9	33.7	-5.3	3.39	-12.9
Adult paperbound	29.8	19.7	39.5	21.9	6.89	4.2	5.0	8.7	6.3	10.5	.97	-7.6
Children's hardbound	30.0	-15.3	35.6	-16.4	4.70	-22.3	48.6	-27.1	57.6	-27.2	7.87	-33.4
Children's paperbound	2.7	-3.6	3.7	.0	2.78	38.3	1.5	-21.1	2.1	-22.2	1.67	17.6
Religious	23.7	4.9	30.1	5.6	3.71	-2.4	12.2	3.4	17.1	4.9	2.46	-3.9
Hardbound	20.6	5.1	26.7	6.0	2.51	-2.7	8.6	3.6	12.6	5.0	1.08	-4.4
Paperbound	3.1	3.3	3.4	3.0	1.20	-1.6	3.6	2.9	4.5	4.7	1.38	-3.5
Professional	267.4	28.0	316.4	27.1	12.14	18.6	27.7	10.4	29.1	10.2	1.09	5.8
Hardbound	232.3	29.2	276.2	28.2	8.25	19.0	22.9	8.5	23.9	8.1	.65	.0
Paperbound	35.1	20.6	40.2	20.4	3.89	17.5	4.8	20.0	5.2	20.9	.44	15.8
Book club	.0	.0	.0	.0	.00	.0	.0	.0	.0	.0	.00	.0
Hardbound	.0	.0	.0	.0	.00	.0	.0	.0	.0	.0	.00	.0
Paperbound	.0	.0	.0	.0	.00	.0	.0	.0	.0	.0	.00	.0
Mail order publications	5.4	.0	7.3	.0	.66	1.5	1.3	-13.3	1.6	-15.8	.16	
Mass market paperbacks	8.7	3.6	11.6	2.7	4.55	-5.6	54.5	4.2	74.6	4.3	26.48	-3.6
University presses	23.5	3.5	29.4	4.3	1.93	-1.0	1.5	.0	1.8	.0	.13	-7.1
Hardbound	21.6	3.8	27.3	4.6	1.55	.6	1.1	.0	1.4	.0	.07	.0
Paperbound	1.9	.0	2.1	.0	.38	-7.3	.4	.0	.4	.0	.06	-14.3
Elhi text	12.7	8.5	14.3	8.3	2.20	1.4	1,002.9	8.0	1,002.9	8.0	231.18	-2.1
Hardbound	11.7	7.3	13.2	7.3	1.91	.0	550.6	6.8	550.6	6.8	94.17	-.2
Paperbound	1.0	25.0	1.1	22.2	.29	11.5	452.3	9.6	452.3	9.6	137.01	-3.4
College text	81.1	5.3	87.5	5.3	5.39	-5.4	82.6	4.3	82.9	4.3	7.17	-6.6
Hardbound	73.7	5.3	80.0	5.3	4.63	-5.7	64.1	4.2	64.4	4.2	4.88	-6.9
Paperbound	7.4	5.7	7.5	5.6	.76	-3.8	18.5	4.5	18.5	4.5	2.29	-6.1
Subscription reference	17.3	4.2	17.3	4.2	.04	.0	19.9	3.6	19.9	3.6	.04	.0
Total	619.0	10.3	751.2	10.0	62.42	-5.7	1,283.2	5.3	1,329.6	4.9	282.61	-3.7

TABLE 4 Estimated Publishers' Book Sales and Domestic Consumer Expenditures on Books by Type of Book and Market, 1982 (cont.)
(Millions of Dollars and Units)

	Direct to Consumer						Other Domestic					
	Publishers' Sales		Consumer Exp.		Units		Publishers' Sales		Consumer Exp.		Units	
	$	% Change from 1981	$	% Change from 1981	No.	% Change from 1981	$	% Change from 1981	$	% Change from 1981	No.	% Change from 1981
Trade	41.6	14.9	41.6	29.2	6.07	7.4	38.6	35.4	77.2	28.0	50.04	14.1
Adult hardbound	23.9	2.6	23.9	2.6	2.61	−7.1	26.3	4.8	52.6	4.8	28.58	−2.4
Adult paperbound	16.3	35.8	16.3	35.8	3.03	19.3	5.0	25.0	10.0	25.0	4.15	8.6
Children's hardbound	1.4	55.6	1.4	55.6	.40	48.1	4.8	71.4	9.6	71.4	6.30	34.9
Children's paperbound	.0	.0	.0	.0	.03	.0	2.5	47.1	5.0	47.1	11.01	80.5
Religious	37.3	7.8	37.3	7.8	5.34	1.9	4.1	7.9	8.2	7.9	3.80	4.7
Hardbound	29.8	7.6	29.8	7.6	2.81	1.1	3.6	9.1	7.2	9.1	2.36	7.3
Paperbound	7.5	8.7	7.5	8.7	2.53	2.8	.5	.0	1.0	.0	1.44	.7
Professional	330.9	1.1	330.9	1.1	13.18	−6.5	9.8	14.0	12.3	13.9	1.01	7.4
Hardbound	284.1	1.5	284.1	1.5	8.62	−7.6	8.0	14.3	10.0	13.6	.60	5.3
Paperbound	46.8	−1.3	46.8	−1.3	4.56	−4.2	1.8	12.5	2.3	15.0	.41	10.8
Book club	564.5	1.7	564.5	1.7	180.40	−14.3	.0	.0	.0	.0	.00	.0
Hardbound	438.3	1.6	438.3	1.6	56.94	−12.5	.0	.0	.0	.0	.00	.0
Paperbound	126.2	2.0	126.2	2.0	123.46	−15.1	.0	.0	.0	.0	.00	.0
Mail order publications	545.9	−9.1	545.9	−9.1	46.78	−9.9	3.4	−22.7	5.7	−21.9	2.11	−22.7
Mass market paperbacks	67.2	18.5	67.2	18.5	33.92	10.1	14.4	27.4	24.0	27.7	17.99	19.3
University presses	8.8	14.3	8.8	14.3	.79	6.8	1.1	.0	2.8	.0	.75	−6.2
Hardbound	6.8	15.3	6.8	15.3	.40	11.1	.8	.0	2.0	.0	.37	−5.1
Paperbound	2.0	11.1	2.0	11.1	.39	2.6	.3	.0	.8	.0	.38	−7.3
Elhi text	15.7	7.5	15.7	7.5	3.59	−2.4	2.1	5.0	2.6	4.0	1.20	−3.2
Hardbound	8.6	6.2	8.6	6.2	1.46	−.7	1.2	.0	1.5	.0	.50	−7.4
Paperbound	7.1	9.2	7.1	9.2	2.13	−3.6	.9	12.5	1.1	10.0	.70	.0
College text	31.4	6.8	31.4	6.8	2.16	−4.4	4.6	12.2	7.6	10.1	1.82	−1.6
Hardbound	23.8	7.2	23.8	7.2	1.43	−4.0	3.5	12.9	5.8	11.5	1.16	−1.7
Paperbound	7.6	5.6	7.6	5.6	.73	−5.2	1.1	10.0	1.8	5.9	.66	−1.5
Subscription reference	295.2	1.2	295.2	1.2	.92	.0	.8	.0	1.0	.0	.07	.0
Total	1,938.5	−.8	1,938.5	−.6	293.15	−10.0	78.9	13.2	141.4	19.8	78.79	13.3

TABLE 4 Estimated Publishers' Book Sales and Domestic Consumer Expenditures on Books by Type of Book and Market, 1982 (cont.)
(Millions of Dollars and Units)

| | Publishers' Export Sales | | | | All Publishers' Sales | | | | All Consumer Expenditures | | | |
| | Dollars | | Units | | Dollars | | Units | | Dollars | | Units | |
	$	% Change from 1981	No.	% Change from 1981	$	% Change from 1981	No.	% Change from 1981	$	% Change from 1981	No.	% Change from 1981
Trade	151.8	5.5	41.04	3.0	1,447.7	1.4	449.68	3.1	2,278.1	2.7	408.64	3.2
Adult hardbound	93.2	-2.7	17.74	-10.4	798.2	-6.9	157.01	-15.8	1,225.6	-8.1	139.27	-16.5
Adult paperbound	35.2	24.8	10.63	8.6	387.3	20.3	117.58	3.2	648.3	21.9	106.95	2.7
Children's hardbound	20.5	15.2	8.72	8.5	199.5	2.8	85.70	9.6	286.9	9.0	76.98	9.7
Children's paperbound	2.9	38.1	3.95	77.1	62.7	15.5	89.39	55.9	117.3	16.0	85.44	55.0
Religious	31.5	15.0	8.22	8.0	383.1	8.6	106.62	2.6	632.6	11.4	98.40	2.2
Hardbound	23.5	14.6	3.76	7.4	271.5	8.3	43.42	1.6	442.5	9.6	39.66	1.1
Paperbound	8.0	15.9	4.46	8.5	111.6	9.5	63.20	3.3	190.1	11.2	58.74	2.9
Professional	231.5	13.9	12.09	9.0	1,245.1	11.2	67.22	6.6	1,223.7	11.3	55.13	6.1
Hardbound	187.5	12.7	6.75	3.8	992.3	10.2	35.96	1.4	958.1	10.1	29.21	.9
Paperbound	44.0	19.2	5.34	16.3	252.8	15.2	31.26	13.3	265.6	15.7	25.92	12.7
Book club	12.6	17.8	4.03	2.5	577.1	2.0	184.43	-14.0	564.5	1.7	180.40	-14.3
Hardbound	10.1	20.2	1.31	3.1	448.4	2.0	58.25	-12.2	438.3	1.6	56.94	-12.5
Paperbound	2.5	8.7	2.72	2.3	128.7	2.1	126.18	-14.8	126.2	2.0	123.46	-15.1
Mail order publications	11.3	-5.8	1.10	-1.8	599.7	-8.7	55.63	-8.8	617.4	-8.6	54.53	-8.9
Mass market paperbacks	119.9	22.5	80.71	14.6	990.1	12.2	663.28	4.6	1,549.5	10.9	582.57	3.4
University presses	16.9	3.0	1.95	-2.5	87.4	7.5	11.75	.9	94.0	8.5	9.80	1.7
Hardbound	14.0	2.9	1.14	-.9	64.1	7.6	5.26	3.3	65.8	8.8	4.12	4.6
Paperbound	2.9	3.6	.81	-4.7	23.3	7.4	6.49	-.9	28.2	8.0	5.68	-.4
Elhi text	26.5	-.4	4.70	-7.7	1,091.4	7.7	251.95	-2.3	1,075.0	7.9	247.25	-2.2
Hardbound	25.2	-.8	4.32	-7.9	614.5	6.3	106.03	-.7	595.5	6.6	101.71	-.4
Paperbound	1.3	8.3	.38	-5.0	476.9	9.6	145.92	-3.4	479.5	9.6	145.54	-3.4
College text	121.7	6.0	10.98	-5.1	1,179.5	10.0	108.96	-.6	1,338.5	10.6	97.98	-.1
Hardbound	93.7	6.5	7.36	-4.4	884.7	9.2	70.02	-1.7	997.6	9.8	62.66	-1.3
Paperbound	28.0	4.5	3.62	-6.5	294.8	12.2	38.94	1.4	340.9	13.3	35.32	2.3
Subscription reference	26.9	-.4	.08	.0	360.1	1.4	1.08	.0	333.4	1.5	1.00	.0
Total	750.6	10.4	164.90	7.9	7,961.2	5.8	1,900.60	.3	9,706.7	6.2	1,735.70	-.4

Source: TRENDS Update, October 1983 © 1983 Book Industry Study Group, Inc. Reprinted with permission.

TABLE 5 Estimated Acquisitions by U.S. Libraries of Domestically Published Books, 1981
(Millions of Dollars and Units)

	Direct		Thru Wholesalers		Total		% Change from 1980 Direct		Thru Wholesalers		Total	
	$	Units	$	Units	$	Units	$	Units	$	Units	$	Units
College & university libraries												
Trade	15.6	2.04	67.3	8.50	82.9	10.54	3.3	−8.9	4.0	−6.6	3.9	−7.0
Professional	22.5	.85	43.0	1.56	65.5	2.41	4.7	−10.5	7.0	−4.3	6.2	−5.5
University press	4.5	.39	13.0	.84	17.5	1.23	2.3	−2.5	1.6	−1.2	1.7	−1.6
Subscription reference	7.4	.02	.0	.00	7.4	.02	5.7	.0	.0	.0	5.7	.0
Other	25.0	2.25	29.4	2.94	54.4	5.19	2.9	−26.2	6.9	−17.6	4.8	−21.5
Total	75.0	5.55	152.7	13.84	227.7	19.39	3.9	−16.2	5.1	−8.6	4.7	−10.9
Public libraries												
Adult trade hardbound	11.4	1.62	58.8	7.69	70.2	9.31	4.6	5.9	5.6	2.3	5.2	2.9
Adult trade paperbound	4.9	1.07	10.6	2.14	15.5	3.21	−12.5	−31.0	−13.1	−35.3	−12.9	−31.4
Juvenile	12.2	1.96	34.1	6.10	46.3	8.06	3.4	3.7	−6.6	.3	−4.3	1.1
Professional	15.8	.90	7.6	.79	23.4	1.69	3.3	−5.3	−19.1	−14.1	−4.9	−9.6
Mass market paperback	1.4	.60	9.9	4.22	11.3	4.82	7.7	−3.2	2.1	−8.5	2.7	−7.8
Subscription reference	8.0	.02	.0	.00	8.0	.02	.0	.0	.0	.0	0	.0
Other	3.5	.44	8.2	.88	11.7	1.32	2.9	−26.7	−15.5	−16.2	−10.7	−20.0
Total	57.2	6.61	129.2	21.82	186.4	28.43	1.4	−7.7	−3.0	−6.4	−1.7	−6.7
Special libraries												
Trade	11.2	1.23	14.0	1.59	25.2	2.82	2.8	−5.4	7.7	−4.8	5.9	4.7
Religious	8.1	1.40	10.4	1.20	18.5	2.60	5.2	−3.4	13.0	.8	9.5	−1.5
Professional	25.7	1.05	57.9	1.99	83.6	3.04	9.8	−1.9	5.1	−4.8	6.4	−3.8
Other	3.7	.21	8.7	.58	12.4	.79	37.0	−40.0	20.8	16.0	25.3	21.5
Total	48.7	3.89	91.0	5.36	139.7	9.25	8.9	−1.8	7.7	−1.7	8.1	−1.7
School libraries												
Adult trade hardbound	8.2	.87	27.3	3.02	35.5	3.89	1.2	.0	3.4	.3	2.9	.3
Adult trade paperbound	2.2	.39	3.5	.66	5.7	1.05	−12.0	−29.1	−14.6	−30.5	−13.6	−30.5
Juvenile	6.2	.90	75.3	12.34	81.5	13.24	−1.6	−6.2	−13.4	1.2	−12.6	.7
Professional	21.1	.80	5.3	.23	26.4	1.03	2.4	−9.1	.0	−11.5	1.9	−10.4
Mass market paperback	.8	.27	47.1	18.23	47.9	18.50	.0	−12.9	−6.4	−16.9	−6.3	−16.9
Subscription reference	19.2	.04	.0	.00	19.2	.04	4.9	.0	.0	.0	4.9	.0
Other	17.4	2.06	18.2	2.30	35.6	4.36	1.8	−7.2	21.3	15.6	11.3	3.6
Total	75.1	5.33	176.7	36.78	251.8	42.11	2.0	−8.7	−6.0	−8.8	−3.7	−8.8
Total all libraries	256.0	21.38	549.6	77.80	805.6	99.18	3.7	−9.3	−.2	−7.7	1.0	−8.0

**TABLE 6 Estimated Average U.S. Consumer Expenditures
on Books per Unit, 1981 and 1982
(Millions of Dollars and Units)**

	1981	1982	% Change
Trade	5.60	5.57	−.5
Adult hardbound	7.99	8.80	10.1
Adult paperbound	5.10	6.06	18.8
Children's hardbound	3.75	3.72	−.8
Children's paperbound	1.83	1.37	−25.1
Religious	5.96	6.42	7.7
Hardbound	10.28	11.15	8.5
Paperbound	2.99	3.23	8.0
Professional	21.16	22.19	4.9
Hardbound	30.04	32.80	9.2
Paperbound	9.98	10.24	2.6
Book club	2.63	3.12	18.6
Hardbound	6.62	7.69	16.2
Paperbound	.85	1.02	20.0
Mail order publications	11.28	11.32	.4
Mass market paperbacks	2.47	2.65	7.3
University presses	8.98	9.59	6.8
Hardbound	15.35	15.97	4.0
Paperbound	4.57	4.96	8.5
Elhi text	3.94	4.34	10.2
Hardbound	5.46	5.85	7.1
Paperbound	2.90	3.29	13.4
College Text	12.33	13.67	10.9
Hardbound	14.31	15.92	11.3
Paperbound	8.79	9.65	9.8
Subscription reference	328.50	333.40	1.5
Total	5.24	5.59	6.7

Adult trade paperbounds, on the other hand, enjoyed sales increases in 1982, although price inflation was a factor here also. The fact that operating income of adult paperbounds shrank to 2.1% in 1982 (the 1981 sample had reported 6.0%) appears superficially due to two factors: manufacturing cost increases and a decline in "other" income. But remembering the steep inflation in this category, coupled with the sturdy sales increase of 20.3% in dollars and 3.2% in units, I suspect that manufacturing costs rose more than is apparent from the table, that operating costs, too, moved to a higher plain, but that "other" income remained relatively stable.

The cost increases, in turn, were probably due to the less discriminating and too optimistic wave of paperbacking to which I alluded earlier. My suspicion is reinforced by the substantial increases in the cost ratios for editorial expense and plant costs (the latter not shown in Table 7 but listed elsewhere in the AAP report) that adult paperbounds experienced in 1982.

The key factor in publishers' operating expenditures are, of course, salaries, for which up-to-date figures have in the past been hard to come by. For this edition of *The*

Book Publishing Annual, however, the editors at R. R. Bowker have developed a new survey that not only sheds light on the 1983 salary experience, but promises to become a useful indicator of salary movement during the coming years. The survey utilizes data from four employment agencies serving the industry and while agency-brokered positions may be compensated, on the average, at somewhat above routine rates, the information is still helpful when analyzing salary trends in the field.

The positions covered in Table 10 were selected for their representativeness and significance. Salaries reported apply to fully qualified employees, not trainees, and do not include fringe benefits. Note the definitions of the positions supplied with the table, which conform generally to those used in AAP compensation surveys.

Since this is the first survey of its kind, its structure is of the simplest: no stratification has been supplied to segregate data by size of publisher, geographical location or other criteria that might contribute useful distinctions. It is hoped that in future years such refinements can be added; they will make the results even more informative and productive.

TABLE 7 Operating Data of Trade Book Publishers, by Type of Book* (Thousands of Dollars)

| | All Publishers | | | Your Data | | |
| | | % of Net Sales | | | % of Net Sales | |
	$	Average	Mid-range	$	Average	Mid-range
Gross sales	588,670	122.5	113.5 to 127.1			
Returns and allowances	108,242	22.5	13.5 to 27.1			
Net sales	480,428	100.0	100.0 to 100.0			
Cost of sales						
Manufacturing	194,124	40.4	33.5 to 46.5			
Royalties	76,254	15.9	8.5 to 17.8			
Total cost of sales	270,377	56.3	47.4 to 60.9			
Gross margin on sales	210,051	43.7	39.1 to 52.6			
Other income	51,340	10.7	2.9 to 14.3			
Operating expense						
Editorial	28,758	6.0	4.6 to 7.6			
Production	9,747	2.0	1.4 to 2.8			
Marketing	77,355	16.1	14.0 to 19.6			
Fulfillment	56,344	11.7	7.9 to 13.1			
General & admin.	69,646	14.5	11.0 to 16.9			
Total operating expense	241,850	50.3	44.5 to 57.7			
Net income from operations	19,541	4.1	−3.3 to 16.6			

| | Adult Hardbound | | | Adult Paperbound | | |
| | | % of Net Sales | | | % of Net Sales | |
	$	Average	Mid-range	$	Average	Mid-range
Gross sales	259,439	129.6	117.3 to 133.6	107,571	117.2	111.5 to 120.1
Returns and allowances	59,185	29.6	17.3 to 33.6	15,813	17.2	11.5 to 20.1
Net sales	200,254	100.0	100.0 to 100.0	91,758	100.0	100.0 to 100.0
Cost of sales						
Manufacturing	81,441	40.7	33.2 to 45.7	33,982	37.0	32.9 to 40.4
Royalties	39,867	19.9	12.2 to 23.6	13,759	15.0	9.8 to 18.2
Total cost of sales	121,308	60.6	47.4 to 69.9	47,741	52.0	46.3 to 54.0
Gross margin on sales	78,946	39.4	30.1 to 52.6	44,017	48.0	46.0 to 53.7
Other income	31,457	15.7	6.0 to 20.8	4,948	5.4	0.5 to 10.4
Operating expense						
Editorial	14,689	7.3	5.3 to 9.7	4,643	5.1	3.1 to 7.7
Production	4,356	2.2	1.6 to 3.1	1,857	2.0	1.4 to 2.8
Marketing	35.647	17.8	15.2 to 19.1	14,024	15.3	12.6 to 18.6
Fulfillment	23,819	11.9	6.1 to 13.6	12,024	13.1	8.4 to 19.4
General & admin.	26,946	13.5	8.9 to 19.0	14,461	15.8	12.6 to 22.0
Total operating expense	105,457	52.7	47.5 to 60.8	47,009	51.2	43.9 to 63.5
Net income from operations	4,947	2.5	−8.7 to 22.9	1,956	2.1	−16.6 to 17.0

| | Juvenile | | | Religious | | |
	$	Average	Mid-range	$	Average	Mid-range
Gross sales	106,611	110.0	108.3 to 113.5	25,659	128.5	110.6 to 158.6
Returns and allowances	9,710	10.0	8.3 to 13.5	5,686	28.5	10.6 to 58.6
Net sales	96,901	100.0	100.0 to 100.0	19,973	100.0	100.0 to 100.0
Cost of sales						
Manufacturing	36,920	38.1	34.5 to 46.9	8,614	43.1	30.8 to 53.7
Royalties	12,638	13.0	12.6 to 17.4	2,126	10.6	6.9 to 14.6
Total cost of sales	49,558	51.1	47.4 to 62.3	10,740	53.8	43.6 to 62.4
Gross margin on sales	47,343	48.9	37.7 to 52.6	9,233	46.2	37.6 to 56.4
Other income	7,564	7.8	4.3 to 10.3	543	2.7	0.6 to 8.7
Operating expense						
Editorial	4,646	4.8	4.3 to 8.0	836	4.2	2.6 to 8.0
Production	1,361	1.4	1.6 to 2.7	459	2.3	2.1 to 2.9
Marketing	12,798	13.2	12.2 to 17.6	3,174	15.9	12.6 to 21.0
Fulfillment	11,645	12.0	9.2 to 17.1	2,188	11.0	8.0 to 13.5
General & admin.	14,631	15.1	11.9 to 20.3	2,747	13.8	10.5 to 27.9
Total operating expense	45,082	46.5	39.8 to 68.9	9,404	47.1	39.9 to 69.1
Net income from operations	9,825	10.1	−11.9 to 16.5	373	1.9	−8.6 to 5.4

Source: Association of American Publishers 1982 Industry Statistics. © 1983 by Association of American Publishers, Inc. Reprinted with permission.
*As reported by 27 publishers.

TABLE 8 1982–1983 Departmental Data of College Stores
Comparison of Averages as a Percent of Net Sales

Stores with Net Sales ($)	Under $500,000	$500,000 to $1 Million	$1–$3 Million	Above $3 Million
		Percent of Net Sales		
New course books	66.6	60.5	54.7	40.4
Used course books	6.0	9.4	12.1	8.8
Course books	72.6	69.9	66.8	49.2
General books	3.4	3.3	4.4	10.2
Total book sales	75.9	73.2	71.1	59.4
Student supplies	12.4	13.2	15.8	15.8
Insignia items	4.3	5.4	5.6	8.3
Other merchandise	7.4	8.2	7.5	16.4
Total nonbook sales	24.1	26.8	28.9	40.6
Total net sales	100%	100%	100%	100%
Beginning Inventory	29.6	23.3	24.4	19.6
Net purchases	75.8	74.1	72.4	71.7
Freight in and out	1.9	1.8	1.7	1.5
−Ending inventory	−31.7	−24.6	−24.6	−20.9
Cost of sales	75.7	74.7	73.9	71.8
		Gross Margins by Department		
New course books	21.4	21.7	20.6	20.0
Used course books	36.1	31.6	32.4	31.2
Course books	23.3	23.5	22.8	21.7
General books	36.9	33.3	29.5	29.5
Total book gross margin	23.6	23.0	23.7	22.9
Student supplies	33.3	36.2	38.4	39.6
Insignia items	30.2	32.4	34.2	40.9
Other merchandise	26.0	29.6	30.9	30.6
Total nonbook gross margin	30.7	32.9	35.1	36.0
Total store gross margin	24.3	25.3	26.1	28.2
No. of stores responding	19–43	30–58	48–67	60–86
		Stock Turnover by Department		
New course books	4.0	4.3	4.5	4.0
Used course books	3.8	6.1	5.3	5.7
Course books	3.8	4.3	4.6	4.4
General books	1.9	1.4	1.7	2.2
Total book stockturn	3.6	3.9	4.2	3.7
Student supplies	1.4	2.0	2.1	2.8
Insignia items	1.8	1.6	2.0	2.8
Other merchandise	2.7	4.2	4.3	4.7
Total nonbook stockturn	1.8	2.4	2.2	3.1
Total store stockturn	2.8	3.6	3.4	3.5
No. of stores responding	18–38	23–48	45–68	51–77

Source: *1982–1983 Merchandising/Operating Survey* compiled by NACS Financial Survey Committee © 1984 by National Association of College Stores. Reprinted with permission.

**TABLE 9 1983 Operating Income and Expenses of College Stores
Comparison of Averages as a Percent of Net Sales**

Stores with Net Sales ($)	Under $500,000	$500,000 to $1 Million	$1–$3 Million	Above $3 Million
Net sales	100%	100%	100%	100%
Cost of sales	75.7	74.7	73.9	71.8
Gross Margin	24.3	25.3	26.1	28.2
Salaries	11.9	12.0	12.0	13.1
Mandatory insur. & taxes	1.0	1.0	0.9	1.0
Employee benefits	1.2	1.4	1.4	1.4
Personnel costs	14.2	14.4	14.3	15.5
Rent	3.1	2.9	2.7	2.2
Maintenance, repair, clean- ing	0.3	0.3	0.3	0.7
Real Estate tax & insur.	0.0	0.0	0.1	0.1
Utilities	0.3	0.4	0.6	0.5
Occupancy costs	3.7	3.7	3.7	3.5
Advertising	0.1	0.1	0.3	0.6
Telephone & communica- tions	0.3	0.3	0.3	0.4
Stationery & supplies	0.7	0.6	0.6	0.7
Data processing	0.3	0.2	0.4	0.4
Depreciation	0.5	0.4	0.4	0.8
Professional services	0.2	0.5	0.3	0.4
Educational & buy mtgs.	0.3	0.2	0.1	0.1
Insurance	0.1	0.0	0.1	0.1
Other taxes	0.1	0.0	0.1	0.1
All other operating ex- penses	0.8	1.1	1.4	1.8
Misc. operating expenses	3.5	3.5	3.9	5.3
Total operating expenses	21.4	21.6	21.9	24.3
Gross margin	24.3	25.3	26.1	28.2
Operating income	2.9	3.7	4.2	3.9
+ Other income	+0.8	+0.9	+1.1	+1.2
− Other expenses	−0.4	−0.5	−0.6	−0.9
Net income before taxes	3.3	4.1	4.7	4.2
Number of stores responding	88	112	118	101

Source: *1982–1983 Merchandising/Operating Survey* compiled by NACS Financial Survey Committee © 1984 by National Association of College Stores. Reprinted with permission.

To round out our review of the industry's economic condition, we look at data from the recently released *1982–1983 Merchandising/Operating Survey of the National Association of College Stores.* Our excerpts from the report show sales and operating ratios by size of store reported by 419 NACS members, most of which are among the larger, institutionally owned stores.

Table 8 shows the share of total sales, gross margins, and stock turnover of the major merchandise divisions recognized in the NACS survey. Significantly, the share of total book sales, and of total and new course book sales, declines with the increasing size of the stores reporting. (Course books are defined as all books, text or

otherwise, chosen by faculty for course use.) The share of used course book and general book sales tends to increase with the larger store sizes. Margins on new coursebooks are considerably smaller than those on used and general books, and student supply items carry better margins than books as a whole. On the other hand, book stockturns are more rapid than those of nonbook merchandise. In general, the larger stores in the sample enjoy better total gross margins than the smaller stores do (Table 9), although their operating expenses are also higher. Relatively narrow gaps separate the smaller from the larger stores in bottom-line profitability.

TABLE 10 Selected Annual Salary Ranges Paid by Book Publishers in 1983*
(Thousands of Dollars)

Position†	Adult Trade	Scientific, Technical, Professional	Elhi	College
Executive editor	—	—	42–60	42–60
Senior editor	30–45	33–50	28–35	—
Acquiring editor	—	—	—	28–40
Editor	25–30	28–40	25–30	—
Developmental editor	—	—	—	20–25
Associate editor	20–26	20–26	20–26	—
Assistant editor	14–20	15–20	15–20	15–18
Regional sales manager	22–40	35–40	30–40	30–40
Sales representative	18–20	20–25	20	15–20
Advertising copywriter	14–20	16–25	15–20	14–20
Publicist	15–20	15–22	18–20	15–20
Copy editor	15–18	15–22	15–18	12–18
Production mgr./coordinator	17–35	30–40	15–40	30–35
Art director	25–30	20–35	30–35	30
Designer	15–25	16–25	14–25	18–25

*Based on data supplied by four employment agencies. Salaries reported are applicable to full-time, fully qualified new-hire employees, and include direct compensation only, not bonuses or fringe benefits.

†See accompanying definitions.

Note: Dash indicates position not applicable for this type of publishing.

Position Descriptions

Executive editor. Responsible for assigned sales, profit, return on investment results in a publishing company or division. Acquires manuscripts; manages development projects and author relations; publishes books meeting quality and salability standards for a designated market within time and expense budgets. May manage and approve acquisitions of other editors.

Senior editor. Acquires, evaluates, and develops manuscripts for a market. Develops project guidelines and schedules. Consults with authors; edits and rewrites. Directs copy editing, design, production. Advises marketing and sales on appropriate strategies. May supervise work of other editors.

Acquiring editor. Acquires, develops, and revises books. Develops and recommends publishing strategies through market knowledge. Works with authors; acts as liaison with design, copy editing, production. May have profit and loss responsibility.

Editor. Selects, evaluates, and develops manuscripts for a market. Consults with authors. Advises other departments on design, production, sales and promotion strategies. Establishes and coordinates editorial and publication schedules.

Developmental editor. Responsible for editorial development. Edits and rewrites to meet market requirements, works with reviewers and analyzes competing books. Coordinates editorial work with design and production.

Associate editor. Rewrites, clarifies manuscripts, consults with authors. Plans artwork; supervises production to specifications. May also copy edit.

Assistant editor. Screens manuscripts. May consult authors on changes in content, style, format. Works under close supervision of project or senior editor.

Regional sales manager. Responsible for maximizing sales and editorial acquisitions. Supervises district sales forces, establishes goals and performance objectives for a geographic area; may modify and implement national strategies on a regional basis.

Sales representative. Sells within a defined geographic area. Responsibilities may differ with products or markets.

Advertising copywriter. Originates and prepares advertising, publicity, and promotion materials. Schedules copy development to fit marketing plans. Works with artists to coordinate copy with layout.

Publicist. Books authors, press interviews. Writes press releases; handles travel arrangements.

Copy editor. Edits manuscript for style, accuracy, consistency, and so on. Supervises index preparation. Confers with other editors on these matters.

Production manager/coordinator. Prepares type specifications, page layouts. Coordinates copy editing, art, compositor and printer schedules. May also copy edit, proofread, design books or jackets.

Art director. Manages development of design and art concepts. Develops and recommends art and design plans; cost estimates. Supervises purchase of artwork.

Designer. Designs projects from conception to finished product. Commissions and supervises free-lance illustrators. May suggest printing and binding methods. May review proofs.

Outlook

With 1983—a year tainted by recession—behind us, we can look forward to a solidly productive 1984 and beyond. General retailers should once again lead the industry in gains, both in the volume of books sold and in the expansion of outlets. Institutional and educational markets will perform less vigorously although they, too, will be improving in the economically more favorable environment ahead.

The major liability in an otherwise encouraging picture remains the high price inflation affecting all sectors of the book field. In earlier forecasts, I had assumed a moderation of that inflation in line with declines in the general inflationary pattern, counting on significantly improved unit sales as a result. When book prices remained stubbornly high despite the moderating inflationary trend, I had to revise my unit sales forecasts substantially downward.

My preliminary 1984 projections for BISG call for gains in publishers revenues of 12.9% in dollars and 5.1% in units in 1984, setting a pace that I expect will continue through 1987. General retailers' sales will increase by 13.8% in dollars and 8.7% in units, while college stores will post gains of 13.0% in dollars and 3.6% in units in 1984. Libraries will show an 8.7% growth in dollars but suffer a 3.9% decline in units, and schools will, similarly, record a 7.6% dollar gain but experience a 0.5% unit loss. Direct to consumer sales should be much improved, with a 10.7% increase in dollars and a 4.8% gain in units. General consumer markets promise to continue moving at the established pace, while educational and institutional sectors should show further, gradual improvement during the next five years.

13

Title Output and Average Prices

CHANDLER B. GRANNIS

American book title output continued its moderate annual rise in 1983, while average per volume prices were holding steady or even beginning to drop very slightly in a number of subject categories for the first time in several years, according to R. R. Bowker Company computations.

Of U.S. book output in 1983, nearly 42,000 titles had been accounted for by the end of the year. Many more will be added as computations continue, and the final total, to be completed by late summer, will probably exceed the final 1982 total of about 47,000. Figures are compiled and computed under the direction of Peter Simon and Beverly Lamar of Bowker's Data Services Division, using the data base of the *American Book Publishing Record (BPR)* and *Weekly Record* for hardcover and trade paperback books, and the *Paperbound Books in Print* data base for mass market paperbacks.

So far, as can be seen in Table 1, the 1983 output comes to 41,888 titles, of which 3,825 are mass market paperbound volumes (Table 2) and 10,962 are paperbacks other than mass market (Table 3). The principal addenda in the final report will probably occur in the hardcover and trade paperback groups.

Table 4, showing imported books (hardbound and trade paperbound volumes only), is a report that had been missing from these surveys for several years because only incomplete data could be extracted from the *BPR* data base. The situation is now rectified, and import totals similar to those of the late 1970s (in the 4,500 to 5,000 range) can be expected in the final report for 1983.

The reader will doubtless conclude from Table 2 that a breakdown between new books and new editions could not be given for mass market books; this information is not available in the *Paperbound Books in Print (PBIP)* data base, from which mass market figures are derived. Similarly, the *PBIP* data base does not now provide information on imported titles, so mass market titles are not included in Table 4. Even if they were, however, the number probably would not be great.

Table A deals with average prices of hardcover volumes and indicates, at least for this preliminary report, an overall price increase of 50 cents above the 1982 final figure of $30.34. Table A-1, showing average hardcover prices of all volumes priced below $81, shows—again, on a preliminary basis—an increase of only 12 cents over the final 1982 average, $23.26.

Table B, giving per-volume averages in the mass market field, presents a highly erratic picture, with overall average 21 cents above the 1982 final average of $2.93.

Table C, per-volume average prices of trade paperbacks, indicates, in the preliminary compilation for 1983, a decline of 68 cents, or 5.5%, from the 1982 final average of $12.32. *This overall decline, however, is attributable almost entirely to declines in two categories, Biography and Sociology/Economics,* where, for reasons not traced, the 1982 averages turned out to be abnormally high. The only other category where the average per-volume price of trade paperbacks fell off was in Technology, with a 51-cent drop from 1982's $14.78.

TABLE 1 American Book Title Production—1981, 1982, 1983
Hardbound and paperbound books, domestic and imported, from listings in Bowker's *Weekly Record* and *Paperbound Books in Print*

Categories with Dewey Decimal Numbers	1981 titles (final) Hardbound & trade paperbound only New Books	New Editions	Totals	All hard- & paperbound Totals	1982 titles (final) Hardbound & trade paperbound only New Books	New Editions	Totals	All hard- & paperbound Totals	1983 titles (preliminary) Hardbound & trade paperbound only New Books	New Editions	Totals	All hard- & paperbound Totals
Agriculture (630–639: 712–719)	393	76	469	474	338	97	435	439	347	86	433	440
Art (700–711; 720–779)	1,450	235	1,685	1,693	1,453	260	1,713	1,722	1,294	172	1,466	1,472
Biography (920; 929; B)	1,407	379	1,786	1,860	1,447	240	1,687	1,752	1,356	203	1,559	2,059
Business (650–659)	1,031	302	1,233	1,342	979	335	1,314	1,327	990	268	1,258	1,266
Education (370–379)	1,006	152	1,158	1,172	887	148	1,035	1,046	739	111	850	856
Fiction	1,906	653	2,558	5,655	2,042	406	2,448	5,419	1,814	273	2,087	4,946
General Works (000–099)	1,428	229	1,657	1,743	2,055	283	2,338	2,398	1,945	222	2,167	2,216
History (900–909; 930–999)	1,813	465	2,278	2,321	1,696	443	2,139	2,177	1,350	368	1,736	1,761
Home Economics (640–649)	848	151	999	1,108	886	133	1,019	1,099	815	113	928	1,006
Juveniles	2,761	201	2,962	3,102	2,677	150	2,827	3,049	2,313	108	2,421	2,651
Language (400–499)	629	112	741	761	447	122	569	576	415	96	511	531
Law (340–349)	1,128	316	1,444	1,448	1,065	385	1,450	1,451	974	269	1,243	1,245
Literature (800–810; 813–820; 823–899)	1,477	256	1,733	1,777	1,454	250	1,704	1,742	1,337	216	1,553	1,597
Medicine (610–619)	3,128	625	3,753	3,788	2,691	510	3,201	3,229	2,352	486	2,838	2,869
Music (780–789)	298	101	397	398	265	77	342	346	265	56	321	323
Philosophy, Psychology (100–199)	1,141	244	1,385	1,465	1,151	242	1,393	1,465	980	207	1,187	1,277
Poetry, Drama (811; 812; 821; 822)	1,047	120	1,167	1,183	925	96	1,021	1,049	867	82	949	967
Religion (200–299)	1,905	347	2,252	2,278	1,762	291	2,053	2,075	1,533	226	1,759	1,781
Science (500–599)	2,781	577	3,358	3,375	2,604	506	3,110	3,124	2,164	424	2,588	2,605
Sociology, Economics (300–339; 350–369; 380–399)	6,627	1,122	7,749	7,807	6,319	1,081	7,400	7,449	5,660	1,056	6,716	6,759
Sports, Recreation (790–799)	921	165	1,086	1,264	832	150	982	1,191	749	135	884	1,056
Technology (600–609; 620–629; 660–699)	1,866	436	2,302	2,313	1,911	400	2,311	2,328	1,772	403	2,175	2,223
Travel (910–919)	372	96	468	472	352	107	459	482	330	94	424	442
Total	**37,259**	**7,359**	**44,618**	**48,793**	**36,238**	**6,712**	**42,950**	**46,935**	**32,361**	**5,692**	**38,053**	**41,888**

NOTE: In all these tables, figures for mass market paperbound book production are based on entries in Paperbound Books in Print. All other figures are from the *Weekly Record* (*American Book Publishing Record*) database.

TABLE 2   Mass Market Paperbound Titles

	1981 final	1982 final	1983 prelim.
Agriculture	5	4	7
Art	8	9	6
Biography	74	65	50
Business	9	13	8
Education	14	11	6
Fiction	3,097	2,971	2,859
General works	86	60	49
History	43	38	25
Home Economics	109	80	78
Juveniles	240	222	230
Language	20	7	20
Law	4	1	2
Literature	44	38	34
Medicine	35	28	31
Music	1	4	2
Philosophy, Psychology	80	72	90
Poetry, Drama	16	28	18
Religion	26	22	22
Science	17	14	17
Sociology, Economics	52	49	43
Sports, Recreation	178	209	172
Technology	11	17	48
Travel	4	23	18
Total	**4,175**	**3,985**	**3,835**

SOURCE: Paperbound Books in Print (R. R. Bowker Co.)

TABLE 3   Paperbacks Other Than Mass Market 1981, 1982, 1983

Categories	1981 titles (final) Totals	1982 titles (final) New Bks.	1982 titles (final) New Eds.	1982 titles (final) Totals	1982 titles (prelim.) New Bks.	1982 titles (prelim.) New Eds.	1982 titles (prelim.) Totals
Fiction	399	238	73	311	281	48	329
Nonfiction	12,011	10,299	2,048	12,347	8,866	1,767	10,633
Total	**12,410**	**10,537**	**2,121**	**12,658**	**9,147**	**1,815**	**10,962**

TABLE 4   Imported Titles, 1983, Hardbound & Trade Paperbound Only
(From Listings in *Weekly Record*)

	New Books	New Editions	Totals
Agriculture	46	14	60
Art	96	9	105
Biography	100	9	109
Business	76	14	90
Education	109	11	120
Fiction	98	18	116
General Works	143	29	172
History	188	29	217
Home Economics	26	8	34
Juveniles	61	4	65
Language	113	16	129
Law	78	16	94
Literature	158	9	167
Medicine	273	18	291
Music	43	4	47
Philosophy, Psychology	115	12	127
Poetry, Drama	124	12	136
Religion	84	2	86
Science	607	72	679
Sociology, Economics	924	81	1,005
Sports, Recreation	69	6	75
Technology	269	47	316
Travel	33	5	38
Total	**3,833**	**445**	**4,278**

TABLE A   Average Per-Volume Prices of Hardcover Books—1977, 1980, 1981, 1982, 1983
(From *Weekly Record* Listings of Domestic and Imported Books)

Categories with Dewey Decimal Numbers	1977 vols. (final) Average prices	1980 vols. (final)		1981 vols. (final)		1982 vols. (final)		1983 vols. (preliminary)		
		Total volumes	Average prices	Total volumes	Average prices	Total volumes	Average prices	Total volumes	Total prices	Average prices
Agriculture (630–639; 712–719)	$16.24	360	$27.55	390	$31.88	299	$33.54	301	$ 9,478.61	$31.49
Art (700–711; 720–779)	21.24	1,132	27.70	1,094	31.87	1,009	31.68	898	31,468.16	35.04
Biography (920; 929; B)	15.34	1,508	19.77	1,348	21.85	1,230	22.27	1,136	25,536.72	22.47
Business (650–659)	18.00	898	22.45	1,045	23.09	976	25.58	890	24,905.80	27.98
Education (370–379)	12.95	626	17.01	697	18.77	621	20.74	507	10,794.11	21.29
Fiction	10.09	2,100	12.46	1,855	15.49	1,972	13.91	1,663	23,618.12	14.20
General Works (000–099)	30.99	1,190	29.84	1,295	35.02	1,165	37.29	1,230	43,781.72	35.59
History (900–909; 930–999)	17.12	1,743	22.78	1,761	23.15	1,558	26.25	1,202	29,923.88	24.89
Home Economics (640–649)	11.16	517	13.31	584	16.07	569	16.42	519	9,139.07	17.60
Juveniles	6.65	2,742	8.16	2,660	8.31	2,290	8.77	2,062	19,997.82	9.69
Language (400–499)	14.96	318	22.16	328	22.95	346	22.85	295	7,109.62	24.10
Law (340–349)	25.04	759	33.25	1,175	36.30	1,047	35.61	826	31,786.30	38.48
Literature (800–810; 813–820; 823–899)	15.78	1,266	18.70	1,190	19.79	1,162	21.40	1,023	23,914.31	23.37
Medicine (610–619)	24.00	2,596	34.28	3,065	36.47	2,559	38.88	2,276	86,612.52	38.05
Music (780–789)	20.13	273	21.79	284	25.82	219	26.42	202	5,256.67	26.02
Philosophy, Psychology (100–199)	14.43	1,045	21.70	982	22.41	964	23.28	802	19,777.20	24.65
Poetry, Drama (811; 812; 821; 822)	13.63	753	17.85	699	19.34	568	19.96	523	12,133.76	23.20
Religion (200–299)	12.26	1,109	17.61	1,147	18.54	991	17.89	950	16,360.50	17.22
Science (500–599)	24.88	2,481	37.45	2,778	40.63	2,437	44.44	1,992	87,704.82	44.02
Sociology, Economics (300–339; 350–369; 380–399)	29.88	5,138	31.76	5,616	29.28	5,089	45.12	4,531	212,844.12	46.97
Sports, Recreation (790–799)	12.28	644	15.92	738	18.82	603	20.20	518	10,397.12	20.07
Technology (600–609; 620–629; 660–699)	23.61	1,742	33.64	1,864	36.76	1,558	40.65	1,458	55,070.49	37.77
Travel (910–919)	18.44	253	16.80	234	19.55	225	22.20	220	5,115.07	23.25
Total	**$19.22**	**31,234**	**$24.64**	**32,829**	**$26.63**	**29,457**	**$30.34**	**26,024**	**$802,726.51**	**$30.84**

TABLE B   Average Per-Volume Prices of Mass Market Paperbacks—1981, 1982, 1983
(From *Paperbound Books in Print*)

	1981 volumes (final) Average prices	1982 volumes (final)		1983 (preliminary)		
		Total volumes	Average prices	Total volumes	Total prices	Average prices
Agriculture	$2.54	3	$3.61	7	$ 35.65	$5.09
Art	5.49	9	8.45	6	27.80	4.63
Biography	3.82	65	4.29	49	227.05	4.63
Business	4.63	13	3.89	8	40.15	5.02
Education	3.96	11	4.25	6	33.25	5.54
Fiction	2.47	2,900	2.72	2,838	8,135.40	2.88
General Works	3.62	49	3.90	48	255.40	5.32
History	3.53	38	4.25	25	110.45	4.42
Home Economics	4.34	78	4.68	77	360.95	4.69
Juveniles	1.79	221	2.04	223	500.30	2.24
Language	3.41	7	3.61	20	68.45	3.42
Law	3.08	1	3.50	2	5.90	2.95
Literature	3.41	37	3.65	32	127.05	3.98
Medicine	3.66	27	5.08	31	160.50	5.18
Music	—	4	5.67	2	10.90	5.45
Philosophy, Psychology	2.83	70	3.57	90	390.55	4.33
Poetry, Drama	3.21	19	3.41	18	88.30	4.90
Religion	2.70	22	3.55	22	84.95	3.86
Science	4.45	14	4.70	17	72.35	4.26
Sociology, Economics	3.43	49	4.05	43	182.70	4.24
Sports, Recreation	3.04	207	2.90	171	592.50	3.47
Technology	4.20	15	4.33	47	188.80	4.02
Travel	3.22	23	7.55	18	178.65	9.92
Total	**$2.65**	**3,882**	**$2.93**	**3,790**	**$11,878.00**	**$3.13**

TABLE A-1. Average Per-Volume Prices of Hardcover Books, Eliminating All Volumes Priced at $81 or More 1977, 1980, 1981, 1982, 1983

Compare indicated classifications with Table A

Dewey Classifications	1977 (final)	1980 (final)	1981 (prelim. only)	1982 (final) Total volumes	1982 (final) Average prices	1983 volumes (preliminary) Total volumes	1983 volumes (preliminary) Total prices	1983 volumes (preliminary) Average prices
Agriculture (630–639; 712–719)				281	$29.08	284	$ 7,434.36	$26.17
Art (700–711; 720–779)				971	26.88	846	22,288.66	26.34
Biography				1,204	19.68	1,156	22,468.72	20.15
Business (650–659)				964	23.48	874	20,541.05	23.50
Education (370–379)				618	20.41	506	10,689.11	21.12
Fiction				1,966	13.57	1,661	23,283.12	14.01
General Works (000–099)	$22.45	$23.34	$25.15	1,095	26.93	1,178	30,710.08	26.06
History (900–909; 930–999)				1,538	23.70	1,189	28,504.38	23.97
Home Economics (640–649)				566	15.80	516	7,602.57	14.73
Juveniles				2,289	8.74	2,058	18,497.32	8.98
Language (400–499)	$14.55	$20.14	$20.65	343	22.09	291	6,620.97	22.75
Law (340–349)				997	29.30	785	23,253.52	29.62
Literature (800–810; 813–820; 823–899)				1,153	20.39	1,012	21,320.81	21.06
Medicine (610–619)				2,353	33.01	2,109	66,803.07	31.67
Music (780–789)				216	25.28	198	4,699.22	23.73
Philosophy, Psychology (100–199)	$14.17	$20.18	$21.61	960	22.75	799	19,152.25	23.92
Poetry, Drama (811; 812; 821; 822)				559	18.12	509	10,025.76	19.69
Religion (200–299)	11.98	15.55	16.58	984	16.61	945	15,260.50	16.14
Science (500–599)	23.78	32.67	33.97	2,200	35.20	1,839	63,935.95	34.76
Sociology, Economics (300–399; 350–369; 380–399)				4,957	23.81	4,405	108,151.68	24.55
Sports, Recreation (790–799)				595	18.61	511	9,694.62	18.97
Technology, (600–609; 620–629; 660–699)				1,433	31.27	1,371	44,586.89	32.52
Travel (910–999)				220	19.29	215	4,082.57	18.98
Total	$17.32	$22.48	$24.33	28,462	$23.26	25,216	$589,607.18	$23.38

TABLE C   Average Per-Volume Prices of Trade Paperbacks— 1977, 1980, 1981, 1982, 1983

(From *Weekly Record* listings of domestic and imported books)

Categories	1977 volumes (final) Average prices	1980 volumes (final) Total volumes	1980 volumes (final) Average prices	1981 volumes (final) Total volumes	1981 volumes (final) Average prices	1982 volumes (final) Total volumes	1982 volumes (final) Average prices	1983 volumes (preliminary) Total volumes	1983 volumes (preliminary) Total prices	1983 volumes (preliminary) Average prices
Agriculture	$ 5.01	104	$ 8.54	96	$ 9.74	116	$11.91	118	$1,729.64	$14.65
Art	6.27	563	9.09	651	10.07	625	12.75	434	6,383.97	13.19
Biography	4.91	363	6.57	444	7.33	414	26.50	368	3,733,13	10.14
Business	7.09	285	9.90	309	10.10	302	12.82	316	4,959.22	15.69
Education	5.72	382	8.42	484	9.54	383	10.22	310	3,538.60	11.41
Fiction	4.20	432	5.71	479	5.81	449	6.70	398	2,855.14	7.17
General Works	6.18	544	8.00	578	10.90	1,120	9.10	855	9,960.95	11.65
History	5.81	478	7.57	634	9.10	525	10.64	467	5,883.44	12.59
Home Economics	4.77	360	6.33	465	7.01	422	7.94	380	3,380.25	8.89
Juveniles	2.68	460	3.50	504	3.35	475	4.04	315	1,508.16	4.78
Language	7.79	215	8.59	252	8.56	208	10.51	198	2,214,40	11.18
Law	10.66	317	11.33	307	12.34	335	12.25	274	3,619.90	13.21
Literature	5.18	424	7.26	477	8.14	504	9.07	476	4,871.23	10.23
Medicine	7.63	682	11.46	814	12.35	573	13.13	503	6,885.06	13.68
Music	6.36	83	9.36	126	10.12	113	10.69	103	1,175.60	11.41
Philosophy, Psychology	5.57	382	7.57	415	9.66	395	10.93	348	4,039.06	11.69
Poetry, Drama	4.71	442	5.09	525	6.00	424	6.87	390	3,002.75	7.69
Religion	3.68	937	6.15	1,142	6.81	1,000	7.63	758	6,038.96	7.96
Science	8.81	630	13.46	648	14.75	605	15.29	510	8,977.18	17.60
Sociology, Economics	6.03	2,016	9.75	2,275	11.56	2,128	18.85	1,923	24,196.26	12.58
Sports, Recreation	4.87	326	7.11	414	7.86	355	9.28	338	3,185.51	9.48
Technology	7.97	601	13.52	918	14.60	673	16.78	593	9,653.51	16.27
Travel	5.21	247	6.73	263	8.20	221	8.17	190	1,769.55	9.31
Total	$ 5.93	11,279	$ 8.60	13,220	$ 9.76	12,365	$12.32	10,613	$123,561.47	$11.64

14

U.S. Book Exports and Imports

CHANDLER B. GRANNIS

United States book exports increased about 6.3% in 1982 over 1981, reaching a total of over $641.3 million (Table A), and book imports increased at a similar rate, about 6.8%, for a recorded total of almost $315 million (Table B), according to the U.S. Department of Commerce. The figures have been extracted and organized by *Publishers Weekly* from printouts supplied by William F. Lofquist, printing and publishing specialist at the department's Bureau of Industrial Economics, Washington, DC 20230.

The Commerce Department data omit export shipments valued under $500 and import shipments valued under $250; the actual amount of those shipments is not known.

In 1981 and 1982, imports were a little under half the value of exports; in 1980 and earlier, annual imports were reported at somewhat *over* half the export total.

Total figures are not available for units—numbers of copies of books exported and imported—since data on children's books are not given.

Broad Fluctuations

In all the Department of Commerce book categories,

year-to-year fluctuations are typically very broad and seldom easy to explain. The key categories, of course, are "Books Not Elsewhere Classified" under exports and "Other Books" among imports; most trade books, presumably, are accounted for in these groups, but in fact the Department of Commerce categories can only remotely be correlated with the book industry's own customary classifications.

The relative positions of the principal countries (Table C) receiving and sending books to the United States fluctuate considerably from year to year, but the top three countries in each column remain the same: Canada, the United Kingdom, and Australia for exports, and the United Kingdom, Canada, and Japan for imports. Canada accounted for about 37% of U.S. book exports in 1982; the United Kingdom was the source of some 27% of book imports by the United States. Small shipments in each case, however, must have accounted for large additional quantities in unknown proportions.

Table D covers total book title output of principal leading book-producing countries. Table E reports numbers of translations, by original language, for the top 25 languages as of 1978.

TABLE A   U.S. BOOK EXPORTS 1980–1982

Shipments Valued at $500 or More ONLY

	TO ALL COUNTRIES, Dollar Values				TO ALL COUNTRIES, Units				TO CANADA ONLY, Dollar Values		
	1980	1981	1982	% chg. 1981–82	1980	1981	1982	% chg. 1981–82	1980	1981	1982
Bibles, Testaments & Other Religious Books (2703020)	$31,867,260	$33,894,757	$31,873,724	− 6.0	43,501,521	35,871,584	34,872,569	− 2.8	$6,848,742	$7,710,272	$7,716,728
Dictionaries & Thesauruses (2703040)	6,018,536	7,098,264	5,750,959	−19.0	1,726,792	2,689,611	1,087,077	−59.6	1,312,839	1,557,846	1,063,469
Encyclopedias (2703060)	27,944,503	25,819,529	25,344,932	− 1.8	6,462,048	4,619,219	4,195,293	− 9.2	9,340,069	7,011,290	6,127,968
Textbooks, Workbooks & Standardized Tests (2703070)	99,657,783	118,716,052	130,785,740	+10.2	——	——	28,297,679	——	37,395,796	41,283,009	51,537,407
Technical, Scientific & Professional Books (2703080)	53,927,278	79,637,779	118,491,757	+48.8	15,807,469	21,678,179	30,606,547	+41.2	11,816,779	15,745,842	19,982,424
Books Not Elsewhere Classified & Pamphlets (2704000)	284,159,654	327,185,497	319,643,723	− 2.3	199,852,375	215,360,345	195,882,465	− 9.1	121,136,963	143,059,209	147,171,845
Children's Picture & Coloring Books (7375200)	8,049,807	10,848,562	9,445,771	−12.9	——	——	——	——	3,451,007	4,718,255	4,191,463
Total Domestic Merchandise Omitting Shipments Under $500	**$511,622,823**	**$603,200,440**	**$641,336,606**	**+ 6.3**	——	——	——	——	**$191,302,195**	**$221,085,723**	**$237,701,304**

source: U.S. Dept. of Commerce, **Printing and Publishing** issue of Spring–Summer 1980 and P&P editors; 1981 and 1982 figures compiled from data supplied to **PW** by U.S. Dept. of Commerce, Bureau of Industrial Economics (William S. Lofquist, Printing and Publishing Industry Specialist).

TABLE B   U.S. BOOK IMPORTS 1980–1982

Shipments Valued at $250 or More ONLY

	Dollar Values				TO ALL COUNTRIES, Units			
	1980	1981	1982	% Change 1981–1982	1980	1981	1982	% Change 1981–1982
Bibles & Prayerbooks (2702520)	$ 5,912,277	$ 5,363,579	$ 7,618,372	+42.0	1,513,528	2,234,254	8,560,438	+283.1
Books, Foreign Language (2702450)	30,100,817	27,021,249	27,081,560	+ 0.2	17,953,146	18,297,425	19,460,202	+ 6.4
Books Not Specially Provided for, wholly or in part the work of an author who is a U.S. national or domiciliary (2702560)	4,152,073	7,178,346	10,306,088	+43.6	1,148,235	15,202,787	38,699,397	+154.5
Other Books (2702580)	257,041,783	246,895,088	260,928,176	+ 5.7	196,199,815	202,306,063	217,021,948	+ 7.2
Toy Books & Coloring Books (7375200)	9,303,476	8,406,121	9,057,181	+ 7.7	——	——	——	——
Total Imports, Omitting Shipments Under $250	**$308,510,938**	**$294,862,383**	**$314,991,377**	**+ 6.8**	——	——	——	——

source: See footnote to Table A.

TABLE C U.S. BOOK EXPORTS & IMPORTS PRINCIPAL COUNTRIES, 1981–1982

U.S. Exports (over $500 shipments only)

	Dollars 1981	Dollars 1982	% Change 1981–82
Canada	$221,085,723	$237,701,304	+ 7.5
United Kingdom	90,109,326	82,570,276	− 8.4
Australia	53,348,172	57,026,542	+ 6.9
Japan	21,343,698	24,909,000	+ 16.7
Nigeria	22,177,822	21,305,568	− 3.9
Netherlands	14,654,782	17,324,325	+ 18.2
Mexico	21,695,165	15,508,370	− 28.5
Rep. S. Africa	10,621,634	12,248,738	+ 15.3
Germany, W.	9,638,096	11,870,388	+ 23.2
Philippines	6,863,202	11,045,829	+ 60.9
Portugal	7,332,287	10,105,811	+ 37.8
Ireland	3,387,508	10,043,952	+196.5
Saudi Arabia	8,442,042	9,131,554	+ 8.2
Brazil	9,795,851	9,058,563	− 7.5
Singapore	8,255,662	8,994,100	+ 8.9
New Zealand	7,757,549	8,200,195	+ 5.7
All others	86,691,921	94,292,091	+ 8.9
Total, all countries	**$603,200,440**	**$641,336,606**	**+ 6.3**

U.S. Imports (over $250 shipments only)

	Dollars 1981	Dollars 1982	% Change 1981–82
United Kingdom	$90,840,357	$85,036,854	− 6.4
Canada	39,252,863	47,500,975	+ 21.0
Japan	44,585,307	46,889,045	+ 5.1
Hong Kong	15,520,380	19,306,161	+ 24.4
Spain	15,157,382	16,575,489	+ 9.4
Germany, W.	16,442,051	16,350,227	− .6
Italy	14,108,956	15,573,855	+ 10.4
Netherlands	8,795,091	9,501,430	+ 8.0
Switzerland	7,861,061	7,026,595	− 10.6
Mexico	5,578,452	6,902,932	+ 23.7
France	5,946,085	6,454,008	+ 8.5
Belgium	2,158,506	5,751,581	+ 58.4
Singapore	5,115,987	5,330,870	+ 4.2
All others	23,499,478	26,990,275	+ 14.8
Total, all countries	**$294,862,383**	**$314,991,377**	**+ 6.8**

SOURCE: See footnote to Table A.

TABLE D TITLE OUTPUT: PRINCIPAL BOOK-PRODUCING COUNTRIES 1978–1980

	1978	1979	1980
AFRICA			
Egypt	1,680	———	———
Nigeria	1,175	———	2,316
NORTH AMERICA			
Canada	22,168	21,793	19,063
United States*	87,569	88,721	86,377
SOUTH AMERICA			
Argentina	4,627	4,451	4,698
Brazil	18,102	———	———
Chile	———	———	1,109
Colombia	———	———	5,492
Peru	968	857	766
Uruguay	———	1,012	857
ASIA			
Bangladesh	1,229	———	———
China	12,493	14,738	19,109
Cyprus	1,054	1,335	1,137
Hong Kong	———	3,386	———
India	12,932	11,087	13,148
Indonesia	2,628	2,402	2,322
Iran	2,657	———	———
Iraq	1,618	1,204	———
Israel	2,397	———	———
Japan	43,973	44,392	45,596
Korea, Rep.	16,424	16,081	20,978
Malaysia	1,328	2,037	———
Pakistan	1,317	1,184	1,279
Philippines	———	———	1,254
Singapore	1,306	1,087	1,406
Sri Lanka	1,405	1,582	1,875
Thailand	———	3,779	4,091
Turkey	———	5,071	3,396
Vietnam	1,721	———	———
EUROPE			
Austria	6,439	6,783	7,098
Belgium	9,012	10,040	9,009
Bulgaria	4,234	4,600	4,681
Czechoslovakia	9,588	10,089	11,647
Denmark	8,642	9,415	9,256
Finland	3,367	4,834	6,511
France	21,225	25,019	32,318
Germany, E.	5,680	5,816	———
Germany, W.	50,950	59,666	64,761
Greece	———	4,664	4,048
Hungary	9,579	9,120	9,254
Italy	10,679	11,162	12,029
Netherlands	13,393	13,429	14,591
Norway	4,407	5,405	5,578
Poland	11,849	11,191	11,919
Portugal	6,274	5,726	———
Romania	7,562	7,288	7,350
Spain	23,231	24,569	———
Sweden	5,256	5,396	7,598
Switzerland	10,077	10,765	10,362
United Kingdom	38,641	41,864	48,069
Yugoslavia	10,509	12,061	11,301
OCEANIA			
Australia	7,658	8,392	———
New Zealand	2,079	2,496	2,850
USSR	**84,727**	**80,560**	**80,676**
Byeloruss SSR	2,618	2,806	3,009
Ukraine SSR	8,259	9,032	9,081

SOURCES: **UNESCO Statistical Yearbook 1982,** Table 8.2 (New York, Unipub, 1983), except U.S.A. figures, which are supplied by R. R. Bowker Co. Data Services and University Microfilms. UNESCO figures are published late.

*Includes books and pamphlets issued through U.S. Government Printing Office (in 1978, 14,814; in 1979, 13,506; in 1980, 13,000 est.); also, university theses (in 1978, 31,529; in 1979, 30,035; in 1980, 31,000 est.).

NOT included in the U.S. figures are publications of state and local governments, publications of numerous institutions, and many reports, proceedings, lab manuals and workbooks.

TABLE E TRANSLATIONS BY ORIGINAL LANGUAGE: TOP 25 LANGUAGES IN 1978

	1976	1977	1978
English	19,264	19,577	23,715
Russian	6,994	6,771	6,745
French	6,105	6,054	6,220
German	4,665	4,656	5,663
Italian	1,323	1,260	1,731
Swedish	1,166	1,158	1,177
Spanish	751	649	879
Danish	589	577	625
Czech	653	715	584
Polish	570	539	578
Hungarian	682	685	565
Dutch	367	448	528
Latin	479	432	508
Serbo-Croatian	463	437	477
Romanian	376	383	454
Classical Greek	496	387	437
Chinese	288	165	352
Arabic	260	227	318
Japanese	157	129	308
Norwegian	235	279	264
Bulgarian	284	289	256
Hebrew	232	215	246
Sanskrit	192	152	221
Portuguese	151	140	215
Ukrainian	216	203	156
Total, all languages	**50,381**	**50,047**	**57,147**

SOURCE: **UNESCO Statistical Yearbook 1982;** Table 8.12.

15

Rights and Permissions

PAUL S. NATHAN

1983 was a year in which the subsidiary rights market regained much of its vitality. Pursestrings that had been drawn tight began to be loosened for books considered especially desirable for reprint, motion pictures, television, or serialization.

There appeared to be two reasons for this relaxation. One was the growing perception of an improving outlook for the U.S. economy, encouraging buyers of rights to spend more freely. Another was the dwindling of inventories and a need for more material to keep presses and cameras turning.

Perhaps because reprinters had become somewhat embarrassed about their lavish outlays of the past, climaxing with the $3.2 million spent for *Princess Daisy* in 1979, the exact amounts for some of 1983's biggest transactions were kept secret. It seemed likely, however, that top money for softcover rights to a hardcover title was commanded by Erma Bombeck's *Motherhood: The Second Oldest Profession*. The price paid by Dell, while less than the $2 million obtained by McGraw-Hill in 1980 from Fawcett for *Aunt Erma's Cope Book* by the same author, was known to be in seven figures.

If *Motherhood* was indeed in first place, the runner-up would then be *August* by Judith Rossner. Warner Books guaranteed $1.165 million for the bestseller interweaving the stories of a psychoanalyst with those of one of her patients. Rossner and her primary publisher, Houghton Mifflin, shared this bonanza on the basis of a 60–40 percent split.

Warner Books made another of the year's more newsworthy purchases in *The Name of the Rose*. A novel that required a certain erudition, including a knowledge of Latin, for full enjoyment, Umberto Eco's *moyenâgeux* ecclesiastical mystery, translated from the Italian, surprised many observers by hitting the number-one spot on national bestseller lists. Remaining at or near the top for better than half the year, it continued as a bestseller into 1984. Equally surprising was that when this dark horse, published under the Helen and Kurt Wolff imprint by Harcourt Brace Jovanovich, was put up for auction, nine reprinters vied for it. Then, most surprising of all, was the size of the winning bid: $550,000. Howard Kaminsky, Warner Books president and publisher, was asked how he expected to get his money back for something still widely regarded as of questionable mass appeal. He indicated that initial publication by Warner might be as a trade paperback, attractive to the same audience that had been buying the hardcover, but that even as a rack-sized reprint he thought it could give good account of itself. He added that he could see *The Name of the Rose* as one of those books that comes along every so often, bought by large numbers of people for its cachet even if not read.

One of the rules for running an auction for reprint rights is to be pretty sure someone out there wants to acquire them. On at least several occasions in 1983 auctioneers set a date for accepting bids—and nobody phoned one in. Such disappointments served to point up a trend of the last several years: reprinters passing over perfectly good material they formerly would have bought. Paperback houses have discovered that, by and large, their readers are satisfied with books—especially in such genres as romance, fantasy, and science fiction—conceived and launched at minimum expense as softcover originals.

Last year's *Publishers Weekly Yearbook* took note of an

aborted auction for reprint rights to *Ancient Evenings.* Hoping for a big sale prior to hardcover publication, Little, Brown invited bids for Norman Mailer's massive Egyptian novel, then, reportedly dissatisfied with what was offered, decided to try again after the book came out in the spring of 1983. The wait proved well advised; Warner Books once more registered one of its decisive bids—a shade over $500,000.

Some reprint deals involved more than one book. In this category none approached Berkley's buy of 35 Agatha Christie titles, a buy that edged out Warner and Bantam with a guarantee of $2.6 million for a seven-year license. Dell, the holder of the expiring license, reportedly attempted to renew it by offering the hardcover publisher, Dodd, Mead, slightly more than $1 million. Paperback rights in another 37 Christie mysteries remained for the time being with Pocket Books.

Judy Blume, the enormously popular young-adult novelist, fared well with a double-barreled deal for her two works of fiction for older readers. Pocket Books bought reprint rights to the new *Smart Women* from Putnam while renewing its license on *Wifey,* both for $1.6 million.

Other titles selling for reprint at good prices included *Almost Paradise* by Susan Isaacs (Harper & Row), to Ballantine for $800,000; Trevanian's *The Summer of Katya* (Crown), also to Ballantine, for $771,000; *The Love You Make* by Peter Brown and Steven Gaines (Crown), an "insider's" account of the Beatles, to New American Library for $750,000; Morris West's *The World Is Made of Glass* (Morrow), to Avon for $575,000; *The Warlord* by Malcolm Bosse (Simon & Schuster), to Bantam for $506,000; *Dream West* by David Nevin (Putnam), to NAL for $500,000; *Fatal Vision* by Joe McGinniss (Putnam), to NAL for $495,000; *Winter's Tale* by Mark Helprin (Harcourt), to Pocket Books for $350,000; and Nora Ephron's *Heartburn* (Knopf), to Pocket Books for $341,000.

Reprint contracts for a number of these included bonus or escalator clauses pertaining to the books' bestseller performance, movie adaptations, and so forth. In certain instances these raised the guaranteed base prices substantially.

Two of the year's major deals covered the acquisition of both hard- and softcover rights in books still being written. Weidenfeld & Nicolson, the English house controlling Mick Jagger's autobiography (a collaboration with John Ryle of the London *Sunday Times*), held a New York auction for U.S. publication rights. The floor from which bidding was supposed to start was reportedly $1.5 million. Bantam emerged the winner, on terms closely guarded by both buyer and seller. For $2 million Simon & Schuster and Pocket Books obtained Clive Cussler's next two novels, both dealing with Dirk Pitt, hero of seven previous intrigue-and-action tales.

The movie and television markets for books remained steady during 1983. Straight purchases, as always, were the exception, with most would-be producers holding material under option while they endeavored to work out financing and releasing arrangements. Among nonfiction titles bought outright for the big screen were three from

Random House. *Eleni,* Nicholas Gage's account of the torture and murder of his mother by Communist guerrillas in Greece, was acquired by Nick Vanoff and Mark Pick for a price that could range from $750,000 to $850,000. *Marie: A True Story,* in which Peter Maas tells of a young woman's courage in blowing the whistle on corrupt government practices in Tennessee, went to Dino De Laurentiis for $650,000. C. David Heymann's *Poor Little Rich Girl: The Life and Legend of Barbara Hutton* was bought by Lester Persky for $350,000 plus 5 percent of the picture's profits. Although the book subsequently was withdrawn from sale by the publisher, Random House, and dropped by the Book-of-the-Month Club (BOMC) on grounds of inaccuracy, Persky indicated that he still had faith in the biography's essential integrity and planned to proceed with filming.

Schindler's List, which falls somewhere between nonfiction and fiction (it was published in England as the former and in the United States by Simon & Schuster as the latter), was announced for production by Universal Pictures—prematurely, as it turned out, since MGM had earlier tied up rights to the true story from which Thomas Keneally had drawn his inspiration. This had to do with the rescue of Jews from the Nazis by a courageous non-Jew, Oskar Schindler. MGM lost interest in making a movie on the subject, and the way was cleared for Universal to buy the book for $500,000.

Ed McClanahan's first novel, *The Natural* (Farrar, Straus and Giroux), went for $100,000, cash on the barrel, to Marvin Mirisch at Universal. And three novels by Arbor House author Elmore Leonard were sold without going through the option phase—one of them, *LaBrava,* to Universal at a price of $400,000 for production by another Mirisch, Walter. The same studio also paid $350,000 for *Stick,* this sum covering the author's services as adapter. Finally, Davis-Panzer, a company with offices at Columbia Pictures, paid $200,000 for *Cat Chaser.* It had been the intention of Leonard's agent, H. N. Swanson, to auction film rights in *LaBrava* just as reprint rights are auctioned—a departure from accepted movie industry procedure. The auction was to take off from a floor of $600,000. But because the floor had not been established by a bid from a potential buyer, and no one was prepared to go that high let alone higher, "Swanie" was obliged to settle for the $400,000 figure. His comment afterward: "It's still a good price."

The discovery of Leonard as a "serious" writer after some 20 novels, accompanied by more and better screen deals, constituted one of 1983's success stories. On the heels of the Hollywood sales of *Stick* and *LaBrava,* his two most recent entries, came the sale of the 1981 *Split Images* to Uxor Productions for $350,000.

Not surprisingly, Leonard's stock has been rising on the reprint as well as the movie market. *LaBrava* was auctioned to Avon for $363,000, with up to $110,000 in possible bonuses if enough hardcover copies are sold.

Not all film options are alike. Certain ones have so much riding on them, either in money invested or in the commitment of stars or directors, that production is virtually assured. A "very substantial sum" put down by

Warner Bros. on *The Little Drummer Girl* was one of the reasons to expect that cameras will turn on the John le Carré novel, probably in 1984. Another was the agreement reached by the studio with George Roy Hill to direct. Assuming the option is in fact exercised, le Carré stands to receive close to $1 million.

For Sidney Sheldon the purchase for a film of his first novel, published by Morrow in 1971, marked the closing of a circle. Finally all his books have found—or are in process of finding—their way to theater or television screens. It will be the theater screen for *The Naked Face*, acquired by Canon Films as a starring vehicle for Roger Moore.

During the year self-confidence gave promise of paying off for Norman Katkov. Offered an option on his St. Martin's/Marek novel about pre–Pearl Harbor Hawaii, *Blood and Orchids,* that could lead to an overall payment of $250,000, he chose to hold out for something better. His gamble was rewarded by another bid for movie rights, from Lorimar Productions: $100,000 option against a total of $400,000 plus 2 percent of profits.

With his *Yentl the Yeshiva Boy,* after long preparation, emerging as a starring-directing vehicle for Barbra Streisand, Isaac Bashevis Singer seemed about to come into his own as a begetter of film projects. Three more works from the pen of the Nobel laureate were optioned—two by one producer, Herbert Kloiberg, who said he would combine them into a single feature, which might show either in theaters or in series form on TV. *The Manor* and *The Estate,* chosen by Kloiberg, portray the period from the middle to the end of the nineteenth century when Jews began to play an important role in Polish industry. The third book (all are published by Farrar, Straus and Giroux) re-creates Jewish life in seventeenth-century Poland. Titled *The Slave,* it was optioned by a group that usually buys for Roman Polanski. The assumption was that Polanski would direct this one, as a theatrical feature.

A British producer, Jack Weiner, took an option on Anne Edwards's biography of Margaret Mitchell, *The Road to Tara.* Whereas Weiner was spending $55,000 to tie up the Ticknor & Fields book for a year and would pay a total of $200,000 to complete the purchase, Mitchell herself parted with the film rights to *Gone With the Wind* for only $50,000. Even allowing for inflation, the deal had its ironic touch.

In an unusual shuffle, the two Jean M. Auel novels published so far in her Earth's Children epic moved from one area of film to another. Instead of being made as a miniseries for NBC-TV, *The Clan of the Cave Bear* and *The Valley of Horses* were taken over by Universal Pictures to be shot as two related theatrical movies. For Auel the change portended a larger financial return— considerably more than the quarter- to half-million dollars she would have earned from the series.

Additional markets were opened for dramatic rights to books with the appearance on the scene of several new motion picture companies. One of these, Vista Films, optioned Larry McMurtry's *The Desert Rose* (Simon & Schuster) well before the author's *Terms of Endearment* blossomed into one of the year's box-office and critical hits. It also optioned *The Franchise,* a football novel by

Peter Gent (Villard Books), and Dick Francis's *Danger* (Morrow).

The Catalina Production Group took options on *The Haven* by Ruth Gruber (Coward, McCann), Hammond Innes's Knopf novel *The Big Footprints; The Man Who Wanted to Play Center Field for the New York Yankees* by Gary Morgenstein (Atheneum), and three other books.

Marton Productions, formed to nurture young writing talent, helped develop seven titles, fiction and nonfiction, and placed all seven with publishers. One book, a collaborative effort by Richard Pierce Greenfield and Herbert Margolis, a partner in Marton, was bought not only by Simon & Schuster but by Universal Pictures. This was *Plunderers of the Gigabyte,* reputedly "the world's first computer espionage novel."

Although not a new company, Kings Road Productions entered a new phase, having raised enough money to be able to finance its own movies. On the Kings Road agenda were two novels by Jeremy Leven, *Creator* (Coward, McCann) and *Satan* (Knopf); Clifford D. Simak's Hugo Award winner *Way Station,* originally published by Doubleday; *Enemy Mine,* a novella in a Berkley collection, *Manifest Destiny,* for which Barry Longyear garnered all three top science fiction awards, and Nelson DeMille's tentatively titled *Dawn's Early Light,* scheduled as a Warner Books hardcover.

Television, both network and pay cable, detected good commercial potential in the fiction of Barbara Taylor Bradford. Early in the year Artemis Productions, a Los Angeles company, bought her first novel, *A Woman of Substance,* and later her second, *Voice of the Heart,* was purchased by producer John Conboy. Each of the Doubleday bestsellers went for six figures. Filming of *A Woman of Substance* was to get under way in February 1984; its release would be on Operation Prime Time. *Voice of the Heart* was scheduled by NBC.

Almost Paradise, the Susan Isaacs novel, added $500,000 in TV money to its $800,000 reprint guarantee. ABC will air the six-hour miniseries.

Robert A. Caro's *The Path to Power,* volume one of the projected trilogy The Years of Lyndon Johnson, was bought for TV by a new partnership, David Geffen and Mary Lazar. An eight-part series was envisioned. The producers expressed the intention of acquiring the second and third volumes as they came along, for similar treatment. Payment is called for in three stages, for a total of $1 million.

Another trilogy still being written, John Jakes's fictional panorama of the Civil War, has taken its first steps toward TV. David Wolper bought *North and South* and also, without seeing it, part 2 of this work, for which Harcourt Brace Jovanovich likewise was waiting.

Magazines found much of interest in the year's books, especially nonfiction, with substantial prices being paid for excerpts from beauty and health manuals. *The Jaclyn Smith Beauty Book,* for example, in preparation for October 1984 publication by Simon & Schuster, was grabbed by *Good Housekeeping* for $35,000. Before that, the same magazine beat out the competition for another title from the same publisher, *The Linda Evans Beauty*

1983 Seven-Figure Sales Involving Subsidiary Rights

Title	Author	Original Publisher	Subsidiary Rights Purchaser	Price
Motherhood: The Second Oldest Profession	Erma Bombeck	McGraw-Hill	Dell	"7 figures"
August	Judith Rossner	Houghton Mifflin	Warner Books	$1.165 million
35 books	Agatha Christie	Dodd, Mead	Berkley	$2.6 million
Smart Women; Wifey	Judy Blume	Putnam	Pocket Books	$1.6 million
Mick Jagger autobiography	Jagger with John Ryle	Weidenfeld & Nicolson	Bantam (hard- and softcover)	believed around $1.5 million
Two unpublished novels	Clive Cussler	S&S/Pocket Books joint purchase	Pocket Books	$2 million
The Little Drummer Girl	John le Carré	Knopf	Warner Bros. (film option)	approximately $1 million if option exercised

and Exercise Book, for which it paid the same amount. Presumably to satisfy "Dallas" star Victoria Principal's desire for an edge over both, *Good Housekeeping* upped the ante to $35,100 when it also acquired *The Body Principal* (Simon & Schuster again).

Just as it had drawn down one of the top prices for reprint, *Motherhood: The Second Oldest Profession* went for big money in a magazine auction: *Woman's Day* took it with a bid of $50,000. Later, *Woman's Day* spent $70,000 for *The Mary Kay Guide to Beauty* by the Beauty Experts at Mary Kay Cosmetics—particularly high for second serial rights.

Glamour paid its "highest price ever"—undisclosed—for *Why Can't Men Open Up?* by Steven Naifeh and Gregory White (Clarkson N. Potter). *Family Circle* decided *The Complete University Medical Diet* by Dr. Maria Simonson and John Heilman (Rawson) was worth $38,000. *US* handed over what may have been the highest amount ever for rights to a book being published in trade paperback: $50,000 for *Loving John* by May Pang (inamorata of John Lennon) and Henry Edwards (Warner).

Redbook continued as one of the more receptive magazines to new writers of quality fiction, though it dropped the regular feature of a condensed novel in each issue. *The New Yorker* also maintained its open-door policy to newcomers; one of its issues carried almost a third of a first novel, *Elisto* by Padgett Powell (Farrar, Straus and Giroux). *Ladies' Home Journal* bought David Nevin's novel about John and Jessie Frémont, *Dream West,* which was also to be a BOMC main selection. *Harper's* condensed J. M. Coetzee's *Life & Times of Michael K* prior to publication by Viking and before it had been awarded Britain's important Booker Prize, while *Vanity Fair* studded its pages with excerpts from books, among them Philip Roth's *The Anatomy Lesson* (Farrar, Straus and Giroux), Luis Buñuel's *My Last Sigh* (Knopf), and *Laura Z.* by Laura Z. Hobson (Arbor House).

The international traffic in rights may have lagged a bit early in the year, but it gained momentum as the months passed. By the time of the Frankfurt Book Fair in October, trade was humming. From England, in addition to the Jagger autobiography, a first novel, *Night Sky* by

Clare Francis, had been bought at auction in the United States for an unusually high advance: Morrow was the winner, bidding more than $500,000. American titles generating particular interest abroad included Norman Mailer's *Ancient Evenings* (Little, Brown) and *Tough Guys Don't Dance* (Random House), *Everything and More* by Jacqueline Briskin (Putnam), *Nop's Trials* by Donald McHaig (Crown), Jackie Collins's *Hollywood Wives, The Legend* by Shirley Conran (both Simon & Schuster), Arthur Hailey's *Strong Medicine* (Doubleday), and two rather similarly titled novels, *WarGames* and *War Day.* The former, a Dell paperback by David Bischoff, had been the source of a popular motion picture; the latter, by Whitley Strieber and James Kunetka, attracted attention abroad at the time of its auction for U.S. publication, when it elicited a bid of approximately $460,000 from Holt, Rinehart & Winston, which is to bring it out this year.

The book clubs, with Book-of-the-Month and Literary Guild having the most money to spend, bought during the year along largely predictable lines. A few of the titles for which they paid above-average amounts were *The Little Drummer Girl* (BOMC, $500,000), *Fatal Vision* (BOMC, $200,000), and Cathy Cash Spellman's Delacorte novel *So Many Partings* (Guild, $40,000).

Significant as a probable trend-setting deal was the licensing to Coleco Industries of material in the books by Richard Scarry, long a staple of the Random House and Western Publishing lists. Coleco, the manufacturer of Cabbage Patch Kids dolls and the Adam computer, obtained exclusive rights to make and market home video games and software based on the author-illustrator's stories and characters. It was also empowered to license his properties for transmission into the home via telephone lines, broadcast and pay cable TV. In addition, Coleco was to become sublicenser or developer of a wide range of Scarry juvenile products, exclusive of books.

Any survey of a given year must necessarily be incomplete. But as may be gathered from even the selective review of highlights in the foregoing paragraphs, last year was a lively one in the rights market.

16

Financial Summaries of Publicly Owned Book Publishers

JOHN MUTTER

The 14 major publicly held publishing companies or subsidiaries listed below had varied results during the year, but on the whole, they showed fair growth in sales and revenues and significant improvements in net income.

The gains in net income, ranging as high as Harper & Row's 60.9% gain, reflected an improved economy and—more important—efforts taken at most companies in the past several years to cut costs and improve productivity, including such measures as cutting the size of the work force and selling unprofitable operations.

Besides Harper & Row, such efforts paid off at Addison-Wesley, CBS/Publishing, Houghton Mifflin, Macmillan, McGraw-Hill, Thomas Nelson, John Wiley & Sons and Zondervan, all of which had increases in net income of at least 15% and more often in the high 20s.

Lower interest rates and lower losses on foreign exchange transactions also helped publishers' bottom lines.

Harcourt Brace Jovanovich's and Grolier's net income rose dramatically, but both reflected special situations. In the previous year HBJ had written off all the costs of moving its headquarters—$27.7-million. This method of accruing such costs dragged down 1982 earnings to $3.3-million, thus lowering the point of comparison for this year's net income figures.

In Grolier's case, the company recorded an extraordinary gain in the 1983 fourth quarter of $35.4-million from its completed refinancing program, resulting in a large gain over 1982 figures.

Net income at SFN Companies dropped, mainly be-cause the company has been making substantial investments in acquiring and creating companies. The use of money for these purposes instead of depositing in interest-yielding investments sustantially cut into short-term investment income.

Time, Inc., Books had a large loss, largely because of a $20-million writedown on the sale of Time-Life Books's subsidiary in Japan. Other Time publishing subsidiaries, including Book-of-the-Month Club and Little, Brown, had a banner year.

Sales rose between 8.0% and 22.7% at most companies, reflecting a revived economy. Religious publishers Thomas Nelson and Zondervan had the highest sales during the year, and textbook and trade publishers also did well. Sales dropped at only two companies, Time, Inc., Books and Grolier.

Note: For purposes of this survey, the results of John Wiley & Sons, SFN Companies and Harper & Row were taken on a quarterly basis rather than by the fiscal year.

Addison-Wesley

	Year Ended Nov. 30	
	1983	1982
Sales	$114,346,000	$102,226,000
Income	5,648,000	4,556,000

For the year sales rose 11.9% and net income rose 24.0%.

CBS/Publishing Group

	Year Ended Dec. 31	
	1983	1982
Sales	$587,000,000	$538,700,000
Income	55,200,000	38,000,000

For the year revenues rose 9.0% and operating profits rose 45.3%.

The company stated that the improvement reflected revenue and profit gains by each of the group's two divisions, including Holt, Rinehart and Winston, the Dryden Press, Praeger Publishers, W. B. Saunders Co. and Winston Press.

Grolier

	Year Ended Dec. 31	
	1983	1982
Sales	$286,214,000	$333,249,000
Income	46,864,000	4,357,000

For the year net sales and other revenues dropped 9.8% and net income rose substantially.

The company said that the year's drop in sales was attributable to Latin American operations, "where local currency financial statements in Mexico and Venezuela were translated during 1983 at greatly devalued rates," and to a sales drop of 6% in the U.S. and Canada.

Operating income grew 32% in the U.S. and Canada because of cost reduction programs and improved operations, but operating income dropped 41% internationally, mainly because of conditions in Latin America.

In the fourth quarter the company reported an extraordinary gain of $35.4-million from its refinancing program completed last fall.

Harcourt Brace Jovanovich

	Year Ended Dec. 31	
	1983	1982
Sales	$648,827,000	$575,255,000
Income	27,476,000	3,294,000

For the year sales and revenues rose 12.8% and the net gain grew substantially. In the fourth quarter of 1982 the company had a net loss of $15.9-million because of its decision to accrue all the costs of its relocation to Orlando, Florida, amounting to $27.7-million, in that quarter.

During the year elementary and secondary sales and revenues rose 27.0% to $212.3-million and net income grew 105.9% to $22.5-million. University and professional education sales and revenues rose 8.2% to $173.5-million and net income dropped 5.1% to $7.5-million.

Harper & Row

	12 Months Ended Jan. 31	
	1984	1983
Sales	$194,721,000	$180,318,000
Income	6,871,000	4,271,000

For the year net operating revenues rose 8.0% and net income rose 60.9%.

Note: Harper & Row's fiscal year begins May 1.

Houghton Mifflin

	Year Ended Dec. 31	
	1983	1982
Sales	$219,208,000	$189,714,000
Income	13,190,000	10,678,000

For the year net sales rose 15.5% and net income rose 23.5%.

Macmillan

	Year Ended Dec. 31	
	1983	1982
Sales	$430,515,000	$384,311,000
Income	25,061,000	20,833,000

For the year sales of products and services rose 12.0% and net income rose 20.3%.

"Our strong performance in 1983 results from sharply improved profitability in virtually all Macmillan's operating divisions, with publishing and information services particularly strong," Edward P. Evans, chairman and chief executive officer, stated.

The school division had record results, and there were "strong" profit gains in the professional, Glencoe and college divisions. Macmillan Book Clubs had "dramatically improved results" during the year.

McGraw-Hill

	Year Ended Dec. 31	
	1983	1982
Sales	$1,295,175,000	$1,193,587,000
Income	126,478,000	110,018,000

For the year operating revenue rose 8.5% and net income rose 15.0%.

"The newly consolidated worldwide book operations reported a strong increase in operating profits on a modest increase in revenues," Joseph L. Dionne, president and chief executive officer, said. "Domestically significant gains were registered by the Gregg, CTB, general books and health professions units while abroad Canada, Mexico and the Caribbean operations set the pace."

Thomas Nelson

	Nine Months Ended Dec. 31	
	1983	1982
Sales	$43,319,172	$35,304,135
Income	2,648,928	2,191,558

For the nine month period operating revenues rose 22.7% and net income rose 20.9%

President Sam Moore said that "virtually all areas" of the company recorded growth in revenues and income. Bible sales were particularly strong, and bestsellers by both the religious and general book divisions contributed to the growth.

Prentice-Hall

	Year Ended Dec. 31	
	1983	1982
Sales	$448,206,000	$409,731,000
Income	39,035,000	36,266,000

For the year sales rose 7.4% and net income rose 9.4%.

SFN Companies

	12 Months Ended Jan. 31	
	1984	1983
Sales	$302,424,000	$275,065,000
Income	27,804,000	29,492,000

For the year total revenues rose 9.9% and net earnings dropped 5.7%.

John R. Purcell, chairman and president, said that results "were penalized due to aggressive investments in acquisitions, reducing short-term investment income." The financing of new electronic publishing software also caused a greater net loss for part of the year than was anticipated.

During the year, SFN purchased or agreed to purchase a number of companies, including New York Law Publishing, Biomedical Information Corp., Broadcast Advertisers Reports, and a number of television and radio stations.

SFN sold the Fleming H. Revell Co.

Note: SFN's fiscal year begins May 1.

Time, Inc., Books

	Year Ended Dec. 31	
	1983	1982
Sales	$401,300,000	$484,600,000
Income	(13,700,000)	1,600,000

For the year revenues dropped 17.2% and the operating gain became an operating loss.

The company stated that the restructuring of Time-Life Books was completed during the year with the sale of most of the subsidiary's operations in Japan, which "resulted in a writedown of approximately $20-million." Time-Life Books's U.S. and European operations had improved results during the year while Book-of-the-Month Club and Little, Brown had record sales and profits.

John Wiley & Sons

	12 Months Ended Jan. 31	
	1984	1983
Sales	$180,272,000	$156,556,000
Income	12,218,000	8,379,000

For the year net sales rose 15.2% and net income rose 45.8%.

The company noted that it had only a minor charge to net earnings for foreign currency losses this year compared with a charge of $1.4-million in the previous year.

Interest expense was also sharply reduced.

Note: Wiley's fiscal year begins May 1.

Zondervan

	Year Ended Dec. 31	
	1983	1982
Sales	$92,830,000	$75,713,000
Income	4,330,000	3,092,000

For the year net sales rose 22.6% and net income rose 40.0%.

Peter Kladder, Jr., president, said that 1983 sales and profits were at record levels in both publishing and retail operations. Publishing improvements reflect strong book and Bible sales and a turnaround in the music and record business. Productivity improvements, cost-cutting and lower interest rates helped in the earnings growth.

17

New Business Ventures

WILLIAM GOLDSTEIN

Algonquin Books, a trade house "dedicated to publishing good books," announced that it would publish its first list in Fall 1983. The company, located in North Carolina, is headed by Louis D. Rubin, Jr., a writer and professor of English at the University of North Carolina, Chapel Hill. Shannon Ravenal, an editor at Houghton Mifflin (where she was responsible for *Best American Short Stories*), was named senior editor.

Peter Bedrick, who resigned as publisher and executive vice-president of Schocken Books, founded his own company, **Peter Bedrick Books,** in April. The new imprint would concentrate on adult and children's illustrated books, as well as mythology, history, and reference titles, Bedrick said. Harper & Row, it was announced, would handle fulfillment. The publisher's offices are located in New York.

The Book Peddlers was formed in August by Jonathon Lazear and Vicki Lansky to "package, publish, or agent books." Lazear has held various posts at Doubleday, Warner, Harcourt Brace Jovanovich, Simon & Schuster, and Fawcett. Lansky is former co-owner and founder of Meadowbrook Press and author of the bestselling *Feed Me! I'm Yours* and *The Taming of the C.A.N.D.Y. Monster.* The firm is based in Minneapolis.

R. R. Bowker, publisher of *Publishers Weekly, Library Journal,* and *School Library Journal,* announced that it would begin publishing *Small Press: The Magazine of Independent Book Publishing* in September 1983.

Bradford Mountain Book Enterprises was formed by Shirley Sarris and Charles Van Doren to distribute reference books and practical guides that focus on international business and finance, as well as international publishing. Sarris has worked at a variety of publishing companies, and Van Doren was most recently vice-president, editorial, of Encyclopaedia Britannica, of which he remained a member of the board of directors. The company has offices in New York.

Calling book distribution "an appalling calamity for most authors," William F. Buckley, Jr., author, syndicated columnist, and founder and editor of the *National Review,* and Stuart W. Little, author and former editor of the Authors Guild *Bulletin,* formed the New York-based **Buckley-Little Book Catalogue Co.,** in June, to promote the sales of authors' out-of-print books to booksellers, librarians, and others through an annual catalog. The pair solicited the 6,000 members of the Authors Guild. Under the plan, authors would be required to buy overstock copies of their books from publishers at "the remainder price," as the books go out of print. The books will either be warehoused to the Catalogue Co., or by the authors themselves, who will pay a small premium for listing in the annual catalog, the first of which was scheduled for January 1984.

Paula Diamond, formerly associate publisher, marketing, for Harper & Row, opened her own New York literary agency in July. As director of subsidiary rights at Harper & Row, beginning in 1973, she handled the record-breaking sale of *The Thorn Birds* and *Linda Goodman's Love Signs.* Most recently, she was associated with Nat Sobel Associates, where her clients included Allan Sloan and Hillel Levin.

Esquire Press division was formed by *Esquire* magazine

to publish and co-publish books "about wide-ranging subjects of contemporary interest." Priscilla Flood, *Esquire* executive editor, was named managing editor.

Lawrence Freundlich, former publisher of Wyndham Books at Simon & Schuster, formed his own company, **Freundlich Books,** to publish hardcover fiction and nonfiction, with British backing. His company has its offices in New York.

Gelles-Coles Literary Enterprises was established in September by Sandi Gelles-Coles, most recently a senior editor at Dell/Delacorte, where she worked with Danielle Steel, among other authors. The New York-based firm will specialize in book packaging, author representation, and editorial and consulting services.

Mildred Hird resigned as vice-president and director of subsidiary rights at Bantam Books to establish her own New York-based business selling translation rights. She had been with Bantam for 16 years.

InfoSource, a book-packaging company to develop projects for publishers on the business applications of microcomputers, was established in October by D. Michael Werner and Thomas W. Warner, authors of books on computers and business information. InfoSource has offices in Gainesville, Florida.

Asher D. Jason, formerly vice-president of Edward J. Acton, Inc., formed **Asher D. Jason Enterprises** in November, for the purposes of literary representation and book packaging. The firm has its offices in New York.

Alfred van der Marck, former general manager of the McGraw-Hill co-publishing and foreign rights division, formed a new imprint, **Alfred van der Marck Editions.** Sales, distribution, and warehousing will be handled by Harper & Row, San Francisco.

The Evan Marshall Agency was formed in October by Evan Marshall, former senior editor at Dodd, Mead. His firm, located in New York, will specialize in adult fiction and nonfiction.

L. T. Mead & Associates was formed in October by Linda T. Mead, former marketing director of Schocken Books. The firm will represent publishers in subsidiary rights sales, licensing, special sales, and marketing. The agency, it was announced, would also represent authors. Mead is located in Foster City, California.

New England Publishing Associates, a book-producing company and literary agency with a special interest in nonfiction, was formed in September by Elizabeth Frost Knappman, formerly a senior editor at Morrow and Doubleday. Branches of the firm were established in Old Lyme, Connecticut, and Brooklyn, New York.

In July, *The New York Review of Books* and its book

club subsidiary, The Readers' Subscription, announced the establishment of the American Garden Book Club, under the directorship of Pamela Lord, a gardener and owner of Good Garden Books, a bookstore in Bridgehampton, New York.

On-Line Publicity, a company specializing in media and marketing for computer products, was formed in November as a division of M. Lande Promotions, Inc., and Diane Glynn Publicity and Public Relations, Inc. The company is located in New York.

Proscenium Publishers was formed in November by Mel Zerman, former administrative sales manager at Random House. The publisher will "specialize in books on the performing arts," concentrating, initially, on trade paperback reprints under the imprint of Limelight Editions. The company is located in New York.

Thor Information Services, designed to provide a variety of educational services to the "information and publishing communities," was organized in July by three members of the board of the Association of American University Presses, who resigned during the AAUP's annual meeting in June. The three staffers, whose resignations became effective September 30, were Jerome J. Lewis, Larry M. Fees, and Sheila C. Brady.

Thorsons Publishers, Inc., was founded in May as a joint venture of Thorsons Publishers, Ltd., of Great Britain, and Inner Traditions International Ltd., an American house. The new company announced it would specialize in health books, with an output of 50 titles per year. The company is located in New York.

Waldenbooks announced it would publish and distribute to its more than 800 stores, four hardcover volumes of classic novels under the imprint **Longmeadow Press.** The first four titles, which appeared in July, included a one-volume edition of Mark Twain's *The Adventures of Tom Sawyer* and *The Adventures of Huckleberry Finn,* Jack London's *The Call of the Wild, White Fang and The Sea-Wolf, The Invisible Man* and *The Time Machine* by H. G. Wells, and the Brontes' *Wuthering Heights* and *Jane Eyre.* Each book retailed for $4.95.

Werbel & Peck was formed in September to manufacture and sell out-of-print fiction, nonfiction, and young adult books. Its founders were Lawrence Werbel, president of the Hebrew Publishing Co. for the past 10 years, and Ted Peck, of Ted Peck Advertising. The company is located in New York City.

Rhoda A. Weyr, a literary agent at the William Morris Agency for the past 10 years, established her own firm, **Rhoda Weyr Agency,** in August. Among her authors: Lonnie Barbach, Sheila Ballantyne, and Gordon Liddy. The new agency is located in New York.

18

Mergers and Acquisitions

JOHN MUTTER

Merger and acquisition activity in 1983 was quiet in comparison with previous years. Major sales were made by large companies for reasons that often had little to do with the subsidiary's performance or financial health—in sharp contrast with 1982, when three major mass market houses and subsidiaries, several of them ailing, were sold.

In 1983, Mattel agreed to sell its profitable Western Publishing subsidiary after Mattel's electronics subsidiary sustained heavy losses during the year. Times Mirror sold profitable New American Library (NAL) because it wanted to concentrate on professional publishing. Gulf & Western, which already owned a quarter of profitable Esquire, Inc., made an offer to purchase the rest of the company's outstanding stock. Macmillan and Scholastic made acquisitions that bolstered their positions in specialized markets. SFN Companies sold its religious publishing subsidiary.

One last casualty of the gloomy economic scene in 1982 was Doubleday, where the Dial Press subsidiary essentially became an imprint of Doubleday, and Dell and Delacorte's operations were cut back.

Mattel Agrees to Sell Western

Late in the year, Mattel agreed in principle to sell its Western Publishing subsidiary for $75 million and the assumption of various liabilities to Richard A. Bernstein, a New York investor, and certain members of Western management. Mattel had acquired Western in 1979 for $120.8 million in cash and securities.

In addition to publishing Golden Press children's books, Western prints mass market paperbacks—with Dell as its biggest customer, educational kits, newspaper inserts, card games, and sales promotion materials.

Western had been one of Mattel's most profitable subsidiaries. However, the company as a whole had a net loss of $179.4 million on sales of $424.4 million in the six months ended July 30, 1983. In the same period Western had an operating profit of $1.8 million on sales of $104.9 million.

Mattel's problems stemmed from the company's electronics subsidiary, which markets Intellivision home video games and home computers. Suffering from severe competition, the electronics subsidiary lost over $201.1 million with sales of only $25.5 million in the six months ended July 30.

Gulf & Western Agrees to Buy Esquire

In December Gulf & Western, which owns publishers Simon & Schuster and Pocket Books, announced an agreement in principle to buy Esquire, Inc., for about $190 million. Esquire was destined to become the nucleus of the new Simon & Schuster Education Group. Esquire management was slated to remain in place at the company.

Esquire, owner at one time of *Esquire* and *GQ* magazines, is primarily an educational textbook and film and music publisher. Its subsidiaries include Allyn & Bacon, Follett Publishing, Cambridge Book Co., Coronet Instructional Media, Globe Book Co., and Modern Curriculum Press.

At the time the sale was announced, Gulf & Western owned 2.8 million shares of Esquire, about 27 percent of its 10.5 million shares of common stock outstanding. Gulf

& Western offered to buy the remaining stock at $25 a share.

The acquisition marked Gulf & Western's first major presence in educational publishing as well as the company's first major acquisition since the death of its former chairman Charles Bluhdorn early in the year. After his death, the company had sold much of its $750 million stock portfolio and announced a divestiture program that, when completed, would sell off some 20 percent of Gulf & Western's assets.

Times Mirror Sells New American Library

One of the biggest acquisitions of the year was the purchase of New American Library for $50 million in cash from Times Mirror by a private investor group headed by Ira J. Hechler and Odyssey Partners. The transaction, completed in December, included senior management of NAL in the purchasing group.

Odyssey Partners consists of three former senior partners at Oppenheimer & Co.—Lester Pollack, Leon Levy, and Jack Nash—who sold Oppenheimer to British Mercantile House in 1982. The three then founded Odyssey and have been involved in various financing deals, proxy fights, and acquisitions of communications, apparel, real estate, and retail operations. They said they were attracted to NAL by its "excellent reputation, its record of consistent earnings, and its backlist and prospective list that provide for growth in its basic business in an industry that is likely to grow." The new owners hinted that acquisitions, even of a hardcover house, were possible.

Top NAL executives who are now minority partners in the company are Robert G. Diforio, chairman and chief executive officer; Elaine Koster, executive vice-president and publisher; and Marvin Brown, president and chief administrative officer.

Times Mirror sold NAL in an effort to "focus the main thrust of its book publishing activities on the publication of professional books." The sole trade subsidiary Times Mirror will keep is Harry N. Abrams, the art book publisher.

Times Mirror bought NAL from Kurt Enoch and Victor Weybright, its founders, in 1960. Over the past 15 years NAL has been profitable and for the last 10 years its profits were between 10 and 12 percent of pretax sales.

Dial Merged with Doubleday; Dell, Delacorte Cut Back

In one of the larger and more controversial mergers of the year, Doubleday announced major changes in February that severely affected Dell, Delacorte, and the Dial Press.

Relative to its size, Dial was perhaps the most strongly affected: Its operations were moved to corporate headquarters with the loss of 6 out of 18 staff jobs. Subsidiary rights, publicity, and design were thereafter handled by Doubleday departments; sales and manufacturing were already handled by Doubleday. Many in the industry considered the move to signify the "end" of Dial.

Dell and Delacorte were mainly affected by major across-the-board staff cutbacks, precise numbers for which Doubleday would not divulge. However, reliable estimates put the totals at about 100 employees let go in a total work force of about 1,100. Delacorte's output had already been cut back, from about 40 titles a year in 1978 to 10 a year now.

Doubleday executives blamed the cuts on "a substantial growth in the staff over the past few years" as well as "the present economic climate." They also claimed that there would be no redirection of effort in book publishing at Dell.

Other Mergers and Acquisitions

SFN Companies sold the Fleming H. Revell Co. to the Zondervan Corporation in September for $10 million. Three-quarters of that amount was paid in cash; the remaining $2.5 million is to be paid with interest over the next three years.

Revell, which publishes evangelical and motivational trade books and a magazine for women and has annual gross revenues of about $13.5 million, continued to operate as a wholly owned subsidiary under its president, John S. Reno, Jr. The company was founded in 1870 and was bought in 1978 by Scott, Foresman and Company, now an SFN subsidiary.

SFN sharply curtailed its involvement in trade publishing when it sold William Morrow & Co. in 1981. With the sale of Revell, SFN chairman and president John R. Purcell stated, "SFN can now focus its resources on its base businesses and areas targeted for diversification."

Silver Burdett Co., an SFN subsidiary, bought most of the assets of Instructo/McGraw-Hill in August. Instructo, which developed and marketed supplementary educational supplies for the school and school distributor markets, was combined with the Judy Company, the Silver Burdett subsidiary that manufactures and sells educational puzzles and other preschool and primary school teaching aids. The new company is called Judy/Instructo.

Simon & Schuster (S&S) bought the J. K. Lasser Tax Institute, which was founded in 1954 and puts out financial, business, and tax publications. S&S has had a connection with J. K. Lasser since 1937, when it signed Lasser, a certified public accountant, to write a tax guide for consumers. That book, *J. K. Lasser's Your Income Tax*, is updated annually and has had over 26 million copies in print over 46 years.

At the beginning of the year, Macmillan hired Gordon R. Hjalmarson, former chairman, chief executive officer, and president of SFN Companies, to work "in conjunction with Macmillan's top management and development group in the company's expanded efforts to acquire product lines and businesses in publishing and related fields."

At the same time the company announced that it had

made an agreement with a New York bank for a $150 million line of credit to finance the acquisitions.

The hiring of Hjalmarson and the announcement that it was on the lookout for companies to buy marked a major change at Macmillan, which for three years had divested itself of over half the company as constituted in 1979, including such major subsidiaries as Brentano's, Alco-Gravure, and Cassell.

Macmillan made two purchases during the year, both of industrial education and home economics publishing companies.

The first purchase was of the Bennett Publishing Co. of Peoria, Illinois, a vocational-educational publisher that specializes in industrial arts and home economics textbooks for the high school and post–high school markets. After the acquisition, the vocational-educational list of Glencoe, another Macmillan publishing division, was moved to Bennett.

In December Macmillan bought the McKnight Publishing Co. of Bloomington, Illinois, a vocational-educational publisher that specializes in industrial arts textbooks, particularly in such areas as woodworking, drafting, and graphic arts.

In September Scholastic bought International Media Systems (IMS), which operates under the name Great American Book Fairs and is one of the largest book fair companies in the country. IMS became part of Scholastic's book fair division, and its management was retained. The acquisition gave Scholastic book fair representation across the United States.

Time-Life Books dismissed 54 of its 200 editorial staff members in February, with president and chief executive officer Reginald Brack, Jr., calling it "the last step in the painful process of restructuring the company into a smaller business unit." Only weeks before, Time Inc., the parent company, had announced that the book division, including Book-of-the-Month Club and Little, Brown, had seen operating income drop to only $1.6 million from $21.1 million. Time-Life Books also lost more than $10 million in 1982, relating to Mexico's devaluation of the peso and currency export controls.

Later in the year, Time-Life closed 5 of its 18 telemarketing offices—in Boston, Philadelphia, Alexandria (Va.), and Long Beach and Santa Monica (Calif.)—in yet another step to make the operation more efficient.

Clarke Irwin & Co. Ltd., the distinguished Canadian publishing house, was placed in receivership in May and managed by the trustee department of Price Waterhouse until its list and inventory were bought by the Book Society of Canada in July. Fleet Books, which had been acquired by Clarke Irwin just before going into receivership, was sold to Key Porter Books in a separate transaction.

Clarke Irwin's publishing program was about 75 percent trade and the firm represented in Canada such U.S. and British firms as E. P. Dutton, M. Evans, Dial Children's Books, Parents Magazine Press, and Gollancz. Most of the houses moved to other distributors after the company went into receivership.

The company's bank debt had risen to Canadian $1.5 million (about U.S. $1.2 million) and was guaranteed by the Ontario Development Corporation under its Book Publishing Development Program. After the company announced substantial losses early in the year, its bankers requested that the government of Ontario increase the guarantee to $1.9 million. The government refused, and the bank called in the loan, which the government paid.

Werner Mark Linz, president and principal shareholder of the Continuum Publishing Corp., acquired the Cross-road Publishing Co. from W. H. Smith Publishers, the U.S. subsidiary of W. H. Smith & Son, London. Linz had been connected with Crossroad's ecumenical religious publishing program, which had its roots in the Herder & Herder imprint, when he served at Herder & Herder in various executive posts from 1959 to 1973.

Smith executives said that after the sale of Crossroad they would concentrate their efforts in the United States on Mayflower and Sunflower Books, its promotional and remainder book operations.

Linz had founded Crossroad in 1980 while he was still president of the Seabury Press. Soon thereafter, Crossroad was sold to Smith, whose money helped finance the imprint's rapid growth.

In a related development late in the year, the executive council of the Episcopal Church voted to "dissolve" the Seabury Press, which had an annual operating deficit of $250,000. The board of the press resigned and three trustees—Deborah E. Wiley, Matthew Costigan, and the Right Reverend Alexander D. Stewart—were named to wind up Seabury's trade publishing affairs. The press has 400 titles in print and had put out about 60 titles a year. The press intended to do business until June 30 or until it was bought. The church plans to retain the Seabury Press imprint to use if it ever returns to trade book publishing.

Founded in 1952 to publish and market Christian education material developed by the Episcopal Church, the press later began to publish trade books for general bookstores. In the 1960s it introduced a line of children's books. In 1973, after the press had had a few years of red ink, Werner Mark Linz was named president and brought with him a number of Herder & Herder titles that included theological works by Roman Catholic authors. The press sold its Clarion Books children's imprint to Houghton Mifflin in the 1970s, and in 1979 Linz left the press, taking with him some 120 backlist titles, and founded Crossroad.

In July, Zondervan Corporation acquired the remaining two-thirds of Marshall Pickering Holdings and the remaining 49 percent of the Benson Company that it did not own.

In March, William Morrow & Co. bought Fielding Publications, which has published the annual Fielding travel guides since 1948. Temple Fielding, chairman, died not long thereafter. His wife, Nancy, who with Fielding researched, wrote, and revised each year's editions of *Fielding's Europe, Fielding's Selective Shopping Guide to Europe,* and *Fielding's Low Cost Europe,* continued as a consultant. Morrow had distributed Fielding titles to the trade for more than 30 years.

Grolier Enterprises, a subsidiary of Grolier Inc., acquired rights from Random House to publish, market, and distribute the Best Book Club Ever. The acquisition, announced in April, marked Grolier's entry into the children's paperback book club market and supplements Grolier's hardcover book clubs, Disney's Wonderful World of Reading, and the Beginning Reader's Program.

Best Book Club Ever authors include Richard Scarry, Laurent de Brunhoff, and Stan and Jan Berenstain. Grolier expected to generate more than $8 million in sales during its first year operating the book club.

In June, Ten Speed Press, the Berkeley, California, publisher best known for its perennial bestseller *What Color Is Your Parachute?* by Richard Nelson Bolles, bought Celestial Arts, which publishes many titles connected with the human potential movement. Celestial's sales were reported to be $2 million in 1982, and Phil Wood, president of Ten Speed, expected to do much better, mainly by ordering large print runs of popular Celestial titles that have gone out of print. The backlist amounted to about 200 titles, with over 20 of them selling more than 1,000 copies a month. Popular titles include *Love Is Letting Go of Fear* by Gerald Jampolsky and a number of family therapy books by Virginia Satir.

M. John Storey, an executive at Garden Way, Inc., bought the company's publishing operations in June. Storey moved publishing, marketing, and editorial offices to Bennington, Vermont, from Charlotte, Vermont, where customer service and order fulfillment continue to be provided. Recent Garden Way titles include *The Compact House Book* by Don Metz and *Award-Winning Passive Solar House Designs,* co-published with McGraw-Hill.

Joan Kahn, who moved her mystery imprint to E. P. Dutton from Ticknor & Fields in 1982, left Dutton in January and joined St. Martin's Press. She has published such authors as Patricia Highsmith, John Ball, Dick Francis, Dorothy L. Sayers, John Creasey, Nicholas Blake, and Tony Hillerman.

In January, Truman M. Talley moved his imprint to E. P. Dutton from Times Books, where it had been for four and a half years. His first titles scheduled for Dutton included *The Exploding Suns* by Isaac Asimov, *The Endless Migrations* by Roger Caras, *The Dragon Hunters* by Frank Graham, Jr., and *The Future of Banking* by Martin Mayer.

In August, Wang Laboratories, the office automation company, bought Dictronics Publishing, the software publisher of such leading reference works as the Random House and Oxford dictionaries and *Roget's International Thesaurus.* Dictronics was merged into Wang Electronic Publishing.

There were two major filings for reorganization under federal bankruptcy laws in 1983. One involved A&W Publishers, which filed June 8, listing total assets of $1.5 million and liabilities of $4.2 million. Its largest unsecured creditor was Simon & Schuster, with $377,000 at issue.

The company stated that it got into trouble when it did not meet 1982 sales forecasts and wound up with an oversupply of inventory, forcing it to close out excess inventory at low margins. The resulting reduced cash flow with fixed costs caused a financial crisis, at which point many suppliers refused to extend credit. A&W stated that it intended to reduce general trade publication activities and rebuild sales in its strong areas: the Information Please and Galahad Promotional divisions.

The other publisher to file under Chapter 11 was Hastings House, which reported total liabilities of $1.3 million and total assets of $1.2 million. During its previous fiscal year it had sales of about $1.9 million.

In its initial filing, the company blamed much of its troubles on a contract it had signed several years earlier to distribute all titles published by Focal Press, Ltd. The company had to hire more employees and rent extra warehouse space, increasing overhead just as the recession was in full swing. Cash-flow problems were a prime consideration in the filing, particularly after a printing company won a $32,000 judgment against Hastings House.

Hastings said it thought it would be able to operate profitably under reorganization because it would be able to concentrate on selling profitable titles, it could cut its overhead, it presumed that sales would improve as the economy improved, and it hoped to interest a third party in investing in the company.

Changes in Book-related Companies

Clark, Wulf & Levine, the New York public-interest law firm that fought many significant First Amendment cases, disbanded in February. Partners Alan H. Levine, former attorney general Ramsey Clark, and Melvin Wulf cited "economic pressure," particularly escalating rent and operating costs, for their decision to disband.

They had established the firm in 1978 and sometimes charged no fees. Among their cases: the successful challenging of the Island Trees book banning, the defense of former CIA agent and author Philip Agee, the defense of *Snapping* authors James Siegelman and Flo Conway, and the defense of Lawrence Hill and several authors against a $120 million libel suit brought by a former CIA agent.

After sales for the holiday season in 1982 fell short of projection by $1.5 million, Brentano's management decided to close the ailing chain, which by early 1983 was operating only 8 stores, down from 28 when the chain filed for reorganization under federal bankruptcy laws in May 1982. Several months later, the company accepted a Waldenbooks offer to buy three of the chain's remaining four stores, effectively ending the life of the company.

Follett Corporation, the book distribution company, acquired United Art Company in September. United's primary operation is United College Bookstores Co., which runs 54 college bookstores. United continued in business as a Follett subsidiary separate from Follett Stores Corporation, another Follett subsidiary that operates 72 college bookstores.

Fraser, Inc., bought a major interest in Research Books, a wholesale distributor of scientific, technical, and management books and other information services to special libraries.

Book Trade Mergers and Acquisitions, 1983

Bennett Publishing. *See* Macmillan

The Benson Co. *See* Zondervan

Richard A. Bernstein bought Western Publishing.

The Book Society of Canada bought the assets of Clarke Irwin & Co.

Celestial Arts. *See* Ten Speed Press

Clarke Irwin & Co. *See* the Book Society of Canada

Continuum Publishing bought Crossroad Publishing.

Crossroad. *See* Continuum

Dictronics Publishing. *See* Wang Laboratories

Esquire, Inc. *See* Gulf & Western

Fielding Publications. *See* William Morrow & Co.

Fleet Books. *See* Key Porter Books

Follett Corporation bought United Art Co.

Fraser, Inc., bought a major interest in Research Books.

Garden Way. *See* M. John Storey

Grolier Enterprises bought the rights to Random House's Best Book Club Ever.

Gulf & Western agreed to buy Esquire, Inc.

Instructo/McGraw-Hill. *See* Silver Burdett

International Media Systems. *See* Scholastic

The J. K. Lasser Tax Institute. *See* Simon & Schuster

Key Porter Books bought Fleet Books.

McKnight Publishing. *See* Macmillan

Macmillan bought Bennett Publishing and McKnight Publishing.

Marshall Pickering. *See* Zondervan

William Morrow & Co. bought Fielding Publications.

New American Library. *See* Odyssey Partners

Odyssey Partners bought New American Library.

Random House's Best Book Club Ever. *See* Grolier Enterprises

Research Books. *See* Fraser, Inc.

Fleming H. Revell Co. *See* Zondervan

Scholastic bought International Media Systems.

Silver Burdett bought most assets of Instructo/McGraw-Hill.

Simon & Schuster bought the J. K. Lasser Tax Institute.

M. John Storey bought Garden Way's publishing operations.

Ten Speed Press bought Celestial Arts.

United Art Co. *See* Follett Corporation

Wang Laboratories bought Dictronics Publishing.

Western Publishing. *See* Richard A. Bernstein

Zondervan bought the Fleming H. Revell Co. and acquired complete interests in Marshall Pickering and the Benson Co.

Other Activity

A&W Publishers filed for reorganization under federal bankruptcy laws.

Brentano's closed its doors.

Clark, Wulf & Levine disbanded.

Doubleday made the Dial Press an imprint.

Hastings House filed for reorganization under federal bankruptcy laws.

Joan Kahn moved her imprint to St. Martin's Press from E. P. Dutton.

The Seabury Press was "dissolved" by the Episcopal Church.

Truman M. Talley moved his imprint to E. P. Dutton from Times Books.

Books and the Law

19

The First Amendment

HOWARD FIELDS

The decision to bar the news media from covering the U.S. invasion of Grenada may have garnered the most First Amendment attention in 1983, but months earlier the government made another decision: to require prepublication review of certain writings, which could have a far greater impact, especially on the book world and federal employees who would write for it.

Otherwise, the year saw a continuation of many of the same censorship activities that dominated the previous year, though tempered somewhat. People continued to try to ban books and censor textbooks while their opponents coalesced and attempted to fight them with greater effectiveness.

New wrinkles were brought to censorship when a public figure brought suit claiming exclusive rights to any book on his life and trying to stop an author before she could even put a word down on paper, and publishers themselves took steps to censor colleagues.

Congress finished the year undecided about whether to protect legitimately published books from a legal reaction to child pornography, and the Supreme Court put on its agenda for 1984 several potentially important libel cases.

Attacks continued on the Freedom of Information Act, but while defenders stood fast against encroachments, some of those who would weaken it made progress in one important attempt to get relief from disclosure requirements.

Prepublication-Review Directive

At the beginning of 1983, books by Spiro Agnew, James Bamford, Taylor Branch, Joseph Califano, Jimmy Carter, Jeane Kirkpatrick, Henry Kissinger, and Richard Nixon were still in bookstores.

By a stroke of the pen on March 11, President Ronald Reagan launched a government-wide directive that, if it had been in force when those authors had served in government, would have meant that none of those books would be in the stores in their published form. Some might not even have been published.

National Security Decision Directive 84 was entitled "Safeguarding National Security Information" when Reagan signed it. Although innocuous sounding, the directive would have the effect of putting at least 127,000 government employees under the same constraints as Frank Snepp after he lost a Supreme Court battle in 1980.

Like Snepp, a former CIA agent who wrote *Decent Interval* (Random House), those employees were to be placed under a cloud of government censorship for the rest of their lives if they chose to put anything on paper.

The key paragraph read:

> (b) All persons with authorized access to Sensitive Compartmented Information (SCI) shall be required to sign a nondisclosure agreement as a condition of access to SCI and other classified information. All such agreements must include a provision for prepublication review to assure deletion of SCI and other classified information.

Another paragraph did not mention prepublication review, but could include it, and was intended to cover "all persons with authorized access to classified information." That presumably would add hundreds of thousands of employees to the restriction.

Officials of the Justice Department, who drew up the order for Reagan to sign and who would implement it, made clear that the intent was that nondisclosure agreements including prepublication review would be "such as were approved by the Supreme Court in United States v. Snepp."

The nondisclosure agreement that Snepp signed was an agreement the CIA requires of all its employees and covers the employee for the rest of his life. Even novels must be submitted in manuscript for review, in case they expose secrets.

Townsend Hoopes, president of the Association of American Publishers (AAP), made the tie of the directive to the book publishing world when he submitted testimony in October before one of several congressional hearings held on the order. He served as under secretary of the Air Force in the last years of the administration of Lyndon Johnson, who was succeeded by Nixon.

After leaving that office, Hoopes wrote *The Limits of Intervention,* a book critical of the U.S. handling of the six months prior to and just after the Vietnam war's Tet offensive in 1968. Hoopes said in his testimony:

> Had I been subject to the Reagan directive requiring prior review of the manuscript by the Nixon administration, there is every reason to believe that efforts would have been made to blunt the thrust of the book, to soften the criticism, to find fault with specific facts, to allege that certain information was still classified, and possibly to prevent publication. . . .
>
> At the very least, I believe this adversarial process would have been prolonged, with the governmental authorities seeking by means of delay to discourage the author and to erode the economic prospects for the potential publisher.

To make matters worse, the previous year Reagan had signed another directive allowing the reclassification of information that previously had been declassified.

In other testimony, AAP submitted a list of 49 books by authors who had held security clearances during government service, who published books from 1970 through 1982, and who would have been required to submit their manuscripts for review had they signed a similar nondisclosure agreement. "The prepublication review process contemplated by the new directive and its 1982 predecessor will cast a total chill over the whole publishing process," Hoopes said.

As with CIA clearances of written material, the directive would require review of manuscripts by the government before a publisher could see them. Several former CIA agents have agreed that they experienced delays in their efforts to publish books under those circumstances. They also agree the CIA has been nitpicking and erred on the side of secrecy when there were any doubts. Several also have accused the agency of excising passages out of embarrassment, not because secrets were revealed. Asked repeatedly in the hearings for estimates of the number of secrets revealed by persons who otherwise would be covered, government officials could offer only a few, none of them of any great consequence. Both houses of Congress passed legislation in the waning days of the 1983 session to place a moratorium on the executive order until April 15, 1984, when they will consider the case.

A New Form of Censorship

Although the prepublication-review directive was potentially the greatest censorship threat that emerged during 1983, one new form of censorship was created when singer Frank Sinatra sued to halt the research and publication of a book on him by bestselling author Kitty Kelley (*Jackie Oh!* and *Elizabeth Taylor—The Last Star*). In addition to trying to place a prior restraint (which the U.S. Supreme Court has taken a dim view of) on an author's research, the Sinatra suit, filed in a Santa Monica, California, court, also claimed that only he and his corporation, Camden Enterprises Ltd., had the "right to commercially exploit the name and likeness of Frank Sinatra, including the right to publish the authorized biography or autobiography of "Sinatra's life."

The leader of one of several writers' groups that formed a coalition to support Kelley said that under Sinatra's reasoning, "Henry Kissinger could have silenced Seymour Hersh, the Kennedy family could have silenced William Manchester, the 'Brethren' on the Supreme Court could have quashed Armstrong and Woodward, and the late Mayor Richard Daley could have paralyzed Mike Royko." The authors' groups said the attack on Kelley was an attack on all authors whose First Amendment rights would be threatened if the charges were upheld.

In addition to seeking $2 million in damages from Kelley, Sinatra sought a court injunction to stop her work on the book because she would "continue to make false and misleading representations and statements and to deceive certain persons and the public." That referred to allegations that Kelley had misrepresented herself to prospective interviewees as having Sinatra's blessing for the book. Sinatra's real reasons for bringing the suit were believed to be his suspicion that "she intends to focus upon sensational, controversial, and deprecating events, real or imagined, of Sinatra's life," and to serve notice on his friends and acquaintances to refuse to talk to Kelley. Kelley, who received a $1 million advance from Bantam for the Sinatra book, said that despite the suit she would continue researching the book. "Yes, I'm scared," she said. "I am worried about the lawsuit, not just for myself, but for all of us" authors.

Child Pornography Bill

The publishing world received some good news in the First Amendment area in 1983 when the House of Representatives voted just before quitting for the year to safeguard the interests of legitimate publishers in a new crackdown on child pornography. The bad news was that differences between the House and a less lenient Senate version passed earlier remained unresolved.

The House vote of 400–1 for the bill did not reflect the debate that had been waged for more than a year on whether to try to protect legitimate publishing interests. The vote was seen only as one against child pornography.

The question of the propriety of the bill and its safeguards was reflected by the one vote against the bill, cast by Representative Ted Weiss (D., N.Y.), who said the language was still too broad. Language barring "lewd exhibitionism," he said, could be used to ban National Geographic, which "has documented tribal rites which involved displays of genitals which could be considered 'lewd exhibitionism.' "

But the language in the House version was expected to protect adequately such books as St. Martin's Press's *Show Me!*, which was removed from circulation after the 1982 Supreme Court ruling upholding a New York state pornography statute that did not require a finding of obscenity. The book remained out of circulation at year's end because Congress had not taken final action.

The House bill would exempt visual depictions in a book of "simulated conduct if there is no possibility of harm to the minor, taking into account the nature and circumstances of the simulation, and there is redeeming social, literary, education, scientific, or artistic, value."

The Senate version, passed in July, would not provide protection for books, not even those judged to have scientific or educational value. It would allow courts to confiscate all profits and assets used in the production of the material.

St. Martin's president Tom McCormack repeatedly stated in congressional hearings that *Show Me!* was a sex-education book for children produced by a German psychologist. It features photographs of nude children.

Censorship actions were intense enough during 1983 that Banned Books Week gained a lot of attention in several cities during the September 10–17 observance. Many public broadcasting stations showed a videotape produced by the American Library Association (ALA), which centered on censorship of books in the public schools. Many libraries featured displays of books that had been banned or were the subject of banning efforts somewhere in the United States.

Publisher Censorship

A new wrinkle in book banning occurred within the publishing industry itself, serious enough to generate a rebuke by the Freedom to Read Committee of the Association of American Publishers.

Dodd, Mead & Co. was bought by Thomas Nelson, Inc., the world's largest publisher of Bibles and a publisher of mostly religious books. In late summer, Nelson informed Dodd, Mead that it was no longer to publish "objectionable" books and ordered two novels in process canceled, and a poetry collection recently published withdrawn.

The novels were *Tip on a Dead Crab*, by William Murray, and *Skim*, by Thomas Henege. The poetry was *The Devil's Book of Verse*, edited by Richard Conniff.

Thomas Harris, senior vice-president of Nelson, denied it was acting as censor, any more than certain magazines censor when they choose not to publish material they find offensive.

But the Freedom to Read Committee disagreed. In an unusual statement, it said it was disturbed by the reported circumstances that led to the suppression.

What troubles the committee is the potential abridgement of the freedom to read by the cancellation of the book—in the absence of any new information regarding the validity of the work—after it has been accepted, printed and readied for distribution.

The committee is convinced that such a practice, rare as it may be, is contrary to the best interests of authors, publishers, readers and indeed of our culture as a whole.

In another case involving allegations of publisher censorship, Simon & Schuster sought to have a look at another publisher's book before publication. The book was *Media Monopoly*, by Ben H. Bagdikian, who charged that 50 corporations control public opinion. Simon & Schuster is mentioned in it. Before the May publication date, Simon & Schuster threatened legal action if the book were published with defamatory passages about the publisher. It asked to be able to scan the book in advance. Beacon Press refused to comply with the request. In a Berkeley, California, news conference in April, Bagdikian said Simon & Schuster's action "demonstrated the theme of my book, namely that excessive concentrations of power are, in themselves, a threat to freedom of expression."

School Censorship Activity

Although lacking the public intensity of the previous year, censorship efforts also continued in the nation's school systems.

Some of the most important action took place in Texas, where at year's end the state board of education was considering a ruling to allow the evolution theory of Charles Darwin to be ignored in textbooks. (It decided in January that the theory could be ignored and, where it was mentioned, equal weight had to be given to other theories, including the Bible's "creationist" theory.) The publishing industry watches what Texas does to its textbooks because its statewide buying system acounts for $60 million worth of sales by the industry, including 10 percent of all biology text sales. Thus, what Texas decides influences the textbook choice the rest of the country has.

A study being prepared as 1983 closed accused textbook publishers of yielding too much to the Texas board. Released by the People for the American Way in January of this year, the report said, "An embarrassing number of leading publishers have significantly decreased coverage of—and emphasis on—evolution and related topics" during the past ten years. In October, the Louisiana Supreme Court supported the state legislature in its 1981 vote to require the teaching of creationism alongside evolution. Thus, Louisiana became the only state in the union to have a creationism law. Similar efforts have been unsuccessful in other states.

In other school censorship activity, the Island Trees School Board on Long Island, the center of attention the previous year because of an important U.S. Supreme Court anticensorship decision, gave up the fight early in 1983 and returned to library shelves the nine books it had banned in 1976, leading to the court case. But essentially the same issue returned to another court at about the same time when an Elk River, Minnesota, girl sued the school board for restricting her access to five books, three by Judy Blume.

A survey released in March concluded that 34 percent of 860 high school librarians polled reported challenges to books during the previous year. The figure had risen 4 percent since the previous survey. But the biggest increase, from 1 to 17 percent, was recorded in the reports of censorship pressure from local groups.

A la Studs Terkel the previous year when he confronted the Pennsylvania school censors of his book, Barbara Beasley Murphy traveled from New York to Calhoun County, Alabama, to confront a school board that wanted to remove seven books from library shelves. In light of the Island Trees decision, the board decided to require parental permission for access to the books. Murphy's *No Place to Run* was among the seven books, so the PEN America's Right to Read Project chose her as its first author to be sent into the community to challenge censorship. She reported qualified success.

Public Library and Bookstore Censorship

Public libraries also were not free of censorship efforts, some of them instigated by the libraries themselves. Libraries in Chicago, Milwaukee, and San Francisco, which together have 115 libraries, refused to circulate *Jake and Honeybunch Go to Heaven*, by Margot Zemach (Farrar, Straus & Giroux), a winner of ALA's Caldecott Medal. All three library systems objected to the book on the grounds that it perpetuated racist stereotypes.

Because of the censorship efforts, the American Society of Journalists and Authors issued its first Open Book Awards in 1983, giving them in March to a teacher, an author, a public librarian, a high school student, a bookstore manager, and a bookstore buyer for "courageous personal actions to combat censorship of books." The buyer, Faith Brunson of Rich's Department Store in Atlanta, had been named plaintiff in a suit against Georgia's "minors' access" law, the subject of action in several states in 1983. Max Lillienstein, general counsel of the American Booksellers Association, said the Georgia bill was so broad it would "effectively bar minors from stores selling admittedly non-obscene materials."

Moves to close adult bookstores were made in practically every community with varying success. One statewide effort in New Jersey found the governor and general assembly grappling over a bill that would make display or sale of material deemed obscene a criminal nuisance and grounds for closing the offending establishment. A Massachusetts law allowed towns to regulate adult bookstores by requiring special zoning permits.

The U.S. Supreme Court could have intervened in another censorship case but chose in mid-summer to refuse to hear the suit of an Iowa library trying to protect the confidentiality of readers. The Polk County attorney, investigating a rash of animal mutilations, had demanded to see a list of those who had been checking out books on the occult. The Des Moines library refused him access, he took the case to court, and the library board of trustees appealed to the Supreme Court.

Those who lead many of the censoring efforts had their own complaints in 1983. The Reverend Jerry Falwell, president of the Moral Majority, and his outspoken vice-president for communications, Cal Thomas, complained in April that conservative writers had been the victims of library and bookstore censorship. Falwell said a survey showed that only 2,000 of the nation's 30,000 libraries carried conservative books. "It looks a bit as though censorship and book banning have been practiced by someone," he said.

Libel Cases

The Supreme Court was busy during the year with several libel cases, mostly hearing oral arguments in cases to be decided this year. The Supreme Court cases, heard in November, included one against *Consumer Reports*, accused of libeling Bose Corp., maker of stereo equipment, when the magazine reviewed sound systems. That case centered on a choice of words in an article.

Another case was overshadowed when the central figure, Larry Flynt, publisher of *Hustler* magazine, shouted obscenities in the courtroom and was ousted. The case, however, held important ramifications for the book-publishing industry since it centers around the ability of a plaintiff to bring a libel suit in the state of his or her choice. Several press organizations joined *Hustler* in the appeal to the high court. On the same day, the Court heard another case featuring residency, this time the home of the author of a piece. Actress Shirley Jones had filed a suit in a California court against the Florida-based *National Enquirer*.

One decision by the Supreme Court had at least a tangential effect on censorship. The Court ruled in March that a selective tax on publishers was unconstitutional because it could be used to censor the press. The case applied to Minnesota newspapers, but the principle involved could affect book publishers. The state had levied a special tax on newsprint and ink. The majority opinion, written by Sandra Day O'Connor, said there was too much potential for the government to use the tax as "a censor to check critical comment by the press, undercutting the basic assumption of our political system that the press will often serve as an important restraint on government."

In other courts, a U.S. Court of Appeals judge ruled in a Maryland case that opinion published as fact may be subject to libel suits, and a U.S. District Court in the District of Columbia threw out a $2 million libel verdict issued by a jury the previous year against the *Washington Post*. The judge ruled that William P. Tavoulareas, president of Mobil Oil Corp., had not been libeled because "actual malice" had not been shown and Tavoulareas was considered a "public figure."

One case that gained notoriety, but did not make it to the high court, occurred in South Dakota where Governor William J. Janklow asked bookstores in May to remove copies of *In the Spirit of Crazy Horse* by Peter Mathiessen (Viking) on grounds that it libeled the governor. The bookstores refused.

In another libel case, Nathaniel Davis, who was U.S. ambassador to Chile at the time of the 1973 military coup there, filed suit against Harcourt Brace Jovanovich, Avon Books, and the author and movie producers for *The Execution of Charles Horman: An American Tragedy*, by Thomas Hauser. Davis claimed that the book and the movie *Missing*, based on it, libeled him in recounting his alleged involvement in the disappearance of an American during the coup.

Government Secrecy

The remaining First Amendment issue refused to go away in 1983, although it did not make progress. As the new Congress took office, new legislation was introduced to restrict access to government files, usually obtained under the Freedom of Information Act (FOIA). The year began with a bill in the Senate that originally was considered softer from a publisher point of view than previous versions. As the year and Senate consideration of the bill continued, however, changes were made and finally a bill was sent to the Senate floor over publisher objections.

AAP centered its objections on a provision that would allow the government to charge a "fair value fee or royalties, or both" for technological information with commercial value generated or procured by the government. The bill also included, AAP said, language that "creates a new authority for the government to withhold, by imposing prohibitive charges for its release, govern-ment information that should be freely available to the public. This, we submit, has the potential for imposing a vicious 'means-test' form of government censorship."

Although House leaders have given assurances that the Senate efforts will go nowhere, piecemeal attacks on the act did gain movement. Chief among them was a bill passed by the Senate on the penultimate day of the 1983 session to exempt CIA disclosure of material in its "operational files" from FOIA.

As a compromise, the Senate Intelligence Committee added a clause that would prevent the CIA from reducing the number of personnel or amount of funds allocated to fulfilling the FOIA requests for other files. It also retained the right of scholars, writers, and other researchers to bring court challenges of CIA denials of material.

Critics claimed the bill would allow the CIA to hide illegal covert operations. The House then scheduled early 1984 hearings.

The FOIA year began with a Justice Department decision to require requesters to prove they qualify for the fee-free search of files beyond the claim that they are researchers or plan to write a book. The new restriction could prove a problem for a first-time author without a book contract.

AAP claimed the new rule "will provide a shield behind which agencies wishing to hinder access to materials deserving of wide dissemination and public attention may hide."

Ironically, a report issued in May by the General Accounting Office showed that the Justice Department had a poor record for complying with the FOIA, even though it is the government agency responsible for instructing the rest of the government on compliance with the law.

20

Washington Report

HOWARD FIELDS

The beginning of activity, rather than the conclusion of it, shaped the impact the federal government had on the book-publishing industry in 1983. A few changes were made, most of them advantageous to the industry, but in most of the activities begun, the results will not be known for years.

Publishers won protection from U.S. Postal Service, (USPS) crackdowns on mail fraud, postal rates received only one increase, and the U.S. Supreme Court made decisions that had some impact on publishers or at least special interest to them. That was about it. Most of any action had to come from Congress. Many bills were introduced during the period and many hearings were held, but Congress did little.

Usually, inactivity is to the advantage of publishers. Since they depend little on government largess or favors, they generally consider themselves better off if the government does nothing that will have an impact on them. But sometimes publishers need government initiative. Among the actions begun in 1983 that publishers favored and that could be resolved this year were renewed efforts to obtain relief for publishers from an Internal Revenue Service (IRS) policy to tax publisher backlists at full value; to allow publishing house participation in Small Business Administration (SBA) loan programs; and to achieve greater involvement on all fronts in the effort to combat adult functional illiteracy.

As in other years, publishers and their Washington representatives fought to preserve their First Amendment rights (see Chapter 19) and to obtain greater funding for education programs that might lead to more textbook sales. The Library of Congress (LC) began a technological

test about which publishers are concerned, and in another technological area, a long-range project was begun to develop standards for computerized publishing houses.

Public Lending Right

One arm of the federal government provided a forum in 1983 for discussion of a topic that could have a far-reaching impact on the publishing industry. At least the discussion promises to get livelier in the future.

Within a 35-year period since 1946, ten nations—Denmark, Norway, Sweden, Finland, Iceland, the Netherlands, the Federal Republic of Germany, New Zealand, Australia, and the United Kingdom—have adopted various versions of what has become known as a public lending right. Generally, the plans compensate authors and/or their publishers for library loans. Last September, for the first time in the United States, publishers, authors, and librarians got together under the auspices of the Library of Congress's Center for the Book to discuss the possibility of instigating a similar plan.

Two months later, a bill was introduced by Senator Charles McC. Mathias, Jr. (R., Md.) to establish a two-year commission to study the idea. The Mathias bill was a suggestion of Robert Caro, author (*The Path to Power*, Knopf) and former president of the Authors Guild, where the idea was first broached in the United States, and a participant in the symposium. No conclusions were reached at the meeting, but it was generally agreed that no one's special turf would be tread on. Librarians, led by Robert Wedgeworth, executive director of the American Library Association (ALA), had no objection to the idea as long as the payments did not come from libraries.

Somewhat of a pessimistic air crept into the discussion, however, as it was pointed out that U.S. authors are not exactly a dying and poverty-stricken breed since they are not harmed by foreign book imports, and that a public lending right would be looked on as a sort of welfare program for writers. One participant suggested that in light of such drawbacks, the idea should be pressed as one of the right of authorship. Some suggested calling it an "author's lending right" instead of "public lending right." Another cited an Authors Guild survey that disclosed that the average author earned less than $5,000 a year from writing. That type of author would benefit a great deal from public lending royalties, he said; with even the British ceiling, some authors would double their income.

In Great Britain, where the same public discussion raged in a controversy between librarians and authors, the two-year-old public lending right operates government-funded royalties of up to $7,500 per author based on library surveys. Other European systems do not give the money directly to the authors, but fund such programs as pensions for authors. In Australia, both publishers and authors share the royalties. None of the countries with public lending rights requires the library user to pay a fee.

Dorothy Schrader, general counsel of the U.S. Copyright Office, suggested that the public lending right question also was a copyright question, since copyright owners have the exclusive right to lend their works as long as the work is not sold. That is the protection movie producers have when they lease their movies to theaters. If authors who do sell their books want to retain copyright lending rights, Schrader said, perhaps they should try for inclusion in a congressional effort to have sound recordings included in the commercial lending right that movies now enjoy.

Hearings were held in Congress during the year on proposals to amend the "first sale doctrine" of the 1976 Copyright Act to prohibit the rental of phonograph records for commercial purposes. Although Schrader suggested that inclusion in commercial restrictions might be a first step in obtaining a public lending right, no noticeable movement took place.

Sony Betamax VCR Decision

Also begun but not concluded during 1983 was a copyright issue decided one block away at the U.S. Supreme Court. The court issued a decision this January on the side that publisher and author groups had opposed in the question of whether videocassette recorders (VCR) could be used without compensation to the movie producers whose works VCR owners record.

A year, almost to the day, before the Court's 1984 decision, the nine justices heard arguments in the case involving the Betamax VCR of Sony Corp. of America and movie producers led by Walt Disney Productions and Universal City Studios. It was apparent from those arguments that the justices were ill informed about copyright law. Thus, the spring, when a decision was expected, came and went without a ruling. At mid-summer the justices said they needed to hear the case again. The arguments were held on the opening day of the new term, the first Monday in October. The justices appeared better prepared this time.

The Association of American Publishers (AAP) and the Authors League of America, on the side of the movie studios, and the American Library Association, on Sony's side, were not allowed to give oral arguments in the case, but did file friend-of-the-court briefs. AAP said the matter involved the "fair-use doctrine" of the Copyright Act and that "fair use can never excuse copying which, as here, threatens to reduce existing, emerging, or potential markets for the work copied." The authors termed the practice of using VCRs "home-counterfeiting" that "displaces the sales of commercially produced cassettes licensed by the author or film company, and deprives those copyright owners of income from such sales." ALA argued, however, that the real issue was "the public's right of access to information and entertainment."

The justices ruled, 5–4, on the side of Sony, saying the sale of Betamaxes violated neither the fair-use doctrine nor the doctrine of contributory infringement cited by the producers. Writing the opinion for the majority, Justice John Paul Stevens said, "Any individual may reproduce a copyrighted work for a 'fair use'; the copyright owner does not possess the exclusive right to such a use."

That and other interpretations of fair use contained in the Stevens opinion disturbed the member of Congress most responsible for the 1976 act. Representative Robert Kastenmeier (D., Wis.) said he thought the justices had broadened the intended definition of fair use, the doctrine that protects publishers from unlimited photocopying of published works. Charles Lieb, who wrote the AAP brief as an attorney in the New York firm of Paskus, Gordon & Hyman, said he was disturbed by the decision, but optimistic there would not be much impact on the copyright community. However, problems "are going to arise," he said.

"Fair Use" in Photocopying

The fair-use interpretation of publishers received an important endorsement from the Copyright Office just before the court's first Betamax argument. The office said the intended balance between the rights of owners and the needs of users of copyrights had not been achieved. The office was talking about photocopying.

In a report to Congress, the office recommended changes in the Copyright Act to make it clear that any photocopying that exceeds the fair-use doctrine specified in the act should include a copyright notice that carries the name of the copyright owner. Congress also might consider, the report said, a possible surcharge on some photocopying machines (a solution the movie studios had recommended at one point for VCR use) and a royalty system similar to the public lending right idea. The 363-page report covered the first five years of experience with the major revisions in the act, which took effect in 1978. In all, the tone of the report was on the side of publishers, who had made a major issue in 1982 of copyright violations by photocopying.

The "Work-for-Hire" Controversy

In November, the action publishers feared most was taken. Senator Thad Cochran (R., Miss.) introduced work-for-hire legislation that would tend to discourage work-for-hire contracts. Publishers on one side and authors and artists on the other girded for a major battle over the issue in 1984. Cochran's bill, a stronger version of one he introduced the previous year, would make it illegal to treat contributions to collective works, supplementary works, and instructional texts as work for hire. An exception would be works in which the treatment is specified in the contract with the contributor and waived by him or her for a fee.

Publishers argue that such legislation would have no real effect, since they would contract only with authors willing to waive their right to copyright privileges for their material. Such arrangements are already standard in contracts with free-lance contributors, except for the fee, which presumably would be taken out of the price paid for the contribution. The Cochran bill would also allow the contributor to own the rights to the work two years after first publication.

The Manufacturing Clause

Although the decision came too late to do book publishers any immediate good, the International Trade Commission (ITC) issued a report in July that sided with the publisher view of the impact of the manufacturing clause in the Copyright Act on the U.S. economy.

The previous year, Congress had voted an extension of the clause—due to die in mid-1982—until mid-1986. As part of that action, it required a report from ITC, and the publishers and the printing industry argued their sides before the commission in March. Congress decided on the extension when labor groups joined with the printers to predict the loss of hundreds of thousands of American job opportunities in the printing and allied industries to foreign competition if the clause, which bars copyright protection to books written by Americans and printed abroad, were allowed to die. ITC agreed that some job opportunities would be lost, but claimed that the number was closer to 2 percent of the estimate, or 1,400 to 6,850.

The report could have an impact on a case that was pending in the U.S. District Court of Manhattan during 1983. The Authors League sued to have the extension of the clause declared illegal on the grounds that the extension violated the Fifth Amendment (due process).

Other Copyright Issues

In other copyright action during 1983, publishers won a battle when Kastenmeier's subcommittee decided in December not to try to change the Copyright Act's language in an effort to incorporate protection for computer chips. In hearings earlier in the year in both the House and the Senate, a publisher representative argued that chips should be protected in a separate part of the act. Jon Baumgarten, of the Washington office of Paskus, Gordon & Hyman, argued that technology exists for putting an entire book on a computer chip, which in the near future will be sold to a reader using a "reader-terminal." If the copyright language protecting books were changed to also protect chips, the protection for the book contained on the protected chip might be lost, he argued. Each medium should have its own specific protection, he contended.

Kastenmeier later agreed, indicating at a December 1 hearing that he favored separate legislation to deal with the chips. Kastenmeier's panel also looked at, but took no action on, the impact that some of the new technologies may have on the Copyright Act.

Publishers also won an important protection for their works in the 28 Caribbean nations. Congress, led by Representative Thomas Downey (D., N.Y.), attached to a bill embodying President Ronald Reagan's Caribbean Basin Initiative granting aid to those countries a proviso that they be denied aid unless they take steps to protect the intellectual property, including copyrights of other nations.

The provision became law in August. By the end of the year, publishers began pressing for a similar proviso in bills providing aid to developing nations, and were getting ready to take action against plans to aid an unspecified country considered in violation of the restriction.

Shortly after the beginning of 1983, Reagan signed into law a bill implementing an international pact designed to allow books to be imported into signatory countries free of tariffs. The Nairobi Protocol to the 22-year-old Florence Agreement had been agreed to in 1976, but it took that long for the United States, under pressure from publishers, to finally sign it.

Fighting Illiteracy

A major effort that could have an impact in the decades ahead was begun in 1983 when various groups took a look at the alarming rise in the rate of functional illiteracy among U.S. adults and decided to do something about it. The Reagan Administration, B. Dalton Booksellers, ALA, and Harold McGraw, Jr., retired chief executive officer of McGraw-Hill, took action during 1983 to tackle a problem that until last year had been given a lot of lip service but little attention on a broad scale.

ALA brought together 11 organizations, including B. Dalton's and library, education, and literacy groups, to form the Coalition for Literacy to combat the problem said to cost the United States $224 billion a year in welfare payments, crime, and poor job performance. ALA estimated that there are more than 23 million functionally illiterate adults in the United States, and 2.3 million are added to the rolls each year. Reagan gave the new campaign, centered now around a national advertising campaign offering help to those who need tutoring, a boost of publicity in September when he held a White

House ceremony to honor some of the members of the coalition. He singled out Sherman Swenson, chief executive officer of B. Dalton, for pledging $3 million to help fund volunteer programs to promote literacy over the next four years.

Despite B. Dalton's help, volunteer programs on the local and national level will need millions of dollars in order to carry on. Townsend Hoopes, president of AAP, had tried during the previous year to get publishers and other corporate executives to form an organization to raise private funds to underwrite many of those programs. Hoopes was unsuccessful and gave up on the idea, but McGraw picked it up and, using his business ties as chief officer of a large corporation, got executives to agree to join him in creating a foundation, the Business Council for Effective Literacy. McGraw pledged $1 million of his own money for the effort. And Congress passed a bill to add $50 million to a college work-study program that supports part-time jobs for students, to be used in part to help students train illiterates.

Postal Legislation

On the legislative front, book publishers could count two major victories during the year, both on postal matters.

Compared with the roller-coaster ride the postal rates took the previous year, the cost of mailing books remained relatively stable during 1983. Because Congress had failed to come up with the necessary subsidy to keep the rates down, the year began with an increase in the library rate, from 43 cents to 47 cents for the average, two-pound book mailed to or from a library. The cost of the first pound was raised from 32 to 35 cents, the second through seventh pounds from 11 to 12 cents, and each pound over seven remained at 7 cents. It turned out to be the year's only increase. Users of the subsidized rate benefited from a combination of congressional inactivity and, oddly, the raging controversy over abortions.

Each year, Congress decides whether to provide to the U.S. Postal Service the funds to allow it to keep library and other nonprofit rates down, and how much these funds will be. When it misses a deadline, usually at the beginning of the federal fiscal year on October 1, Congress enacts a "continuing resolution" to continue federal spending rates at the level of the previous year. Library-rate users usually benefit from continuing resolutions because in recent years a push has been on to cut the subsidy or wipe it out completely.

The library rate had been scheduled for phasing out over a 16-year period ending in 1987. But phaseout has been ahead of schedule since the years of budget cutting began, and if Reagan's request for a cutback in the subsidy to $400 million last year had been granted, rates would have risen by more than half.

The House of Representatives ignored Reagan's request for a cut and was ready to give (USPS) all the funds it needed—$879 million—to keep the rate the same. The Senate was planning a $720 million funding level, which the Postal Service had said would erase the subsidy. At one point, a compromise of $802 million was projected.

Postal funds are included in an appropriations bill that also provides funds for the Treasury Department, the White House, and independent agencies. While the measure was being acted upon on the House floor, an amendment was attached to bar use of any of the funds to finance abortions. Rather than accept that language, proponents of the bill killed it altogether. Later, a continuing resolution was enacted to continue funding USPS at the level of the 1983 fiscal year, or $879 million. In his 1985 budget request, Reagan asked again for a cutback to $400 million.

While all that was occurring, the Supreme Court ruled in June that the U.S. Postal Rate Commission, one of the agencies that acts on rate requests, does not have to set postage rates strictly according to the cost of the service. Publishers had favored that ruling because not only the library rate but also the unsubsidized special fourth-class "book rate" benefit from that interpretation. Before the year ended, however, the Postal Service decided it would seek increases in all rates as early as October 1, 1984. That would include a two-cent increase in the book rate and a five-cent increase in the library rate.

Publishers also won a three-year battle to protect legitimately published books from possible seizure by USPS agents using newly won powers in a crackdown on mail fraud. Publishers had been concerned that the bill granting new powers would allow the Postal Service to seize a book even if it wasn't part of a scheme to make profits from a claim in the book, such as an unsubstantiated cure for an illness. Such actions are usually taken on the basis of advertising in newspapers and magazines that make certain claims for the contents of a book. Publishers asked Congress to include the "mirror image doctrine" used by the Federal Trade Commission. This doctrine holds that an advertisement is not false if it accurately reflects the contents of a book, regardless of the claims made in the book.

Publishers had stated in testimony at the beginning of the year that books had been seized at the rate of one a year over the past 20 years even without the new powers USPS was seeking. Just a few days before adjourning for the year, Congress took final action on the bill, adopting the mirror image doctrine.

Publishers lost on another postal matter, at least for the present. AAP had asked that floppy discs for computers be allowed to qualify for the book and library rates. USPS responded that it would like to, but a change of that nature would have to go through lengthy procedures by two agencies before it could be made. Such a request would be filed, the Postal Service said.

Tax Changes

In the tax area, publishers sided with at least three requests for changes. One was the oft-repeated request to get relief from Internal Revenue Service policy imposing taxes on publishing house backlists according to the full original value of the book. Publishers have been seeking redress for this IRS decision known as the "Thor Power

Tool Decision" since the Supreme Court upheld the IRS policy in 1980, but each year the effort has died in Congress.

The effort was renewed during 1983, first when Representative Ed Jenkins (D., Ga.), a member of the tax-writing Ways and Means Committee, introduced a bill to reverse the decision to free all "excess inventories." Later, Senator Patrick Moynihan (D., N.Y.) introduced a bill to free book inventories only. The effect of a rollback would be to allow the publishers to again deduct the depreciated value of the books while they are sitting in the warehouse, regardless of whether the book later was sold for its full "list price."

Publishers supported a move by authors to allow them to deduct the full fair-market value of donations of their works to libraries, archives, museums, and other nonprofit institutions. A similar effort the previous year died in the Senate.

Publishers met with IRS representatives during the year to resist a change in rules that would require capitalization of prebook publishing expenses. Now, publishers can deduct those costs as a business expense during the year in which the expense is incurred. The IRS wanted to allow deductions of those expenses only in the year in which the book is actually published.

Publishers also renewed a battle to end discriminatory practice by the Small Business Administration against businesses engaged in dispensing information. Policy denies SBA programs, particularly loans, to any business, including publishers, engaged in First Amendment activities. David Godine, president of David R. Godine Publisher, Inc., told a House subcommittee considering the proposal that about 90 percent of U.S. book publishers are small enough to otherwise qualify for SBA programs.

New Technologies

Washington also was the site of two publishing-related efforts to deal with some of the new technologies. One was instigated by publishers, the other endorsed by them, with some reservations.

One reason publishing houses have not joined the computer age in their relations with authors is that there is no standardization of the codes and other operations that make different computers and computer systems compatible. AAP announced in 1983 its sponsorship of a $250,000 project carried out by the Aspen Institute to develop a standardized computer coding that authors can use to make their material compatible with the house's computers. Under the plan, libraries would also be able to use the code, primarily for bibliographical purposes.

In addition to giving authors more control over the preparation of their manuscripts, standardization is seen as a way for publishers to widen business opportunities, such as entry into data-base publishing and automated indexing and cataloging.

Another technology is being developed by the Library of Congress that would enable it to copy books, journals, sound recordings, photographs, and movies by using a laser beam to transfer an image of their content onto an optical disk. The user would call up the image on a computer screen and read it there or copy it on a photocopying machine. LC brought together a group of journal publishers, including those owned by book-publishing houses, to ask their cooperation. In general, the publishers agreed to allow their journals to be used for a two-year test, but book-publisher representatives cautioned against giving LC a blank check.

At a second meeting, William Welsh, deputy librarian of Congress, announced that he was naming one panel of publishers and another of librarians to protect the interests of the two groups.

Funding for Education

1983 also was the time to focus on the quality of education in the United States. For the most part, it was a repetition of the national scare that followed the launching of the first satellite, Sputnik, by the Soviet Union in 1957. A study by the National Commission on Excellence in Education, *A Nation at Risk,* blamed part of the U.S. decline on a 50 percent decline in textbook expenditures and other instructional materials since the mid-1960s. The report also criticized publishers for not taking greater care to ensure the quality of textbooks.

In his 1984 budget message, delivered at the beginning of 1983, President Reagan proposed cuts in many programs favored by publishers. Publishers generally support these programs because they tend to promote reading and literacy, or because they tend to mean more textbook sales. Reagan said the burden of improving American education was that of the state and of local school systems, not the federal government.

Happily, from the publisher point of view, Reagan's attempts failed in many areas. In fact, several programs were increased. Reagan wanted to cut back federal assistance to libraries to practically nothing. Instead, Congress voted $80 million for public library services, an increase over the previous year. Proponents of legislation to provide federal aid for public library construction failed to get it included in the same bill, but the House Education and Labor Committee sent to the floor for action this year a bill that would restore the $50 million that had been provided the previous year.

Also during the year, Congress passed a bill to provide $1 billion for improvement in math and science education, triple what the administration had sought. Congress took initial action to increase arts and humanities endowments by 30 percent more than the administration requested.

Publishers fought Congress on another matter. In a move to centralize the printing of government information within the Government Printing Office (GPO), a congressional panel proposed including all information produced with the aid of government funds. Publishers argued that the inclusion was too sweeping, that as proposed it could logically reach to much of nonfiction work since much of it relies on government-supported research. That would make GPO the exclusive publisher in competition with private publishers, AAP said in testimony to the Joint Committee on Printing.

Technology and Design

21

Book Design

JEROME P. FRANK

1983 was a "settling down" period for both interior and exterior book design as publishers and manufacturers learned to work within the constraints of a difficult economic period that reached its depths in 1982, to produce books at less cost, but without cheapening the product either physically or graphically. In fact, several art directors of major publishing houses agreed that 1983 was the start of a trend toward better-looking books.

However, not everyone in the publishing business would agree with that point of view—in particular, some of the book show judges who, in spite of their delight with some books, found much to complain about in books produced in 1983.

How pronounced is the movement toward handsomer books? Robert Scudellari, vice-president, graphic arts, Random House, pronounces it a subtle movement, but one from which there is no turning back. Frank Metz, vice-president and art director for Simon & Schuster, thinks that his firm's search for designers and illustrators to give first and second novels of younger authors a look that will attract attention began upgrading the quality of S&S graphics in 1983. The same is true at David R. Godine Publishers, says William Luckey, production manager, who points out that Godine began creating a different graphic look in 1983 that plays down typography and plays up a more commercial approach.

Still, if one reads the general conclusions of the judges of book shows across the country, it appears clear that books in 1983 pleased them more than the ones entered in their shows the year before. Their more positive criticisms may be another signpost on the way to better-made, handsomer books. At no time did art directors and book show judges complain, as they did in 1982, that designers were being placed in an adversarial role with respect to the manufacturing function. If designers still felt that way, perhaps the sharp edge had dulled as they learned how to work within the new economic climate.

That is Scudellari's contention. Viewing 1983, he claims there is no doubt that economic decisions made by publishers in 1981 and 1982 that affected all departments "reached a nice kind of resolution in 1983." Through that year, he states, art directors and designers "settled in" and refined their work; manufacturers realized there was profit to be made even when buying cheaper materials and simply did their job better. The art director also maintains that one of the reasons for the movement toward better-looking books can be ascribed to the younger editors, who have been asking for changes in the appearance of their books. "Because publishers are listening to them," Scudellari said, "they are beginning to reap the benefits of subtle changes in book jackets and packages that say to the public, 'We are no longer making things look the same.' "

If 1983 was a generator of a subtle shift in the appearance of books, then Random House, Simon & Schuster, and David R. Godine, among others, may be regarded as the generators of important components of that change. But the approaches being taken do not have much in common. For example, Random House is toning down its covers, S&S is reaching for a different look that has no fixed theme or "feel," and Godine is going more commercial and more "shiny."

Scudellari remarks that publishers are no longer so convinced that every cover and jacket has to be laminated

Robert Scudellari, vice-president, Graphic Arts, Random House, feels designers have refined their work during 1983.

with a shiny plastic film, while Luckey explains that one of Godine's books, published this past February, uses a glossy lamination rather than a matte jacket, "which," says Luckey, "is another way of saying we are moving into the 20th century." But the fact is that Godine is moving in both worlds—today and yesterday—since it is using a matte-coated cover for another of its upcoming books.

The Matte Look

The low-key, matte look for book jackets and paperback covers was a strong part of the Random House design direction in 1983. That year, the firm introduced a new and unique liquid-matte laminate (or coating) for some of its paperback covers. To do a paperback line like the one that was introduced by Random House's Vintage Books last year—that is, to produce a paperback without a fully protective gloss coating on it for the semi–mass market or trade paperback market—was, as Scudellari puts it, "unheard of."

Vintage Books art director Judy Loeser explained that she had designed three books at first, introducing them in 1983—two mass market–size books with a ten-point matte-coated cover stock supplied by Longacre Press in New Rochelle, New York, *Freud and Man's Soul* by Bruno Bettelheim and *Selected Poetry of Rainer Maria Rilke,* and a 6⅛ × 9½ inch book, *Twentieth Century French Poetry.* She also used it for the first six paperback volumes of Vintage's new Aventura series of works of contemporary non-Anglo-American writers, which were published last year.

The low-key, elegant matte look also appealed to Louise Fili, art director of Pantheon Books, another Random House imprint. Fili, who is gaining an enviable reputation as a book designer and art director, used matte stock for paperbacks in a number of series last year, including WPA (Work Projects Administration) series; the Modern Classics series, which included such titles as *The Leopard* and

Young Torless; and the Norberg Elias series, which included *The History of Manners, Power and Civility,* and *The Court Society.*

Fili, like her colleague at Vintage, plans to use the matte-coated cover stock for several of her 1984 books, including the covers of a Simone de Beauvoir series and a book titled *Feminist Theorists,* edited by Dale Spender. She experimented with the matte-coated cover in 1983, when she used it on a book entitled *When Things of the Spirit Come First.*

Simon & Schuster's approach is to individualize books by its younger authors. "These books require a look different from those of more established authors," art director Metz said, "so we try to find designers and illustrators who will give the first and second novels of these newer authors a look that will attract attention to them from reprinters, book clubs and the eventual book buyer."

Breaking the Rules

Simon & Schuster is making a conscious effort to break away from the formula look. Just as Random House is leaving the responsibility for the new look to individual art directors, so also is S&S banking on its art directors to "put in their own individuality so the book look doesn't fall into a mold." Metz cited a paperback, *Restaurants of New York* by Seymour Bridgski, that S&S published last year (hardcover was published by Random House earlier) as a case in point. "The art director did an unusual and special design and the reception of the book after the original had been published some years before was a revelation to us because it did so well. It just doesn't look like a typical guide book." Metz also stated that one of his favorite jackets of 1983 was on S&S's *The Europeans* by Luigi Barzini, which was designed by Louise Fili in her capacity as a free-lance art jacket designer.

Fili has her own ideas about what might act as a constraint on book designers—and the cause lies not with the manufacturing department, but rather with marketing. "It's one of the reasons why I can't always use a matte stock when I feel it is appropriate. If I'm designing a big book or an important paperback book, like *Italian Folktales* by Italo Calvino a couple of years ago—the hardcover by Harcourt Brace Jovanovich had a matte jacket—and I decide to use a matte paperback cover, marketing may decide, as they did in the case of the Calvino book, that because the printing was so large and because they didn't want the book to get dirty on the bookstore shelf, we would have to go with a laminated cover." That battle is still being waged today, according to Fili, but she does notice that though more is expected of her, she is basically on her own and doesn't feel "too much pressure either from the marketing or the manufacturing side."

How does an art director take her books in a new or different direction? Fili, who claims to have quite a bit of freedom, constantly tries to break the rules. That was particularly true in 1983, when she designed one of her favorite jackets for a book titled *Light* by Eva Figes. "It has a Monet painting on the cover as well as the smallest title I have ever designed before. The letters are about a quarter of an inch high and [the size] violates set policy about size of letters on jackets." The cover is striking and according to Fili has gotten a lot of attention, but she points out there is no way she can prove to the sales people that many people have bought it because of the cover.

Preprinted Covers for Juveniles

At Viking/Penguin, Barbara Hennessy, art director for Viking, Penquin, and Puffin imprints, points out a number of directions the firm has been moving in, starting in 1983, particularly designing books that will be produced by Toppan Printing in Japan and published here this spring. One juvenile picture book on the 1983–1984 list, *Jump All the Morning* by P. K. Roche, will be designed with a preprinted cover and a jacket—a first for Viking. The impetus for the preprinted cover came from the firm's sales and marketing department, whose people felt strongly that for a picture book for children a laminated picture cover does better than an unillustrated paper-over-boards cover with an illustrated jacket. "This book will be printed and bound in Japan and by going there we could afford to design *Jump All the Morning* with preprinted cover and jacket as well," Hennessy maintained, "but it would be too costly to do that in the U.S."

Why the jacket? "Our editors felt it was necessary because they wanted to be able to use the flaps to explain about the nursery rhymes that form the text—and also, librarians seem to favor jacket copy," Hennessy explained.

Looking for Illustrators

David R. Godine Publishers, in Boston, was also involved in creating a different graphic look for its books in 1983, its jackets becoming a bit more commercial and a little less typographic and, in a trend counter to that in the large houses, becoming less "quiet." "It's a kind of evolution for Godine," William Luckey, production manager, said. "First we used line drawings and typography and now we are searching for illustrators whose work is somewhat commercial."

Luckey explained that in the Boston area there are many illustrators to choose from and not necessarily much competition to get them. "If you are in New York and you want a particular look, you go to, say, Fred Marcellino, and you know that everyone will love his work and, what's more, he's the only one who does it the way he does—but you pay for that." He added that because Godine is a small publisher, it has to search for new talent—in competition with the art directors of the major houses for illustrator/designers, it either has to compete on their money level or to get someone particularly interested in a project, or bow out and acknowledge that it must get younger people who are just getting started and whose craft is not quite as highly developed as some of the more

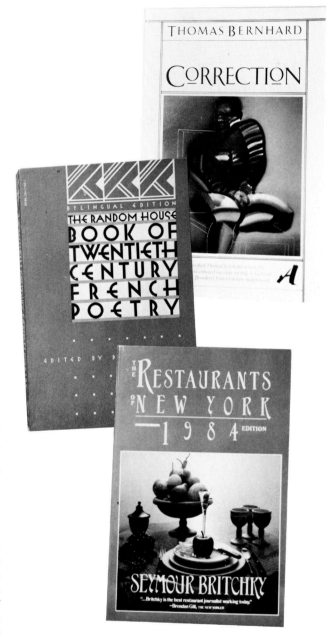

Vintage has also used the matte laminate for its covers on its new Aventura series introduced in 1983. Correction *is one of six titles introduced that year.* © *1983 Jerome Frank.*

An elegant, soft look for a trade paperback is achieved by Vintage Books of Random House by using a new liquid matte laminate over the cover. This title, The Book of Twentieth Century French Poetry, *one of the first to use the new look, was published in 1983.* © *1983 Jerome Frank.*

Simon & Schuster achieved an "individual" look with its paperback edition of The Restaurants of New York. © *1983 Jerome Frank.*

established artists. "But [when] you go with them," Luckey continued, ". . . you take a chance on an unknown, on someone who has not had much work reproduced or used for jackets. He or she may not be sensitive to the differences between fine art and book-jacket illustrations."

As is the case with Simon & Schuster, Godine sees all visiting artists and illustrators on the theory that you never know when someone can provide exactly what is needed. Luckey explained how Godine discovered, in 1983, that it pays to check the portfolio of everyone who knocks on the door. "An artist visited us without an appointment, but I decided to see her, busy as I was," Luckey related. "She had just returned from Italy with watercolors and engravings she had done there. It was perfect timing because we were considering what to do for a jacket for a book titled, *The War in Valdorcia,* a memoir kept by Iris Origo that had never been published in the U.S. As it turned out, the events in the memoir took place in the same area in which the artist painted. On the strength of her paintings, we decided to bring out the book simultaneously as hardcover and paperback, which we proceeded to do last year and published the work with her illustrations in February." He also explained how a chance Godine took with another woman artist, an illustrator by the name of Jeanne Titherington, paid off handsomely. Many art directors had thought her work "too weird." "We decided that she would be perfect for illustrating several books we were bringing out, including a paperback, *The Chronicles of Pantouflia* by Andrew Land, a collection of fairy tales, and *The Story Teller: Thirteen Tales by Saki.*"

Book Show Jurors Cast a Critical Eye

As creative as publishers try to be, they don't always meet with critical success. Certainly, in 1983, their work was under stringent critical appraisal, more critical than in

Jeanne Titherington—The Chronicles of Pantouflia—and Iris Origo—War in Val D'Orcia—are two artists "discovered" by David R. Godine Publishers in its search for new, lesser-known artists for its juvenile and adult books. © *1983 Jerome Frank.*

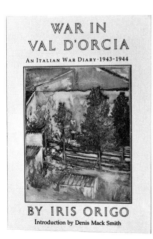

Although many art directors felt Jeanne Titherington's work was too "weird," Godine used her work to critical acclaim in The Story-Teller—Thirteen Tales by Saki. © *1983 Jerome Frank.*

earlier years. Traditionally, judges of the American Institute of Graphic Arts (AIGA) Book Show pay close attention only to the graphics. In the 1982–1983 show, however, they were as critical of bindings and endpapers as they were of graphic expertise—and they rejected overproduced entries "as readily as those that were poorly produced."

According to the 1982–1983 book show report in *Graphic Designs U.S.A. 4,* the AIGA annual, which covers books published in 1982 but not reported on until 1983, some of the overproduced entries seemed competently designed from a graphics standpoint, but were, by their "oddball" formats, virtually unreadable, "which made them not well designed at all." The report stated that while this type of book was more apt to be from a limited edition by a private press, "some trade houses were also guilty of overproduction." Book show judges found designers in conflict with marketing people "whose hearts may be in the right place, but whose eyes are firmly fixed on the bottom line."

The report sketches briefly some key questions publishers ask themselves as they judge "as accurately as possible the intersection of those two marketing curves—cost-plus-profit and consumer affordability. Will a parent really spend $15 for a hardcover storybook for his child, or $25 for himself? Which areas of production can be compromised, and how many, before value and marketability begin to suffer? At what point does less-expensive begin to look cheap?" The AIGA report clearly agrees with Scudellari's observation about the industry's settling in in 1983, as it stated that "publishers and designers are finding their own answers to these questions as hard times in publishing assume the status quo."

Books published in 1983 drew strong criticism, yet the judges were also quick to distribute praise. In fact, for the first time in years, the praise outweighed the negative judgments. Overall, and consistent with earlier years, textbooks took a beating for all kinds of reasons. Yet Ed Bedno, partner in Bedno/Bedno, Inc., judging at the Chicago Book Clinic, pointed out that "textbook judging is not the same as book judging. If you bring preconceived ideas to the judging about the 'Book Beautiful,' you are going to be disappointed. Given the extraordinary constraints affecting content needs, publishing needs and production needs, one does not wonder that it was done well—one wonders that it was done at all."

Bedno said that when judging textbooks, he looks first for a demonstration of the publisher's ability to pull together enormous amounts of information about a complex subject and have it come out clear and organized. "If the book can do that," he said, "and in addition look handsome, or even exciting, or even not ugly, then design has triumphed over adversity."

At the same show, reviewer Patrick Clinton, writer and editor for the *Chicago Reader,* was acerbic: "Why are textbooks the way they are? Why are they so cumbersome? Why do they all succumb to the same false luxuries—too much color, too much graphic rigmarole?"

He chose as an example of his complaint the attractive and wittily illustrated *Building Spelling Skills* of McDougal, Littell. "Surely dazzling four-color spellers shouldn't exist at all, not just because they are wasteful, but because the extravagance of the sugar coating is apt to persuade children that the medicine is nastier than it really is."

At the New England Book Show, judge Frank Mahood, a book designer who was art director for the University of New Mexico Press and senior designer and assistant design department manager at Princeton University Press, was initially impressed by the high quality of the cover/jacket designs of college textbooks. "The concept that 'less can be more' (never attempted in the interior design) seems to be a standard approach on the covers. Excellent use of professional color photography and graphics, with strong simple display typography, seemed abundant, but too often it was merely superficial and pretty and bore little relevance to the subject matter." He liked Susan Marsh's *Contemporary Cultural Anthropology,* which he thought exhibited a good sense of organization and flow to the text design, using the second color to make clear delineations between kinds of textual material and giving appropriate weight and attention to the chapter opening spreads. "This is good, traditional two-color college text design that has not run amuck," said Mahood.

At the Philadelphia Book Show, textbooks did somewhat better, and, in fact, captured the highest marks; top awards went to Lea & Febiger's medical books—*Differential Diagnosis in Dermatopathology* and *Skeletal Injury in the Child*—and W. B. Saunders's *Structure and Function in Man.* In each case, the text was set in the old, conservative, tried-and-true typefaces—Baskerville, Caledonia, and Palatino.

Elementary and high school books also drew some spirited remarks, particularly from Quentin Fiore, book designer and illustrator, who prefers working with limited edition and university press books and who studied drawing and painting with Hans Hoffmann and George Grosz. Fiore stated that elhi books cannot be judged by the same standards that apply to, for example, specialty books. "The el/hi book is not meant to be read in the solitary, private way a novel is read; using it is a shared, public experience. Further, el/hi books are now more often being used in relation with other teaching devices in the classrooms, such as computers, film and video." He said their shared use and their relation to TV film and computer imagery greatly affect books designed for school use. Fiore points out that this interdependence of technologies doesn't exist in other categories. It is his opinion that since some now-outdated conventions inhibit better textbook design, such as the sometimes arbitrary regulations regarding type designs, textbooks should be singled out for some special consideration. One suggestion for improvement that Fiore makes would be a more venturesome approach to type presentation, "taking a leaf from the sometimes sprightly type styling that accompanies film/TV computer printed literature, screen titles, and so on. Students are more than ready for livelier stuff!"

College texts continued to be dissected, this time by Mary Mendell, design and production manager at the University of Massachusetts Press, at the New England show. Her remarks were significant in the sense that, because there were fewer examples of successful design in that category, she delved into the problems more analytically. She found covers often unrelated in content or design approach to interiors. Second colors used unselectively destroyed the expected effect of contrast. Front matter was often ill-designed, overdesigned, and/or unrelated to the text design.

Her questions are posed for college textbook publishers and they are couched sensitively: "When a category of books fails so completely to provoke aesthetic interest, there must be some explanation. Is it a self-perpetuating tradition of poor design which cannot be shed, or the strong influence on design by people with little graphic or typographic sensitivity? It is hard to believe that it represents a genuine response to 'market' demand, for the taste of college professors and their students cannot be so very different from that of other readers. In fact there is quite an overlap in the readership of the professional, typographic and college text categories." Mendell cannot believe that text sales would plummet because of good graphic design. "At worst," she added, "it might be unrecognized by unsensitized eyes. Surely the only way people develop sensitivity is through acquaintance with quality."

She chose as one of her favorites, *Foundations of Wave Theory for Seismic Exploration Methods,* which she found fresh and although designed with some attention to every detail, unpretentious. "Despite the title, it invites reading."

Worthy of special merit is a sociological study designed by Harvard University Press's Marianne Perlak, *Before Color Prejudice* by Frank M. Snowden, Jr., which drew applause from several judges, who found the book, as summed up by Mahood, "a solid, handsome design by any

Marianne Perlak of Harvard University Press designed this sociological study, Before Color Prejudice, *which was deemed a standout by several judges at the New England Book Show last year.* © 1983 Jerome Frank.

standard. I think all the judges were particularly drawn to it because its clean straightforward look made it a standout among the others." Designed by Perlak and published by Harvard University Press, *Before Color Prejudice* was set 10/13 Melior Metroset II by American-Stratford Graphic Services, with Carolus Roman Bold and Outline display. The book was sheetfed offset in one color by Maple-Vail Book Manufacturing Group on 55 pound Glat Offset by Glatfelter Company. The book was Smyth-sewn case-bound, also by Maple-Vail, with a Joanna Western Mills Arrestox B brown #31500 cover. The 6 × 9 inch book retails for $17.50.

As usual, Godine's *A Constructed Roman Alphabet* won attention, but Quentin Fiore struck a petulant note when he noted that the linecuts of the individual Greek characters in the portfolio were struck too hard, which resulted in a "disturbing 'offset' on the characters on the reverse side of the sheet—shiny black passages on matte-black characters. I also felt the case was overdesigned."

Richard Bartlett, a free-lance designer and production consultant and former art director at D. C. Heath, production manager at Beacon Press, and director of publications at Harvard's Peabody Museum, among many other credits, summed up the New England show by pointing out one common flaw in the submissions, which was inappropriateness. "Should a medical book's jacket look like a vanity press belles-lettres number?" he asked. "Should a book on design have folios of billboard size? Can a book with radical errors in the scaling and proportioning of elements be redeemed by adding over-sized dingbats, color panels, or devices? Are these the paths to design integrity?"

In his opinion, many entries seemed to be designed to dazzle jaded jurors rather than to meet the basic design challenge of making books that combine function with beauty. "Coherence and rightness should be our goals. Pretentiousness is a sad thing to look upon."

He wonders whether this designer entrapment occurs because throughout the years jurors have failed to note and reward the "solid accomplishments of those who have put a checkrein on the urge for novelty for its own sake. Competence and craftsmanship are not exciting virtues; they are passed over in a book show, although valued in the real world. Perhaps success in a book show and success in the marketplace are less related than we would like to believe."

Designers were hit roughly at the 1983 design and production show of the Association of American University Presses, when Hans Schmoller, retired production director of Penguin Books—a juror—leveled the accusation that "many designers lack basic equipment and do their work in blissful ignorance of typographic history and traditions and many of the unchanging ground rules." Out of 254 books submitted, the jurors chose 22 classed as typographic and 15 as illustrated; 36 jackets were chosen out of 323 submitted.

Schmoller, who thinks that designers handle text and makeup perfunctorily, sees the rapid change from hot metal to film and digital typesetting playing havoc with type design, quality of spacing, and other elements that until a few years ago could be taken for granted. He argued that a current practice by publishers of letting designers see proofs only of title pages and a few other special elements is "not healthy." He insisted that "designers fight for the right to see a book through all its stages [otherwise] they cannot be held responsible for the way the final product looks or functions."

At the Chicago Book Clinic, reviewer Patrick Clinton affirmed that university press and trade books were almost without exception satisfying. He pointed out that *Willa Cather: A Bibliography,* from the University of Nebraska

Hans Schmoller, retired production director of Penguin Books, speaking at last year's design and production show of the Association of American University Presses, hit out at unknowledgeable designers. © Tony Faust.

Press, reworks a "dusty old reference book style into something sleek and startling; the extreme leading, which could have turned into self-parody, is elegant, understated and functional."

TABA's Graphic Award Winners

The 1983 Graphic Awards selections of the American Book Awards will be the last such awards for a while, since this section of the event is being eliminated together with many other categories. The eight winners received a specially designed Louise Nevelson sculpture. The winners by category were:

- **Book Design (Pictorial):** *Lewis Carroll's Alice's Adventures in Wonderland,* published by University of California Press; illustrated by Barry Moser; art director, Stephen Revich
- **Book Design (Typographical):** *A Constructed Roman Alphabet,* published by David R. Godine Publishers; designer/illustrator, David Lance Goines; art director, William F. Luckey
- **Book Illustration (Collected Art):** *John Singer Sargent* by Carter Ratcliff, published by Abbeville Press; designer and art director, Howard Morris; editor, Nancy Grubb; production manager, Dana Cole
- **Book Illustration (Original Art):** *Porcupine Stew* by Beverly Major, published by William Morrow Junior Books; illustrator, Erik Ingraham; designer and art director, Cynthia Basil
- **Book Illustrations (Photographs):** *Alfred Stieglitz: Photographs and Writings,* by Sarah Greenough and Juan Hamilton; published by National Gallery of Art/Calloway Editions; designer, Eleanor Morris Caponigro
- **Cover Design/Illustrated (Mass Market Paperback Books):** *Key Exchange* by Kevin Wade, published by Avon Books; designer, Martha Sedgwick; art director, Matt Kepper
- **Cover Design/Illustrated (Trade Paperback Books):** *Bogmail* by Patrick McGinley, published by Penguin Books; illustrator, Doris Ettlinger; designer/art director, Neil Stuart
- **Jacket Design/Illustrated:** *Souls on Fire* by Elie Wiesel, published by Summit Books of Simon & Schuster; designer, Fred Marcellino; art director, Frank Metz

Return to Design Fundamentals Urged

Abe Lerner, for 35 years a worker in book design, production, and editing, presently with Dodd, Mead in production, speaking before the Typophiles in 1983, pointed out a number of obstacles that he sees lying in the path of good bookmaking:

- as yet unmastered new technologies;
- in typesetting on film, the need for more good faces and better versions of standard designs;
- the need for more good border rules and decorative type pieces—fleurons and typeflowers, for example;

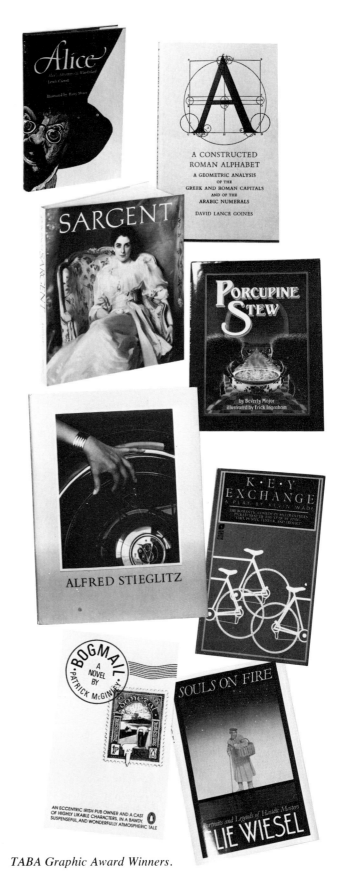

TABA Graphic Award Winners.

• a need for looser letter fitting and tighter word spacing by typesetters;
• poor adhesive binding—the backs of adhesive bound books are too tight;
• the need for more interesting surfaces on less costly papers for noncloth cover materials.

Lerner opposes the pressures to make books "lively" or "jazzy." He thinks that kind of pressure comes from advertising concepts that have no place in the making of books.

The year 1983 may be remembered as the fountainhead of new trends—spinning off better-looking books and giving publishers and manufacturers the time needed to get used to working within tough economic constraints. New design directions will enable major publishing houses to become more competitive in the bookstore marketplace. What strikes one most about 1983 design trends is the welcome attitude by publishers that they will not give in to crassness and cheapness in the creating of their books—and their attempt to continue to attain the delicate balance between content and form.

22

Book Manufacturing

New manufacturing technology in 1983, except for electronic communication of manuscripts between authors and publishers and publishers and typesetters, was of less interest to publishers and manufacturers than were solutions to the problems of poor administrative productivity in manufacturing departments, rising costs of materials, and, for some printer/binders, sheer survival.

Not that the bookmaking industry wasn't aware of and even researching new technological advances, but the expenditure of hard cash was put off in favor of coping with day-to-day problems. Of course, such major manufacturers as R. R. Donnelley & Sons Company and Rand McNally & Company continued to spend capital dollars for new equipment. Of note was the huge, block-long Toshiba press at Rand McNally's Versailles (Ky.) plant, installed last year to print the Encyclopaedia Britannica. And Donnelley continued its long-term program of upgrading its various book-manufacturing plants with the installation of new equipment in the press and bindery departments.

Among publishers keeping a close watch over advancing technology was Houghton Mifflin Company (HM), which last year set up a "new technologies" committee to investigate current and future advances in the bookmaking state of the art as they might impact on HM's publishing programs. Committee members include Marilyn Stevens, vice-president and editorial director, mathematics and science, chair; Stephen Pekich, production director, trade publishing group; Howard Webber, publisher, Reference Division; Richard Bueschel, president, Time Share Corporation; and Patricia Thoma, vice-president and director, art and production, School Division. They are starting to

take a close look at such technologies as computer-generated graphics for the preparation of text art; in-house photocomposition; laser printing and its impact on traditional printing, binding, and distribution methods; and on-demand printing.

Transmitting Manuscripts by Computer

A technology already on the publishing scene, at least in a checkerboard pattern that claimed more attention in 1983, is the telecommunication of authors' manuscripts to typesetters. While scientific book publishers have for several years accepted disks from authors, run them on compatible hardware for editing, and then communicated the completed text in converted tape form to phototypesetters, trade publishers are considerably less advanced in the technique. In fact, even science book publishers are not exactly expert yet.

To do it right, publishers would have to spend a minimum of $10,000 for terminals and screens for each distant author, plus the cost of their own computers (which would probably already be on premises handling other-than-editorial chores), plus the cost of telecommunication of signals from author (if he or she does not mail in the disk) to publisher. In a number of cases, those costs are considered too high at a time when bookmaking is plagued with rising costs and publishers are trying to discover new areas in which to trim more fat from their operations. Others try it and give it up because of problems met early in the word-processing cycle.

One publisher got off on the wrong foot by neglecting to inform a book author that language accents had to be inserted into the manuscript. When the disk arrived at the publishing house, the absence of accents was discovered during initial editing, which meant that someone had to go through the entire disk to insert the accents, but, as it turned out, every position on that disk was used up. In that case, the publisher turned back to the traditional typesetting approach by simply printing out a hard copy, inserting accents on the pages, and having the typesetter compose from paper rather than electronic signals.

Houghton Mifflin, with an eye on cutting costs, began experimenting with the word-processing cycle in 1983, according to Stephen Pekich. The idea was to set all of its new guides in the Birnbaum Travel Guide series on word processor and transmit the edited copy on tape to the typesetter. "We set some of our then newest guide, *U.S.A.,* on a Wang word processor in our New York office and it worked so well that we decided to do an entire book that way," Pekich said. "We are presently inputting our upcoming guide, *France,* on the Wang. Output is disk, which is converted to magnetic tape and sent to the typesetter." But this was in HM's trade book department. At company headquarters in Boston, the School Division had been using word processing for a few years and has its own word-processing manual. Emulating its sister division, the trade book division is rewriting the Association of American Publisher's primer for word processing to conform with the (HM) division needs. "It will be used whenever a book is done on a word processor," Pekich said. "And I'm learning that our own people, who used to be afraid of word processors, now say that once they use one they never want to go back to their typewriters."

As much as publishers want to solve the problem of author-to-typesetter communication, however, it is a complex task, since not all personal-computer hardware and software are compatible. Sometimes, even computers made by the same company will not communicate. As pointed out by one expert in the field, the exacting requirements of leading, kerning, character widths, and line-ending tolerances, lead to sophisticated software that operates at higher levels than authors' word-processing software. So, when an author sends a manuscript on floppy disk from, say, an IBM Personal Computer (PC), the publisher must transfer the manuscript into his composition system using communication software and telephone lines (in some cases, the floppy disk may not be compatible with the publisher's disk, or with magnetic tape used in the system). This means that someone must call up the file and insert composition codes, and this can be as time-consuming as rekeying the entire manuscript.

Some publishers have asked their authors to insert codes during the writing process, but this requires careful proofreading on the publisher's part, and the electronic files that are then composed on the typesetter cannot be sent back to the author for examination and approval.

Although publishers last year were still being frustrated by these problems, some took specific action. For example, Macmillan in some cases has supplied word processors to authors of reference books for manuscript preparation. Its college and school divisions have been accepting floppy disks from 10 percent of their authors. Macmillan uses third-party conversion service to convert the disks to compatibility with its own typesetting equipment. HP Books specifies in its contracts that its authors must use an optical-character-recognition readable font on their typewriters and follow special formatting instructions. The resulting manuscript is then scanned into the publisher's composition system for editing and typesetting. The final manuscript is stored on floppy disks and the author keeps a hard-copy printout. Authors who don't follow instructions are charged for any retyping that is needed. At John Wiley & Sons, authors submit a hard-copy manuscript from their word processors, together with the floppy disk. Wiley inserts its own generic coding and manuscript and disk go together to the conversion service, which converts the disk into compatibility with the publisher's typesetting system, while inserting the codes. This process eliminates the need for rekeying; however, Osborne/McGraw-Hill on the West Coast, specializing in computer books, hasn't keyboarded a manuscript in seven years. Disks arrive from authors and software specially developed by the company translates them into compatibility with the typesetting equipment.

The ease of revising and updating a book stored in an electronic memory, or of carrying on a correspondence about a manuscript with an author on the other side of the country, was demonstrated last year by North River Press, which had been concerned about typesetting costs and the time it took to turn a manuscript into type. William Cowan, president of the small publishing house in Ossining, New York, experimented with word processing by pretending he was an author and using the facilities of a typesetting service called Dial-A-Typesetter. Keying in on

Author/publisher William Cowan (foreground), guided by owner of typesetting operation, Henry Levine, inputs copy on Micom 2000 in the first step of telecommunicating electronic manuscript over great distances to teletypesetter.

a Micom 2000 word processor provided by the service, Cowan set a passage from a manuscript, already committed to type, to see how close it would come to the conventional product. He keyed in the sample passage, which contained about 5,000 characters—perhaps four pages of conventional manuscript—all stored on a single "electronic page." Next he directed the Micom to print out a hard copy to edit.

Because Cowan's authors are scattered across the country, the question was how to simulate the distance between, say, an author on a university campus perhaps a thousand or more miles away and the publisher, based in Westchester Country in New York. The answer in this case was to send the text via modem (local telephone lines) to a time-sharing computer network available to individuals and businesses. Cowan dialed the local access number to the system and "uploaded" the author's file directly from the Micom's disk to the "electronic mailbox"—a process that took less than one minute.

He then restored the phone link with the time-sharing network, this time assuming the guise of the publishing house editor receiving a manuscript from an author. This "downloading" produced an entirely new file on floppy disk, consisting of the author's manuscript, formatted precisely as the author typed it. All that remained was for the publisher to process the manuscript and have it typeset. Mnemonic codes were embedded in the manuscript to command the typesetting computer to select fonts, sizes, leading, line lengths, and other typesetting parameters. Cowan then dialed the network once more and uploaded the marked-up text, complete with typeset-

At Compugraphic MCS typesetter, edited copy is checked on terminal screen to verify that the editor has inserted mnemonic codes correctly.

ting instructions. He then called Dial-A-Typesetter and reported that a job was waiting for them at the time-sharing network. Dial-A-Typesetter merely dialed the network and downloaded the appropriate message. All that remained was to enter the file into the typesetter's queue for printing at, in this case, 150 lines per minute. The result was galleys received by the publisher. If it were preferred, the type could have been run out in page form with crops, running heads, and folios in place. Costs were: a dedicated word processor ($10,000); hardware and software to permit telecommunication ($2,500), telephone modem ($800), and rented electronic mailbox at the time-sharing network ($100)—a total capital cost of $13,400.

Administration by Computer

Computers also came into play at the manufacturing departments of publishing houses, where managers in 1983 were extremely interested in learning as much as they could about computer assistance in the administration of their departments. Last year several companies, including Harper & Row, Prentice-Hall, CBS Educational & Professional Publishing, and McGraw-Hill Book Company, created successful computer operations to control a number of functions within the manufacturing groups, operations that, before 1983, had to be done manually.

Harper & Row, for example, introduced a stand-alone IBM Personal Computer to administer book-manufacturing operations, and particularly cost estimation. The production manager, Ann Rudich, first used the computer in day-to-day manufacturing control by writing a system in BASIC language to estimate manufacturing costs and generate all paperwork for ordering the manufacturing of books. From BASIC, the department moved to dBASE (data-base management) programs, which enabled the system to be run by menu and eliminated the need to learn a command language. Programs written in 1983 included a publication report listing all titles scheduled by ready date and a projection of Harper & Row's manufacturing by supplier, units, and dollars. This gives the capability of calling up cost status by department, which allows for pinpointing problems and tightening controls. The system also prints out consolidated reports, updated monthly, that indicate by department the number of books printed at each supplier and track composition and author's alteration costs. Rudich upgraded her IBM PC to an IBM XT, which uses a hard disk that holds more information than the floppy and enables the system to store data and develop data bases from the estimating system, something the PC could not do.

At Prentice-Hall, Gerard Scanlon, vice-president for book manufacturing, wanted to eliminate repetitive work, such as cost-analysis development, preparation of manufacturing orders (especially where there are many standardized products), control of book-paper inventory, and the creation and monitoring of schedules. These were considered prime candidates for computer assistance. In 1983, Scanlon found a consulting/programming organization, Printers Software, and bought a package originally

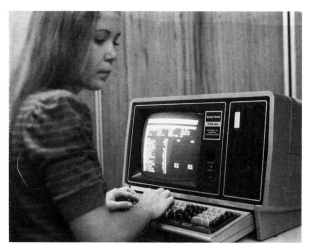

Prentice-Hall buyer used Tandy TRS 80 Model 2 computer to check manufacturing inventory using spread-sheet software.

developed for estimating by printers. The system was geared to a microcomputer and Scanlon acquired a stand-alone Tandy TRS 80 Model 2 with display terminal, floppy disk storage, and printer at a cost of between $9,000 and $10,000, plus additional floppy disk storage capacity. Using a VisiCalc program, Prentice-Hall created a spread sheet, entering vertically on the left all elements of book manufacturing, from composition to binding, and horizontally at the top the various estimated quantities. A system was also built in to segregate plant cost from running cost and to calculate reprint data.

Unlike Prentice-Hall and Harper & Row, CBS Educa-

tional and Professional Publishing uses not a stand-alone microcomputer but a corporate data-base system, although initially the manufacturing-control program was set up with an independent time-sharing service. When the model program grew to 10,000 titles, stated Lymon O. Louis, vice-president for manufacturing, it was moved in-house. The present system (still a time-sharing function in that the department uses a dataphone, which it pays for) is used for estimating and for such specification jobs as purchase-order generation and manufacturing and strategic planning. Every October the manufacturing department publishes its entire manufacturing schedule for the next year, by month. The schedule includes such items as paper type, printer, hours on press, and so forth. When contractors bid on the firm's book business, the manufacturing department gives them a readout of a profile of the number of units, sizes, colors, and types the department ran the year before, segmented by month so a contractor can know what activity has looked like and base his estimates on solid information.

A mainframe computer is also used at McGraw-Hill Book Company's manufacturing department to control printing, binding, and paper-inventory control. Dion von der Lieth, vice-president and director of manufacturing and inventory management, explained that in 1983 the program enabled his department to bring in the entire forecast-driven inventory management system and use the marketing forecasts both to drive inventory management and to bring the schedules that come out of inventory management over into manufacturing. This allowed for

IBM XT microprocessor will be used by McGraw-Hill to capture daily data from suppliers.

the projection of manufacturing orders into the future and gave the division capacity planning for printing and binding and for paper needs on a book-by-book basis. As von der Lieth explained, the capability to do this lay in the fact that the specifications of each product existed in the data base. For von der Lieth, the computer's biggest advantage is in price negotiations, since it gives him a much better idea of where the department is going, and the kind and number of products it will be making in the future.

According to von der Lieth, his department's next major communication phase will be with its printers and binders. He is setting up microprocessor-to-microprocessor communication, using standard IBM PC-to-XT units, with his major suppliers. His idea is to capture the daily data from suppliers' PCs onto McGraw-Hill's more advanced XT microprocessor in New York, review the data, and then automatically download it into the mainframe, eliminating keystrokes.

The computer activity generated by manufacturing departments last year will undoubtedly trigger significant productivity strides in 1984, and continued experience with computers will go a long way toward keeping bookmaking costs in line.

Of course, publishers are taking other courses, too, to make their manufacturing operations more efficient. One piece of new equipment that captured the imagination of some publishers last year was Dai Nippon's "mini" video system, which takes 8mm and 16mm film and converts it into a high-quality transparency. Houghton Mifflin has seized on the concept and is planning to convert transparencies made from motion film into printable books, bringing back a series of H. A. Rey books that hasn't had a new edition for some years. No titles have been decided on, but it is understood that the project is already underway and that books will be published in the fall of 1984.

Super-Short-Run Printing

1983 was also a year of great significance to a number of scholarly publishers, particularly university presses, because of the appearance of several super-short-run printing lines that allowed them to reprint some of their out-of-print titles at an acceptable price in quantities down to 35 or 50 copies.

Although the first such line was created in 1982, it wasn't until last year that the market really began growing and saw at least three firms printing and binding the super-short runs—the first, Westview Press in Boulder, Colorado, and then Thomson-Shore, Inc., in Dexter, Michigan, and C & M Press in Denver. Westview, a scholarly publisher with publishing and typesetting divisions, set up a super-short-run division after its founder and president, Frederick A. Praeger, saw the need for a low-cost way to print scholarly titles, since scholarly publishers were dropping many titles from their lists because of the high cost of reprinting.

In order to set up a super-short-run operation, Praeger

Printing super-short runs of scholarly reprints at Thomson-Shore on the "System 5"—a combination of A.M. Total Copy System Model 2975 (perfecting offset press), shown here, and A.M. Plate Camera Model 875.

bought an A.M. Total Copy System Model 2975 perfecting offset press, collating towers, an A.M. Plate Camera Model 875 (all of which form the A.M. System 5), and a Muller-Martini Baby Pony adhesive binder, and began printing economically runs of 50 to 300 copies. Both C & M

Thomson-Shore operator prepares to shoot page on the platemaker, which bypasses the negative stage to create plates directly.

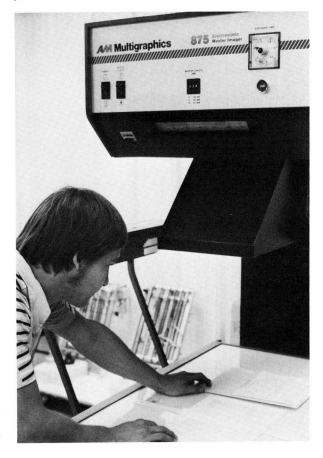

and Thomson-Shore followed suit and by the end of 1983 demand was so intense that at least two of the firms added more equipment to expand capacity—Westview another Model 875 press and Thomson-Shore a Sulby perfect binder.

One reason System 5 can produce books at a low unit cost lies in the ability of the platemaker to bypass the negative stage and shoot the pages of an original book directly. This saves the time and manpower needed to create and strip negatives.

Numbering among the customers of super-short-run presses in 1983 were such prestigious institutions as Harvard University Press, the University of California Press, Cornell University Press, Hoover Institute of Stanford University, the University Press of America, and the University Press of New England. Owners of the super-short-run presses think that some publishers may decide to stop reprinting in 300-to-500 quantities and move to the short-short run in order to save money and avoid the possibility of sales slackening on certain titles, which would leave books languishing in the warehouse.

The Paper Market Strengthens

As the economy began to pick up in the third quarter of 1983, so, too, did the fortunes of a number of manufacturers, who benefited from the greater number of bookmaking orders coming in from their customers. This was a welcome turnaround, since the book-manufacturing community had been suffering from excess capacity for several years—to the point where several printer/binders had to close their doors during 1982. Although it could have been predicted as a natural outcome of more prosperous times, the abrupt rise in paper costs that followed this strengthening of the economy surprised, even shocked, manufacturers and publishers alike, who had gotten used to a buyer's market over the course of three years, from 1980 to 1983. Customers had gotten used to receiving paper practically whenever they wanted it, and paper prices were depressed.

By the end of 1983, however, the pickup in the use of paper grades of all types was unmistakable, primarily because better business meant more paper use; inventory pipelines were filling up at printer, converter, and publisher levels; and customers were hedging their buying in most grade categories, getting in one last shot before possible price increases.

What had happened was a rise in the mills' capacity rate: In the last half of 1982 the rate was running in the high 80 percent area, but toward the end of 1983, mills were running at a 94–95 percent rate. Printing and writing papers had continued to grow faster than the economy. Uncoated free sheet on average exceeded the economic trend as depicted by the gross national product (GNP) by .6 percent per year, the result of an above-average growth in paper demand for office copying, word processing, and computer printouts. Coated paper use increased an average of 1.6 percent over the GNP as a result of

increases in magazine advertising, catalog sales, and inroads into uncoated paper markets.

Robert G. Spicer, vice-president for marketing of Fine Paper for Carpenter/Offutt Paper, Inc. (Long Beach, Calif.), last year predicted that changes in capacity trends over the next three years will be much different from those experienced over the last three. He explained that from mid-1980 to mid-1983, uncoated free sheet capacity increased 4 percent, while coated paper moved up 22 percent. However, he said that in the next three years— mid-1983 to mid-1986—the magnitude of the changes will reverse, with uncoated free up 14 percent and coated up only 5 percent.

All this adds up to higher prices for manufacturers who stock paper on their plant floors and for publishers who buy their own paper. To keep control of the price situation and to assure themselves of a continuing paper supply, manufacturers and publishers were given the following advice by Spicer last year: Anticipate needs as far in advance as possible; don't trust to luck that you can obtain paper when you need it; treat your supplier as a partner; be as flexible as possible in selection of grades, shades, basis weights, and so forth; be open to suggestions from suppliers; and assume that paper-supply times will continue to be short.

Photocomposition from Abroad

1983 was also the year that firms from England and Ireland invaded the U.S. photocomposition market, promoting their capability to phototypeset scientific fonts. In October, two contingents appeared in New York City: Arrowsmith Phototype from London and Alden Press from Oxford, exhibiting at the Folio Show, and three phototypesetters from Ireland (Intercontinental Photocomposition, Ltd., and Scanway Graphics International, Ltd., both from Dublin, and Doyle Photosetting, Ltd., of Offaly), exhibiting at the offices of the Irish Export Board.

Interest was high among representatives of U.S. publishing houses who visited the exhibits. At the Irish show, Ruth Weine, senior editing supervisor for McGraw-Hill's Professional Reference Division, was searching for a firm that could phototypeset a 1,300-page chemistry book that contained 800 pages of tables—a text, she said, "that is a necessity for every freshman taking college chemistry." Weine had not been able to find a domestic typesetter that had the capability and capacity (and low cost) to do the job.

As it turned out, the Irish exhibit payed off for at least two firms, McGraw-Hill and Holt, Rinehart & Winston, both of which are having technical books phototypeset by several of the Irish companies. Both firms contracted the typesetting with Cobb/Dunlop, a publisher service based in New York City (David E. Dunlop, co-owner of that company, also had attended the exhibit), which in turn contracted the jobs out to two of the Irish phototypesetters attending the event. Because other publishers were also on hand at the Irish Export Board, some of whom had had books typeset in Ireland, it seemed clear that McGraw-Hill and Holt would not be the only publishers to have their typesetting done by the phototypesetters in Ireland.

For Holt, this new typesetting job will be the third done in Ireland, according to Deborah Moore, editor of electrical engineering and computer information systems, College Department. The book being set at present is Amnon Yariv's *Introduction to Optical Electronics,* 3rd edition; the earlier books were Chen's *Linear System Theory and Design,* 2nd edition, and McGillem & Cooper's *Continuous and Discrete Signals System Analysis,* 2nd edition.

Was the "invasion" successful? It appears that it was and conversations with the English and Irish contingents revealed that they think the American market is ripe for the picking, primarily because many U.S. phototypesetting houses do not specialize in scientific and chemical fonts and specialized hand-done technical typesetting.

Report on Textbooks

The concern of elementary and high school educators that adhesive-bound books would not stand up to the daily pounding these books take from students was abated in 1983 when a study found that adhesive-bound textbooks after three years of use in metropolitan areas in Massachusetts, New Jersey, Illinois, and Indiana were holding up satisfactorily.

The finding was part of a three-area status report on such textbooks made by the subcommittee on casebound adhesive binding of the Advisory Commission on Textbook Specifications (ACTS). The report covered the "open territory"—the northern tier of states—and two "closed" states—West Virginia and Texas—where textbooks are under the jurisdiction of the National Association of State Textbook Administrators (NASTA). (Other closed, or administered, states are Alabama, Arizona, Arkansas, California, Florida, Georgia, Idaho, Kentucky, Louisiana, Nevada, New Mexico, North Carolina, Oklahoma, Oregon, South Carolina, Tennessee, Utah, and Virginia.)

The northern-tier test was on the Houghton Mifflin textbook *Geometry;* the southern text was *Essentials of Economics,* published by Addison-Wesley. Half of the books were Smyth-sewn, the other half casebound adhesive bound, and the books were evenly mixed within cartons and distributed. The books tested in West Virginia and Texas were used for only one semester, but were found to be holding up well and their condition tended to reinforce the experience of the northern-tier schools. Michael Bodden, vice-president and director of manufacturing for Houghton Mifflin, reported to the subcommittee that during the three years in which the books were in use in the northern tier, his firm had not received a single customer complaint. Bodden inspected 110 books, two of which were dismissed for obvious student abuse; of the 108 remaining, 61 had been sewn and 47 adhesive bound. Of the sewn books, 85 percent were judged to be in

good-to-excellent condition; 81 percent of the adhesive-bound books were judged to be in good condition. Of the latter, Bodden concluded that virtually all will be serviceable for the beginning of the fourth year of classroom use and that, if any should fail during the 1984 school year, the books would nonetheless have achieved an acceptable longevity.

In the southern-tier test, Stanley Robinson, manufacturing manager for Addison-Wesley, and Gerald Perry, NASTA representative from West Virginia, checked 180 Smyth-sewn and 224 casebound adhesive-bound books. In the former, they observed a slight loosening of the front signature in 5–10 percent of the books. Otherwise they were said to be in excellent condition. In the latter, they observed a separation between leaves 1 and 2 in 36 percent of the books, which, they claimed, "has no bearing on the adhesive binding itself." Thus, there was no evidence of overall failure of the book block (the bound pages before attachment of the cover), or of individual pages falling out. In Texas, J. Henry Perry, NASTA representative; Tom Bayer, division general manager, books, for W. A. Krueger Company; Frank Stark, plant manager of the Rand McNally Versailles (Ky.) plant; and Jim Hofferth of Van Hoffman Press examined about 600 each of adhesive-bound and Smyth-sewn copies used for one semester at two schools. They were found to be in excellent shape; although a separation between leaves 1 and 2 in 10–15 percent of the books was apparent, there was also no evidence of book block failure or individual pages falling out. The adhesive binding was said to be performing well.

ACTS members were disturbed by the use of college textbooks in high schools and a report by R. Jerry Rice, NASTA representative from Tennessee, pointed out the technical problems that such use caused: namely, that college textbooks did not have to conform to ACTS specifications as set out in the ACTS "bible," *Manufacturing Standards and Specifications for Textbooks* (MSST), and often fall apart quickly under high school use. This is a recurring problem experienced by public secondary schools that buy college-level textbooks for use in college

In tests of adhesive binding by the Advisory Commission on Textbook Specifications, two books were used: Houghton Mifflin's Geometry *and Addison-Wesley's* Essentials of Economics. © *1983 Jerome Frank.*

credit or advanced placement courses. The source of the problem, according to the 1983 report, appears to center around the fact that el-hi divisions of publishing companies are separate from college divisions and that the MSST are designed only for el-hi textbooks. "In reality, however," Rice stressed, "the public high schools of America offer both secondary and college courses. In fact, more and more schools have begun to offer advanced placement courses for college-bound students." Since secondary schools are required to use a college-level textbook in order for students to receive college credit in advanced placement courses, ACTS is faced with purchasing books that are not required to meet MSST standards. "Most consumers do not understand this differentiation in manufacturing specifications," Rice went on, "and have even become hostile toward publishers as a result of the problems they have encountered with these adhesive bound books. Not only have the school districts formed some negative opinions about adhesive bound books, they have also formed some adverse opinions about future purchases from certain publishers who have sold and replaced books that have literally fallen apart within three months."

Although Rice saw no clear-cut answer to the dilemma since it involves a group that operates independently of ACTS—the college division of each publishing company—he made three suggestions that he hoped would bear fruit in 1984 and beyond:

> I would like to suggest to publishers that they consider the following possible ideas. Is it not possible for the el-hi and college divisions to form a cooperative arrangement so that books that are accepted for use in advanced placement courses be labeled or identified so that the binder would manufacture them according to MSST? This might first of all require a few minor changes to the MSST to include such books as a part of the standards. For example, the definition of "textbook" should include "books for advanced placement courses being taught to secondary students."
>
> Secondly, some cooperative arrangements should be attempted with the College Board that governs the advanced placement programs nationwide to identify those books that have been accepted for use in advanced placement programs and to develop a system for identifying those books written for this purpose so that the publisher and binder can insure that they will meet MSST standards before they are sold to public schools.
>
> Another possibility is that NASTA members could call for bids in Advanced Placement subjects each year and specify that the books would have to meet MSST specifications. This would signal to the publisher that if the books were approved their products would have to meet the el-hi standards rather than college specifications.

Rice noted that in his state of Tennessee, advanced placement courses are offered in urban school districts and that the judgment emerging from conversations he has had with educators there is that the presumed savings of adhesive-bound books over the traditionally sewn binding is more false economy than anything else. Also, he claims there are no accurate data to reflect the actual costs to school systems and publishers of these "inferior books,"

which have to be picked up, rebound, and returned to the schools two or three times. "In addition to these dollar costs," he added, "it is impossible to calculate the value of lost instructional time to the students, school system, and taxpayers."

In Rice's opinion, school systems will be willing to pay the "small additional costs" of quality binding for these textbooks rather than having to deal with the frustration and disruption caused by inferior quality. One school system has proposed the possibility of buying the signatures and binding the books to MSST standards.

The subject will undoubtedly arouse controversy among publishers, NASTA, book manufacturers, and school administrators, and specific solutions may be proposed by ACTS in 1984.

Growing Use of Flexibook

Although the binding innovation called Flexibook introduced into the United States by A. Horowitz & Sons, Inc., of Fairfield, New Jersey, first appeared in 1982, it wasn't until 1983 that publishers began to accept self-binding as an option between hardcover and paperback. Flexibook is an integrated, semirigid, boardless cover made on special machinery at the Horowitz plant. The idea is to reduce costs for the hardcover publisher by eliminating boards, cloth, and binding material as well as cover stamping and book jackets, and to enhance the appearance of paperbacks by using a semirigid cover that overhangs the book block in the manner of a hardcover book. A number of publishers have already committed themselves to long runs of books covered in the Flexi binding and in 1983 Flexi-bound titles such as *Madame: My Misbegotten Memoirs* (Dodd, Mead); *Keeping Close* (Citadel Press); *The Bible* (King James Version published by C. R. Gibson); *The Bible* (New King James Version published by Thomas Nelson); *Cats* (Harcourt Brace Jovanovich); *The Three Bears* (a juvenile by Harper & Row); *When Parents Die* (Bantam Books); *Publishers Weekly Yearbook* (R. R. Bowker Company); and *The Velveteen Rabbit* (David R. Godine Publishers) appeared.

To date, Bantam has reordered three titles in Flexi binding—*How to Survive the Loss of a Love* and *When Lovers Are Friends* (both published in 1982), and *When Parents Die*. By the end of December 1983, Horowitz had bound between 800,000 and 1 million books in the Flexi binding. Gearing up for large Flexi runs in 1984 are Houghton Mifflin, which is planning to mark the fiftieth anniversary of the publishing of Petersen's *Field Guides to the Birds* with a 100,000-copy edition in Flexibook in spring; and Western Publishing, with a 40,000-copy printing of each of 12 spiral-bound volumes of its Betty Crocker Cook Book series, also in the spring.

Manufacturer Gears Up

In mid-1983, John D. Lucas Printing Company, defying the trend toward the low profile in the book-manufacturing area, dedicated its $3.1 million, 175,000-square-foot, humidity- and dust-controlled and air conditioned plant in Holabird Industrial Park, in Baltimore, Maryland. The massive plant has a $40 million capacity in three eight-hour shifts and did about half that amount in 1983 in two-shift days, turning out books, magazines, and commercial work for a balanced marketing approach.

The Lucas equipment roster is impressive and includes a wide variety of sheetfed and web presses, including a 39″ × 55″ Roland 800 four-color press with densitometer-controlled inking system.

The Roland press is a complex machine capable of 7,500 to 8,000 impressions per hour on light stock and approximately 10,000 impressions on heavier stock. The ink fountains are a series of slides, each set either automatically by computer, or opened and closed by a pressman from the control panel.

At the end of 1983, a number of publishers were talking about consolidating their suppliers and turning to fewer manufacturers for all of their bookmaking work. Almost

in response to this incipient trend, some of the larger book manufacturers were investigating the process of doing the total bookmaking job—including all component work as well as printing and binding.

Stephen Pekich of Houghton Mifflin believes that single sourcing will become the norm for individual jobs in 1984, a course that will undoubtedly cause manufacturers to tighten up their own operations in order to merchandise their most important assets—high efficiency, excellent quality control, and bull's eye scheduling. With business picking up in the last quarter of 1983, both manufacturers and publishers may become more adventuresome in experimenting with new technology in order to keep a tighter rein on costs.

A number of leading publishers, attracted by the design potential of the Flexibook binding, in 1983 bound a wide variety of titles in that semi-rigid cover. © *Jerome Frank.*

Retailing

23

Issues in Bookselling, 1983

ALLENE SYMONS

Booksellers were concerned with several issues in 1983, among them the increasing presence of discount bookstore competition and changes in distribution. The latter included the new ZIPSAN shipping system (which met with failure after only five months of operation), Ingram Book Company's new warehouse concept, and—of great interest to booksellers and the industry overall—the experimental Booksellers Order Service (BOS), devised by the American Booksellers Association (ABA). ABA not only faced the challenge of the innovative BOS project, but also contended with a number of legalities throughout the year. Toward the end of the year it came as a surprise to the industry when both the executive director, G. Roysce Smith, and the associate executive director, Robert Hale, announced their plans to retire from leadership of the organization.

The Widening Reach of Discount Bookselling

Discount bookselling increased markedly throughout the United States in 1983. Discount book chains opened new locations, major chains competed by offering bestsellers at marked-down prices, and many department stores and independent booksellers faced the competition by adopting similar off-price policies. Discounting is no longer the exception in book retail, and the line can no longer be clearly drawn between discount outlets and nondiscount; rather, the distinction is now made between full-line stores—which often mark down selected titles—

and full-discount stores, which discount all titles and aggressively advertise their off-price policies.

The confusion between full-line stores and discount stores became evident in the summer of 1983, when B. Dalton began offering selected "Hot List" (bestseller) titles in the Los Angeles area, a market where Crown had opened 50 stores by the end of the year. During the Christmas season, Waldenbooks joined B. Dalton in the discount war against Crown in Southern California by offering bestsellers at a 35 percent discount; in addition, Dalton offered discounts in its Denver and Dallas stores, and Waldenbooks began spot discounting in various areas (including Portland, Maine, and Miami, Florida) in a program that merchandise director Michael Meyer of Waldenbooks described as a matter of "meeting the competition." Regarding its Los Angeles/Denver/Dallas discount policies, B. Dalton spokesperson Shirley Kitzman stated that the firm was merely "testing the discount concept" and did not intend to extend the program.

Although the exact meaning of the term *discount bookseller* is rapidly becoming amorphous, the full-discount chains are growing and new companies are entering the market. The full-discount format as popularized by Crown Books—although Crown was not the first—back in 1981, is a no-frills approach to bookselling intended to keep overhead low and sales volume high. To accomplish this, sites are usually in lower rent retail areas, such as strip malls (versus enclosed malls); staff is kept to a minimum and in-store signing is used to facilitate customer self-service. High volume is accomplished by emphasis on bestsellers, with only a representative selection of backlist and slower-moving titles. The discount bookseller also devotes a large percentage of selling space to remainders, displayed as bargain books. Advertising campaigns highlight the reduced price on bestselling titles, comparing these with full or list price as currently offered in other bookstores.

The pricing policies of full-discount bookstore chains generally use the following formula, with some variations: *New York Times* bestsellers are discounted between 35 and 40 percent; the top three books on the fiction and nonfiction hardcover lists are often offered at 40 percent off list price. Paperback bestsellers are usually offered at a 25 percent discount, with other titles 10–15 percent lower than the suggested retail price.

Among the full-discount operations, expansion was evident as Crown Books reached a total of 126 stores by the end of the year, compared with 100 at the end of 1982 and only 50 in 1981. Based in Landover, Maryland (a suburb of Washington, D.C.), Crown has locations throughout the country in such markets as Los Angeles, Chicago, San Francisco, San Diego, Houston, Washington, D.C., and San Jose (Calif.). At the end of 1983, Crown opened outlets in Seattle, Washington; other markets under consideration were Pennsylvania and New York State.

On the East Coast, where the Barnes & Noble bookstore chain has been discounting since 1975, expansion plans were also under way. At the end of 1983, the New York City–based Barnes & Noble operation had 31 discount outlets (New York, New Jersey, and the Boston area), with plans to open at least 10 to 15 stores in the coming year.

Also located on the Eastern seaboard is the Massachusetts-based Lauriat's bookstore chain, which has 16 full-line locations. In 1982, this firm opened a pilot store in Quincy, Massachusetts, with the purpose of establishing a discount subsidiary called Royal Discount Books. Royal follows the standard discount policy: 35 percent off all *New York Times* hardback bestsellers, 25 percent off paperback bestsellers, 20 percent off all other hardcover titles, and 10 percent off other paperback books. The Quincy store also offers some nonbook merchandise, such as cards and gift wrappings. Although plans were to open three or four Royal Discount locations in the greater Boston area during the latter part of 1983, only one other location was actually opened. The second Royal Discount location, in the Marshfield suburb of Boston, opened in November; unlike the first, the Marshfield store's inventory is exclusively books. According to Lauriat's operations director, Edward Diamond, the firm is continuing to look for locations in the greater Boston area; availability of suitable real estate is a major determinant in expansion, not only for Lauriat but for all discounters. If sites are found, Lauriat's plans to open two or three locations a year.

In the Midwest, where Crown has a strong discount position in the Chicago area, Pickwick Discount Books announced in 1983 that it was ready for rapid expansion. Pickwick is a special operating company of B. Dalton and both have corporate headquarters, a few miles apart, in Minneapolis, Minnesota. After four years of testing in Columbus, Ohio, Pickwick intends to instigate a 20-store rollout in three market areas during 1984. Although the market areas were not disclosed at the time of the announcement, it was stated that 10 stores would be in one market area, while 10 locations would be in the other two markets. According to Pickwick's vice-president and general manager, Jack Ford, although B. Dalton and Pickwick Discount Books are under the same corporate umbrella (Dayton Hudson), and while competition between the two is inevitable, nonetheless there is a difference in format (size, location, store design) that should allow both Pickwick and B. Dalton to prosper, as they are intended to serve different market segments.

Pickwick Discount Books regards Crown as its real competition, since both are backed by huge parent corporations and presumably each could hold out in case of a discount war. In this regard, Barnes & Noble (B&N) is potentially more than an East Coast regional chain, since the B&N corporation includes several large subsidiaries (among them: a wholesale division, a huge mail-order operation, the Marboro remainder division, and 31 college store lease operations). But other regional discounters are emerging and expanding, hoping to wrap up their respective regions before the national discounters close in. One of these regional discounters is Encore Books, based in Philadelphia. Established in 1973, Encore has 15 stores with a new location targeted for early 1984 and plans for another 7 to 10 sites before the end of the year, according to its president, David Schlessinger. Encore Books expects to have around 30 locations within the next two or three years within its current territory, which includes greater Philadephia, encompassing South New Jersey and Delaware.

On the West Coast, Bookmania® has five stores in the Bay Area, including San Jose, Saratoga, Oakland (the most recent), and a flagship store in downtown San Francisco. Although Crown Books is now established in the area, Bookmania plans to open two or three new stores each year. By offering in-store events and customer services, Bookmania is trying to compete with Crown's no-frills operation. In the Southwest, two discounters are already in place. One is Book Stop, based in Austin, Texas. This firm has two locations (Austin and San Antonio) and plans to add two stores a year within the state. The other discounter, with two locations at present and plans to add more, is Spectrum, based in Houston.

Despite the expansion of discount operations around the country during 1983, so far there is little head-to-head competition between the full-discount chains. But this situation is certain to change in the near future, since the projected growth of these companies points to eventual overlap. The national book discounters (Pickwick and Crown) and regional retailers (Barnes & Noble and Encore, along with small but aggressive companies such as Bookmania, Book Stop, and Spectrum) could eventually be in direct competition, at least in some markets. When this occurs, the aggressive advertising strategy begun by Crown—"Now, you'll never have to pay full price again"—is likely to be taken for granted by consumers, and full-price bookstores (with the possible exception of specialty stores and retailers in lower-volume markets) may become increasingly rare. On the subject of discounting, the outgoing executive director of the American Booksellers Association, G. Roysce Smith, offered this observation: "I think prices are high enough on books that people can afford to do some discounting without killing themselves. . . . I think discounting is here to stay this time. Even if there were not discounters in the area, people will discount."

Challenges and Change for Booksellers Associations

Over the course of the year, the regional booksellers associations continued their pattern of growth, with several groups enlarging their trade-show programs to include additional days. Several of the 20 associations added or expanded services for their members; among these services, regional advertising efforts resulted in several cooperative newspaper and catalog advertising campaigns targeted to the holiday retail season.

The antagonism between the national and regional groups that had marked the past few years lessened somewhat in 1983. The major cause of recent disharmony had been the controversial discriminatory-pricing-practices lawsuit against Avon Books and Bantam Books, which was initiated by the Northern California Booksellers Association (NCBA) and two other plaintiffs in 1982; NCBA members made it clear at the time that ABA was not able to provide financial and moral support.

The lawsuit moved slowly through several stages during the year. The widely held belief among independent booksellers that many publishers offer advantageous discount terms to large bookstore chains—the allegation in the pricing-practices lawsuit—still had not been proven in court by the end of 1983.

The discriminatory-pricing suit was originally filed in 1982 against Hearst Corporation, publisher of Avon Books, by co-plaintiffs Northern California Booksellers Association, Cody's Books of Berkeley, California, and Bookplate, Inc., of San Francisco. Just prior to the end of 1982, NCBA had filed a complaint that added Bantam Books as a co-defendant in the suit against Avon Books.

In January of 1983, Bantam Books filed an answer to the complaint, making a motion to the effect that its case be severed from that of Avon. According to William Petrocelli of Himmelstein, Savinar, Petrocelli & Curtis, NCBA's counsel, one justification for treating the defendants in a single lawsuit was the fact that both used the same kind of cost-justification defense under the Robinson-Patman Act.

Yet in February, the presiding judge in the case, U.S. District Court Judge Thelton E. Henderson, severed Bantam Books from the suit brought by the three plaintiffs. This decision was based on Henderson's agreement with Bantam that disclosure of pricing information in legal proceedings might damage Bantam's competitive position with Avon or open the two publishers to allegations of price-fixing.

In May of 1983, the plaintiffs in the suit against Hearst/Avon agreed to suspend further discovery proceedings in the case while Avon conducted a six-month study, undertaken at its own expense, of its pricing practices. When the study was nearing completion in October, the Hearst Corporation gave the plaintiffs a preliminary draft analysis of the costs of selling books to chain and independent stores. At that time, Petrocelli said that NCBA and the other two plaintiffs would give serious thought to settlement of the case. The suit against Bantam Books was at that time in the deposition stage and not scheduled for a court date until February 1984. At the end of the year, talks between Avon and NCBA had reached a "dead end," according to Petrocelli, and in a reversal of its October prediction of a settlement, NCBA took steps to move the action back toward trial.

Among the other legal issues commanding ABA attention this year were several censorship cases, the outcome of which could impact member book retailers and the products they sell. As a member of the Media Coalition, ABA worked with the Upper Midwest Booksellers Association to fight a proposed amendment to the Minneapolis civil rights ordinance that would broadly redefine pornography as a form of discrimination against women with the effect that a significant number of books would be banned from sale in the Minneapolis area. In a South Dakota contest, three booksellers were included in a lawsuit brought against Viking by Governor William Janklow. Janklow alleged that *In the Spirit of Crazy Horse* by Peter Matthiessen was libelous; the booksellers were named in the suit for continuing to sell the book. At the end of the year, several retailers were included in a similar libel suit filed against Random House for material in *Poor Little Rich Girl: The Life and Loves of Barbara Hutton* by David Heymann. Among the retailers cited in the suit were Crown Books and the California bookstore chain Hunter's Books.

ABA's G. Roysce Smith Resigns, Rath Appointed New Director

The regional and national bookselling associations were united in their efforts to protect First Amendment rights and to protect retailers from being subjected to unjust and costly lawsuits. Yet there was another issue in 1983 that caused an ongoing rift between ABA and a segment of its membership. This occurred when ABA executive director G. Roysce Smith and associate executive director Robert Hale announced in October their intentions to retire from the organization. Smith had been head of the organization for 12 years, while Hale had served as second in command for six years. The need to find a new executive director

Newly appointed ABA executive director Bernard Rath. ©
Susan Rath.

and associate director spurred a movement within the general membership of ABA, and a splinter group proposed its own slate of candidates for the ABA board of directors (although a new board would not be selected until May 1984). In November, after deliberation and interviews of candidates, the ABA board of directors announced that it had recruited a new head for the organization from the outside—Bernard Rath, director of the Canadian Booksellers Association (CBA). Nationalism seemed a nonissue regarding this choice of leader, for when Rath's name was announced in December, the decision seemed to meet with the general approval of the ABA membership.

After 12 years as executive director of the American Booksellers Association, G. Roysce Smith announced his decision to retire from the organization effective March 1, 1984. At the time of his announcement in October, Smith said that his choice not to renew his contract as ABA director was actually the result of a decision made three years ago when his contract last came up for renewal. Due to organizational pressures resulting from the discriminatory-pricing lawsuit at that time, Smith deferred his retirement plans. He noted that now, with the lawsuit no longer as divisive an issue for ABA, and with the Booksellers Order System in its final testing phase, he believed this was an opportune time to retire and pursue other interests.

Smith was appointed ABA executive director in 1972, after serving as acting director following the death of Joseph A. Duffy, who held the post for 19 years. Prior to his position as acting director, Smith was the ABA's educational project director (1971) and he also served on the ABA board of directors. Smith's bookselling career began in 1949 as a Christmas temporary at Davison's, a Macy's Atlanta affiliate. He became assistant buyer and remained at Davison's until 1957, when he joined the Yale Cooperative Corporation in New Haven, Connecticut, where he became book department manager that same year. Actively involved in the National Association of College Stores (NACS) from 1957–1971, Smith was instrumental in the formation of the NACS Booksellers School in 1965, a program in which ABA began to participate in 1969. During that same time he wrote a weekly column of book news that appeared in the New Haven *Register;* he also produced and moderated a weekly half-hour TV talk show, "The Opinionated Man," on WNHC-TV in New Haven (1966–1971), and was host of a daily radio program featuring interviews and book news. Smith has also contributed numerous articles on bookselling to trade journals, including *Publishers Weekly,* for which he served several years as a contributing editor.

During Smith's tenure as executive director, the association expanded in membership and services. Membership increased from around 3,000 to over 5,000. Since membership is based on a single corporate registration for chain stores, the total number of outlets represented is much larger, or around 9,000, according to Smith.

Among the expanded services ABA developed for its membership under Smith's leadership was the weekly newsletter informing members of book and author promotions, the *Newswire* (1973). More recently, *Newswire* has been expanded to include other publishing news in digest form. In addition, ABA introduced the *American Bookseller* magazine in 1977.

During the 12 years of his tenure, the organization Smith headed faced major changes and challenges to its membership. One of these was the emergence and rapid expansion of national bookstore chains and, a few years later, discount retail operations. Since ABA membership includes both independent booksellers and chains, increasing competition between the two categories of retailer required circumspection by ABA—and by Smith as its executive director—in order to serve its entire membership and to ensure competitive equitability.

Among steps taken toward this end were efforts to improve bookstore profitability through encouragement of changes in publishers terms, and the implementation of freight pass-through. But perhaps the greatest challenge to ABA under Smith was the question of how ABA should and could respond to membership pressure for legal action against publishers for allegedly discriminatory pricing practices. This pressure was complicated by the fact that the alleged price discrimination was in favor of other ABA members (in particular, the national chains).

As Smith prepared to hand the ABA leadership to Bernard Rath, he offered a few observations about his twelve years as ABA head:

- On ABA/membership tensions: "It's been tricky, keeping tempers calm and keeping the membership happy. We've not always been successful at it. I haven't always been too pleased about the constraints that are placed on trade associations. I would have liked to have been able to speak more freely. It has made ABA a particularly easy target for people who have had their own agenda."
- On the annual ABA trade show: "Over the years, the number of exhibits grew, the parties grew, and the pressure on the executive director grew. The convention always gets good press—Memorial Day is a dead weekend and there's no news so they cover us like crazy. But the main purpose is to get publishers and booksellers together. Problems still persist: the problem of space assignments still hasn't been resolved; the question of attendance—is quality or quantity most important, that is always the debate. But the quality people are always in attendance, wherever the trade show is held."
- On ABA changes since 1972: "It was a time of dramatic change in retail and in publishing as well. I think one thing ABA needed when I came in was to be more democratic—at least, that was the perception of the membership—and I think it became more service-oriented toward its members as well, it produced more things to use, more booksellers schools, became more training oriented."
- On ABA failures: "One was the Give A Book program—I think it was a real tragedy that it didn't catch on. And it didn't catch on in 1949 either, so I guess we shouldn't have been too surprised. It needed industry support and it couldn't operate without publishers being enthusiastic as well."

Retiring ABA associate executive director Robert Hale. Bachrach.

- On future ABA challenges: "The Booksellers Order Service. And I think one of the challenges is going to be a matter of restructuring the role of executive director. I was practically tied to the office while Bob Hale handled membership on the road. In the last five years I practically became an inaccessible man. Bob and I realized that his job wouldn't be continued. The executive director should get help in various areas so that it will free him to do what Bob Hale was doing."
- On industry trends: "Net pricing is probably the next big thing to have to face up to. I think more and more booksellers are beginning to price books any way they want to. A lot of independents are lowering prices on some books, raising it on others. It will be a hotly debated issue."

When announcing his retirement, Smith stated that his plans included relocating to San Diego, California, where he plans to write several books and spend around one-third of his time as manager of nonbook shows for small trade and professional associations.

Retiring American Booksellers Association executive director G. Royce Smith. Bachrach.

Smith's impending retirement was not the only leadership change announced in ABA during the year. Associate executive director Robert Hale resigned on November 1 to return to bookselling as owner of the Westwinds Bookstore in Duxbury, Massachusetts, where he began his retailing career in 1954. Hale was director of the Connecticut College Bookshop in New London from 1962 to 1969, and president and general manager of the Hathaway House Bookshop in Wellesley, Massachusetts, from 1970 to 1978. He was founder of the New England Regional

Booksellers Association and was its president in 1973–1974. Subsequently he was ABA president from 1976 to 1978 during which time he began the tradition of children's book and author breakfasts at ABA conventions. As ABA associate executive director from 1978 to 1983, Hale was instrumental in the establishment of Banned Books Week, and in the development of regional bookselling associations.

Although Hale's resignation was announced only a month before its effective date, a period of two months (January and February 1984) was planned for transition of leadership from Smith to the new executive director, Bernard Rath. Rath has served as executive director of the Canadian Booksellers Association since 1978. CBA represents a retail membership approximately one-tenth the size of ABA.

Under Rath's leadership, CBA membership increased by two-thirds and its annual trade show doubled in size, as did its contribution to association income. Other changes in the organization included the development of the association magazine, *Canadian Bookseller,* from a typewritten broadsheet to a professionally produced magazine. In 1979 Rath founded, incorporated, and served as general manager of the Canadian Booksellers Co-operative Inc., a buying group for CBA members. The annual volume of the co-op, which was $30,000 its first year of operation, was expected to reach $400,000 by the end of CBA's current fiscal year. As a member of the task force on distribution, Rath was instrumental in implementing an industry freight consolidation program. He also played an active role in the establishment of the Canadian Telebook Agency, which is the first international data base, and worked with others on the Wintario Halfback Program, a program wherein losing lottery tickets can be used as credit toward purchase of books. Another project planned under Rath's direction is a consumer-oriented book show (similar to the *Boston Globe* book fair), which will be held for the first time in June 1984 in Toronto, just prior to the CBA trade show. CBA member stores will sell books out of the publishers' booths, with proceeds going to a fund for promotion and travel subsidies to enable out-of-town CBA members to attend the trade show.

In his new position as executive director of ABA, Rath plans to restructure the executive position and the association's support staff. Trade-show coordination is a duty that has been handled by the executive director in the past, and that due to the size of the trade show has become a job warranting a separate title. One of the intentions of this staff restructuring is to provide more travel time for the executive director, so that he may consult with regional bookselling organizations and participate in such activities as the joint NACS/ABA Booksellers Schools. As part of this restructuring, the position of associate executive director (recently held by Robert Hale) will be eliminated.

Experiments in Book Distribution

In the area of book distribution, the industry watched expectantly during 1983 as two controversial new systems—ZIPSAN and the Booksellers Order Service—were proposed to improve the flow of merchandise into book retail outlets. By year's end, ZIPSAN had been instituted and had failed; Booksellers Order Service remained in the approval and development phases, with testing to begin in February and full operation projected for late spring, 1984. Yet a third innovation was introduced by the Nashville (Tenn.) based Ingram Book Company, which opened a huge new warehouse designed to expedite distribution of books that are frequently handled by retailers on a per-customer or special-order basis.

ZIPSAN began operation in early July, after a few months of industrywide recruitment to persuade publishers and booksellers that orders would be more expeditiously and more cheaply transported by using the system. ZIPSAN was announced as an alternative transportation system (alternative to the U.S. postal system, United Parcel Service, and other forms of contract shipping). The system was designed and headed by an executive team with many years of publishing and transportation experience: Thomas F. Farrell, formerly with Baker & Taylor and W. R. Grace, and De Witt C. Baker, who has held executive positions at R. R. Donnelly & Sons, Elsevier/Dutton, Random House, and Western Publishing.

In its New Jersey warehouse, ZIPSAN utilized freight consolidation principles effected by a sophisticated, computer-monitored sorting procedure that separated books by zip code and standard address number (SAN) for routing to retailers. Despite a generally positive reception to the idea by booksellers, who were urged to specify that publishers use ZIPSAN for shipping, problems arose after only a few months of service. The underlying principle of shipping consolidation requires that volume be sufficient to warrant regularly scheduled deliveries. In its early months of operations, volume (and therefore service) fell below ZIPSAN's projections. A problem that contributed to low volume was the fact that not all publishing houses utilize SAN in their invoicing and shipping documentation. Receiving this data was important to the system in order to meet its optimum level of efficiency, even though freight could be processed without SAN (via a cross-referencing program built into the computer system). Another reason for lack of freight volume was that many publishers, accustomed to controlling their own stock transportation, were reluctant to turn this function over to ZIPSAN. On December 8, 1983, ZIPSAN terminated its book-industry delivery service due to insufficient volume.

In a different approach—one with broader aims—Booksellers Order Service continued to discuss and explore ways to institute its service, and at the end of the year it was announced that a final phase of testing would begin in February 1984. When the plan was first proposed (in November 1982), it was called Booksellers Clearing House (BCH); however, it was discovered that the name was already in use by another company. Renamed Booksellers Order Service, this proposed system (as a wholly owned subsidiary of the American Booksellers Association) was described as an order-and-fulfillment service designed to streamline traditional methods of shipping, ordering, and payment. In particular, the tele-communications-based system is intended to provide such services to participating ABA member bookstores as reduction of paperwork, a centralized ordering system (which has the potential of maximizing discounts earned by individual stores), and consolidated shipping. Reduction of paperwork on the publisher's end is another proposed benefit, as well as BOS participation in shipping and fulfillment (via consolidated shipping) and management of other details, which could include accounts payable, returns, and credit.

In February 1983, ABA announced that it had completed a feasibility study of BOS, and that two user councils—one for publishers and one for bookstores—had been established to further explore the details of the BOS proposal. Following a presentation at the ABA convention in Dallas, ABA reported that over 300 bookstores had expressed interest in the plan. In October, the ABA board of directors voted to allot $90,000 for a six-month test of the system, and at the same meeting it elected its first BOS board of directors. At the end of the year, the participants in the test, 25 bookstores and 5 publishers, were announced. The 5 publishers are Macmillan, New American Library, CBS/Holt, Scholastic, and St. Martin's Press. The 25 booksellers, according to the ABA, represent a "diversity in type of store, geographical region and creditworthiness." The largest retailer among the participating bookstores is Kroch's & Brentano's, which has 16 stores in the Chicago area. At the first of the year, the BOS board appointed as credit director M. Leo Chambers, who was formerly credit director for Harlequin Sales Corporation and who previously held a similar position at W. W. Norton.

ABA announced an expanded test (with 25 additional bookstore participants) to proceed in April, with national availability of the service targeted for July 1, 1984. Further details of the telecommunications system were also announced. During the testing phase, participants would not be charged (except for the usual cost of books plus shipping expenses); when BOS is in full operation, booksellers may lease or purchase a turnkey system, which may be upgraded to become IBM-compatible. All bookstore participants are to have a mailbox for receiving publishers' promotional plans, special stock offers, media schedules, and information on local author appearances.

Just as BOS grew out of an analysis of problems within the book industry (specifically, in the area of ordering and fulfillment), the superwarehouse concept of Ingram Book Company offered a new way of handling an old problem: special orders and in-print titles not readily available through distributors. In October, the Nashville (Tenn.) based distributor opened a warehouse in Jessup, Maryland, with an inventory of 40,000 supplementary titles in addition to its regular stock of 30,000 titles. Promoted by Ingram as "Superstock," the new warehouse was established to offer a selection of backlist and more unusual titles, which are routed to retail accounts through Ingram facilities in Nashville and Southern California. The Ingram superstock warehouse has several advantages: avoiding single-copy orders with accompanying low discounts, minimizing paperwork (since these titles combine with others on a regular Ingram invoice), and faster delivery than when ordering directly from a publisher. On the one hand, this service makes special ordering easier for independent book retailers; on the other hand, it opens the way for chain operations that have previously avoided this kind of customer service to more aggressively promote special ordering.

24

Software Comes to the Bookstore

ROBERT DAHLIN

The year 1983 was a testing period for booksellers beginning to merchandise computer software, and by year's end the question of whether it was a good idea to sell computer software as well as books was still unanswered. Some booksellers had tested the market by placing software on their bookstore shelves, but few of the 20 independent retailers surveyed by *Publishers Weekly* as 1983 drew to a close had reached any definitive answer to the question. The chains—B. Dalton, Waldenbooks, and Barnes & Noble—were aggressively positive, but they too were still testing through 1983. Few experiments anywhere had yet yielded clear results. Nevertheless, it was certain by the end of the year that the prevailing drift of booksellers' attitudes was toward the affirmative.

Sparking bookseller interest in software were the sales of computer books, which had been growing over the last few years at a highly rewarding rate. In the fall of 1983, Book Centers of Western Maryland, a 3,000-square-foot general bookstore in downtown Cumberland, Maryland, multiplied its stock of computer-related books tenfold—from 30 to 300 titles—to meet burgeoning customer interest in the subject. "These books take up only about 5 percent of our inventory, if that," said Book Centers' Lee Schwartz, "but they account for an average of 8 percent or higher of a day's book sales." These book sales persuaded Schwartz to cater more fully to this audience, and he began selling software in his store by mid-November. By the end of the year he had over 125 titles on hand.

At the Book Exchange in Morgantown, West Virginia,

Art Shipe reported that his computer book sales grew about 20 percent a month in the fall and early winter of 1983. This swelling business convinced him to add software to his stock mix as well.

Probably the most impressive computer book department in a general bookstore was to be found in the Canadian emporium that has been called the largest bookstore in the world. This 75,000-square-foot Toronto outlet of the Coles chain (numbering 253 stores, of which 62 are in the United States) has a 3,000-square-foot computer book section. Bill Ardell, president of Coles, reported that his flagship store first added software to this department in October. It was a major commitment—some 500 software titles representing an inventory of $100,000 (Canadian)—but it was purely a test, this being the only Coles store carrying software in 1983.

Just one of Barnes & Noble's outlets, a college store in California, was focusing in depth on software in 1983, but major plans were afoot to open a new outlet in New York City to be called Barnes & Noble Computer Bookstore & Software Center. The 25,000-square-foot store was expected to open in March 1984 with a full complement of computer books and a monumental number of some 2,000 software titles to sell.

Virtually all retailers reported a keener consumer demand for computer books as the variety and quantity of computer hardware boomed. Introductions of lower-priced and more easily understandable computers by a variety of manufacturers induced many people, including some who were formerly fearful of the new technologies, to purchase the equipment for home use, and this broadened the market both for computer books and for software. In fact, many of the booksellers' first tentative steps into the software market came from stocking computer books, which more and more frequently in 1983 were published by houses such as Prentice-Hall, dilithium, and Barron's in conjunction with software packaged within the book itself.

Computer stores, booksellers discovered, did not usually represent tough competition. They were generally less interested in handling software—or computer-oriented books—than in merchandising the significantly more expensive computers themselves. Ned Densmore, of the Village Book Store in Littleton, New Hampshire, noted, "Computer stores aren't really interested in marketing software. They want to sell hardware because that's where the big money is. Software gets shuffled into the corner. If an exciting piece of software comes along, it may be quite a while before the hardware dealer gets on to it. That's why the bookstore is so important." Densmore devoted 100 feet of his bookstore shelving to software.

Ron Jaffe, software marketing manager at Waldenbooks, reported that 15 to 20 of its stores in a total of five cities tested software in 1983, and 11 B. Dalton outlets experimented with the product, according to Dorothy Goldie, that chain's computer software buyer.

"Software is a natural extension to computer books," said Jim Scott of Lauriat's, an 18-store chain in southern New England (14 of the 18 outlets carried software). "It's an information package, just as a book is."

While this assertion was undeniably true, the obvious differences between books and software were becoming even clearer to most booksellers handling both. Sal Cimilla, from his Little Professor bookstore in Great Neck, New York, observed, "Software is not a passive sideline. You have to learn the terminology. It's not like greeting cards or video. Software is a whole thing."

The newness of software and the uncertainty of taking on a product that they did not fully understand worried many booksellers, who wondered about making correct choices. Which software titles should be ordered and from whom?

This concern was addressed in the summer of 1983 when Ingram began distributing software to bookstores. If one of the major U.S. book distributors decided to venture into software, a number of retailers reasoned, perhaps it was time for them to do so too. And because many had frequently dealt with Ingram in the past, the need to locate new and untried distributors of software was eliminated.

"After I talked to Ingram at the [1983] ABA convention in Dallas, I decided it was something I just couldn't pass up," said Glenda Elam, whose Village Book Shoppe in Addison, Indiana, brought in software to sell in September of that year.

James Goolsby was considerably more knowledgeable about software than were most of his bookselling peers because, before running a bookstore, he was a computer programmer. After seeing the strengthening position

afforded software at the Ingram booth and those of other software distributors at the 1983 American Booksellers Association convention, he changed the name of his El Dorado, Arkansas, store from The Book Shelf to Books & Bytes.

Goolsby's experience told him what kinds of software to stock, and he even created his own programs to sell, but other retailers relied on Ingram for the merchandise and for selection. Terms were similar to those Ingram offered on books, and initially the software was fully returnable. A suggested introductory assortment of programs relieved the bookseller of having to choose an opening inventory. By the end of 1983, some of these policies were being reconsidered at Ingram, but the fact remained that the distributor had contributed greatly to a growing acceptance of software within the bookstore community.

More adventurous booksellers began investigating the programs available from companies specializing in software distribution, firms such as Sofsell and Softsmith. Some retailers sought out software producers located in their own towns, although, as many pointed out, the matter of acquiring programs of high quality could be difficult when dealing with unknown firms and commodities. Several booksellers called in high school students in 1983, and these young people, familiar with and enthusiastic about computers, supplied their expertise in helping select software programs to stock. Other retailers scanned such computer magazines as *Byte* to ascertain what programs were receiving the most advertising support from manufacturers.

In an effort to gauge just what kinds of programs would be popular in a given city, the experimenting bookseller often ordered software for a variety of computers because what will operate on one brand will not necessarily operate on another. Both Waldenbooks and B. Dalton stocked software for four machines: Atari, Apple, Commodore 64, and IBM. Other stores offered programs for seven or eight different kinds of computers, and those that did not sell were subsequently phased out. The retailer then concentrated on the kinds of programs suitable to the hardware most widely used locally. If the city's school system had acquired a number of Apple computers, for example, programs for this hardware would be among the more profitable to stock. The concensus was that a bookseller would be able to fulfill most customer needs with programs for only three or four kinds of computers. The problem was in discovering just what those were within a given geographical area. Software created for Apple and for Commodore 64 were among those cited by the retailers interviewed as the biggest 1983 sellers in their bookstores.

The computer literacy of the surrounding community also had a strong effect on what kind of materials sold best in a bookstore. If the level of sophistication was low, games usually represented the sort of software to specialize in. These were also the least expensive investment for the bookseller, for the retail price of a computer game can dip below $20. Advancing into educational software, which many booksellers believed was the area of greatest growth potential, the price approached or surpassed $100 a program, and business applications could cost hundreds of dollars. In an effort to hold down inventory investments, however, the majority of booksellers experimenting in the field were reluctant to sell complicated and expensive programs, preferring to special order if a customer wished one. Another reason booksellers were loathe to stock the highly sophisticated software was their lack of experience with such materials.

It was true that most programs were unfamiliar to most booksellers, and therefore they often felt threatened by their inability to discuss and demonstrate software knowledgeably. The matter of demonstrations, which tended to become more necessary with software selling at higher price points, could be a problem. Ideally computers should be available for demonstrating a variety of software, said some booksellers, although neither B. Dalton nor Waldenbooks conceded that demonstrations were required in the proper merchandising of software.

James Goolsby had four demonstration computers in his store: Commodore 64, Vic 20, Timex, and TRS 80. Other booksellers, including David Kidd of Deseret Books in Logan, Utah, occasionally brought their own computers into the store to show just what the programs could do. The new Barnes & Noble software store in New York City was expected to have nine different computers for demonstration.

An opposite—and minority—viewpoint among independents is expressed by Lou Coniglio of the Book Shelf in Slidell, Louisiana, who introduced software into his store early in 1983. "There is absolutely no need to demonstrate the programs," he claimed. "My primary emphasis is on games and educational systems for home use. I have the software available, and my intention is to sell Johnny what he already wants."

Coniglio's theory had it that potential software buyers had already seen a desired program in action, which certainly could have been true in a number of instances. However, the majority of booksellers carrying software embarked on self-education programs that would enable them to sell the products more surely and aggressively.

"I'm not as knowledgeable as I will be," said Tom Daugherty of The Bookcase in Lancaster, Ohio. "Right now I don't know much more about the software than my customers do, and that worries me about getting into the business in a big way."

When they did get into it, booksellers most often displayed the software along with their computer books. Some, like Art Shipe from the 4-store Exchange chain in Morgantown, West Virginia, erected pegboard, from which the software hangs. Others placed it right on the shelves beside the books. "We have no special fixtures," said Sal Cimilla of the Little Professor in Great Neck. "We just put the software and the computer books together. Some people may not even recognize the software as software because, in their packages, they often look like books."

There was an ongoing debate about the best way to display the material. Some booksellers insisted that they could sell the software only if it is out and available for customers to browse through. The potential buyer wanted to handle the package and read about the program and its requirements in terms of equipment and computer memory, they insisted.

Other booksellers were concerned about pilferage of a piece of goods that is often vastly more expensive than a book. These retailers installed special locked cases, and the software was displayed behind glass or acrylic doors. Another attempt to thwart theft was seen in the cases constructed of plastic that had holes in the front just large enough to insert a hand. A customer could handle a software package in this way, but the hole was not large enough to permit withdrawal of the hand while clutching a package. There was no uniformity of display among the experimenting Waldenbooks stores; the software is either behind locked doors or behind the cash register or shelved beside books, in each case depending on the local manager's wishes.

"We had cabinets specially designed for the games we carry," said Tom Daugherty. "We never locked them, though, until one day I saw a kid in the back of the store with a game stuffed in his pants. Then, on went the locks."

Frequently the software was displayed near the front of the store. Because this was a heavy traffic area, customers were invariably brought face-to-face with the merchandise that they might otherwise have missed. Also, the front was where the cash register was located, and its proximity to the software meant that a cashier was better able to keep an eye on the section, whether or not it was kept under lock and key.

Cris Popenoe, whose Yes! Bookshop is located in Georgetown in the District of Columbia, dealt with possible theft in another fashion. In her store, the packages of software were opened, and the discs or cartridges that were the actual computer programs removed and placed in a compartment at the cash register. The boxes and the documentation were left on the display shelves. The packages were keyed to the software, so when a customer wished to buy a piece of software, the disc or cartridge was retrieved from its place of security and reunited with the package.

This method was considered unworkable by some booksellers, who believed that people were reluctant to buy anything that no longer looked sealed and pristine.

Even though it was generally acknowledged that customers would more frequently buy software if they could handle and examine the package, it was even more universally argued that software packages were too often poorly designed. Not only might the graphics be unappealing, but vital information could be lacking altogether. The words on the outside of a package often did not reveal what kind of computer the program was suitable for, did not explain the computer capacity necessary, or did not specify just what sort of adjunct equipment was required to operate the software.

From Addison, Indiana, Glenda Elam complained, "Many of the packages have absolutely no information on the box. There should be information on graphics, on interest level and ability level. They should specify what accessory may be needed, such as a joy stick."

Sal Cimilla had taken it upon himself to remedy the situation. He said, "Now we put our own labels on the packages—discs, cassettes, cartridges—to tell what kind of computer memory is necessary for that software, whether any kind of peripheral material is necessary."

To inform customers that software was available in their stores, most booksellers relied on signs, both in the window and within the store itself. Some advertised in local papers. Dalton advertised software in two of its catalogs. Others took booths at local computer shows or organized user groups and workshops. Barnes & Noble worked up a number of promotions for its new store, including vendor days, during which a software manufacturer would create an in-store event simply by being on hand to demonstrate his or her programs.

James Goolsby ran an adult computer education course in his store. In Logan, Utah, David Kidd built a mailing list by hanging a clipboard in his computer book and software section on which customers could indicate their interests. "We have about 150 names," Kidd said, "and we segregate our mailings, so we can send out new product news on Commodore software, for example, to the people who have Commodores. People appreciate a service like this, which is something they can't get from a store like K-Mart."

Even though their experience was still in the infant stages in 1983, a number of booksellers were finding that customers who may have first come into the store to purchase computer games returned to buy educational software. More book sales were likewise being made.

"When word first got out that we were carrying games in July, we got the game-players coming in," said Ned Densmore from Littleton, New Hampshire. "They were often people who hadn't bought books before, which they started to do. The recent trend we're seeing is that game-players are wondering what else their machines will do. Not only are they buying educational software, they're getting into doing their own programming. They can then make their own games."

Another invitation to return visits that several bookstores found profitable was in the stocking of computer accessories, such as joy sticks or blank diskettes. A box of discs could be purchased at around $20 and then resold for something in the area of $35, which meant that a retailer could add both a customer service and a tidy profit.

As is true in many areas of software, however, the volatility of the marketplace made it important for the bookseller to be careful. Glenda Elam said, "I sell joy sticks, but the prices vary, almost on a daily basis. Just a while ago I bought some joy sticks for $12.95 and sold them for $19.95. Now they're available at $9.95."

Another aspect of the business that requires caution is a major distributional difference. Booksellers are accustomed to being able to return unsold books to publishers for cash or credit. In most cases, software returns are permitted on a much less liberal basis. Software distributors and manufacturers rarely allow a retailer to unload unsold merchandise, unless it is exchanged for alternate software. Therefore, it is imperative that a bookseller be as attuned as possible to the most salable software in his or her area. Research and a concerted effort to grow familiar with local needs were frequently advised by those already trying to merchandise software.

Despite the initial difficulties, however, booksellers—even while awaiting the results of their experiments and testing—were hopeful that software would mean a new source of revenue for them.

"It's a business that we're committed to in the long term," said Art Shipe, "even though the market will take some time to mature."

"No, there is not yet a strong enough consumer base for responsible and profitable consumer retailing," said Ron Jaffe of Waldenbooks. "But that doesn't mean we should not get into it and prepare for the explosion in the consumer base."

"By 1985, I expect software to become a major department in our stores," said Jim Scott of Lauriat's.

But during the period of 1983 testing, it remained to be seen when—and if—the rocky road of experimentation would lead to the realization of such optimistic expectations.

Milestones

25

Publishing Firsts, 1983: As Reported in PW

WILLIAM GOLDSTEIN

Thanks to Barbara Tuchman and three other donors, the New York Public Library was **open on Thursdays for the first time since 1975,** beginning in January. The first book requested was Clive Bingley's *The Business of Book Publishing.*

Louis L'Amour's *The Lonesome Gods,* published by Bantam in February, was the enormously popular western writer's **first hardcover book and his first hardcover bestseller.** In October, L'Amour became the **first novelist to be awarded the Congressional Gold Medal,** presented to only 70 persons since George Washington received the first. (Robert Frost is the only other literary figure to get the award.)

Workman Publishing published its **first reprint** in March, when it issued a paperback edition of Kit Williams's *Masquerade,* the treasure hunt storybook. Workman passed up original publication of the book (as did 20 other publishers) before Schocken published it in hardcover in 1981, selling more than 400,000 copies.

The **first Alfred Harcourt Award in Biography and Memoirs,** which carries a $10,000 prize and goes to a published work, was announced in March. The winner was Elisabeth Young-Breuhl's *Hanah Arendt: For the Love of the World* (Yale University Press). The **first Ellen Knowles Harcourt Award in Biography and Memoirs,** which goes to a doctoral dissertation on the "life, diaries, letters and memoirs of an American woman" and carries a $5,000 cash award and a $5,000 advance against royalties, was

won by Sharon N. White for her *Mabel Loomis Todd: Gender, Language and Power in Victorian America,* due from Columbia University Press.

A French chateau among vineyards was home in the Spring to Ron Hansen, the author whose second novel, *The Assassination of Jesse James by the Coward Robert Ford* (Knopf), was **the first winner of the annual Bordeaux Artist-in-Residence Award.** The author received a $1,000 grant, as did the Bread Loaf Writers' Conference, which administered the program.

Beginning with its Fall 1983 list, Crown announced it would **charge no return penalty on first novels.** This is the first time a publisher has offered such a policy. Booksellers could combine first novels with other titles to obtain a maximum discount, the publisher announced, but its first novels would be exempt from its usual return penalty.

The **first books from Pocket Books' new trade paperback division, Long Shadow Books,** would be published in Fall 1983, the publisher announced. The imprint is under the direction of Marty Asher.

Publishers Weekly Yearbook, 1983 edition, published in May, was the first reference work to use A. Horowitz & Son's new Flexibook binding.

"First Edition," a Book-of-the-Month Club-sponsored half-hour cable television series with host John Leonard, **first aired on May 9.** The show featured reviews (some negative) and interviews, mainly with authors, but also with editors and/or executives when appropriate. The show was scheduled for a limited, 12-week run.

In May, for the **first time in its eight-year history,** the $7,500 Ernest Hemingway Foundation Award for first fiction went to a short story collection, *Shiloh and Other Stories* by Bobbie Ann Mason (Harper & Row). In addition, a $1,500 award was given to Susanna Moore for her first novel, *My Old Sweetheart* (Houghton Mifflin).

For the first time, there were **two winners of the Seal Books $50,0000 First Novel Award,** announced in Canada in May. David Kendall, author of *Lazaro,* and Jonathan Webb, author of *Pluck,* each received $25,000.

Warner Books announced in June that it would publish **its first Young Adult series,** Two by Two, in the Fall. Each book in the series featured two versions of the same love story: one told from the boy's point of view, the other, the girl's. The tales would be issued upside down and back to back, in the manner of the Ace Double Novels of the 1950s.

In June, *Return of the Jedi* (Random House), an illustrated storybook based on the successful *Star Wars* movie, became the **first children's book** to appear in the number-one position on the *New York Times Book Review* bestseller list its first week on the list.

Launched in June by IMS International, a medical publisher, the Medical Book Club of America is believed to be the **first full-service book club for physicians only.**

Thomas Congdon, of Congdon & Weed, signed for **the first book ever written by a robot,** *My Life As a Robot,* although no publication date has been set. The four-foot tall robot, with flashing red eyes and a red cape, meant to call attention at the American Booksellers Association meeting in Dallas to Time-Life's book *Life in Space,* was in the booth next to Congdon's when they got to talking. "His stories were wonderful," Congdon said. (Ed Fish, an employee of ShowAmerica, Inc., of Elmhurst, Illinois, was the man behind the robot.)

Dream West by David Nevin (Putnam), the Book-of-the-Month for March 1984, would be **the first first novel to be a BOMC selection in five years,** it was announced in August.

In October, Harlequin Books published **its first trade paperback,** *Wild Concerto* by Anne Mather, one of its most popular authors.

The first full-time officer to fight book piracy was appointed by the British Publishers Association in September. He was David Winsor, who was hired to travel around the world investigating reports of piracy, gathering evidence, making representations to governmental authorities, and initiating legal actions.

For the first time, a handling fee of $20 was charged for nominations of books for Pulitzer prizes in the five "Letters" categories. The decision was made out of "economic necessity" said Robert C. Christopher, secretary of the Pulitzer Prize board, and not to discourage entries. Journalism nominations were first charged a fee in 1982, he said, and entries did not decline.

For what may be the first time in recent publishing history, senior management of an acquired house were among the purchasers of New American Library from Times Mirror, in November. A private investor group led by Ira Hechler and Odyssey Partners (known on Wall Street as "the deal people") bought the company for $50 million in cash; included in the group were Robert G. DiForio, chairman and chief executive officer at NAL; Elaine Koster, publisher; and Marvin Brown, president and chief administrative officer.

The International Spy Society announced its first annual Oppy Awards, named in honor of E. Phillips Oppenheim, "one of the pioneers in establishing the spy novel as an important part of literature." *The Last Supper* by Charles McCarry (Dutton) won the fiction prize, *The Rosenberg File* by Ronald Radosh and Joyce Milton (Holt, Rinehart & Winston) won the nonfiction prize, and *The Puzzle Palace* by James Bamford (Houghton Mifflin), was the special-achievement award.

26

People on the Move

WILLIAM GOLDSTEIN

Judy Appelbaum, since last year assistant editor in charge of paperbacks at the *New York Times Book Review,* resigned that position in November. Previously, she had been managing editor at *Publishers Weekly.*

Marty Asher, editor-in-chief of Pocket Books, was named head of a new Pocket imprint, unnamed at the time, but later named Long Shadow Books. **William R. Grose,** vice-president and editor-in-chief of New American Library, joined Pocket Books as vice-president and editorial director at the same time.

Robert E. Baensch joined the Macmillan Publishing Company in November as its vice-president of marketing, a new position. He was formerly vice-president of marketing at McGraw-Hill International, and before that president and chief executive officer of Springer-Verlag New York.

Barbara Bannon, executive editor of *Publishers Weekly* and for many years head of its Forecasts review section, left the magazine in November after 37 years.

Allan Barnard, vice-president and associate editorial director at Bantam Books, announced his retirement in April, after 19 years with the company. Among his acquisitions: *The Day of the Jackal; Everything You Always Wanted to Know About Sex; Chariots of the Gods?; The Amityville Horror,* and *All Creatures Great and Small.* (During his years at Dell, Barnard also acquired *Peyton Place.*)

Marvin S. Brown, president of Atheneum since 1977, was named president and chief executive officer of New American Library, effective February 1. **Robert G. Di-**

forio, who had been NAL president, was promoted to chairman of the board. He retained the title chief executive officer.

Ross Claiborne, for less than two years vice-president and publisher of Warner Books' hardcover division, left the company in July. Before joining Warner, Claiborne had been associated with Dell Publishing for more than 25 years, where he was last vice-president and editorial director.

Walter Clemons, who had been an editor at *Newsweek* for 11 years before becoming an editor at *Vanity Fair* in 1982, returned to his old position at *Newsweek* in October, after only 16 months at *Vanity Fair.* The following week, founding editor **Stephen Rubin** also left *Vanity Fair.*

John P. Dessaur, statistical and financial management consultant, was named director of the newly established Center for Book Research at the University of Scranton, in March.

Joseph Dionne, president of McGraw-Hill since 1981, was promoted to chief executive officer in April, following **Harold W. McGraw's** vacating the position. McGraw, whose grandfather founded the company, continued as chairman of the board and chairman of the executive committee.

Arnold Dolin, formerly executive editor at NAL, in February was named vice-president and editor-in-chief of Plume, Meridian, Mentor, and Signet Classics, all NAL imprints.

Jean Feiwel, editorial director of Books for Young Readers at Avon, left that company in June to join

Scholastic Inc., where she was named divisional vice-president and editorial director of the company's Arrow and TAB book clubs and the young people's trade publishing program.

Donald I. Fine, president, publisher, and chief executive officer of Arbor House, the company he founded but sold to Hearst Coroporation five years ago, was abruptly "terminated" on October 24. **Eden Collinsworth,** who joined Arbor seven years ago as publicity director and was most recently vice-president and associate publisher, was named publisher.

Bill and Helen Fisher, founders of HP Books in 1964, left that company in November, four years after selling it to the Knight-Ridder chain of newspapers. The couple had served as co-publishers since that sale, with Bill Fisher as president and Helen Fisher as vice-president. HP Books is known primarily for its line of bestselling paperback cookbooks.

Richard Fontaine resigned as president of B. Dalton Bookseller at the end of August, in order, he said, "to pursue other interests." He had joined Dalton in 1968 and had been president since 1981.

In October, **Donald L. Freuhling** was named president of the newly combined domestic and international book companies of McGraw-Hill, which became known as McGraw-Hill Book Company. **Alexander J. Burke, Jr.,** who has been president of both operations, was appointed executive vice-president, staff services, and **Edward T. Reilly, Jr.,** was named executive vice-president, international group.

Arlene Friedman, former vice-president and editor-in-chief of Fawcett Books, was appointed senior executive editor of Macmillan's general books division in January. **Joan B. Sanger,** who held that post since June 1982, was named senior editor in the hardcover trade division of the Putnam Publishing Group.

In September, **Erwin A. Glikes,** senior vice-president/editorial and president and publisher of Touchstone Books at Simon & Schuster, left the company to become president and publisher of the Free Press, a division of Macmillan. Glikes was also named a vice-president of the parent company. Before joining S&S, Glikes was president and publisher of Basic Books and, simultaneously in 1976 to 1979, publisher of Harper & Row's general trade books division.

Irving Goodman resigned in September as president and chief operating officer of Viking Penguin, Inc. He was temporarily replaced by **Peter Mayer,** chief executive of Penguin Books International and executive chairman of Viking Penguin, who named himself acting president. By the end of the year, amid editorial and administrative shake-ups galore (including the firing of nine longtime employees), **Allan Kellock,** who had come to Viking from Waldenbooks in 1982, was named president of a newly streamlined Viking Penguin.

Paul Gottlieb, president, publisher, and editor-in-chief at Abrams, was elected chief executive officer as well, following the departure of **Seymour Turk** to Book-of-the-Month Club, where Turk is responsible for all of the company's financial, manufacturing, and fulfillment activities.

Also in November, **Phyllis E. Grann** was named president of G. P. Putnam's Sons, the adult hardcover and trade paperback division of the Putnam Publishing Group. She was elected at that time to the Group's board of directors and continued as publisher.

Bruce Gray, vice-president and publisher of R. R. Bowker Magazine Division, was named Bowker president in November, following the promotion of **Joseph Riccobono** to vice-president and general manager of the Xerox Information Group. Xerox owns Bowker.

Robert Hale resigned his position as associate executive director of the American Booksellers Association effective November 1. He purchased the Westwinds Bookshop in Duxbury, Massachusetts—the store where he began his retailing career in 1954—and said he hoped to combine bookselling with writing, editing, and lecturing. Hale had been ABA president from 1976–1978, when he became associate executive director.

Gordon R. Hjalmarson joined Macmillan in January "to work in conjunction with Macmillan's top management and development group in the company's expanded efforts to acquire product lines and businesses in publishing and related fields." Hjalmarson had resigned in 1982 as chairman, chief executive officer, and president of SFN Companies.

Byron Hollinshead, former president of Oxford University Press, was named president of the American Heritage Publishing Company, in April. He had been with Oxford for 27 years, the last six as president.

Marc Jaffe became the first editorial director of Villard Books, the fourth hardcover imprint at Random House, in February. He joined Random House in 1980 as executive vice-president of Ballantine Books and Random House after a long association with Bantam Books. Jaffe's first appointment was **Peter Gethers,** as executive editor of the new imprint. (The Villard Houses in New York were for many years Random House headquarters.)

Peter Jovanovich, who moved in 1982 to San Diego in order to direct Harcourt Brace Jovanovich's relocated trade book department, was transferred in June to London, to manage Academic Press, a far-flung HBJ subsidiary. The move was described by Peter's father, William, chairman of HBJ, as temporary, though possibly for as long as two years. The move was seen as part of a broadening of responsibilities, leading to his eventual accession to the chairmanship of HBJ.

Joan Kahn, who had brought her personal imprint to Dutton from Ticknor & Fields in February 1982 (after 34 years at Harper & Row), left Dutton in February 1983. She had been asked to leave Dutton "out of the blue," she told *PW.* She joined St. Martin's Press later in the month.

Joseph Kanon was appointed publisher of adult books at E. P. Dutton in May, following the recent departure of John Macrae III for Holt, Rinehart & Winston. Kanon, it was announced, would continue as editor-in-chief of adult books. In August, he replaced **Ivor A. Whitson,** who resigned as president of the company. Kanon again continued his other accumulated duties. In September, however, **Bill Whitehead** became editor-in-chief at Dutton, while Kanon continued as president and publisher. Whitehead had joined Dutton in 1974 as senior editor.

In August, **Laurence Kirshbaum** returned to Warner Books as the firm's publisher and chief operating officer after a brief stint as vice-president and director of circulation at Condé Nast Publications. Before that he had been vice-president of marketing, Warner Books.

Also in August, **Richard Koffler,** executive director of the Association of American University Presses for the past three years, resigned (effective the end of 1983) to form his own consulting company, Book Counsel, Inc.

Richard A. Krinsley left his post as executive vice-president, marketing and corporate development, at Random House in April to join Scholastic, Inc., as executive vice-president, responsible for direction of all U.S. book operations. The position is a new one.

In January, **John Leonard** left the *New York Times,* where he had served in a variety of capacities for 15 years, to become a columnist and general cultural writer for *Vanity Fair.* **Renata Adler,** too, was named to the staff. Both resigned within six months.

Mitchel Levitas, editor of the Week in Review section of the *New York Times,* became editor of the *Times Book Review* on October 10. **Harvey Shapiro,** *Book Review* editor for eight years, would become a deputy editor of the *New York Times Magazine* and *Times* literary critic, it was announced.

Harry A. McQuillen was named president of the CBS Educational and Professional Publishing Division (which includes Holt, Rinehart & Winston and Praeger Publishers, among others) in May. He succeeded Dr. Stanley D. Frank, who resigned. In June, **Robert P. Rainier** was appointed to the new position of vice-president, editor-in-chief, college publishing, at CBS.

In March, **John Macrae III** left his position as publisher and editor of Dutton's adult book division to become editor-in-chief of Holt, Rinehart & Winston's general book division. MaCrae, whose grandfather, father, and uncle had all worked at Dutton, had been at Dutton for 15 years.

Steven J. Mason was named president and chief operating officer of Ingram Book Company. He had formerly been vice-president and general counsel at Ingram Industries.

Nansey Neiman, a senior editor at Warner Books since 1980, was named that company's vice-president and editor-in-chief, hardcover division, in November.

Leona Nevler was appointed editor-in-chief of the mass market division of Fawcett Books, at Ballantine, in February.

Sandra Ordover, formerly vice-president of creative affairs at Marble Arch Productions, was named editor-in-chief of Pinnacle Books in January. Previously, she had been editor-in-chief at Jove. In October, she was promoted to president and publisher, following the resignation of **Stanley L. Reisner.**

Marianne Orlando, a vice-president and director of John Wiley & Sons, retired October 1. She began her career in publishing in 1951 with Interscience Publishers, where she was a vice-president when that company merged with Wiley in 1961. She would continue as a consultant to Wiley, it was announced.

Jane Pasanen, associate publisher of E. P. Dutton's adult trade division, left that position in April to become director of marketing at Holt, Rinehart & Winston. She was the second Dutton person to join Holt this year, following John Macrae III.

Alvin B. Reuben was named president of the newly created Promotional Book Publishing Division of Simon & Schuster in March. At the same time, **Steve Dorsky** was named vice-president, director of marketing at S&S. He was formerly vice-president, marketing and subsidiary rights, at Holt, Rinehart & Winston.

In February, **Franklyn Rodgers** was named president of Warner Publishers Services, Inc., the world's largest distributor of magazines and paperback books. Rodgers had been president of Scribner Book Companies for the past five years.

Charles Scribner, Jr., also chairman of the board, was named president of Scribner Book Companies. At the same time, **Alred Knopf, Jr.,** was named president of Atheneum Publishers, while continuing as Atheneum chairman and vice-chairman of Scribner's. **Jacek Galazka** was named president of Charles Scribner's Sons Publishers. Both Atheneum and Scribners are divisions of Scribner Book Companies.

William Shinker was appointed publisher of the trade paperback division of Warner Books in February. He continued as vice-president, director of marketing, for the hardcover, mass market, and trade paperback lines. He joined Warner in 1978, but "abruptly resigned" from his new position and "left the premises of Warner Books," August 8.

G. Roysce Smith announced his resignation as American Booksellers Association executive director, effective March 1, 1984. It was a "complete coincidence" that Smith's announcement followed by one week Robert Hale's resignation as associate executive director. Smith began his retailing career in 1949 as temporary Christmas help at Rich's, Atlanta, rising to become book department manager at Yale Co-op, a position he held until 1971, when he joined ABA. Set to take his place was **Bernie Rath,** since 1978 executive director of the Canadian Booksellers Association.

Wendy J. Strothman was named director of Beacon Press, effective July 15. Strothman, at 32 the youngest director of the company in its 129-year history, came from the University of Chicago, where she had been assistant director and general editor.

The imprint of **Truman Talley Books** moved to Dutton in February, after four and a half years at Times Books. Mr. Talley was the founder of Weybright and Talley Books and was, before that, associated with New American Library.

Victor Temkin, who left his post as president of Berkley Publishing at the end of 1982, became head of the new Consumer Products Group of Berkley's parent company, MCA, in January 1983.

Richard W. Young, formerly executive vice-president and director of worldwide marketing at Polaroid Corporation, was named president of Houghton Mifflin Company in January; he had been a member of the board of directors of the company since 1981.

In February, **Robert Wyatt** was named editor-in-chief of the mass market division of Ballantine Books (he continued as editor-at-large at Random House). At the same time, **Marilyn Abraham** was appointed executive editor of the Ballantine mass market imprint.

27

Obituaries

WILLIAM GOLDSTEIN

Curtis G. Benjamin. Bachrach.

Curtis G. Benjamin, who built the fledgling McGraw-Hill Book Company into a world-straddling giant, died following a heart attack on November 5. He was 82. He had started his career at McGraw-Hill as a salesman in 1928, was elected chairman in 1961, and retired in 1966.

Robert J. Benowicz, author and biochemist, died of a heart attack in New York on November 16. He was 42.

Corrie ten Boom, Dutch survivor of a Nazi concentration camp and bestselling writer of inspirational books, died April 15 in California at the age of 91.

Charles R. Byrne, a founder of Berkley Books (in 1954) and a literary agent, died October 4 of a stroke. He was 67.

Kenneth Clark, art historian, museum director, television narrator, and author of *Civilisation*, died May 21 in an English nursing home. He was 79.

Lord Kenneth Clark. © London Sunday Times.

William F. "Fred" Cody, founder of Cody's Books in Berkeley, California, died of lung cancer on July 9. He was 66.

Paul Dimmitt, special markets manager for Rand McNally, died December 6, after a long illness. He was 52.

Temple Hornaday Fielding, the well-known travel writer, died of a heart attack May 18, at home in Palma, Majorca. He was 69. His guide, first published in 1948, has sold more than 3 million copies in all editions. **Nancy Parker Fielding,** his wife and collaborator, died October 31, at the age of 70.

Joe Flaherty, journalist, novelist, and one-time campaign manager for Norman Mailer when he ran for mayor of New York in 1969, died October 26 of cancer. He was 47. His second novel, *Tin Wife,* due in February 1984 from Simon & Schuster, was named a Book-of-the-Month Club selection shortly before his death. His wife, Jeanine Johnson Flaherty, is publicity manager at Putnam.

Keith A. Foiles, senior vice-president of Harcourt Brace Jovanovich, died March 5 in New York. He was 56.

William Goyen. © *J. Gary Dontzig.*

William Goyen, novelist and short story writer, died of leukemia August 30 in Los Angeles. He was 68. His first novel, *The House of Breath,* was published in 1950; his most recent, *Arcadio,* was published posthumously in October.

David Greenhood, writer, editor, and a founder of Holiday House, Inc., died March 26 in Santa Fe, New Mexico. He was 87.

Charles Haslam, owner of Haslam's Bookstore in St. Petersburg, Florida, and a past president of the American Booksellers Association, died October 10 of a rare form of malaria contracted while on vacation in East Africa. His wife, who also suffered from the disease, recovered. With 25 employees, his store is one of the largest in the region.

Eric Hoffer, the longshoreman/philosopher who wrote 11 books, including *The True Believer,* died May 21 in San Francisco. He was 80.

Norman Hoss, editorial director of the Times Mirror Magazines Book Clubs, died November 18 in New York City. He was 60.

M. J. Jossel, director of advertising and promotion at Dell, died June 8. She was 62. She is credited with creating the first television commercial for a mass market paperback.

Ezra Jack Keats.

Ezra Jack Keats, illustrator of 33 children's books, died of a heart attack May 6, in New York. He was 67.

Arthur Koestler, author of *Darkness at Noon,* was found dead with his wife in an apparent suicide pact in their London apartment, March 3. Koestler, who suffered from leukemia and Parkinson's disease, was 77.

Jonathan Latimer, author of numerous murder mysteries, died June 23 at the age of 76. On one day in the 1930s, he earned $19,000 selling three stories to the movies and one to *Collier's* magazine. Later, he adapted 50 Erle Stanley Gardner books for the television series "Perry Mason."

Erich Linder, one of the world's leading literary agents, died in Milan following a heart attack, on March 22. He was 58.

Richard Llewellyn, the novelist most famous for *How Green Was My Valley,* died of a heart attack in Dublin, Ireland, on December 2. He was 76.

Norah Lofts, historical novelist and biographer, died September 10 at home in Bury St. Edmunds, England. She was 79. Two posthumous books, *Saving Face and Other Stories* and *Pargetters,* a novel, remained to be issued by Doubleday, her longtime American publisher.

Ross MacDonald, whose series of detective novels featured the hardboiled private eye Lew Archer, died July 11, at 67. He suffered from Alzheimer's Disease. The first Lew Archer novel, *The Moving Target,* was published in 1949, by Knopf. The last, *The Blue Hammer,* was published in 1976, also by Knopf, his lifelong publisher.

Ross MacDonald. © *Hal Boucher.*

John Macrae, Jr., former chairman of E. P. Dutton, died October 7 at his summer home on Nantucket Island. He was 86.

Catherine Marshall, whose inspirational books have sold more than 18 million copies, died March 18. Widow of the late Reverend Peter Marshall, she was 68. Her most famous book is *Christy,* a novel based on her mother's life.

John Masters, the novelist whose work dealt with the role of the British in India, died at 68 on May 6.

Marion Monroe, a child psychologist and co-author of the "Dick and Jane" books read by schoolchildren from the 1940s through the mid-1970s, died June 25, at 85. The long sovereignty of "Dick and Jane" ended when they were criticized for being racist and sexist and for stressing memory instead of phonics.

Scott Nearing, author with his wife, Helen, of *Living the Good Life,* died August 24. He had turned 100 just two weeks before.

Robert Payne, author of more than 100 books, including biographies of Lenin, Hitler, Mao, Greta Garbo, Dostoevsky, and Shakespeare, died while on vacation on February 18. He was 71.

Robert C. Preble, former president of Encyclopaedia Britannica, died at his home in Chicago on November 26. He was 86.

Joseph H. Reiner, vice-president of Crown Publishers and Outlet Book Company who founded Outlet's Bonanza division, died October 2 in Miami Beach. He was 71.

Mary Renault. © *Philip De Vos.*

Mary Renault, historical novelist of Ancient Greece, died in South Africa, where she had lived since World War II, December 13. She was 78. As a past president of PEN, she opposed all forms of censorship, and as a resident of South Africa, had been a foe of apartheid.

Andrea Rizzoli, former president of the Rizzoli publishing empire, died of heart failure May 31 in Nice. He was 69.

A. Milton Runyon, retired first vice-president of Doubleday, who was largely responsible for the growth of the company's book clubs, died May 3, following a heart attack. He was 77.

Kyrill Schabert, one of the founders of Pantheon Books in 1942 and its president for 20 years, died April 7 at the age of 74.

Christina Stead, the Australian novelist whose most famous work is *The Man Who Loved Children* (1940), died March 31 in Sydney, Australia. She was 80.

Tennessee Williams, the playwright, died February 25.

Christina Stead. © *Mark Gerson.*

28

The Book Industry Abroad

HERBERT R. LOTTMAN

Although the U.S. publishing industry is more self-sufficient than most others—less dependent on exports, for example, than its nearest counterpart, the British—foreign sales of finished books and the licensing of rights abroad can be significant income producers. The largest American publishing groups maintain international divisions and sometimes operate overseas subsidiaries for stocking and distribution; foreign rights make a contribution to the balance sheets of trade publishers and literary agents. Foreign sales are of course a year-round preoccupation, but much of this activity can be observed at one time and place: the autumn Frankfurt Book Fair, the biggest market of its kind, where nearly all American publishers—trade, paperback, scientific and technical, and academic—are represented on the stands, usually by their chief executives and by their sales and subsidiary rights managers.

Not surprisingly, the Frankfurt fair is the ideal place to take the temperature of the world book trade. At the most recent fair, held October 12–17, 1983, an observer could have learned a great deal about the state of international publishing. Certainly this observer would have concluded that things are looking up for books. After resisting the downward slide of the business curve for a long time—those were the days when publishers told each other optimistically that book sales were "anticyclical"—publishing had gone the way of the world economy in the late 1970s. The persistent recession in Europe and Japan led publishers in those countries to reduce their acquisitions

from the United States; there was increasing resistance, for example, to the high advances on royalties that American publishers and agents were demanding for their potential blockbuster bestsellers à la Judith Krantz. And the unpredictability of inflationary rises in production costs from country to country all but put an end to what had once been a thriving trade in co-production, for who dared guarantee a price quotation for the year or two it would take to move from the dummy stage to delivered books? The atmosphere at recent Frankfurt fairs seemed unpromising, if not downright gloomy.

So the return to optimism at the 1983 Frankfurt fair seemed a sign of better times to come. The optimism expressed itself concretely in an increased willingness of fairgoers to commit themselves to new investment; if in the recent past American publishers found it difficult to interest foreign partners in new projects, this time the partners were dropping by the American stands to ask what was new. The bounciness of the book trade was also evident in the increased publisher participation at the fair: 5,890 exhibitors against 5,688 the previous autumn, 4,195 individual exhibitors (4,076 in 1982). The fair's director, Peter Weidhaas, who once more could not provide stands for all those who requested them, pointed out that most of the newcomers to his fair were medium-sized or small firms, which was a sign that things were looking up again: "These firms, which use much sharper pencils in their calculations than do their large and established colleagues, see realistic chances of success." While American visitors were not obtaining the record offers for translation rights that they had obtained at earlier fairs, they seemed to be making it up in the *quantity* of deals.

Those with their ears to the ground had detected the new international mood as early as last March, when an observer at the Bologna Children's Book Fair, Macmillan president Bruno Quinson, described the atmosphere as one of "quiet enthusiasm." But at Bologna, at Frankfurt, and all year long American book traders seeking to do business abroad were faced with a new challenge: the rise in the value of U.S. dollars against all other currencies. For the dollar has been soaring. Between January 1981 and the latest Frankfurt fair, French francs lost 80 percent of their value with respect to dollars, German Deutschmarks 33 percent; last year alone the dollar rose 20 percent against the franc by the time of the Frankfurt fair, and 12 percent against the Deutschmark. During the fair, attorney and literary agent Morton Janklow, who represents many of the biggest U.S. fiction stars, reported: "Almost every foreign publisher with depressed currency is making smaller offers apologetically, telling us that it's as much money in their own currency as for the last book." Those whose business it is to sell finished books abroad faced the identical problem, as Paul Feffer, president of the New York export firm Feffer & Simons, explained: "Most American hardcover books sold abroad go to institutional customers with fixed budgets in their own currencies; if the original dollar price rises, the customer buys fewer books."

In those countries where American paperback reprints have a large potential market, such as in Scandinavia and the Netherlands where significant numbers of book buyers can read English and like to, and an American paperback reprint of, say, Norman Mailer's *Ancient Evenings* can reach local bookshops faster and can be priced at less than that particular country's translation of the same book, the high cost of dollars has made American imports less attractive. In an open market such as the Netherlands— where American and British books compete—British paperbacks are now edging out American ones. An article in the London trade journal *The Bookseller* last December 17 described how Britain's leading paperback houses— Penguin, Pan, Granada—have taken over the top spots on Dutch bestseller lists, while the leading American contender, Bantam Books, slips down. This is a trend that is expected to continue well into 1984.

The Book Pirates

There is one area in which American and British publishers don't compete, and in which Americans now seem ready to help their British colleagues. Until now, U.K. publishers have been in the vanguard of the global campaign against book piracy, for the good reason that the piracy has been occurring in many of their vital overseas markets. Since American publishers traditionally licensed Commonwealth rights to the British, they felt less concerned, and only a handful of American scientific, technical, and medical publishers were sufficiently active

in the pirates' Third World lairs to be affected in their balance sheets. But in 1983 the American publishing community offered a helping hand to the British, announcing that it would contribute to a war chest to combat piracy in Asia and Latin America, although the hope is that effective investigative and legal action will be combined with efforts at persuasion. Feffer & Simons's Paul Feffer, wearing his other hat as chairman of the International Division of the Association of American Publishers (AAP), was quoted to this effect: "You can't bang on the table anymore with Indians or Filipinos. We have to show them that copyright is a mutual benefit."

In the United Kingdom, the Book Development Council of the Publishers Association now includes an Anti-Piracy Committee, which in 1983 launched its Campaign against Book Piracy to which 108 member publishers pledged £150,000 a year for three years (note that a British pound is now worth $1.40 in U.S. currency). The campaign announced that it would soon have £500,000 at its disposal. In August it engaged a full-time antipiracy officer in the person of David Winsor, formerly with the U.K.'s Van Nostrand Reinhold; although based in London, he will be spending most of his time traveling to trouble spots to gather evidence, contacting local governments and, when appropriate, initiating legal action. Already the Campaign against Book Piracy has a branch office in Hong Kong run by antipiracy officer Yiu Hei Kan, who is also marketing director for Macmillan Publishers (Hong Kong). His area of responsibility includes Taiwan and Korea, and he will keep an eye on the Philippines as well. The campaign is also working with an antipiracy group in Taiwan called the Copyright Holders Association; back in London, it issues the *Anti-Piracy Newsletter*.

Responding to the needs of their own constituencies, both the International Group of Scientific, Technical, and Medical Publishers (STM) based in Amsterdam and the International Publishers Association (IPA) have been engaged in year-round lobbying at copyright meetings and other international conferences on behalf of creators and owners of copyrights, and the problem was high on the agenda at IPA's quadrennial congress, held in Mexico City in March 1984. At the International Forum on the Piracy of Broadcasts and of the Printed Word, held in Geneva last March under the auspices of the World Intellectual Property Organization (which supervises the Berne copyright convention), IPA distributed an impressive dossier entitled "Book Piracy" containing reports on deliberate copyright violations in a wide range of countries, notably India, Pakistan, Taiwan, Korea, Indonesia, Mexico, Peru, and the Dominican Republic, together with a map on which different colors were used to identify offender countries, their victims, and those countries where illegal imported books hamper the growth of local publishing. In a statement to the Geneva Forum, IPA secretary general J. A. Koutchoumow pointed out that book piracy was a more serious matter than illegal reproduction of cassettes and other consumer goods since it is often treated with indulgence in the Third World in the belief that it is favorable to development (i.e., that it makes books available to more people because pirated editions are cheaper). On the contrary, declared Koutchoumow, book piracy is "the most shocking and the most injurious" copyright violation, because of the resultant loss of authors and publishers to creative and cultural activities.

The British themselves estimate that book piracy, which they call "an international conspiracy," costs copyright holders some £500 million annually. Moreover, it destroys the viability of legitimate publishing in the countries in which it occurs, while the pirates, when and if they are caught, are subject to fines hardly proportionate to the quick and easy profits they make. That piracy is not a phenomenon of the Third World alone was made clear when a West German publisher, Christoph Schlotterer of Munich's Carl Hanser Verlag, described to *Publishers Weekly* the extent of piracy taking place in his own country. Popular but expensive novels, such as Umberto Eco's *The Name of the Rose* and Michael Ende's *The Neverending Story,* are ripped off (in softcover facsimiles from which the name and copyright of the publisher have been eliminated), for sale out of suitcases at university campuses for less than half the catalog price of the legitimate publisher.

United Kingdom

A careful observer would have detected positive vibes in London publishing circles all through 1983. At the March 1983 Bologna Children's Book Fair, the British contingent was all smiles. There seemed to be two main reasons: A lower rate of inflation had made it possible for institutional buyers to spend more money for acquisitions than had been expected (most had apparently allowed in their budgets for a 10 percent price rise), and publishers who don't count on institutional purposes had won over book buyers with a number of innovations, including a new generation of pop-ups and construction kits. The early optimism was confirmed during the October Frankfurt Book Fair. It sounded as if Britain's trade leaders had drawn some lessons from several years of adversity. They had shaken down; they were "publishing better," as Penguin's chief executive Peter Mayer explained it, "paying more attention to the right quantity, the right price." Another London publisher, Heinemann's chairman Tom Rosenthal, agreed that one could prosper by paying more attention, but one had to work twice as hard as ten years ago to do that. British publishing had once been an occupation for gentlemen, that is, for amateurs. Those days were over.

Still, the good news seemed to be confined to those at the top of their profession, for rank-and-file publishers had not yet climbed out of their slump. As late as August 1983, London's *Bookseller* headlined a report that comparative results showed a continuation of the downward trend in turnover through 1982. So for indications of better times ahead it was necessary to read the half-year reports of the Penguins and the Heinemanns (although another British giant, Hutchinson, which had been in the red for some

time, was being turned around, and the situation at Collins had also improved).

One thing that becomes clear from a look at the balance sheets is the continued dependence of the biggest U.K. imprints on overseas markets in traditional English-reading members of what is still called the Commonwealth. At Collins, for example, 47 percent of sales in the last full business year reported (1982) were made overseas. When things go bad in foreign climes, the London headquarters feels it, and quickly. Longman blamed some of its own financial problems on the decline of exports, particularly to Nigeria. Indeed, the decline in the price of Nigeria's main export, crude oil, has wiped out that country's buying power, and it was estimated that Nigerian booksellers, as well as Nigerian affiliates of British publishers, owed U.K. publishers some £25 million at the beginning of 1983. Note that the 1982/1983 annual report of Britain's Publishers Association attributed its members' woes to "deepening recession in important [overseas] markets," but also blamed the "virtual dumping of cheap copies of US editions, leading to a reduced share in important countries like Australia." The association added that its members were meeting the challenge with better pricing and services. All in all, it concluded, "the trade looks well placed for the renewed period of expansion forecast by some of the economic model makers."

The resilience of British publishing could also be seen in the year's production figures (see Table 1). For a new record had been set in title output: 51,071 books, of which 38,980 were new (compare the 1982 totals: 48,307 and 37,947); this amounted to a rise of 5.7 percent (2.7 percent for new books alone). Still, it was widely felt that this is too much of a good thing: The retail markets both domestic and overseas could absorb only so many books, and if more titles were produced, there were smaller sales per title. Despite these misgivings, the Publishers Association's Clive Bradley predicted that when all results are in, sales will be seen to have risen 4 percent in real terms, thanks to more units as well as higher list prices. He expressed optimism in a year-end statement as reported in *The Bookseller:* "With the trade coming out of recession, sales improving, publishers giving tauter management and a lot of imagination showing through, 1984 should prove a pretty good year."

Down Under

Long considered only an outlet for British books, then for British *and* American books, Australia has been demonstrating the ability to be a significant book-producing nation in its own right; it is even finding profits in the export trade. Indeed, Australian publishers have been selling books not only to neighboring New Zealand but all the way across the oceans to the former mother country. This past autumn the largest exhibition of Australian books ever sent abroad—1,000 titles—went on display in London, with invitations sent out to 6,000 British booksellers and wholesalers, librarians, publishers, the press, and the academic community. Much of the export effort

TABLE 1 British Publishing Output, 1982 and 1983

The table shows the total title output for 1982 and 1983 with the numbers of new editions, translations, and limited editions.

	January–December 1982				January–December 1983			
Classification	Total	Reprints & New Edns.	Trans.	Ltd. Edns.	Total	Reprints & New Edns.	Trans.	Ltd. Edns.
Aeronautics	238	39	—	—	206	36	1	—
Agriculture and forestry	512	90	7	1	427	68	18	2
Architecture	384	74	6	3	426	62	9	—
Art	1,279	176	36	10	1,312	186	30	9
Astronomy	155	39	3	—	171	40	5	—
Bibliography and library economy	776	151	2	—	675	136	3	—
Biography	1,491	314	67	2	1,969	734	78	5
Chemistry and physics	754	121	26	—	697	115	30	—
Children's books	2,917	535	100	7	3,449	790	194	11
Commerce	1,493	384	3	1	1,377	345	3	1
Customs, costumes, folklore	172	30	8	—	172	37	6	—
Domestic science	776	190	8	—	781	209	29	—
Education	1,175	181	5	—	1,421	245	5	—
Engineering	1,662	382	27	—	1,714	315	22	1
Entertainment	717	102	29	—	598	102	16	1
Fiction	4,879	2,033	178	3	5,265	2,156	204	6
General	777	104	7	1	856	97	2	—
Geography and archaeology	683	109	9	3	437	118	5	—
Geology and meteorology	418	65	7	—	348	40	27	—
History	1,503	310	70	4	1,740	361	46	1
Humor	215	29	2	—	242	43	2	—
Industry	569	113	4	—	612	109	9	1
Language	664	138	10	1	708	129	7	4
Law and public administration	1,464	387	17	—	1,787	403	8	—
Literature	1,612	217	79	6	2,187	1,013	79	3
Mathematics	924	180	21	—	1,011	142	22	—
Medical science	3,274	583	17	2	3,165	520	27	—
Military science	143	21	4	—	167	44	2	—
Music	498	95	29	1	489	113	22	—
Natural sciences	1,507	178	18	1	1,177	169	44	3
Occultism	193	41	5	—	188	35	17	—
Philosophy	521	104	50	—	695	167	59	—
Photography	268	44	5	—	294	40	2	6
Plays	253	77	24	—	381	201	35	2
Poetry	794	87	90	49	925	222	72	31
Political science and economy	4,263	849	146	—	4,177	823	92	—
Psychology	834	161	20	—	705	127	13	—
Religion and theology	1,856	452	157	7	2,257	394	189	3
School textbooks	1,807	312	12	—	1,964	288	9	—
Science, general	58	14	8	—	76	16	4	—
Sociology	1,174	137	34	—	1,162	172	16	1
Sports and outdoor games	541	120	6	1	610	123	2	3
Stockbreeding	297	53	2	1	265	53	7	—
Trade	606	125	2	—	563	127	2	2
Travel and guidebooks	869	348	28	1	956	379	24	5
Wireless and television	342	66	3	—	267	47	1	—
Totals	48,307	10,360	1,391	105	51,071	12,091	1,499	101

Tables 1 and 2 are taken from *The Bookseller,* January 1 and 8, 1983, and January 14, 1984.

TABLE 2 Growth in British Title Output Since 1947

Year	Total	Reprints & New Edns.
1947	13,046	2,441
1948	14,686	3,924
1949	17,034	5,110
1950	17,072	5,334
1951	18,066	4,938
1952	18,741	5,428
1953	18,257	5,523
1954	18,188	4,846
1955	19,962	5,770
1956	19,107	5,302
1957	20,719	5,921
1958	22,143	5,971
1959	20,690	5,522
1960	23,783	4,989
1961	24,893	6,406
1962	25,079	6,104
1963	26,023	5,656
1964	26,154	5,260
1965	26,358	5,313
1966	28,883	5,919
1967	29,619	7,060
1968	31,470	8,778
1969	32,393	9,106
1970	33,489	9,977
1971	32,538	8,975
1972	33,140	8,486
1973	35,254	9,556
1974	32,194	7,852
1975	35,608	8,361
1976	34,434	8,227
1977	36,322	8,638
1978	38,766	9,236
1979	41,940	9,086
1980	48,158	10,776
1981	43,083	9,387
1982	48,307	10,360
1983	51,071	12,091

nica, Field Educational Enterprises, and Grolier). The Australian Book Publishers Association bases its data on questionnaires returned by publishing houses responsible for about 80 percent of that country's book market, and it turns out that 88 percent of new titles published by these 119 respondents were wholly Australia-originated, and they accounted for 36 percent of the total book market in 1982. Still, in general publishing for the domestic Australian market, imported books were outselling locally produced titles by a 5:4 ratio. In 1982, 4,826 titles were produced in Australia, 2,432 of them new; Australian-owned firms published over 57 percent of these new books, U.K.-owned firms 30.9 percent, and U.S. firms 10.4 percent.

Japan

A nation of extraordinary literacy, Japan also enjoys one of the book world's best-regulated retail networks—with 12,250 shops and stands for books spread over that island chain, supplied by highly automatized publisher-owned distribution companies; all new titles go out on consignment, making it certain that everybody's books go everywhere. In the early 1970s when things began to go wrong with the business cycle, it became evident that the

A Japanese ambassador to the international book world: Toshiyuki Hattori, chairman of Tokyo's giant Kodansha book and magazine empire and president of the Japanese Publishers Association.

depends on government assistance, and Australia's small population base and distance from most potential markets make it necessary to subsidize local creations.

Meanwhile, Australian book traders watch for signs that their domestic publishing industry is meeting the needs of Australian book buyers, and it can be said that they are receiving more and more of these signs. Statistics put together for 1982 by the Australian Book Publishers Association showed that sales of Australian-published books exceeded sales of imported books—if only by 1 percent (and the ratio would have been less positive if figures had been available from a number of large foreign companies that sell directly, like Encyclopaedia Britan-

Japanese system was too perfect: Too many books were going out and coming back; today returns are running at 35.5 percent. Japan shares the economic problems of its sister industrial nations, and during 1983 the decline in consumption was particularly rough on the book trade. The caution of book buyers has been expressing itself in a shift of customer preference to cheaper lines of books, not only Western-style paperbacks but also a strictly Japanese format known as *bunko* for lighter fare, comics and romances and practical books, and serious fiction and nonfiction too. More of these cheaper books are being sold than ever, as hardcover sales decline; the slight rise in aggregate turnover has not matched skyrocketing labor and production costs. Since most large Japanese book publishers also publish magazines, publishers have been flooding the market with new magazine titles, but even that solution has its limits, as 1982 balance sheets suggest. To meet the deteriorating financial situation of distributors and retail outlets as well as that of the publishers themselves, all segments of the industry are now working in concert to do something about the problem of returns.

Japan's publishing community was responsible for 41,134 titles in 1982, 31,523 of them new, in an estimated 432.7 million copies. The number of copies actually sold that year was 796.9 million, worth 708.8 billion yen (a current quotation: $1 = 233 yen). The publishers' 1,911 monthly periodicals and 60 weeklies sold 2.5 billion copies, accounting for additional sales of 620 million yen.

In a series of projections prepared for *Publishers Weekly Yearbook* by the president of the Japanese Publishers Association, Toshiyuki Hattori, chairman of the board of the Kodansha book and magazine empire, it can be seen that the industry's slump persisted all during 1983. Publishers met the challenge by publishing more than ever—about 9 percent more titles, and more of them in cheaper format; sales are expected to show an 8 percent rise when all reports are in, and once more that won't be sufficient to offset skyrocketing payrolls and transportation costs. The present estimate is that 860.3 million copies of books were sold in 1983, representing 714 billion yen.

Japanese publishers translate a good deal from Western publishing nations—nearly all American bestsellers, for example, and a great many books in category fiction. But the Japanese also read a great deal in English, particularly in professional and academic subjects, and Japan sees itself as the world's number-one importer of foreign books. To show more foreign books to more potential book buyers, the Japanese are launching an international book fair of their own, to be held May 18–21, 1984, in Tokyo, after which the exhibits are to circulate to six other Japanese cities.

The Federal Republic

Among Western publishing nations, Germany remains the publishing giant, holding the record for title output: 61,332 in 1982, 48,730 of them new (of the higher figure, 8,602 appeared in trade or mass market paperback formats). It is also one of the world's most highly structured book trades, with one of the most reliable and thoroughgoing distribution networks, and when all reports are in, it accounts for 8.25 billion Deutschmarks in sales (divide by 2.5 to get an approximate U.S. dollar value). More than 1,800 publishers and 3,000 retail and wholesale booksellers belong to the German Publishers and Booksellers Association, the Börsenverein, which is responsible for the trade's leading journal, *Börsenblatt,* and the world's number-one book fair, Frankfurt.

The German economic scene is characterized by stability—disquieting stability, some say. The cost of living rose a bare 3 percent last year, in a climate of caution. Publishers complain that booksellers are responsible for the low level of business activity because they are maintaining stocks as low as possible; paradoxically, the country's efficient ordering and delivery systems make this possible. Note also that German publishers issued 6,773 translations in 1982, 4,511 of them (or 66.6 percent) from English originals, 883 (13.1 percent) from French.

Another characteristic of the German scene is the rivalry between two groups, Bartelsmann and Holtzbrinck (whose founder, Georg von Holtzbrinck, died last spring, leaving control in the hands of son Dieter). Each of the groups operates major book clubs both in Germany and abroad. The Bertelsmann clubs are not only the biggest in Germany, but in neighboring France, in Spain, and in a number of Latin American states as well; tests for a Bertelsmann club in the United States are being carried out. Both groups continue to grow by acquisition. Thus in 1983 Holtzbrinck, already owner of S. Fischer Verlag and Droemer and a major textbook publisher, Schroedel, purchased 100 percent of Rowohlt, one of the country's leading publishers of foreign fiction—from Faulkner and Hemingway to Sartre and Camus.

As for Bertelsmann, whose worldwide net sales for the 1981/1982 business year topped 6 billion Deutschmarks, it had been keeping a low profile on the German domestic scene because of the opposition of that country's antitrust authorities to further concentration in the book trade. So Bertelsmann's important recent acquisitions took place elsewhere; for example, it has expanded its interest in one of Spain's largest trade houses, Plaza y Janes, to full ownership; the German giant already owned Spain's largest book club, Circulo de Lectores, and the ubiquitous book-manufacturing company called Printer. For the first time, Bertelsmann's sales abroad exceeded its turnover in Germany (by 51–49), in part because of the higher value of U.S. dollars but also because of the growth of business in its foreign subsidiaries. Sales outside Germany accounted for 60 percent of the income of Bertelsmann book and record clubs, 59 percent of book publishing, 47 percent of printing and manufacturing, 54 percent of music, films, and television, 38 percent of magazine publishing. In the United States it owns paperback publisher Bantam Books, *Parents' Magazine* and *Young Miss,* Brown Printing Company, and Offset Paperback Manufacturers.

Still, when it began to look as if Germany's trustbusters were going to relax their grip, Bertelsmann began moving

Opening day of Spain's first international book fair, the Salón Internacional del Libro, held in October 1983 in Madrid.

within its own frontiers again. So far it has announced the acquisition of 75 percent of Severin & Siedler, whose main asset is publisher Wolf Jobst Siedler, formerly publisher at Berlin's Ullstein; he will continue to work (as Siedler Verlag) in Berlin, far from the Munich headquarters of Bertelsmann's trade publishing division.

Spain

Certainly no Western publishing nation changed as much during 1983 as Spain did, but some of the changes won't show up on any balance sheet. The Spanish book trade made more progress in its transition to democracy, shedding the vestiges of the Francisco Franco years, when the industry was organized along corporate lines. The export trade, for example, which is vital to most large Spanish publishing enterprises, was under the thumb of the governmental Spanish National Book Institute; even the country's book trade journal was published by that organization. Publishers now have their own trade association, and are planning to publish their own trade journal.

Alas, the period of transition has also been one of economic crisis, for the disastrous economic situation in many of the largest countries of Spanish America had an immediate effect on the Spanish publishing industry. Until recent years, 40 percent of all Spanish books were sold abroad, a proportion that has been declining, although a few industry leaders continued to sell half of their production to Latin America. In 1979, the latest year for which comparative data are available, Spain was the world's fourth largest book exporter (after the United States, the United Kingdon, and West Germany); as a percentage of gross national product, Spain could claim the highest ratio of book exports among book-producing nations. And 70 percent of its exports were going to the Western Hemisphere, principally to Mexico (17 percent), Venezuela (14 percent), Argentina (11 percent), Colombia (9 percent). With the total collapse in the exchange value of local currency in Mexico and Venezuela, two of Spain's chief markets were all but wiped out, local distribution affiliates all but written off; with political and economic upheaval in Argentina, that highly literate nation ceased to exist on the Spanish distributors' maps. At least two major Spanish publishers, Madrid's Aguilar and Barcelona's Bruguera, just barely survived the crash (Aguilar, a large general and reference book publisher, had actually been selling *twice* as much in Latin America as in Spain itself; with $3 million in unpaid accounts, it was obliged to announce a suspension of payments).

Spain's publishers have not given up on Latin America, and certainly not on Spain. In October 1983 they even staged their first international book fair in Madrid, largely aimed at the Spanish American trade (it is true that the fair was originally conceived before Spain's traditional Western Hemisphere markets evaporated). Over 50 importers of Spanish books were invited to the fair (the hosts paid half the air tickets and timed the Madrid event—

October 4–9—to make it easy for their visitors to go on to the Frankfurt Book Fair).

A visitor to the Madrid Book Fair also had an opportunity to see how that country's book trade was facing up to the domestic economic crisis. Book production continues to rise—to 32,213 titles in 1982, of which 21,355 were new—although the number of copies printed per title is lower than the European average. (Note that of the 32,213 total, 8,079 books were translations, 3,863 of them from English-language titles.) With inflation running at 12 percent and unemployment at two million (16.5 percent of the active population), Spain's consumers were suffering from a shortage of cash. If that was hurting trade publishing, it seemed not to be dampening customer interest in multivolume reference works sold on credit, and most large publishers continue to produce a wide range of encyclopedias. At the other end of the scale, the crisis has given birth to a new kind of publishing: mass market hardbacks sold via newsstands and other mass distribution outlets. This new kind of book is actually a derivative of Spain's traditional part-work publishing (which usually manifests itself in the form of weekly installments of reference books, sold on newsstands for the price of a magazine). The mass market hardbacks were launched by a recently established company called Orbis, which is a 50–50 partnership between Germany's Bertelsmann and Julián Viñuales Solé (formerly of Barcelona's Salvat); soon giant Salvat and fast-moving Planeta were launching their own lines. Books range from fiction (including classics and selected works by Nobel prize winners) to ambitious works of economics or philosophy, packaged to sell at about U.S. $1.40 a copy; sales of these weekly releases are now averaging 50,000 copies, an incredible performance in a country whose book-buying public has often disappointed ambitious publishers.

France

In the context of a depressed business cycle, chronic unemployment, an increase in business failures, and a lack of confidence in the Socialist government's management of the economy, France's publishers appear relieved that things are not worse than they are. At a time when growth would have been welcomed, the French book trade found itself saddled with the government-enforced retail price maintenance it had been lobbying for. The new system managed to reduce sales in chains and supermarkets without stimulating sufficient sales in traditional retail outlets to compensate for that loss. Still, publishers and booksellers claim to be pleased with fixed prices, and the government has issued one victory proclamation after another; one is reminded of another victory proclamation: "The treatment was successful but the patient died." In figures: Total industry turnover rose 1.6 percent in constant francs in 1982 (to 7.4 billion francs, at the time when a U.S. dollar was worth about 7 francs). Title production rose by 2.9 percent, or 4.6 percent in copies.

Concerning 1983, the best guess is more of the same. Jean-Manuel Bourgois, president of the French Publishers Association, has been quoted to the effect that with inflation running at 10 percent and growth at 6 percent, the year might well end with a 4 percent decline in volume. Meanwhile, a few trade leaders have performed well, above all France's number-two group, Presses de la Cité, whose imprints include Plon, Julliard, and Christian Bourgois; Presses made most of its money with France Loisirs, a 50–50 partnership with Germany's Bertelsmann; with its 3.8 million members, France Loisirs has been called the biggest book club in the world.

The traditionally stable French publishing world has seen some takeover action. The year began with the purchase of small but innovative Ramsay by Gaumont, the country's leading film company. Gaumont also set up a joint venture with general publisher Gallimard to exploit the latter's backlist in visual media (and soon after that Gaumont crossed the Alps to set up a similar venture with Milan's Feltrinelli). At the end of the year it was announced that France's number-three publisher, the encyclopedia house of Larousse, had sold itself to the Compagnie Européenne de Publication (CEP), already a majority shareholder in Fernand Nathan (children's books, textbooks, games); CEP is itself partly owned by an advertising agency belonging to the French government, and opposition critics are complaining that the Mitterrand regime is involving itself in areas where free governments don't belong; the other example cited is Hachette, France's top communications group, which is run by the founder of Matra, the arms and space communications manufacturer now majority-controlled by the government. Note that the Larousse and Nathan families will be minority shareholders in a new holding company set up by CEP to run both Larousse and Nathan.

Italy

Most of the news out of Italy last year was bad. The year began with the unraveling of the Rizzoli affair, a political-financial scandal that had placed the group's president Angelo Rizzoli in jail; fortunately, the year ended with some better news about that ill-starred book, magazine, newspaper, and film group. The company was faring well under Chapter 11 supervision; it had reduced its deficit sufficiently to move creditors to approve a continuation of Chapter 11. Book publishing under new publisher Michele Norsa has been performing respectably in the context of Italy's publishing recession (with sales down 10–15 percent, inflation running at 16–17 percent). Rizzoli continues to release 300 new titles annually to the domestic market, and remains very much in the international market as well, as a serious bidder for major foreign books.

Then came the announcement, in autumn 1983, of a financial crisis at another prestigious Italian imprint, Einaudi of Turin, which for half a century had been doing some of that country's most ambitious works in literature and the social sciences; indeed, Einaudi played a leading role in the renaissance of Italy's cultural life after the fall of Fascism. And now Italians were being told that the firm was wallowing in debt—interest payments were equivalent to a fourth of turnover; apparently the situation had been known to some for a long time, for a literary agent was quoted: "The capacity of Einaudi to avoid bankruptcy has always been the best proof of the existence of God." The situation seemed insurmountable, and for another firm it might have been; but leaders of Italy's cultural and financial communities joined forces in an attempt to keep the company together; at year-end it looked as if they would succeed.

Not only for companies was it a sad year. Italy's pioneer literary agent, Erich Linder, who represented many internationally known Italian authors as well as the bulk of English-language translation rights sold into that country, died suddenly shortly before his fifty-ninth birthday; his Agenzia Letteraria Internazionale was to continue under the direction of his son, Michael Dennis Linder. In Florence, Giunti group president Renato Giunti, a familiar face in international publishing because of his sponsorship of major facsimile projects in co-production, died a month before his seventy-eighth birthday. Ljubivoje Stefanović, a Yugoslav by birth and Florentine by adoption, responsible for bringing American publishers such as Harcourt Brace Jovanovich into the world of international co-publishing, died at 59. His contribution to the book world was commemorated at an unprecedented memorial reception sponsored by a number of major publishers during the October 1983 Frankfurt fair. Stefanović died as the first volumes of his most recent achievement, the Vatican Library facsimile program, were being released by co-publishers Harcourt Brace Jovanovich and Belser Verlag of Germany.

In 1982, Italian publishers issued 20,560 titles, only a handful more than in the previous year (20,504); 11,280 of the books were new. There were 4,630 translations, new and reprint, of which 2,079 were from English-language titles—thus one book in ten published in Italy was of English-language origin. (Runner-up languages: French, with 983 books; German, with 648.) Italy's trade statistics tell us something more: The average printing of an Italian original was 7,310 copies, the average of a translation 7,223, while the average printing for translations from English was 8,443, showing that it makes business sense to buy rights.

Elsewhere in Europe

With its two languages fighting for cultural supremacy, tiny Belgium sometimes seems to be an international market all by itself. Much of the reading matter of the country's French-speaking half comes in across the border from France; its Dutch-speaking Flemish population gets its books from northern neighbor the Netherlands. Within Belgium, 136 publishers cater to the French-reading minority, another 128 to the Flemish majority (actually, 55 of the French-language publishers also produced books in Dutch, 48 of the Flemish publishers do some in French). Yet regional rivalry is bitter, cooperation virtually nonexistent between the rival cultures; there are separate

associations for French- and Dutch-language publishers, and inadequate cooperation within the federation, which in principle should be speaking for both sides.

Publishing statistics are necessarily influenced by those permeable borders. Thus we are told that 8,041 titles were produced in Belgium in 1982, of which 7,207 were new, but after announcing this, Julien de Raeymaeker, head of the French-language Belgian Publishers Association and the most reliable source of book trade data in his country, adds that 703 of those titles were actually produced in the Netherlands (by imprints such as Elsevier, Kluwer, and Spectrum); they get caught in the net spread by Belgium's national library because they carry the name of a Belgian city on the title page, or have a Belgian distributor. Actually, Raeymaeker counts only 4,438 titles produced by professional publishers, and he estimates the total book market at 11 billion Belgian francs, about evenly divided between books for domestic consumption and exports (62 percent of Belgium's French-language production was exported in 1982, by companies such as Casterman, Dargaud, and Marabout—all of them familiar logos in French book stores). (A recent quotation brought 55 Belgian francs for one U.S. dollar.) It is also true that Belgians buy more foreign books than domestically produced ones (at retail prices, 11.9 billion Belgian francs' worth of imports to 8.8 billion francs in local production); in all, ten million Belgians paid 20.7 billion francs for their reading matter in 1982.

Last year *PW* visited another small nation—Sweden, with a population of 8.4 million. In the business year ending March 31, 1982, 2,479 titles were published by members of that country's publishers association, 2,165 of them new, with a wholesale value of 755 million Swedish krona (at that time one krona was worth U.S. 23 cents). The total book market, which includes the production of a book club phenomenon called Bra Böcker, was estimated at 1,130,000,000 krona, for 30.2 million copies sold. The survey in *PW* on August 12, 1983, stressed the role of book clubs, representing 23 percent of the sales of members of the Swedish Publishers Association. But the big story out of Sweden is the titanic struggle between the five clubs belonging to Sweden's largest trade publisher, Bonnier, and maverick Bra Böcker, which sells to its members via a three-books-in-a-package offer (and one of them is usually one volume of an encyclopedia). Bra Böcker has captured a market of its own, consisting of heretofore unreachable readers; its success has allowed this club to outbid the traditional Swedish publishers for bestselling fiction from abroad (e.g., they made an unprecedented $100,000 offer for Swedish rights to Norman Mailer's *Ancient Evenings*). As part of their counterattack against upstart Bra Böcker, trade publishers who normally wouldn't give each other the time of day work together in a book-of-the-month club called Månadens Bok. It is estimated that the Bonnier clubs and Månadens Bok serve half the country's aggregate club membership of 1.2 million; Bra Böcker gets the other half. The partners of Månadens Bok now also operate the country's main mass market paperback line, called MånPocket, set up in order to discourage the sprouting of competing paperback lines in a country whose readership base hardly allows for that.

The Netherlands is only slightly larger than Sweden (14 million population), but this small nation has given birth to giant communications groups, all with international interests—Kluwer, Elsevier-NDU, VNU, and Wolters Samson. Some of them are active in trade publishing, a particularly soft sector in the Netherlands these days, but all are strong in sci-tech and/or professional publishing, where the money is; all reported profits up for the first half of 1983. As an example of how the Dutch move around: Elsevier has so much business in the United States that it has relocated a member of its executive board, D. P. van de Merwe, to the United States. Its flagship is Elsevier Science Publishing in New York, headed by an American with European publishing experience, Charles R. Ellis; but it also owns Congressional Information Service in Washington, D.C.; Greenwood Press in Westport, Connecticut; Excerpta Medica in Princeton, N.J.; and Medical Examination Publishing Company in New Hyde Park, New York.

The Second World

Publishing in the Communist bloc is operated or closely watched by the state; it is also distinguished by its nearly complete lack of contacts with the book trades of the West. Only at the time of international book fairs does it seem possible for East and West to meet, but even at these times true exchanges are rare. This is the way it seems to American trade publishers, who once again stayed away from Moscow's biennial book fair, held in 1983 from September 6 to 12. Actually the boycott was violated by U.S. scientific and technical publishers, whose sales in the Soviet Union are less affected by the ups and downs of politics; it is also true that the contents of their books are less likely to meet objections by the censors, who go about their business with ferocity before, during, and after the book fair.

Still, the leading Western book-producing nations were present at the September fair in Moscow, and trade books—current fiction and nonfiction—continued to attract crowds. In the absence of most American competitors with trade lines (with the exception of the Times-Mirror group and Harper & Row), Britain's Penguin and Pan drew the crowds. Once again, the collective stand run by Israeli publishers and another sponsored by the Association of Jewish Book Publishers from New York were literally besieged by Soviet Jews. The chief business of the fair took place between VAAP, the Soviet copyright agency (which controls everything produced in the USSR except for the work of dissident writers), and foreign publisher participants. VAAP's omnipresent agents distributed requests for options around the fair as if they were lottery tickets: A foreign publisher had to attend the fair in order to receive an option request, but as with lottery tickets, holding one was no guarantee that one was a winner. Those who know how to do business with the Soviets continue to speak of the Moscow fair with enthusiasm, and if the world doesn't fall apart it is likely that the major publishers of the United Kingdom, Germany, and France—and American sci-tech houses too—will be present at the next Moscow fair in 1985.

Although it may seem hard to believe, there was also a book fair in Warsaw last spring, the twenty-eighth International Book Fair, held in the Polish capital. For publishers outside that country, the fair is their best opportunity to obtain year-round orders for scientific, technical, medical, and academic books—but little else. Only 10 American firms showed up this time, but there were 99 imprints from the Federal Republic of Germany, including scientific publishers Springer-Verlag and Georg Thieme.

The Third World

As the largest noncommunist nation of the Third World, India makes a noble effort to maintain ties with the publishers of the major industrial nations of the West, notably via its World Book Fair in New Delhi. The fair attracts leading American and British scientific and technical publishers, who sell and occasionally co-publish in that territory. Thus the February 1984 fair included a marketing seminar sponsored by the International Group of Scientific, Technical, and Medical Publishers, with the participation of Indian publishers as well as representatives of the Indian affiliates of such houses as the U.S.'s McGraw-Hill and John Wiley, the U.K.'s Butterworth, and Germany's Springer-Verlag.

The most recent figures available cover the 1981–1982 business year, when 16,796 new books were issued in India, 6,983 of them in English, 2,556 in Hindi, 7,257 in a variety of other languages (statistics are not compiled on reprints, so these figures are not quite comparable with those of other countries). There are over 10,000 publishing imprints, although only a few hundred are considered significant; most English-language publishing is done in Delhi, and schoolbook publishing is a state monopoly. O. P. Ghai, president of the Federation of Indian Publishers (and head of Sterling Publishers, a large general publisher in New Delhi), reports that India's book exports have been increasing significantly. University-level textbooks, for example, can be produced in India for a fourth of the list price of their American or British equivalents, and there are promising markets in Singapore, Malaysia, Sri Lanka, Bangladesh, Nepal, and even further away in the Middle East and Africa. Yet Indians continue to import $2 worth of books from Britain and the United States for every $1 they manufacture for export; imports represent 16 percent of that country's total trade turnover.

International Book Fairs 1984

Fair Name & Place	Date/ Frequency	Fairgoers at Last Fair Countries with Exhibits	Book Categories Total Exhibit Space % Space for Books	Contact Address for Reserving Exhibit Space
16th Cairo International Book Fair International Fair Grounds Cairo, Egypt	Jan. 26-Feb. 1 Annual	1.8-million 27	All categories 12,652 sq. m 90%	Samir Saad Khalil General Egyptian Book Organization Corniche El Nil, Boulac Cairo, Egypt Cable: GEBO Misc; Telex: 93932 BOOK UN
The Sixth World Book Fair Hall of Nations Exhibition Grounds New Delhi, India	Feb. 4-14 Biennial	— 28	All categories — —	The Exhibition Executive National Book Trust, India A-5 Green Park New Delhi 110 016, India
5th International Book Fair of Mexico Palacio de Mineria Mexico City, Mexico	Mar. 10-18 Annual	200,000 18	All categories 2500 sq. m. 80%	Teresa Sanchez 5th International Book Fair of Mexico Apartado Postal 2400 01000 Mexico D.F., Mexico Telephone: 550-7413, 554-7501 Telex: 177-29-72 BOOKME
21st Bologna Children's Book Fair Bologna Fair Grounds Bologna, Italy	Apr. 5-8 Annual	10,700 (public not admitted) 60	Children's books 12,800 sq. m.; 100%	G. C. Alberghini, Secretary General Bologna Children's Book Fair Piazza Constituzione 6 40128 Bologna, Italy Cable: Bolognafiere— Bologna; Telex: FIERBO 1 511248
The London Book Fair The Barbican Arts Centre London EC2, England	Apr. 10-13 Annual	11,500 (public not admitted) 15	All categories 8000 sq. m.; 90%	Katy James The London Book Fair 16 Pembridge Road London WII, England Telephone: 01 229 1825; Telex: LOBOF 896 691
Quebec International Book Fair Quebec Municipal Convention Center; Quebec, P.Q., Canada	May 1-6 Annual	102,800 18	All categories 65,000 sq. m.; 100%	M. Lorenzo Michaud, General Director Quebec International Book Fair 2590 Boulevard Laurier Suite 860 Ste-Foy, Que., Canada G1V 4M6 Telephone: 418-658-1974
29th Warsaw International Book Fair Palace of Culture & Science Warsaw, Poland	May 23-28 Annual	50,000 21	Primarily scientific, technical medical books 10,000 sq. m.; 50%	Warsaw International Book Fair Ars Polona, Wladyslaw Bienkowski Krakowskie Przedmiescie 7 00-068 Warsaw, Poland Telephone: 17-86-41 Telex: 81 7503 AP PL
84th American Booksellers Association Convention and Trade Exhibit Washington, D.C. Convention Center Washington, D.C.	May 26-29 Annual	15,240 (public not admitted) 15	All categories — 90%	G. Roysce Smith, Executive Director American Booksellers Association 122 East 42nd Street New York, N.Y. 10168 Cable: AMBASSONEW; Telephone: 212/867-9060
103rd American Library Association Conference Dallas Convention Center Dallas, Tex.	June 23-29 Annual	11,083 (public not admitted) 25	All categories 70,000 sq. ft.; —	C. J. Hoy, Conference Manager American Library Association 50 East Huron Street Chicago, Ill. 60611 Telephone: 312-944-6780
35th Frankfurt Book Fair Frankfurt Fair Grounds Frankfurt/Main Federal Republic of Germany	Oct. 3-8 Annual	173,467 79	All categories 79,700 sq. m. 100%	Mr. Fenke Frankfurt Book Fair P.O. Box 2404, Kleiner Hirschgraben 10-12 6000 Frankfurt/Main 1 Federal Republic of Germany Cable: BUCHMESSE; Telex 416265 BUCHM-D Telephone: 611-2102-225
28th International Book Fair in Belgrade Belgrade Fair, Halls I and XIV Belgrade, Yugoslavia	Oct. 25-31 Annual	250,000 48	All categories 37,000 sq. m.; 100% for books	Vojislav Vujovic Association of Yugoslav Publishers and Booksellers International Book Fair Kneza Miloša 25, P.O. Box 883 11000 Belgrade, Yugoslavia Telephone: 011 642-248/533

29

Education for Publishing

ELIZABETH A. GEISER

The Leading Summer Introductory Institutes

DENVER PUBLISHING INSTITUTE

A four-week program combining "hands on" workshops in editing, marketing, and production with lecture/teaching sessions covering every phase of the book publishing process. Concentrates just on books. Ten reading, research, and writing assignments must be completed prior to course. Accepts 85 students; most are college graduates, although occasionally those without degrees but with commensurate working experience are admitted. Admission competitive with selections made by a committee of three. Six hours of graduate credit granted by Graduate School of Librarianship and Information Management, University of Denver. Director actively works on job placement. Founded in 1976. Held annually. 1984: July 9–August 3. Tuition: $1,350 plus $295 for room and $295 for meals. Contact: Elizabeth A. Geiser, Director, University of Denver Publishing Institute, 150 E. 50 St., New York, NY 10022. Tel. 212-751-3033.

HOWARD UNIVERSITY PRESS
BOOK PUBLISHING INSTITUTE

A five-week program examining four major aspects of the publishing process—editorial, design and production, marketing, and business. Concentrates just on books. One reading and one written assignment must be completed prior to attending program. Accepts 30 students with college degrees and also accepts students who have completed the junior year of study. Admission competitive with selections made by a committee of three. Provides placement service. Founded in 1980. Held

annually. 1984: May 30–July 3. Tuition, room, and board: $1,000. Contact: Janell E. Walden, Program Administrator, Howard University Press Book Publishing Institute, 2900 Van Ness St., N.W., Washington, DC 20008. Tel. 202-686-6498.

NEW YORK UNIVERSITY SUMMER
PUBLISHING INSTITUTE

A six-week session covering both books and magazines, involving lectures, workshops, seminars. Software publishing will be included in 1984. As at Radcliffe, students prepare a prototype of a new magazine including editorial and business plans. Students also break into book publishing workshops, filling all the various positions as publisher, editor-in-chief, and so on, and eventually "publish" a book. Several assignments are sent to students prior to the program. Accepts 60 to 75 students on a first-come-first-served basis. Selection by an admissions committee. Provides placement service. Founded in 1977. Held annually. 1984: June 11–July 20. Tuition: $2,100 plus about $25 per day for room and meals. Contact: Barbara J. Meredith, Director, Center for Publishing, School of Continuing Education, 2 University Place, Room 21, New York, NY 10003. Tel. 212-598-2371.

RADCLIFFE PUBLISHING PROCEDURES COURSE

A six-week program covering both books and magazines. The first half concentrates on books; the second half deals with magazines, with students divided into publishing workshops, one group creating a prototype of a new magazine, the other working on a mock-up book. Reading, research, and writing assignments to be completed prior to program. Accepts 86 students with college degrees. Admission competitive with selections made by a committee of ten. Director actively works on job placement. Founded in 1947. Held annually. 1984: June 25–August 3. Tuition: $2,840 (includes room and board). Contact: Frank Collins, Course Administrator, Radcliffe Publishing Procedures Course, 6 Ash St., Cambridge, MA 02138. Tel. 617-495-8678.

THE RICE PUBLISHING PROGRAM

A four-week course divided between books and magazines, concentrating on trade book publishing. For books, students are organized into mock publishing houses, with students holding different positions. For magazines, students create a prototype for a new magazine, much as in the Radcliffe program. Emphasizes regional/specialized publishing. Admits 50 to 80 students with college degrees but will also accept promising students who have completed the junior year. Admission competitive with selections made by a committee of three or four. Founded in 1978. Held irregularly (in 1978, 1979, 1981, and 1983. Will not be held in 1984). Contact: Patricia S. Martin, Director, The Rice Publishing Program, Box 1892, Houston, TX 77251. Tel. 713-527-4803.

A Guide to Some of the Continuing Education Programs

CITY UNIVERSITY OF NEW YORK, GRADUATE CENTER, EDUCATION IN PUBLISHING PROGRAM

Evening sessions conducted each spring and fall with a curriculum based on the guidelines developed by the Association of American Publishers Education for Publishing Committee. Each course meets two hours once a week for the term. Typical courses: computer technology in publishing; book editing workshop; economics of publishing for the nonspecialist; marketing specialized books. A special effort is made to review applicants' credentials and place students in appropriate courses. Approximately $175–$275 per course. Founded in 1978. Contact: Peg Rivers, Administrator, Education in Publishing Program, Graduate Center, City University of New York, 33 W. 42 St., New York, NY 10036. Tel. 212-790-4453, 4454.

COALITION OF PUBLISHERS FOR EMPLOYMENT (COPE)

This workshop provides basic training in the publishing processes, which includes design, editorial, and production. The program is designed for employees of publishing companies who wish to upgrade their skills. It is an affirmative action program primarily for minority students; however, others are accepted into the program. Accepts 30 students who work in teams to produce four to six books a year. Funds and materials are contributed by the publishing community. Tuition of $300 per student

required. Scholarships available to qualified students. Founded in 1970. Classes held at Cooper Union, New York City, every year from mid-September to the end of January. Interested students may inquire in May of each year for applications. Contact: Judith Mathisen, Assistant Vice President and Director, Personnel, Macmillan Publishing Co., 866 Third Ave., New York, NY 10022. Tel. 212-935-2000.

GEORGE WASHINGTON UNIVERSITY PUBLICATION SPECIALIST PROGRAM

A 240-hour evening program awarding a certificate to those completing two 16-week semesters (fall and spring) and an eight-week summer session. Fall and spring semesters are each divided into two eight-week sessions with students taking two courses every eight weeks. Certificate students must take 10 courses to graduate (6 required, 4 electives) and may choose from 20 electives, including association publishing; audiovisual publishing; computer graphics; computer publishing; creative editing; finance and accounting; magazine design and production; public relations; and writing. Students can also apply for individual courses. 1983–1984: September 17, 1983–August 11, 1984. Tuition: $2,110. Individual eight-week course: $255 to $270. Founded in 1974. Contact: Sharon W. Block, Director, Publication Specialist Program, George Washington University, Suite T409, 801 22 St. N.W., Washington, DC 20052. Tel. 202-676-7273.

NEW YORK UNIVERSITY CENTER FOR PUBLISHING (CREDIT COURSES)

Diploma Program in Magazine Publishing, designed for junior to mid-level personnel who must have BA degree. Offers four evening courses in the fall and five evening courses in the spring. Students must apply for entire program or enroll in individual courses. Topics include magazine publishing management; advertising, sales, and promotion; magazine manufacturing management; magazine editing. Grants 18 matriculatable college credits. Tuition: $1,690 for 6 to 10 credits, or $217 per credit. Prices will be raised slightly by summer 1984. Since fall 1983, in cooperation with NYU's School of Education, Health, Nursing and Arts Profession, a master's degree in graphic arts management and technology with a concentration in magazine publishing is offered. Contact: Barbara J. Meredith, Director, Center for Publishing, School of Continuing Education, New York University, 2 University Place, New York, NY 10003. Tel. 212-598-2371.

NEW YORK UNIVERSITY CENTER FOR PUBLISHING (NONCREDIT COURSES)

The School of Continuing Education also offers 25 to 30 noncredit evening courses, workshops, and seminars in book and magazine publishing each fall and spring semester, and 6 to 8 courses in the summer semester covering such topics as international publishing; free-lance indexing; copy editing and proofreading; the information industry. Approximately $230 per course. Founded in

1944. Contact: Barbara J. Meredith, Director, Center for Publishing, School of Continuing Education, New York University, 2 University Place, New York, NY 10003. Tel. 212-598-2371.

STANFORD PUBLISHING COURSE

A two-week program covering books and magazines for experienced professionals who want to learn about components in the process other than their own specialty. Designed for those edging into middle management, but has also attracted heads of houses. Students must complete six case studies before the course. Accepts about 150 students who are divided into two tracks, magazines or books, with several general sessions for all. Founded in 1978. 1984: July 9–20. Tuition: $950 including lunches and two dinners. Housing available for the 60 percent who stay on campus. Contact: Della van Heyst, Director of Publications, Bowman Alumni House, Stanford University, Stanford, CA 94305. Tel. 415-497-2021.

UNIVERSITY OF CALIFORNIA, CERTIFICATE PROGRAM IN PUBLISHING

A certificate program spanning the academic year. Those seeking certificate must take 120 hours of required courses and 80 hours of electives—all of which must be academic courses. The four required courses are Working as an Editor in the Book Business; Marketing in the Book Business; Printing Techniques; Computers in Publishing. Elective courses (15-, 30-, or 45-hour courses) include Editorial Workshop; Technical Writing and Editing; and Book Design. Founded in 1978. Prices range from $90 (for a 15-hour course) to $165 (45 hours). Contact: Ruth Majdrakoff, Director, Certificate Program in Publishing, University of California Extension, 2223 Fulton St., Berkeley, CA 94720. Tel. 415-642-4231.

Institutions Offering a Degree with a Concentration in Publishing

HOFSTRA UNIVERSITY

The Publishing Studies Program provides English undergraduate majors with a concentration in book publishing. Students must take 39 credits in publishing and literature and 3 credits in history. They have opportunities to serve internships in publishing houses between their junior and senior year. Built around a two-semester core program on book editing, the program covers every aspect of the publishing process. Courses toward a certificate may be taken by those not admitted to the university. Founded in 1976. A master's program is under development. Contact: Arthur Gregor, Director of Publishing Studies, English Department, Hofstra University, Hempstead, NY 11550. Tel. 516-560-5468.

NEW YORK UNIVERSITY'S GALLATIN DIVISION

The Oscar Dystel Fellowship in Book Publishing is a graduate program leading to a master's degree in book publishing. It combines courses selected from the many schools within NYU with a tutorial program led by participating publishing executives. The program is individually tailored to the interests and needs of the student and provides opportunities for internships and independent study. Established through an endowment from Bantam Books to honor its former president and first awarded in the fall of 1982. Winner of the fellowship receives approximately $2,000 to $2,500 toward the total cost of about $6,000. Contact: Joan Goulianos, Director, MA Degree Program, New York University, Gallatin Division, 715 Broadway, New York, NY 10003. Tel. 212-598-7075.

More Help for Students and the People of Publishing

Employees and students of book publishing now have a new resource center—the William H. and Gwynne K. Crouse Library for Publishing Arts at the Graduate Center of the City University of New York established through the generosity of the Crouses. Designed especially for those employed in the publishing industry, the library is expected to become the authoritative source of publishing materials in the field. It is the first and only comprehensive collection of materials pertaining to the book publishing industry that is fully open to all users and available in the evening as well as during working hours. Mr. and Mrs. Crouse said that they see the library as providing the opportunity to bring "some of the best and brightest kids into the publishing business, to help them and to keep them in it, because they are satisfied, learning, growing." Crouse is the author of more than 50 books published by McGraw-Hill. The library, more than two years in the planning, opened its doors for business in September 1983, with Alfred H. Lane, former head of Gifts and Exchange for the Columbia University Libraries, as director.

30

The Publisher's Basic Library

MARGARET M. SPIER

Bibliographies of the Book Trade

Gottlieb, Robin. *Publishing Children's Books in America, 1919–1976: An Annotated Bibliography*. New York: Children's Book Council, 1978. $15.

Lee, Marshall. *Bookmaking: The Illustrated Guide to Design/Production/Editing*. New York: R. R. Bowker, 1980. $32.50. Bibliography is divided into four parts: Part 1 covers books and includes a general bibliography as well as extensive coverage of books on all technical aspects of bookmaking; Part 2 lists periodicals; Part 3 lists films, filmstrips, etc.; Part 4 lists other sources.

The Reader's Adviser: A Layman's Guide to Literature. 12th ed. 3 vols. New York: R. R. Bowker, 1974–1977. $120 (3-vol. set); $45 (each vol.). Vol. 1. *The Best in American and British Fiction, Poetry, Essays, Literary Biography, Bibliography, and Reference*, edited by Sarah L. Prakken. 1974. Chapters "Books about Books" and "Bibliography" cover history of publishing and bookselling, practice of publishing, bookmaking, rare book collecting, trade and specialized bibliographies, book selection tools, best books, etc. Vol. 2. *The Best in American and British Drama and World Literature in English Translation*, edited by F. J. Sypher. 1977. Vol. 3. *The Best in the Reference Literature of the World*, edited by Jack A. Clarke. 1977.

Tanselle, G. Thomas. *Guide to the Study of United States Imprints*. 2 vols. Cambridge, Mass.: Belknap Press of Harvard University Press, 1971. $70. Includes sections on general studies of American printing and publishing as well as studies of individual printers and publishers.

Trade Bibliographies

American Book Publishing Record Cumulative, 1876–1949: An American National Bibliography. 15 vols. New York: R. R. Bowker, 1980. $1,975.

American Book Publishing Record Cumulative, 1950–1977: An American National Bibliography. 15 vols. New York: R. R. Bowker, 1979. $1,975.

American Book Publishing Record Five-Year Cumulatives. New York: R. R. Bowker. 1960–1964 Cumulative. 5 vols. $150. 1965–1969 Cumulative. 5 vols. $150. 1970–1974 Cumulative. 4 vols. $150. 1975–1979 Cumulative. 5 vols. $175. Annual vols.: 1978, $59; 1979, $59; 1980, $59; 1981, $82.50; 1982, $82.50; 1983, $82.50.

Books in Print. 6 vols. New York: R. R. Bowker, ann. $169.

Books in Print Supplement. New York: R. R. Bowker, ann. $85.

Books in Series 1876–1949. 3 vols. New York: R. R. Bowker, 1982. $150.

Books in Series in the United States. 3rd ed. New York: R. R. Bowker, 1980. $175.

British Books in Print: The Reference Catalog of Current Literature. New York: R. R. Bowker, 1983. $160. (plus duty where applicable).

Canadian Books in Print, edited by Marian Butler. Toronto: University of Toronto Press, ann. $50.

Canadian Books in Print: Subject Index, edited by Marian Butler. Toronto: University of Toronto Press, ann. $50.

Cumulative Book Index. New York: H. W. Wilson. Monthly with bound semiannual and larger cumulations. Service basis.

El-Hi Textbooks in Print. New York: R. R. Bowker, ann. $49.50.

Forthcoming Books. New York: R. R. Bowker. $67.50 a year. $18 single copy. Bimonthly supplement to *Books in Print.*

International Books in Print. 3rd. ed. 2 vols. Munich: K. G. Saur, 1983. Distributed by R. R. Bowker. $175.

Large Type Books in Print. New York: R. R. Bowker, 1982. $49.50.

Paperbound Books in Print. New York: R. R. Bowker, 3 vols. $75.

Publishers' Trade List Annual. New York: R. R. Bowker, ann. 5 vols. $95.

Robert, Reginald, and Burgess, M. R. *Cumulative Paperback Index, 1939–59.* Detroit: Gale, 1973. $48.

Small Press Record of Books in Print, edited by Len Fulton. Paradise, Calif.: Dustbooks, 1983. $25.95.

Subject Guide to Books in Print. 4 vols. New York: R. R. Bowker, ann. $110.

Subject Guide to Forthcoming Books. New York: R. R. Bowker. $45 a year. $95 in combination with *Forthcoming Books.*

Subject Guide to International Books in Print. 2 vols. Munich: K. G. Saur, 1983. Distributed by R. R. Bowker. $175.

Book Publishing

EDUCATION AND PRACTICE

Association of American University Presses. *One Book—Five Ways: The Publishing Procedures of Five University Presses.* Los Altos, Calif.: William Kaufmann, 1978. $19.95. pap. $11.95.

Bailey, Herbert S., Jr. *The Art and Science of Book Publishing.* Austin: University of Texas Press, 1980. pap. $7.95.

Bodian, Nat G. *Book Marketing Handbook: Tips and Techniques for the Sale and Promotion of Scientific, Technical, Professional, and Scholarly Books and Journals.* New York: R. R. Bowker, 1980. $45.

Bodian, Nat G. *Book Marketing Handbook, Volume Two: 1,000 More Tips and Techniques for the Sale and Promotion of Scientific, Technical, Professional, and Scholarly Books and Journals.* New York: R. R. Bowker, 1983. $60.

Brownstone, David M. *The Dictionary of Publishing.* New York: Van Nostrand Reinhold, 1982. $18.95.

Crutchley, Brooke. *To Be a Printer.* New York: Cambridge University Press, 1980. $22.50.

Dessauer, John P. *Book Publishing: What It Is, What It Does.* New York: R. R. Bowker, 1981. $23.95. pap. $13.95.

Glaister, Geoffrey. *Glaister's Glossary of the Book: Terms Used in Paper-Making, Printing, Bookbinding, and Publishing.* 2nd ed., completely rev. Berkeley: University of California Press, 1979. $75.

Grannis, Chandler B. *Getting into Book Publishing.* New York: R. R. Bowker, 1983. Pamphlet, one free; in bulk 75¢ each.

Grannis, Chandler B., ed. *What Happens in Book Publishing.* 2nd ed. New York: Columbia University Press, 1967. $30.

Greenfield, Howard. *Books: From Writer to Reader.* New York: Crown, 1976. $8.95. pap. $4.95.

Hackett, Alice Payne, and James Henry Burke. *Eighty Years of Best Sellers, 1895–1975.* New York: R. R. Bowker, 1977. $18.95.

Kaufman, Henry R., ed. *Book Publishing 1981.* Patents, Copyrights, Trademarks and Literary Property Course Handbook series. New York: Practising Law Institute, 1981. $30.

Peters, Jean, ed. *Bookman's Glossary.* 6th ed. New York: R. R. Bowker, 1983. $21.95.

ANALYSIS, STATISTICS, SURVEYS

ANSI Standards Committee Z-39. *American National Standard for Compiling Book Publishing Statistics, Z-39.8.* New York: American National Standards Institute, 1978. $4.

Altbach, Philip G., and Eva-Marie Rathgeber. *Publishing in the Third World: Trend Report and Bibliography.* New York: Praeger, 1980.

Arthur Andersen & Co. *Book Distribution in the U.S.: Issues and Perceptions.* New York: Book Industry Study Group, 1982. $60.

Association of American Publishers 1982 Industry Statistics. New York: Association of American Publishers, 1983. Nonmemb. $250.

Association of American Publishers. 1982 Survey of Compensation and Personnel Practices in the Publishing Industry. Prepared and conducted by Sibson & Co., Inc. New York: Association of American Publishers, 1982. Participant $45. Nonpart. $90.

Benjamin, Curtis G. *A Candid Critique of Book Publishing.* New York: R. R. Bowker, 1977. o.p.

Book Industry Study Group, Inc. *Special Reports.* New York: Book Industry Study Group. Vol. 1, No. 1. Lambert, Douglas M. *Physical Distribution: A Profit Opportunity for Printers, Publishers, and Their Customers.* August 1982. $25. Vol. 1, No. 2. Noble, J. Kendrick. *Trends in Textbook Markets.* 1983. $50. Distributed to nonmembers by R. R. Bowker.

Bowker Annual of Library and Book Trade Information. New York: R. R. Bowker, ann. $55.

Bowker Lectures on Book Publishing. New York: R. R. Bowker, 1957. o.p.

Bowker Lectures on Book Publishing, New Series. 10 vols. New York: R. R. Bowker, 1973–1982. $3 each. No. 1. Pilpel, Harriet F. *Obscenity and the Constitution.* 1973. No. 2. Ringer, Barbara A. *The Demonology of Copyright.* 1974. No. 3. Henne, Frances E. *The Library World and the Publishing of Children's Books.* 1975. No. 4. Vaughan, Samuel S. *Medium Rare: A Look at the Book and Its People.* 1976. No. 5. Bailey, Herbert S. *The Traditional Book in the Electronic Age.* 1977. No. 6. Mayer, Peter. *The Spirit of the Enterprise.* 1978. No. 7. De Gennaro, Richard. *Research Libraries Enter the Information Age.* 1979. No. 8. Dystel, Oscar. *Mass Market Publishing: More Observations, Speculations and Provocations.* 1980. No. 9. Giroux, Robert. *The Education of an Editor.* 1981. No. 10. Martin, Lowell. *The Public Library: Middle Age Crisis or Old Age?* 1982.

The Business of Publishing: A PW Anthology. New York: R. R. Bowker, 1976. $18.50.

Cheney, O. H. *Economic Survey of the Book Industry, 1930–31.* The Cheney Report. Reprinted. New York: R. R. Bowker, 1960. o.p.

Compaine, Benjamin. *The Book Industry in Transition: An Economic Analysis of Book Distribution and Marketing.* White Plains, N.Y.: Knowledge Industry Publications, 1978. $29.95.

————, ed. *Who Owns the Media?* 2nd ed. White Plains, N.Y.: Knowledge Industry Publications, 1982. $45.

Coser, Lewis A., Charles Kadushin, and Walter W. Powell. *Books: The Culture and Commerce of Publishing.* New York: Basic Books, 1982. $19.

Dessauer, John P. *Book Industry Trends 1983.* New York: Book Industry Study Group, 1983. Distributed by R. R. Bowker. $150. *Book Industry Trends 1982* also available from R. R. Bowker.

————. *Trends Update* (monthly). Expands on statistics in the annual compilation and explains forecasting techniques. $240 a year. $25 single copy. Both publications distributed to nonmembers by R. R. Bowker.

Gedin, Per. *Literature in the Marketplace.* Translated by George Bisset. Woodstock, N.Y.: Overlook, 1977. $12.95.

Machlup, Fritz, and Kenneth W. Leeson. *Information through the Printed Word: The Dissemination of Scholarly, Scientific, and Intellectual Knowledge.* 4 vols. Vol. 1. *Book Publishing.* Vol. 2. *Journals.* Vol. 3. *Libraries.* Vol. 4. *Books, Journals, and Bibliographic Services.* New York: Praeger, 1978. Vol. 1, $31.95. Vol. 2, $33.95. Vol. 3, $29.95. Vol. 4, $34.95.

Shatzkin, Leonard. *In Cold Type: Overcoming the Book Crisis.* Boston: Houghton Mifflin, 1982. $17.95.

Smith, Roger H., ed. *The American Reading Public: A Symposium.* New York: R. R. Bowker, 1964. o.p.

Whiteside, Thomas. *The Blockbuster Complex.* Middletown, Conn.: Wesleyan University Press. Distributed by Columbia University Press, 1981. $16.95.

Yankelovich, Skelly, and White, Inc. *The 1978 Consumer Research Study on Reading and Book Purchasing.* New York: Book Industry Study Group, 1978. Apply for price scale.

HISTORY

Bonn, Thomas L. *Under Cover: An Illustrated History of American Mass-Market Paperbacks.* New York: Penguin Books, 1982. $12.95.

Briggs, Asa, ed. *Essays in the History of Publishing: In Celebration of the 250th Anniversary of the House of Longman, 1724–1974.* New York: Longman, 1974. $15.

Cerf, Bennett. *At Random: The Reminiscences of Bennet Cerf.* New York: Random House, 1977. $12.95.

Crider, Allen Billy. *Mass Market Publishing in America.* Boston: G. K. Hall, 1982. $35.

Haydn, Hiram. *Words & Faces.* New York: Harcourt Brace Jovanovich, 1974. $8.95.

Hodges, Sheila. *Gollancz: The Story of a Publishing House.* London: Gollancz, 1978. £7.50.

Kurian, George. *Directory of American Book Publishing: From Founding Fathers to Today's Conglomerates.* New York: Monarch, 1975. $25.

Lehmann-Haupt, Hellmut. *The Book in America.* 2nd ed. New York: R. R. Bowker, 1951. o.p.

Madison, Charles. *Jewish Publishing in America.* New York: Hebrew Publishing Co., 1976. $11.95.

Moore, John Hammond. *Wiley: One Hundred and Seventy-five Years of Publishing.* New York: Wiley, 1982. $25.

Morpurgo, J. E. *Allen Lane: King Penguin.* New York: Methuen, 1979. $25.

Mott, Frank Luther. *Golden Multitudes: The Story of Best Sellers in the United States (1662–1945).* Reprint ed. New York: R. R. Bowker, 1960. o.p.

Norrie, Ian. *Mumby's Publishing and Bookselling in the Twentieth Century.* 6th ed. London: Bell & Hyman Ltd., 1982. Distributed by R. R. Bowker. $35.

O'Brien, Geoffrey. *Hardboiled America: The Lurid Years of Paperbacks.* New York: Van Nostrand Reinhold, 1981. $16.95.

Regnery, Henry. *Memoirs of a Dissident Publisher.* New York: Harcourt Brace Jovanovich, 1979. $12.95.

Schick, Frank L. *The Paperbound Book in America: The History of Paperbacks and Their European Background.* New York: R. R. Bowker, 1958. o.p.

Schreuders, Piet. *Paperbacks U.S.A.: A Graphic History, 1939–1959*. Translated from the Dutch by Josh Pachter. San Diego: Blue Dolphin Enterprises, 1981. $10.95.

Stern, Madeleine B. *Books and Book People in 19th-Century America*. New York: R. R. Bowker, 1978. $28.50.

———. *Publishers for Mass Entertainment in Nineteenth Century America*. Boston: G. K. Hall, 1980. $28.

Tebbel, John. *A History of Book Publishing in the United States*. 4 vols. Vol. 1. *The Creation of an Industry, 1630–1865*. Vol. 2. *The Expansion of an Industry, 1865–1919*. Vol. 3. *The Golden Age between Two Wars, 1920–1940*. Vol. 4. *The Great Change, 1940–1980*. New York: R. R. Bowker, 1972, 1975, 1978, 1981. $37.50 each.

Scholarly Books

Gaskell, Philip. *From Writer to Reader: Studies in Editorial Method*. New York: Oxford University Press, 1978. o.p.

Harman, Eleanor, and Ian Montagnes, eds. *The Thesis and the Book*. Toronto: University of Toronto Press, 1976. pap. $8.50.

Horne, David. *Boards and Buckram: Writings from "Scholarly Books in America," 1962–1969*. Hanover, N.H.: University Press of New England, 1980. $10. Distributed by American University Press Services, Inc., New York.

Nemeyer, Carol A. *Scholarly Reprint Publishing in the United States*. New York: R. R. Bowker, 1972. o.p.

Scholarly Communication: The Report of the National Enquiry. Baltimore: Johns Hopkins University Press, 1979. $15. pap. $5.95.

Electronic Publishing

Martin, James. *Viewdata and the Information Society*. Englewood Cliffs, N.J.: Prentice-Hall, 1982. $29.95.

Neustadt, Richard M. *The Birth of Electronic Publishing: Legal and Economic Issues in Telephone, Cable and Over-the Air Teletext and Videotext*. White Plains, N.Y.: Knowledge Industry Publications, 1982. $32.95.

Spigai, Frances, and Peter Sommer. *Guide to Electronic Publishing: Opportunities in Online and Viewdata Services*. White Plains, N.Y.: Knowledge Industry Publications, 1982. $95.

Tydeman, John, and Hubert Lipinski. *Teletext and Videotext in the United States: Market Potential, Technology and Public Policy Issues*. New York: McGraw-Hill, 1982. $34.95.

Editors, Agents, Authors

Appelbaum, Judith, and Nancy Evans. *How to Get Happily Published*. New York: Harper & Row, 1978. $11.95.

Berg, A. Scott. *Max Perkins: Editor of Genius*. New York: Pocket Books. pap. $2.95.

Commins, Dorothy Berliner. *What Is an Editor? Saxe Commins at Work*. Chicago: University of Chicago Press, 1978. $5.95.

Henderson, Bill, ed. *The Art of Literary Publishing: Editors on Their Craft*. Yonkers, N.Y.: Pushcart, 1980. $15.

Madison, Charles. *Irving to Irving: Author-Publisher Relations: 1800–1974*. New York: R. R. Bowker, 1974. $15.95.

Meyer, Carol. *Writer's Survival Manual: The Complete Guide to Getting Your Book Published*. New York: Crown, 1982. $13.95.

Plotnik, Arthur. *The Elements of Editing: A Modern Guide for Editors and Journalists*. New York: Macmillan, 1982. $9.13.

Reynolds, Paul R. *The Middle Man: The Adventures of a Literary Agent*. New York: Morrow, 1972. $6.95.

Unseld, Siegfried. *The Author and His Publisher*. Chicago: University of Chicago Press, 1980. $12.50.

Watson, Graham. *Book Society: Reminiscences of a Literary Agent*. New York: Atheneum, 1980. $10.95.

Book Design and Production

Grannis, Chandler B. *The Heritage of the Graphic Arts*. New York: R. R. Bowker, 1927. $24.95.

Lee, Marshall. *Bookmaking: The Illustrated Guide to Design and Production*. 2nd ed. New York: R. R. Bowker, 1980. $32.50.

Mintz, Patricia Barnes. *Dictionary of Graphic Arts Terms: A Communication Tool for People Who Buy Type & Printing*. New York: Van Nostrand Reinhold, 1981. $17.95.

Rice, Stanley. *Book Design: Systematic Aspects*. New York: R. R. Bowker, 1978. $18.95.

———. *Book Design: Text Format Models*. New York: R. R. Bowker, 1978. $18.95.

Roberts, Matt T., and Don Etherington. *Bookbinding and the Conservation of Books: A Dictionary of Descriptive Terminology*. Washington, D.C.: Library of Congress, 1982. For sale by the Superintendent of Documents, U.S. Government Printing Office. $27.

Strauss, Victor. *The Printing Industry: An Introduction to Its Many Branches, Processes and Products*. New York: R. R. Bowker, 1967. $34.95.

White, Jan. *Editing by Design*. 2nd ed. New York: R. R. Bowker, 1982. pap. $24.95.

Wilson, Adrian. *The Design of Books*. Layton, Utah: Peregrine Smith, 1974. pap. $10.95.

Bookselling

Anderson, Charles B., ed. *Bookselling in America and the World: A Souvenir Book Celebrating the 75th Anniversary of the American Booksellers Association.* New York: Times Books, 1975. o.p.

Bliven, Bruce. *Book Traveller.* New York: Dodd, Mead, 1975. $4.95. o.p.

Manual on Bookselling: How to Open and Run Your Own Bookstore. 3rd ed. New York: American Booksellers Association, 1980. Distributed by Harmony Books. $15.95. pap. $8.95.

White, Ken. *Bookstore Planning and Design.* New York: McGraw-Hill, 1982. $44.50.

Censorship

de Grazia, Edward, comp. *Censorship Landmarks.* New York: R. R. Bowker, 1969. $29.50.

Ernst, Morris L., and Alan U. Schwartz. *Censorship.* New York: Macmillan, 1964. $6.95.

Haight, Anne Lyon. *Banned Books.* 4th ed., updated and enlarged by Chandler B. Grannis. New York: R. R. Bowker, 1978. $14.95.

Hentoff, Nat. *The First Freedom: The Tumultuous History of Free Speech in America.* New York: Delacorte, 1980. $11.95. pap. $2.50.

Jenkinson, Edward B. *Censors in the Classroom: The Mind Benders.* Carbondale, Ill.: Southern Illinois University Press, 1979. $17.95.

Copyright

Copyright Revision Act of 1976: Law, Explanation, Committee Reports. Chicago: Commerce Clearing House, 1976. $12.50.

Current Developments in Copyright Law, 1982. Patents, Copyrights, Trademarks and Literary Property Course Handbook series. New York: Practicing Law Institute, 1982. $30.

Johnston, Donald F. *Copyright Handbook.* 2nd ed. New York: R. R. Bowker, 1982. $27.50.

Lindey, Alexander. *Lindey on Entertainment, Publishing and the Arts.* 3rd ed. 3 vols. New York: Boardman, 1982, $210.

McDonald, Dennis D., and Colleen G. Bush. *Libraries, Publishers and Photocopying: Final Report of Surveys Conducted for the United States Copyright Office.* Rockville, Md.: King Research, Inc., 1982. $25.

Wittenberg, Philip. *Protection of Literary Property.* Boston: The Writer, Inc., 1978. $12.95.

Book Trade Directories and Yearbooks

AMERICAN AND CANADIAN

American Book Trade Directory, 1983. 29th ed. New York: R. R. Bowker, ann. $95.

Book Publishers Directory: An Information Service Covering New and Established, Private and Special Interest, Avant-Garde and Alternative, Organization and Association, Government and Institution Presses. Edited by Linda Hubbard. Detroit: Gale, 1983. $195. Supplement, 1983. $110.

Cassells and the Publishers Association Directory of Publishing in Great Britain, The Commonwealth, Ireland, Pakistan and South Africa 1983. 10th ed. London: Cassell Ltd., 1982. Distributed by International Publications Service. $32.50.

Chernofsky, Jacob L., ed. *AB Bookman's Yearbook.* 2 vols. Clifton, N.J.: AB Bookman's Weekly, ann. $10. Free to subscribers to *AB Bookman's Weekly.*

Congrat-Butlar, Stefan, ed. *Translation & Translators: An International Directory and Guide.* New York: R. R. Bowker, 1979. $35.

Kim, Ung Chon. *Policies of Publishers.* Metuchen, N.J.: Scarecrow, 1982. pap. $15.

Literary Market Place, 1984, with Names & Numbers. New York: R. R. Bowker, ann. $45. The business directory of American book publishing.

Publishers, Distributors, & Wholesalers of the United States: A Directory. New York: R. R. Bowker, 1983. pap. $35.

Publishers Weekly Yearbook: News, Analyses and Trends in the Book Industry. New York: R. R. Bowker, 1983. pap. $29.95.

U.S. Book Publishing Yearbook and Directory, 1981/82. White Plains, N.Y.: Knowledge Industry Publications, 1982. $65.

FOREIGN AND INTERNATIONAL

International Directory of Little Magazines and Small Presses. Paradise, Calif.: Dustbooks, ann. $25.95.

International ISBN Publishers' Directory 1983. Berlin: International ISBN Agency, 1983. Distributed by R. R. Bowker. $99.50.

International Literary Market Place 1983–84. New York: R. R. Bowker, 1983. $55.

Publishers' International Directory. 2 vols. New York: K. G. Saur. Distributed by Gale Research, 1982. $175.

Taubert, Sigfred, ed. *The Book Trade of the World.* 3 vols. Vol. 1. *Europe and International Sections.* Vol. 2. *U.S.A., Canada, Central and South America, Australia and New Zealand.* Vol. 3. *Africa, Asia.* New York: R. R. Bowker. Vol. 1, 1972, $70; Vol. 2, 1976, $70; Vol. 3, 1980, $70.

UNESCO Statistical Yearbook, 1982. New York: Unipub, 1983. $109.75.

Who Distributes What and Where: An International Directory of Publishers, Imprints, Agents, and Distributors. New York: R. R. Bowker, 1983. $55.

Editing

Barzun, Jacques. *Simple and Direct: A Rhetoric for Writers.* New York: Harper & Row, 1976. $12.50.

Bernstein, Theodore. *The Careful Writer.* New York: Atheneum, 1965. $14.95. pap. $9.95.

The Chicago Manual of Style. 13th rev. ed. Chicago: University of Chicago Press, 1982. $30.

Fowler, H. W. *Dictionary of Modern English Usage.* 2nd rev. ed. New York: Oxford University Press, 1965. $15.

Jordan, Lewis. *The New York Times Manual of Style and Usage.* New York: Times Books, 1982. pap. $5.95.

Skillin, Marjorie E., and Robert M. Gay. *Words into Type.* Rev. ed. Englewood Cliffs, N.J.: Prentice-Hall, 1974. $22.95.

Strunk, William, Jr., and E. B. White. *Elements of Style.* 3rd ed. New York: Macmillan, 1978. $7.95. pap. $2.95.

Zinsser, William. *On Writing Well: An Informal Guide to Writing Nonfiction.* 2nd ed. New York: Harper & Row, 1980. $12.45.

Periodicals

AB Bookman's Weekly (weekly including yearbook). Clifton, N.J.: AB Bookman's Weekly. $50.

American Book Publishing Record (monthly). New York: R. R. Bowker. $44.50.

The American Bookseller (monthly). New York: American Booksellers Association. $18.

BP Report: On the Business of Book Publishing (weekly). White Plains, N.Y.: Knowledge Industry Publications. $215.

Copyright Management (monthly). Arlington, Mass.: Institute for Invention and Innovation, Inc. $84.

EPB: Electronic Publishing and Bookselling (bimonthly). Phoenix, Ariz.: Oryx Press. $60.

Electronic Publishing Review (quarterly). Medford, N.J.: Learned Information, Inc. $66.

Publishers Weekly. New York: R. R. Bowker. $68.

Scholarly Publishing: A Journal for Authors & Publishers (quarterly). Toronto: University of Toronto Press. $25.

Small Press: The Magazine of Independent Book Publishing (bimonthly). New York: R. R. Bowker. $18.

Weekly Record. New York: R. R. Bowker. $47.50. A weekly listing of current American book publications, providing complete cataloging information.

For a list of periodicals reviewing books, see *Literary Market Place.*

31

Selected 1983 Publications: Books and Journal Articles

MARGARET M. SPIER

Directories and annuals published in 1983 are included in "The Publisher's Basic Library," Chapter 30.

Books

Carpenter, Kenneth E., ed. *Books and Society in History: Papers of the ACRL Rare Books and Manuscripts Preconference, June 1980, Boston, Mass.* New York: R. R. Bowker, 1983. $29.95.

Carter, Robert A. *Trade Book Marketing: A Practical Guide.* New York: R. R. Bowker, 1983. $29.95. pap. $19.95

Cave, Roderick. *The Private Press.* New York: R. R. Bowker, 1983. $60.

Curtis, Richard. *How to Be Your Own Literary Agent.* Boston: Houghton Mifflin, 1983. $12.95.

Form Aides for Successful Book Publishing. Fairfield, Iowa: Ad-Lib Consultants, 1983. pap. $5.95.

Godine, David R. *The Well Made Book.* Boston: Godine, 1983. $6.95.

Graubard, Steven R., ed. *Reading in the 1980s.* New York: R. R. Bowker, 1983. $14.95.

Joyce, William L., and David B. Hall, eds. *Printing and Society in Early America.* Wooster, Mass.: American Antiquarian Society, 1983. Distributed by University Press of Virginia. $32.50.

Knowledge Industry Publications Staff and Janet Bailey, eds. *Date Base–Electronic Publishing Review and Forecast 1983.* White Plains, N.Y.: Knowledge Industry Publications, 1983. $175.

Lyles, William H. *Putting Dell on the Map: A History of the Dell Paperbacks.* Westport, Conn.: Greenwood Press, 1983. $27.95.

Nelson, Roy P. *Publication Design.* 3rd ed. Dubuque, Iowa: William C. Brown, 1983. $20.95.

Orrmont, Arthur, and Leonié Rosenstiel, eds. *Literary Agents of North America: Marketplace 1983–84.* New York: Author Aid/Research Associates International, 1983. pap. $14.95.

Peabody, Richard, ed. *Mavericks: Nine Independent Publishers.* Washington, D.C.: Paycock Press, 1983. pap. $4.95.

Scherman, William. *How to Get the Right Job in Publishing.* Chicago: Contemporary Books, 1983. pap. $9.95.

Weeks, John, and Jeffrey M. Elliot. *A Superman of Letters: R. Reginald and the Borgo Press.* San Bernardino, Calif.: Borgo Press, 1983. $9.95. pap. $3.95.

Williamson, Hugh. *Methods of Book Design: The Practice of An Industrial Craft.* 3rd ed. New Haven, Conn.: Yale University Press, 1983. $40. pap. $12.95.

Journal Articles

Anthony, Carolyn T. "Is the Publishing Business on the Rebound?" *Publishers Weekly*, July 8, 1983. pp. 30–33.

"Authors Guild Contract Survey: Part I—The Option Clause." *Authors Guild Bulletin*, Summer 1983, pp. 1–16.

Benjamin, Curtis. "U.S. Book Sales Overseas: An Ebbing Tide." *Publishers Weekly*, April 29, 1983, pp. 22–24.

Blanchard, Belle. "The $64,000 Question: Or How Publishers Budget Marketing Costs." *American Bookseller*, February 1983, pp. 74–76.

Bonn, Thomas L. "The First Pocket Book." *Printing History* 5, no. 2 (1983), pp. 3–14.

Carter, Robert A. "Breaking In." *Publishers Weekly*, November 25, 1983, pp. 28–32.

———. "The Human Factor: When Companies Are Sold, Merged or Conglomerated, What Happens to the People Who Work for Them?" *Publishers Weekly*, January 21, 1983, pp. 41–46.

Craig, Gary, Lawrence Buckland, and Barry Yarkon. "Getting Extra Mileage from Your Title Files." *Publishers Weekly*, December 23, 1983, pp. 26–27.

Day, Colin. "The Theory of Gross Margin Pricing." *Scholarly Publishing*, July 1983, pp. 305–326.

Dessauer, John P. "1982 Book Purchases: A Hard Year." *Publishers Weekly*, November 4, 1983, p. 22.

Epstein, Connie C. "The Elusive List Price and the FPT [freight pass-through] Factor." *School Library Journal*, April 1983, pp. 23–26.

Fine, Michael J. "Books/Video/Software—The Next Nexus." *American Bookseller*, July 1983, pp. 30—32.

Frank, Jerome P., ed. "Computers: Manufacturing's Newest Route to Productivity." *Publishers Weekly*, December 2, 1983, pp. 65—74.

———. "Innovative 'Module' Makes Supershort Runs Economically Feasible." *Publishers Weekly*, October 7, 1983, pp. 57–60.

Freilicher, Lila. "Selling by Phone." *Publishers Weekly*, June 3, 1983, pp. 32–37.

Jenkins, John H. "A Regional Publisher Looks at the Future." *AB Bookman's Weekly*, February 14, 1983, pp. 1087–1099.

Lillienstein, Maxwell J. "Current Trends in Censorship." *American Bookseller*, December 1983, pp. 20–23.

Livingston, Barbara. "Charting the Freight Pass-Through Publishers." *American Bookseller*, February 1983, pp. 54–57.

Loftin, Richard. "Publishers Set Out on the Software Adventure." *Publishers Weekly*, May 6, 1983, pp. 34–44.

———. "Software Movers into Bookstores." *PW* Special Report. *Publishers Weekly*, October 7, 1983, pp. 33–48.

Maryles, Daisy, ed. "Magazines in the Bookstore." *PW* Special Report. *Publishers Weekly*, December 2, 1983, pp. 37–62.

Rothman, David H. "Electronic Manuscript Formats for Writers." *Infoworld*, November 28, 1983, pp. 45–49.

Shaw, Bruce. "Financing a Small Publishing Firm." *Publishers Weekly*, July 15, 1983, pp. 16–18.

Sherman, Steve. "Why Certain Titles Are Missing from Bookstore Shelves." *Publishers Weekly*, March 11, 1983, pp. 68–70.

Smith, G. Roysce. "Booksellers Order Service, Phase II." *American Bookseller*, May 1983, pp. 141–144.

Weyr, Thomas. "Rise and Fall of the Blockbuster." *Publishers Weekly*, September 9, 1983, pp. 26–29.

Index